BARUCH

The Public Years

BARUCH
The Public Years

Bernard M. Baruch

HOLT, RINEHART AND WINSTON...NEW YORK

Library of Congress Catalog Card Number: 60-14112

80829-0210

Printed in the United States of America

For my children—

BELLE, BERNARD, JR., *and* RENÉE

Preface

The first volume of these memoirs, which told the story of my origins, early years, and career in Wall Street during its most flamboyant era, was published three years ago. Had I realized then that the completion of this venture into autobiography would take so long, I might have been tempted to abandon it. Not that it has been a disagreeable task; quite the contrary. But after all, it takes more than a normal amount of optimism to plan on bringing out a book in one's ninetieth year.

I have been encouraged to continue with this work, however, by the generous response to the first part of *My Own Story*. Many readers were kind enough to express interest in an account of my experience in public affairs, and some seemed to feel that a review of this experience might provide useful guides to understanding some of the crucial problems confronting us in these difficult times.

This second volume of my memoirs covers the nearly fifty years I have spent in public life. During these years I have witnessed many and been a part of some of the great events and developments of the twentieth century. In World War One, I served as Chairman of the War Industries Board in charge of mobilizing America's industrial resources for the war effort. After the war, I participated in the Paris Peace Conference. A generation later, in a second and even more devastating war, I was again active in the defense program. And when victory had again been achieved, partly through the new and

terrible power of the atom, I was given the task of devising a means
of bringing that power under effective international control.

In the years between the wars, I was actively involved in a variety
of public issues—agriculture, neutrality, preparedness—and took
part in a number of rousing political battles. In those years I was
an interested observer of such phenomena as the great boom that
ended in the great crash. I watched the momentous changes in our
political, economic, and social systems which accompanied the decline of laissez faire.

I have had the opportunity to know many of the men who have
dominated the history of this century. Most of them were unusually
well endowed with character and ability, but I have learned that
human nature in Washington is very little different from human
nature in Wall Street—or Main Street—that, indeed, there is very
little difference between the "great" man and the "common" man.
I have learned the truth of the observation that the more one ap-
proaches great men the more one finds that they are men.

I have learned some other things—affirmations of ancient principles and lessons learned in the hard school of experience—about the
conduct of war and the making of peace, about the role of government in a free society, about the requirements of economic stability.
I hope that some of the things I have learned have meaning for today. I think they do, for the basic problems confronting us, formidable as they are, are not new. Cutting across all of them is the
fundamental question of how to balance human nature with the
nature of things—with the world as it is—of how to get man to employ his reason to so order society that he may live in peace and
dignity. For it is by reason alone that we can find our way.

In writing these memoirs I have relied not only upon my recollections of a busy and crowded life, but have tried to distill the sense
and substance of the great mass of papers—the speeches, articles,

memoranda, and letters—which I have accumulated since entering public life. I have tried, to the best of my ability, to tell the facts as I know them, and to give my opinions as I hold them.

Once again, I am indebted to my friend and associate Harold Epstein, for his invaluable and tireless assistance in writing this book. Robert Lescher, of Holt, Rinehart and Winston, again proved to be an uncommonly patient and helpful editor.

Contents

BARUCH

The Public Years

I

Discontent with Wall Street

PEOPLE OFTEN ASK ME HOW, at the age of forty-seven, after spending more than a quarter of a century in Wall Street, I came to leave a career devoted to business to go to Washington. There was no moment of decision, I always assure them, in which I decided to abandon one career for another. It was, rather, a matter of my own evolution and of chance.

I had entered the financial life of Wall Street as a young man in 1890. Within ten years I had risen from office boy to a partnership in a brokerage house. By the time I was thirty, I had made a fortune. In the process I had come to know and associate with some of the great figures of finance and industry: Thomas Fortune Ryan, one of the most fabulous figures in the history of Wall Street; John W. "Bet-a-Million" Gates, an almost legendary character; James R. Keene, the master speculator who taught me much; Harriman, Rockefeller, Morgan, and the Guggenheims. With these men I had participated in many exciting ventures; the purchase of the Liggett & Myers Tobacco Company for Ryan in his fight to wrest control of the tobacco industry from James B. Duke; the challenge to Morgan for control of the prized Louisville & Nashville

1

Railroad; the dramatic development of the new porphyry copper industry.

Yet, despite these adventures and my material success, I had begun to feel discontent with a life confined to Wall Street. I could not forget my father's look the day I proudly informed him I was worth a million dollars. The kindly, quizzical expression told me, more clearly than words, that in his opinion money-making was a secondary matter. He had always held ethical values and usefulness to the community in higher esteem, and his whole life was a testimony to his convictions. As I came to appreciate my father's values, the satisfactions of Wall Street waned. I found myself wishing sometimes that I had followed him into the practice of medicine, or—as I had once intended—taken up the study of law.

Many were the afternoons when, restless and discontented, I found myself staring down from my office window over Wall Street and Trinity churchyard. The view of the graveyard recalled Gray's melancholy lines from the "Elegy."

Garet Garrett was a frequent visitor on those late afternoons. This small, round, intense dynamo of a man was then with the New York *Evening Post*. Later he was to continue his distinguished journalistic career with the *Tribune* and the *Saturday Evening Post*. Garrett was one of the few men to whom I could unburden myself. Once, after hearing me express my restlessness with Wall Street, he remarked: "I keep telling you, B.M., you don't belong in Wall Street; you should be in Washington." I don't remember my reply; I probably laughed at him. But I thought about his words from time to time, not because they stirred any political ambition but because that phrase, "you don't belong in Wall Street," nourished my discontent.

At that time, during the early years of this century, it was not common for business or professional men to leave their careers for government service. The prevailing doctrine of laissez-faire did not encourage either a high opinion of government service or a sense of social responsibility. It was the gradual awakening of social consciousness in the early years of the new century, and the first great war, which first brought many men like myself into public service. We became instruments through which a revolution, not only in the public attitude toward government but in the role of government, was effected.

Before circumstances led me into the public service, my points of contact with it had been few. I had taken a casual interest in such civic affairs as Boys' Clubs, and had served as an athletic director in a club on West Sixty-ninth Street. I had also tried to further my father's pioneering work in establishing public baths. This brought me into contact with Tammany boss Richard Croker, whom I respected (though he was little deserving of respect in other ways) because he had been sympathetic to Father's ideas. I also came to know his successor in the Wigwam, shrewd Charles F. Murphy, as well as other New York politicians. I met Al Smith when he was still Sheriff of New York County. Later we became close friends. I also knew Mayor William Jay Gaynor, an irascible and erratic man, but an able administrator.

Another of my political acquaintances was William Sulzer, who had served in the New York State Assembly and in the House of Representatives. Sulzer, a flamboyant politician of the old school, was later elected Governor of New York as Tammany's candidate, and soon after gave me a memorable lesson in political courage.

Immediately after his election, Sulzer committed political suicide by rejecting the list of appointees Boss Murphy sent up to him. Murphy was outraged, and such was the power of Tammany in those days, that he succeeded in getting impeachment proceedings instituted against Sulzer. I was indignant at these highhanded machinations and tried to help the Governor by contributing to his defense. But it was useless. He was tried, convicted, and removed from office.

Sulzer's fate was out of character with his professional skill at getting votes in the old-fashioned way. Herbert Bayard Swope used to tell of the night Sulzer went down to New York's lower East

Side to address an audience of immigrant Jews. He assured these
prospective voters that he had personally intervened to bring pressure on the Czar to halt the terrible persecutions in Russia.

"To this day," Sulzer declaimed, trumpeting his alleged success,
"Jews go down on their knees in gratitude to pray for William
Sulzer."

Swope, then a young reporter, was sitting in the front row and
heard this statement with alarm. He leaned forward to whisper
loudly, "Billy, Jews don't pray on their knees."

Sulzer regarded him blandly. "They do when they pray for William Sulzer," he said.

2

My first real introduction to civic affairs came in 1910, when
Mayor Gaynor offered me a trusteeship at my alma mater, the
College of the City of New York. I took this civic task seriously, for
I felt a very deep sense of gratitude to the College for the educa-
tional opportunities it had given me. I kept myself informed about
affairs at the College; often, when a new instructor began teaching,
I would sit down quietly in a back row and see how things were
going.

To this day I retain a deep interest in City College and am a firm
supporter of the tradition of free higher education. Municipal
colleges have educated thousands of men and women who, for
financial reasons, would have been denied the chance for college
training. CCNY graduates include not only such notable men as
General G.W. Goethals, Senator Robert F. Wagner, Justice Felix
Frankfurter, and Dr. Jonas Salk, but thousands of less famous men
and women who have played constructive roles in every walk of life.

My acceptance of the College trusteeship was, as it turned out,
the first link in a chain of circumstances that led me to more
important tasks. It brought me into touch with William McCombs,

a fellow trustee. And it was McCombs who led me eventually to Woodrow Wilson.

McCombs and I were friends from the start. He had been a student of Wilson at Princeton, and was among the first to champion his former teacher for the Presidency. He lost no opportunity to sing Wilson's praises to me and to seek to enlist my support for his candidacy. I listened, although I cannot say that Billy kindled any great enthusiasm in me for his hero.

At this time I had no well-developed political philosophy. As a good Southern Democrat, I had cast my first Presidential ballot in 1892 for Grover Cleveland. In 1896, however, I was so uncertain as to where I stood that I can't say to this day for whom I voted. Like a good many Americans, I was mesmerized by the rich, full voice of William Jennings Bryan when I heard him in the old Madison Square Garden. After I left the place, however, I remembered more of the voice than what it was saying, which is frequently the case when you listen to political addresses. No one I knew intended to vote for Bryan.

McKinley might have had my vote if it hadn't been for Fischel Cohen, my great-uncle. Uncle Fischel, an unreconstructed rebel, who had been on General Beauregard's staff in the Civil War, viewed the marking of a Republican ballot by a native South Carolinian as a base betrayal of the Lost Cause. He could not believe me capable of such incredible treason. But taking no chances, he warned me that my arm would wither if I did such a thing. Father was for John M. Palmer, the gold Democrat, and I suppose I must have voted for him. I don't remember for whom I voted in 1900, but—Uncle Fischel's warning notwithstanding—I probably cast my ballot for McKinley rather than Bryan.

Certainly when Theodore Roosevelt ran in 1904, I felt no compunctions about voting for a Republican. His dynamic personality and ideas appealed greatly to me. I met T.R. only once, and then only casually. But I have always prized a compliment he paid me. During World War One, he wrote our mutual friend, Moe Gunst,

that I was "the ablest man around the Administration." I can't
say that this was true, but I was pleased nonetheless.

As the 1912 presidential election approached, friends of Mayor
Gaynor, who were seeking the Democratic nomination for him,
asked me for help. I admired Gaynor, and I pledged to help
finance his campaign if he were nominated. I went down to the
Party's convention in Baltimore, naïve enough to believe that he
might be chosen. But even a novice on the political scene, as I
was, could soon see that the sweating, clamorous delegates swarm-
ing through headquarters had other ideas in mind.

This was my first convention and I enjoyed the show hugely.
Like all conventions, it was an exhausting carnival of sense and
nonsense, and like all conventions it had its special touch of drama.
In this case the drama lay in the drive to nominate Woodrow Wilson, led by the amateurs Billy McCombs and the tall, explosive,
voluble William Gibbs McAdoo. They were fighting the professionals, including the well-organized forces of Congressman Oscar Underwood of Alabama and Congressman Champ Clark of Missouri,
the leading contenders for the nomination.

In spite of the maneuvering, however, it soon became clear that
one man was the key figure in the convention. Thrice defeated for
the Presidency, William Jennings Bryan, in a black alpaca coat,
sat with his Nebraska delegation, cooling himself with a palm-leaf
fan, aware of everything and waiting for his moment. The Nebraska
delegation was pledged to Champ Clark, but everyone knew that
the Great Commoner was against the coalition of party bosses and
Wall Street financiers who supported Clark and who, according
to Bryan, had been having their own way in the party and expected to go on having it.

The high point of the convention drama for me, as it was for
everyone in the hot and smoky hall, came when Bryan rose to
denounce, as of old, the high priests of finance. Charles Hyde, New
York City's Chamberlain and one of Gaynor's aides, had gotten
me a seat behind the rostrum. From that vantage point I heard

again the mighty voice pouring out the oratory that was more in the style of my father's day than in the manner of the new century. Bryan was absolutely uncompromising. The Democratic Party must not nominate any candidate "of the privilege-hunting and favor-seeking class," by whom he meant such as J.P. Morgan, August Belmont, and Thomas Fortune Ryan.

I could not see Ryan where he sat in the Virginia delegation, and I wondered how he was taking it. But then I saw him stand up, stretch his long, thin neck, and raise his head in a proud, defiant gesture. Here was a man who had been my good friend and business associate in Wall Street; but now in this political world, so different from the business world I knew well, I heard him being character-ized as someone with whom no decent person would be allied.

There was no doubt about how the delegates took it. They hooted, howled, moaned, threatened to lynch Bryan, fought in the aisles, and waved fists in his face. Through it all Bryan thundered on, unperturbed, until at last he came back to the platform, re-trieved his palm-leaf fan, mopped his brow, and by chance sat down beside me. "There, that'll fix 'em," I overheard him say.

It did, indeed, "fix 'em." Bryan's forces refused to give their vote to Clark. As the balloting went on, Clark's strength steadily melted away and Wilson's grew. "I saw that my man Clark was dead," Claude Swanson of Virginia later reminisced in his inimitable style. "I wasn't going to lay down on that ice and get political pneumonia. No, Sir! I got up and cut some fancy didoes and came out for Wilson." So did an increasing number of delegates on each roll call.

At last, on the forty-sixth ballot, Wilson went over the top. The amateurs had triumphed; Wilson was the nominee. Utterly weary and impatient to be off, the delegates perfunctorily nominated Thomas Marshall of Indiana for the Vice-presidency as a reward to Tom Taggart, the first of the state bosses to switch from Clark to Wilson. Then the convention adjourned.

I left Baltimore much better informed than I had been a week before. For the first time I had gotten a good close look at a unique

political institution—the nominating convention. I have attended
many since then, and for me the truly amazing thing about them
is that despite the circus side show and carnival aspects, despite the
second-rate men who at times are selected, so many first-rate, even
great, men are chosen.

3

   Although Roosevelt, for whom I had voted in 1904, was running
again, I intended to vote for Wilson. I was naturally sympathetic
to him as a Democrat. Beyond that, I respected him for his courage
in fighting the snobbery and discrimination of the eating clubs
at Princeton. Remembering my own college days, when the fact of
being a Jew had been enough to bar me from fraternities, I admired
Wilson's blunt attack on the clubs. Moreover, his two years as
Governor of New Jersey had marked him as an imaginative and
effective leader; and the New Freedom he talked about touched
in me an awakening, though still ill-defined, political philosophy.
   Nevertheless, I felt no personal involvement or desire to play a
part in the campaign. To McCombs I pledged to contribute to the
campaign fund, but that constituted my political activity. Thus, I
recall, my first contribution went to the Democratic cause in Maine,
where, I was told, the chances for an upset were bright. In time I was
to learn that the predictions of campaign managers were to be
discounted, in Maine as elsewhere.
   McCombs, however, was not content with campaign contributions. He kept pressing me to meet Wilson. I was reluctant, not
only because I had no taste for the empty amenities accorded campaign contributors, but because I was conscious that my background
might prove embarrassing to a candidate whose hostility to Wall
Street was well publicized. But finally, at McCombs' insistence, I
agreed to let him make an appointment for me to meet Wilson.
   We met, early in October, at the Plaza Hotel, where Wilson had

a suite. In the foyer outside I met James Gerard, soon to be Ambassador to Germany, and Colonel Edward Mandell House, who was present all during my talk with the nominee. I was to see much more of that mysterious, always controversial figure Colonel House, who became the *eminence grise* of the Wilson Administration. House was certainly a devoted aide, an able man who gave unstintingly of his energy and talents to guard the President's political life. His influence on the President was great. Perhaps it was too great and led him at last into believing he was something more than an aide, which cost him his favored position.

From the moment I clasped Wilson's hand, I was taken with him. His lean, somewhat ascetic face was dominated by sparkling clear eyes. He was cordial and forthright and I was quickly impressed by his keen mind.

We talked of the large issues of the day. I recall we discussed monopoly and concentration of economic power. He explained that he was not opposed to bigness in business merely because of the question of size, but because it led to the loss of economic opportunities for others, and led also to political abuse.

There were, however, some business concentrations which were both necessary and proper, Wilson explained. He pointed to the telephone. "Here you have a monopoly," he went on. "But it is a reasonable monopoly. It represents a necessary concentration of capital under private control. But just the same, I believe it should be regulated." We discussed the United States Steel Company's purchase of vast iron ore deposits in the Mesabi range. Wilson said he could see no objection to this unless the steel company used its advantage to restrict competition.

Looking back to that first meeting, I know that I came away profoundly impressed. Although I did not then realize it, I had met a man I would soon regard as one of the greatest in the world.

I followed the last weeks of the campaign with renewed interest. It was an exciting three-cornered race, for Teddy Roosevelt and his Bull Moosers had rebelled against the Republican Party and its candidate, President Taft. It was this split which made Wilson's victory possible, just as a split in the Democratic Party had made possible the election of another great President, Lincoln, in 1860.

Although Woodrow Wilson's election pleased me greatly, it did not alter my life in any way. I played no part, contrary to what some have written, in the introduction of those measures which Wilson called the New Freedom, although I fully supported the Administration in what it sought to achieve.

Wall Street men are popularly supposed to be inimical to progressive ideas. Nevertheless, I knew well the national need for reform. I recognized that the tremendous industrial growth in the decades since the Civil War had made us rich as a nation but had also fostered much social and economic injustice and inequity.

When Wilson became President, national legislation lagged far behind the new social, economic, and political conditions that prevailed. The influence of unbridled laissez faire had restricted the role of government and sanctioned abuses which had accompanied the rapid growth and change in American life.

But Wilson was not bound by obsolete conceptions of government. He launched a vigorous attack against special privilege and monopoly, against economic inequality, social wrongs, and political abuses. In the period from 1912 to 1914, during which Congress was held in almost continuous session, a sweeping program of legislation, then without precedent in our history, was enacted.

The Federal Reserve Act, enacted over the opposition of men who lived to value and praise it, reformed our banking system. The Clayton Anti-Trust Act and the Federal Trade Commission Act, directed against monopolies and unfair trade practices, followed. The Federal Farm Loan Act brought long-term credit at low interest rates to the farmers, and the activity of the Department of Agriculture was greatly expanded to meet the farmers' marketing and production problems. Tariffs were reduced and a tariff commission created.

There was other progressive legislation in the fields of labor relations, child labor, and suffrage for women. With the help of Congressman Cordell Hull, the first income and inheritance tax laws were passed.

Despite the clamor raised against this program, there was nothing radical in it. Wilson did not seek change for the sake of change. As with every true liberal, there was a strong conservative instinct in him. His reforms were not intended to remake the American political and economic system, but to strengthen, preserve, and protect it (from itself, in many respects) by correcting and eliminating the abuses which had grown up about it.

As Wilson put it, he sought new means to preserve old ends. "The New Freedom was only the old revived and clothed in the unconquerable strength of America." The measure of the soundness of his program is to be seen in its permanence. Nothing in it was ever repealed.

There was one occasion in President Wilson's first term when I was able to be helpful. That was during the cotton panic early in the war, when the loss of foreign sales caused cotton prices to collapse. Ship owners, fearing seizure of their cargoes by belligerents, were reluctant to carry cotton. The South, still largely dependent on this one crop, was threatened with disaster. The President, hoping to encourage shipowners, declared that cotton was not contraband. If the private shipping interests still would not carry it, he declared, government ships would. At the same time, he moved to support the price of cotton. For this purpose the bankers were organized to raise a loan fund of $135 million. When McAdoo, then Secretary of the Treasury, told me that the fund threatened to fall short of its goal, I immediately volunteered— as a Southerner naturally much interested in what happened to the cotton growers—to subscribe the last three-and-a-half million. My offer had the effect of stimulating the interest of others. Paul Warburg, formerly of the house of Kuhn, Loeb and then with the Federal Reserve, insisted that Kuhn, Loeb, who had initially held back, take part of my subscription, to which I gladly agreed.

4

The war in Europe, of course, was affecting not only the cotton industry but the whole of American life. Indeed, when the elections of 1916 approached, the war was the nation's overriding concern. I felt strongly that the kind of leadership Wilson could provide was needed in those critical times, and I was prepared to support him whole-heartedly in his bid for re-election.

During the past four years I had gradually become involved in Democratic Party affairs. I had come to know many of the Party stalwarts well. Among those I saw more than casually were "Uncle" Henry Morgenthau, father of F.D.R.'s Secretary of the Treasury; Secretary of the Navy Josephus Daniels; Postmaster General Albert S. Burleson; Secretary of Labor William Wilson; Attorney General Thomas W. Gregory; Daniel Roper; and Homer Cummings. About this time I also met Carter Glass of Virginia and thus began my long friendship with this man so beloved of his friends and respected by his enemies. Glass had a characteristic way of speaking out of the side of his mouth, which once moved Wilson to remark, "Glass says more things out of the corner of his mouth than a lot of people say with the whole thing."

While making these friends, I witnessed the virtual disappearance of another, Billy McCombs. Never robust in health and always inclined to nerves, McCombs had finished the campaign of 1912 physically and emotionally exhausted. McAdoo, in fact, had done most of the headquarters work during the canvass. McCombs had wanted a place in the Cabinet, but Wilson, as I heard later, did not think him physically able to undertake such heavy responsibilities. The President offered McCombs the ambassadorship to France, with the promise to take him into the Cabinet after he recovered his health. This I believe to be true, but McCombs, whose judgment was warped by nervous and physical exhaustion, was not satisfied. He became embittered against Wilson and everyone else. It was my unhappy task to help persuade him to resign the Party chairmanship in 1916. He resisted the idea bitterly. But in the end he consented. He was only forty-six when he died a few years later, a sick and embittered man.

His successor as Chairman of the Democratic National Committee was Vance McCormick, as gallant a little gentleman and as hard and fair a fighter as I have ever known. Short and stocky, looking as pugnacious as he must have looked on the gridiron when he was one of Yale's great football players, he made an ideal campaign manager.

The Democratic Convention renominated Wilson by acclamation. To oppose him the Republicans chose Charles E. Hughes, who left the Supreme Court to accept the nomination. Hughes was a man of impeccable character, immense dignity, and prestige, whose ordinarily reserved personality warmed up somewhat in the heat of campaigning. He proved to be a formidable opponent.

As soon as the campaign got under way I told Charles F. Murphy, the Tammany Hall leader, that I would provide the money that was needed to carry on the campaign in New York. In those days, incidentally, there was no legal limitation on the amount of money a man could contribute to a political campaign. I knew that Murphy was personally bitter toward the President, but nevertheless, I regarded him as a good soldier who would do his best for the Party. He came back to me in a few days and said, "Baruch, I'm going to try to carry the state, but I can't take your money, because I don't think your man can do it."

Vance McCormick felt that Murphy's reply made it clear he wasn't going to try very hard, which proved to be the case. But on the other hand, I think the episode says much in his favor. He could easily have taken the money and returned no more effort for it than he did. Whatever else his critics say he may have been or done, Murphy was always on the square with me.

Tom Chadbourne and I were, according to the records, among the major financial contributors to Wilson's campaign. Chadbourne was a handsome six-foot, six-inch Viking of a man who headed one of the great law firms in the country. As a boy, Tom had shown so little ambition that his father decided he would have to turn him loose in the world to fend for himself. He gave him $100 and sent him off to Chicago. There, after a knockabout career which included a turn on the police force and some prize fighting, Tom met the chewing gum magnate, William Wrigley. Whether it was Wrigley's influence or not, Tom suddenly found himself and quickly rose in the profession of law. He and I were political allies and friends for many years.

Aside from my financial support of the campaign, I spent a good deal of time trying to convince as many members of the business community as I could that Woodrow Wilson was not an avenging angel whose mission on earth was their destruction.

The Republicans fought hard. They criticized the President's domestic program as demagogic. They assailed his Mexican policy on the grounds that he had not acted promptly to protect American lives and honor in that revolution-torn country, despite the fact that he had sent troops into Vera Cruz and in pursuit of General Villa to do just that. His policy of neutrality toward the warring powers in Europe, his patience in the face of German provocation were condemned.

As so often happens, some political opponents stooped to slander and circulated calumnies about Mr. Wilson's private life. His friendship with Mary Hulbert was distorted by sly innuendoes, and all sorts of base canards were whispered about his letters to her. After Mr. Wilson's death, when these letters were offered for sale, I bought them—at the request of Wilson's biographer, Ray Stannard Baker—and gave them to the Library of Congress. There is not a line in any of them to justify the cruel suggestions that were made.

At first Wilson had been inclined to take Hughes lightly. He wrote me on August 19th: "I am inclined to follow the course suggested by a friend of mine who says that he has always followed the rule never to murder a man who is committing suicide, and clearly this misdirected gentleman is committing suicide slowly but surely."

But in the face of the Republican attack, Mr. Wilson had to revise this strategy and campaign hard. Still, he would not pander to any group. When the president of an anti-British group, said to have a record of disloyalty, offered an endorsement, Wilson replied, "I would feel deeply mortified to have you or anybody like you vote for me. Since you have access to many disloyal Americans and I have not, I will ask you to convey this message to them."

On election night, Mrs. Baruch and I attended a large dinner—a victory dinner it was hoped—at the Hotel Biltmore. But as the returns began to roll in, our hopes evaporated. Life and sparkle began to depart from the assembled company. New York was lost, as McAdoo and other practical men had privately granted it would be. But the loss of New Jersey, the President's home state, and of Indiana, where Tom Taggart ran things for the Democrats, were unexpected blows.

Before the night was very old, the New York *World* conceded the election of Hughes. It appeared to be all over, and I paid little attention when my brother, Harty, rushed in to say that things were not as bad as they looked. A telegraph operator at Republican headquarters had told him that returns from some of the Western states were being held up by the Republicans because they seemed so favorable to Wilson. This news did not cheer me because I didn't think it possible to hold up election results. Resigned to Wilson's defeat, my wife and I went home.

About three o'clock in the morning, I was awakened by a telephone call from "Uncle" Henry Morgenthau, speaking from headquarters. "Come on back," he shouted, "we've got Wilson elected."

I dressed hurriedly and rushed over to headquarters. In a room strewn with papers, I found Vance McCormick in the center of a crowd of disheveled men. They had been up all night. They were excited and optimistic at what the returns were now showing. The face of things had begun to change. The Republican states of

Kansas and Ohio were in the Wilson fold, and now the election was in doubt. The result appeared to hinge on Minnesota and California, but as the day lengthened it centered on California alone.

In the early morning hours Herbert Bayard Swope, the *World*'s tall, dynamic, redheaded reporter, burst into headquarters with the news that California belonged to the Democrats unless they let the opposition "steal" it. This was the first time I met this man with whom I was to be associated so intimately for more than forty years. Vance McCormick wired his people in California to be alert to any skulduggery. Gavin McNab wired back that if anyone came around with that idea in mind, they had better bring coffins with them.

That afternoon we had a small conference at the residence of Colonel House and discussed plans for contesting the election, if need be, in some of the close states. A good deal of intemperate talking took place. House impressed me by his tactful and wise handling of the hotheads.

Next day, with California practically nailed down and the election result all but certain, the odds were still as much as two and a half to one against Wilson. A few people, myself not included, made a killing by backing our candidate in California while these odds still held. If anyone had thought of it, that would have been a good way to pare down the campaign debt, as was done later in the New York election of 1922. In that year Alfred E. Smith was running for governor, and Royal Copeland was making his first race for the Senate on the Democratic ticket. Governor Nathan L. Miller was the favorite over Smith, and the odds against Copeland were three and a half to one when Boss Murphy brought to my house a voluminous card index showing the Tammany predictions for New York City. They indicated such large majorities for Smith and Copeland that I asked him to recheck. He returned the next day to assure me that his figures were correct. I told him that in view of his confidence he should get his friends to bet enough to meet the campaign deficit. Murphy followed my advice. His predictions were borne out, Democratic majorities in New York City more than overcoming the Republicans' upstate lead.

Why the odds should have remained against Wilson in California I do not know, because it was clear that Wilson would carry the state. But some people have a way of ignoring unwanted truths. For myself, I have always found it more dangerous to run away from unpleasant truths than to face them. And this is so, not only in the affairs of individuals, but in the affairs of nations.

In the post-election quiet I could assess what lessons I had learned and determine where these exciting events had left me. Certainly they had served to bring me closer to the Democratic Party and its leaders. In the process, I had made some acquaintances who were to become close and valued friends, and I had learned a few things about practical politics.

But above all, the election of 1916 marked the real beginning of my friendship with Woodrow Wilson, one of the most rewarding and in many ways the most significant friendship I have had. Next to my father, Wilson had the greatest influence on my life. He took me out of Wall Street and gave me my first opportunity for public service. His political philosophy helped shape my own. His practical idealism, ability, and conduct still provide the standard by which I measure public men.

II

America Goes to War

As WILSON BEGAN his second term in the White House, one problem loomed above all others—the war in Europe, whose shocks
were being felt with increasing violence in the United States. That
war, we know, was one of the great turning points in history; nothing would ever be the same again. And as America and the world
were irrevocably altered by it, so, too, was my own life. As the war
catapulted America out of her isolation, it lifted me out of the narrow canyon of Wall Street onto the stage of national and international affairs.

From the outbreak of the war, my sympathies were with the
Allies. My distaste for the Prussian military spirit, something of
which I had seen during a youthful visit to Germany, was strong.
Nevertheless, I at first believed, as most Americans did, that we
should stay out of the fight, although I was not sure we could. Many
people thought it inconceivable that America should be drawn into
the conflict. But then, in their innocence, many people had believed
in 1914 that war itself was inconceivable.

Otto Kahn, my dinner companion at the Ritz one night just
after Sarajevo, said in all earnestness that there would be no war

because God would not permit such a terrible thing to happen. I did not share Otto Kahn's belief, and when I saw Europe going up in flames, I began to think that we should be prepared for all eventualities. I am not a martial man, but I have always liked Teddy Roosevelt's idea of having a big stick handy. Weakness is never a virtue and it too often leads to enslavement.

It was my concern, as a private citizen, with the question of preparedness that led me to Washington. This issue had begun to loom large in 1915. Patriotic men were aligned on both sides of it, and the Administration itself was divided. Many Americans were opposed to any measures except those insuring strict neutrality. There were no disasters, like the fall of France in the Second World War, to shock public opinion into awareness; instead, there was a complacent conviction that the Allies were certain to win without any help from us, and that trouble would pass us by if we ignored its existence.

Very early I became an advocate of preparedness, and applauded the efforts of such men as T.R. and Major General Leonard Wood to arouse the country to the need for defense. When an opportunity came to support these efforts, I jumped at it.

One day I attended a luncheon at Henry C. Frick's splendid home on Fifth Avenue, which he had filled with art treasures. I went there frequently to play bridge. After luncheon on this particular day, I found myself sitting next to General Wood. We began to discuss the war in Europe and the problem of American preparedness. He told me of the citizens' military training camp at Plattsburg, New York. This installation was created to turn out future officers for the Army. If the camp was to be opened that year, Wood said, he would have to raise $10,000 to complete road building. When I pledged the money on the spot, General Wood was as surprised as he was grateful.

The need to train officers for an impending emergency could easily be understood. Less readily grasped was the nature of modern war. As the German juggernaut rolled over the Allies in the opening drives of the conflict, it became clear that war was no longer a contest between armies but between nations. Modern war means total war. Armies can wage such a war only with all the nation's resources of men, money, material, and morale mobilized behind them. And this would require a measure of government direction and control never envisaged in the prevailing doctrines of laissez faire.

These ideas were slowly being borne in upon me in the spring and summer of 1915, while the Allies were being pushed back on both fronts. There was a frightful lesson for us in the battles on the Western front, in May and June, when German machine guns mowed down British and French troops who lacked adequate artillery support. And in the tragedy of the Eastern front, huge Russian infantry forces were being thrown almost unarmed against the Germans. What were the brave Russian people to think of a government that asked them to fight for their motherland with little more than their bare hands? More and more, I began to see what we would have to do in our own country if war came.

2

Early in August, I departed on my annual tour of the United States. On these trips it had been my habit to combine business with recreation, visiting enterprises in which I was interested, inspecting other properties, talking to the men in charge; observing, weighing, comparing; trying always to look ahead and see a little farther into the future than the next fellow. For many years the ruling object of these studies had been to make money.

But now, crossing the continent to attend the San Francisco fair, I spent much time thinking about the war—feeling that we would surely get into it, and that we must be prepared. After the fair I took my parents, wife, two older children, and several of their young friends on a trip through Yellowstone Park, Yosemite, and the Grand Canyon. Our trip through Yellowstone was enlivened by a typical Western stagecoach robbery. We were riding in a procession of sight-seeing coaches when the one ahead of us came to an abrupt halt. I could see a man in a blue mask gesturing with a rifle, as the occupants tossed their valuables onto the road. I had a considerable sum of money with me, much of it in large denominations. Quickly I threw most of it under the seat in front of me. My wife threw her pearls there, too.

When the bandit called to us to "Chuck—Chuck," I tossed out a roll of currency containing mostly dollar bills, possibly forty or fifty. I remember looking down at the money on the floor of the wagon. Those big zeros on the old gold certificates looked back at me, getting bigger and bigger.

The bandit ordered us to drive on, and the next wagon came along to be robbed. We had not gone very far before we saw something that made me think we must be actors in a "western." It was a detachment of United States cavalry galloping down the road lickety-split after the bandit. I knew it was no movie, however, when they told us a little later that the "bad man" got away.

James N. Wallace, president of the Central Trust Company, good-naturedly telegraphed me when he learned of the incident, "I see you have been held up. How much did the robber lose?"

On the long ride back East, gazing out the window at the endless fields of corn and wheat, I could not turn my thoughts from the problem of preparedness. I was building and elaborating in my mind a picture of the American economy, mobilized for war. I envisaged our farms and our factories synchronized into a vast machine which, in the event of war, would have to work day and night to maintain a military force in the field and sustain the civilian population. I saw raw materials—the products of field, forest, and mine—marshaled, distributed, refined, and fabricated into all the multitude of products that would be needed in such tremendous quantities. And I visualized a centralized governmental organization, manned by experts, directing the whole vast program.

As soon as I returned home, I took my ideas on defense mobilization to Secretary of the Treasury McAdoo. He was enthusiastic and suggested that I see the President at once. And so it was that in September, 1915, I called at the White House for the first time.

Curiously enough, I recall nothing of the external details of that visit. Not a feature of the room in which the President and I sat has left an impression with me. I must have been too full of my subject or intent on my host to take note of such things. I remember only the keen, preceptive face of Woodrow Wilson as he listened to what I had to say.

My plea was, in effect, for the immediate formulation of plans for putting American industry on a preparedness basis. I proposed the creation of what I called a Defense or Mobilization Committee, on which would be represented the major industries supplying the armed forces. If the government could tap the experience and know-how of industrial leaders on such a committee, I pointed out, it would result in enormous benefit to the Army and Navy.

My suggestion was repeated in a letter I wrote Colonel House a month later. But there was no immediate acknowledgment of my proposal. The Administration was still rent over the preparedness issue. The President, hopeful that he could bring the warring powers to the peace table, and anxious to do nothing to impair our posture of neutrality, opposed a preparedness program. Secretary of War Lindley Garrison, on the other hand, led a determined effort to get a strong Army bill through Congress. Frustrated by his failure to do so, he resigned in February, 1916. Newton D. Baker, who had been an outspoken pacifist, succeeded him.

At every opportunity I pressed my ideas and supported preparedness, even participating in a preparedness parade which marched up Broadway. I wrote again to Colonel House in April, 1916, urging the appointment of a Mobilization Committee. On May 5th, I had this reply from the President:

Mr. House has handed me your letter to him of April twenty-fourth about what I may briefly call industrial efficiency in case of need to mobilize all the resources of the nation. I remember the stimulation I received from our conversation about the matter and it has ever since been at the front of my thoughts. We are now trying to give shape to the matter and I heartily value your generous interest and cooperation.

One day, shortly thereafter, I received a call from the new Secretary of War. Mr. Baker said that President Wilson had requested him to speak to me about my ideas on industrial preparedness. Would it be convenient for me to see him, he inquired, if he came to New York? This unusual suggestion almost floored me, but I managed to say that of course I would go to Washington immediately to see *him*.

Secretary Baker was a small, quiet, pipe-smoking man, a former mayor of Cleveland, who had been a vigorous opponent of preparedness until he took office. The Secretary opened our conversation by alluding to my visit with the President the previous September. He said Mr. Wilson had asked him to show me a copy of a pending bill that provided for the creation of a Council of National Defense and an Advisory Commission. I read the document carefully. The Council, I saw, was to consist of the Secretaries of War, Navy, Interior, Agriculture, Commerce, and Labor. Its object was to concentrate, mobilize, and coördinate the country's resources in time of emergency. To assist it was the Advisory Commission, consisting of seven citizens to be named by the President and to serve without compensation.

I read slowly, with a deepening sense of disappointment. I could see that the Council of National Defense and its Advisory Commission lacked specific authority beyond the making of investigations and recommendations. At best, it might serve to make a beginning at coördinating the preparedness effort.

"Mr. Secretary," I said, "do you think this is all you can get?"

"Yes," he answered bluntly.

I realized that perhaps public opinion would have to be educated before the Administration could set up a body with adequate powers.

"Well," I said, "if this is all you can get, take it and do the best you can with it."

The bill became law in August, 1916, and I gave little further attention to the matter until one morning in October when, on opening my paper at breakfast, I read that the President had announced the personnel of the Advisory Commission and included my name in the list.

I scanned the names of my fellow commissioners. They were a distinguished company: Daniel Willard, president of the Baltimore & Ohio Railroad; Howard Coffin, vice-president of Hudson Motor Car Company; Dr. Hollis Godfrey, president of Drexel Institute; Julius Rosenwald, president of Sears, Roebuck & Company; Dr. Franklin H. Martin, director general of the American College of Surgeons; and Samuel Gompers, president of the American Federation of Labor. They had me down as "Bernard M. Baruch, banker."

I am not a banker, and never have been nor claimed to be. But to many people it seems a convenient label. To this day I am constantly correcting that false impression. In 1916 I regarded myself as a speculator, but I could appreciate what the public might think of my qualifications for a Presidential appointment under that title.

Although I believed myself competent to participate in the work of the Commission, I was concerned that popular inferences drawn from my Wall Street career might prove an embarrassment to the President. With this anxiety in mind, I called on Colonel House to tell him I thought the President was making a mistake in naming me and that I should not accept the appointment. When House conveyed my message to the President, he replied that I had been an ardent advocate of preparedness and that I had to "put up or shut up." I put up.

3

A month after the election, the Advisory Committee convened in Washington. After a few exploratory sessions dealing with the problems of organizing our work, we adjourned to reconvene on the first Monday in January, 1917. I returned to New York glad that I had accepted appointment to the Commission, and hopeful about what we might be able to do to prepare the country to defend itself.

But even before the work of the Commission could get under way, my career in public life nearly ended. I saw how the events of a day, or a single hour, might alter a man's life. I also got my first taste of what it means to be an object of political attack.

It all started on December 12th, when I heard newsboys crying extras about a German peace proposal. That was my first knowledge of the celebrated speech of von Bethmann-Hollweg, the German Chancellor, in which he offered to discuss peace with the Allies. I was not in my office, but I sprang into action like an old fire horse at the clang of the bell. I knew that the stock market must be tumbling, with the "war brides" foremost. Hurrying to a telephone, I called my broker, Harry Content, and instructed him to sell my shares in steel, copper, rubber, and other companies likely to be affected.

For four days I liquidated my holdings on a falling market which at times reached the verge of panic. At the same time I built up a short interest in certain stocks, particularly U.S. Steel, that I believed must inevitably drop still lower on the announcement of another concrete move toward peace.

I was confident there would be such a move, that von Bethmann-Hollweg's speech was the curtain raiser to negotiations that would bring about the end of war. Specifically, I awaited Lloyd George's reply. The Welshman had just overthrown Asquith's government on the issue of a more effective prosecution of the war. I expected that after a certain amount of belligerent rhetoric, he would leave the door open for *pour parlers* on peace.

But I was in for a surprise. No sooner had I established my short position than the silence with which London greeted the German overture and the hostility of Paris steadied the market. To be ready for anything, I reduced my short commitments by about one-half.

Such was my situation on December 19th when I was seated in my office at 111 Broadway, a rather plainly appointed chamber containing a ticker, a switchboard through which I could reach the brokers with whom I did business, and a direct wire to the Stock Exchange floor. With me at the time were William H. Crocker, the famous San Francisco banker, with whom I had been associated in many Western mining ventures; and my then telephone operator, Mary A. Boyle. Miss Boyle became, and still is, my confidential secretary and an assistant so valued and trusted that she has virtual charge of all my affairs.

While we sat talking, the ticker began to chatter. It was a bulletin from London. Lloyd George, speaking before Commons, had asserted that England must fight on to a victorious peace, and Germany must atone for her crimes. The German proposals, the bulletin material went on, were unacceptable, but . . .

There the ticker halted for a moment. I can still see that "but . . ." It seemed to leave the door open for further negotiations, as I had expected.

"This means peace," I said.

Miss Boyle was plugging me through to the brokers.

Crocker arose. He never speculated, never even followed the tape. "I don't know what this is all about," he said and left.

I sold heavily that day, increasing my short account particularly in Steel. But again I was wrong. My interpretation of the Lloyd George speech as increasing the chances for peace was not the interpretation accepted by the markets. Stock prices firmed. So on the following day, December 20th, I bought again to cover about half the stocks I had sold short on the strength of Lloyd George's speech.

This proved to be a premature move. For on the morning of December 21st, great black headlines in the morning newspapers announced that President Wilson had addressed a note to all belligerents asking them to state their terms of peace. The note had been given to the press associations at 12:05 o'clock that morning, having been sent in secret from the telegraph room of the State Department.

This note did to the market what I had thought the Lloyd George speech would do: that day and the next, prices broke in a furious selling wave. Thus my action in cutting my short position on December 20th had been ill-timed. If I had had any advance idea of the President's note, as was later charged, I would have maintained and indeed increased my short position. The note had actually taken me wholly by surprise, and caught me with my guard down. Nevertheless, I had no cause for complaint. Even though I had miscalculated several times, and had been wrong in my judgment that serious peace negotiations were imminent, when I closed my operations and went South for Christmas my brokerage accounts (as later disclosed to the Rules Committee of the House of Representatives) showed a profit of $476,168.47.

On the day before Christmas, stories appeared in the press linking my name to the violent drop in the market, the worst in fifteen years. On January 3rd, Representative William R. Wood, of Indiana, charged on the floor of the House that my recent operations on the Stock Exchange were predicated on prior knowledge of President Wilson's peace note.

Next day my name appeared on the front pages from coast to coast: "Baruch Made Fortune in Big Market Crash," "Baruch Used 'Tip' Rumor, House Hears." Those were the big black headlines in the Charleston *News and Courier,* and they were typical. Beneath them were stories depicting a "big leak" of the President's message from the White House to Wall Street, probably at an alleged breakfast meeting between Joseph P. Tumulty, the President's secretary, and me.

I had never breakfasted with Tumulty. Indeed, I scarcely knew him at the time.

Summoned before the Rules Committee, Mr. Wood produced as authority for his assertion a letter posted in New York and signed "A. Curtis." This communication asserted that secret information on the Wilson note enabled me to "crash the market in all directions."

All sorts of wild stories circulated. In order not to miss the first meeting of the Advisory Commission, I had hired a locomotive to take my private car from South Carolina to Washington. This was construed as a "dash" by special train to obtain secret information in the capital. It was rumored that my "fellow conspirators" and I had made sixty million on our transaction.

All this made a Roman holiday in the newspapers, but as the story developed it turned out that the man who had set off the fireworks was the flamboyant Wall Street speculator, Thomas W. Lawson, who alternated between adventures in finance and muckraking. He had written to Chairman Robert Henry, of the House Rules Committee, charging that a "leak" on the Wilson note had enabled the beneficiaries in Wall Street to make fantastic profits. But when Henry had questioned him privately, Lawson gave no names and told a vague story which Henry publicly dismissed as a "mirage." Now the Curtis letter gave new life to the accusations of Lawson, who blustered all over Washington demanding an investigation and boasting about what shocking revelations he could make.

A lifetime in Wall Street had left me no stranger to rumor or malignant report, but there I knew how to deal with them. Rumors affected me not at all, and I pretended to ignore malignant reports. Nothing, however, had ever hurt me the way this "leak" story did.

Much was made of my connection with the Advisory Commission. The majority of the public had probably never heard of this obscure body until my alleged participation in the betrayal of official secrets brought it into prominence. But the sensational charges brought against me, a member, seemed to me to destroy whatever effectiveness I might have been able to have. Privately I vowed to resign as soon as I had cleared myself of the charges.

From Hobcaw I telegraphed Chairman Henry a brief denial of all the accusations and requested that I be permitted to testify and bring all my records to any investigation upon which his Committee might embark. In due course I was subpoenaed, along with a number of other witnesses. From the outset the Committee had difficulty with Lawson. Only after he had been adjudged in contempt and threatened with arrest did he divulge the names of the persons he accused. Among those he named were Secretary of the Treasury McAdoo; Secretary of State Robert Lansing; Count von Bernstorff, the German Ambassador; Paul M. Warburg; and myself—a distinguished, if somewhat mixed, company. Of course his story lacked any single detail that could be corroborated. Nor was the mysterious "A. Curtis" ever identified.

For days before my turn came to take the stand I was too nervous to sleep. I asked Tom Chadbourne for legal advice. He told me I had nothing to hide, which I knew, and had nothing to fear, about which I was less sure.

One night I was discussing the situation with Eugene Meyer, Jr., and he asked: "When they ask you your business what are you going to tell them?"

I said I hadn't given it any thought.

"Tell them straight out you're a speculator," he advised. I saw the wisdom in this advice and decided to follow it.

Several eminent financiers preceded me on the stand. With an air of virtue, they said they had never sold a share of stock short in their lives. Then my name was called. I was gratified to read in the papers next day that I bore myself with confidence. The truth is that when I stepped to the stand I was frightened half to death. In the audience sat Alice Roosevelt Longworth, the vivacious daughter of T.R. I did not know Mrs. Longworth then, but although she was an exceptionally charming woman, there flashed in my mind a picture of the women of Paris seated about the guillotine, knitting as the heads rolled into the baskets. I thought Mrs. Longworth was there to see my head roll.

Chairman Henry asked my name, address, and business.

"Bernard M. Baruch, 111 Broadway, speculator and investor," I said, but my voice was so low that the Chairman asked the stenographer to repeat what I had said.

"Bernard M. Baruch, 111 Broadway, speculator and investor," he droned without inflection, in the characteristic way of court stenographers. When he said "speculator" the Committee room came alive in a sudden, excited buzz. Speculator! That was the word they wanted to hear; it was as good as an admission of guilt. I was perfectly willing, however, to say I was a speculator. I defined a speculator as a man who observes the future and acts before it occurs.

After I had answered one or two other questions, my confusion left me. I began to tell of my December market activities, short sales and all.

The hearings lasted intermittently for three weeks. Sherman Whipple, an able New England lawyer, had been engaged as counsel for the Committee. He recalled me to the stand for further examination, and I related the story in even greater detail and produced all my books. This time I was perfectly at home on the stand, as I have been ever since.

The upshot of the inquiry was the exoneration of everyone who had been accused. The entire Congress, including the man who had originally brought the charges, voted unanimously to support the report of the Committee. I found myself nationally known, with added prestige in Washington. This was not entirely due to whatever merits I had displayed, but rather to the overzealousness of the President's enemies who had sought to hurt the Administration through me.

I had been hurt by the "leak" investigation. Physically, I had lost twelve pounds in the two or three weeks before the hearing. I went through a good deal of mental suffering before my first appearance in the public spotlight was over; I berated myself many

times for having anything to do with politics or politicians. The
public reaction to my vindication was so gratifying, however, that
I quickly recovered my perspective. I decided not to resign from
the Advisory Commission. But until the Committee reported its
findings I kept away from my colleagues on the Commission, and
from everyone else in official Washington.

I learned several valuable lessons from this experience. If you
have nothing to hide, you have nothing to fear, I saw, because the
big dog of truth always catches up with the little cur of lies. Unfortunately, people may be hurt before that happens. Yet, very
often, unjustified criticism can react to one's advantage. It provides
you with an audience and a chance to prove yourself.

I also realized that I would have to give up my career in Wall
Street if I were going to take an active part in public affairs. I
would have to avoid any semblance of a conflict of interest, a subject
about which we have heard a good deal in recent years. Therefore,
I arranged to dispose, even at a loss when necessity arose, of everything I had which could in any way be affected by the war program,
including my seat on the Stock Exchange. One morning I woke up
about four or five o'clock, thinking about some preferred stocks I
had neglected to sell. I called my broker and offered to sell them
to him well below the market, provided that he took delivery before
the Exchange opened. At the sound of the opening gong, I wanted
it as a matter of record that I had no interest whatsoever in them.

He took them, and on that very afternoon someone raised a
question in Congress about my financial interests. I was able to say
that I no longer owned anything that could be affected by my government work except a few holdings for which there was no market.
The income from these I had set aside for charity.

Among the holdings I disposed of were some which would have
yielded enormous profits if I had held them. But I have never regretted my action.

The problem of conflict of interest is a serious one which frequently bedevils Washington in its effort to recruit able men into

government service. No man can serve two masters; no honorable man would try. A representative of business who betrayed the government would never get another place in business. But many men, ready to serve the government faithfully, are unable or unwilling to divest themselves of financial holdings as the price of service. To some it constitutes a sacrifice—or a penalty. Actually the problem of conflicting interests is not so much a matter of the securities in a man's portfolio, but of his integrity and open-mindedness. The honest and enlightened man in public service will put the government's interest above all others, no matter what his personal financial interests are or may have been. The dishonest or narrow man will not be made otherwise by the temporary disposal of his holdings.

4

When President Wilson took his oath of office on March 4, 1917, America was on the verge of war. The previous December, Washington had learned of German Foreign Secretary Zimmerman's effort to lure Mexico into an alliance if Germany went to war with us, Mexico's reward to be the right to annex New Mexico, Arizona, and Texas. And this brazen act was followed at the end of the month by Berlin's announcement of the resumption of unrestricted submarine warfare.

For three years Wilson had pursued a policy of neutrality. In the face of the earlier U-boat campaign he had refused to be provoked, exclaiming, in justification of his patience, that a nation might be too proud to fight. Through Colonel House, whom he had sent to Europe as his unofficial emissary, through his own appeals, he had tried to find some basis for ending the conflict, for achieving "peace without victory."

But there was no place for a peacemaker in the bitter world of 1917, and no place for a neutral either. Wilson was compelled at last to lead America into war. It was a soul-rending decision. Everything in him cried out against it. To Frank Cobb, the editor of the *World,* he poured out his heart in the early hours of the day Congress was reconvening in special session to hear his war message. He told Cobb that he had sought every loophole of escape and Germany had blocked each with some new outrage. He feared what war would do to American character and American ideals. "If there is any alternative," he cried, "for God's sake, let's take it."

But he knew there was none.

On the historic, tense, rain-washed night of April 2, 1917, I sat in the jammed gallery of the House of Representatives while, below me, Congressmen and Senators, Supreme Court Justices and Cabinet officers, dignitaries of all kinds waited for the President. Then I heard him in his hour of agonized decision, white-faced, his husky voice sounding the evangelical call that struck deep into the heart of everyone in that crowded chamber.

He concluded his half-hour address with a noble statement of American ideals:

> The world must be made safe for democracy. Its peace must be planted upon the tested foundation of political liberty. We have no selfish ends to serve. We desire no conquest, no dominion. We seek no indemnities . . . no material compensation for the sacrifices we shall freely make. We are but one of the champions of the rights of mankind. We shall be satisfied when those rights have been made as secure as the faith and the freedom of nations can make them. . . . It is a fearful thing to lead this great, peaceful people into . . . the most terrible and disastrous of all wars, civilization itself seeming to be in the balance. But the right is more precious than peace. And we shall fight for the things which we have always carried nearest our hearts. . . .

There was a moment of silence when the President finished speaking, and then the chamber echoed to the deafening roar of support.

Four days later, the formal resolutions were passed by Congress. We were at war.

III

The Advisory Commission

THE ADVISORY COMMISSION of the Council of National Defense had been at work for exactly five months when America entered the war. In that interval, it had mapped out a vast program to prepare the nation's economy to fight a war.

When I reread the minutes of the Council of National Defense, the Advisory Commission, and my own memoranda and data, I still wonder how we were able to do what we did. We started out with little knowledge about the workings of government and the requirements of war. Moreover, we began our work at a time when public opinion and the President's policy were directed toward keeping us out of what was generally considered Europe's quarrel.

In this atmosphere of official neutrality, it was difficult to organize a preparedness program. The support we of the Commission got at first was rather desultory and somewhat patronizing. We even had to pay the rent of our own offices in the Munsey Building. This was no burden to me—I have always insisted upon paying my own expenses while in government service—but it did reflect what little weight was attached to the importance of the Commission.

When the Commission met for its first sessions we were, as I have suggested, a somewhat bewildered group of men. In addition, we did not know each other well and were inclined to be wary.

I attach a good deal of importance to personalities, and so I fell to studying my colleagues in those first meetings. Two men stood out at once: Daniel Willard and Samuel Gompers.

Willard, the Chairman of the Advisory Commission, was one of the foremost railroad men in America. Starting as a youth in the industry, he had risen to the presidency of the B. & O. Railroad. A man of great dignity and ability, he was almost universally respected.

From the tales I had heard about Gompers, I was prepared to find nothing congenial in him. I was largely ignorant of the labor movement and suspicious of its leaders. I often reflect how great a part ignorance and suspicion play in our daily lives, how easily they are played upon and we are preyed upon because of them. I was quite prepared to antagonize Gompers, but fortunately for me, he was so unfailingly courteous and coöperative that I soon realized he was not the terrible "eat-em-up" Gompers described by my business friends.

Gompers was a short, squat man, but when he rose to speak he seemed to grow in stature, for he talked well, even eloquently at times, especially when he discussed the needs and problems of labor. I remember well the dramatic and moving meeting at which Gompers informed the Advisory Commission of his summons to labor to rally to the defense of the country.

Gompers sat at one end of the long table, Chairman Willard at the other, and the rest of us were ranged along the sides. Gompers spoke with quiet emotion of his arrival in America as a child, of his experiences in sweat shops for which, as he said, "I have never quite forgiven society." He spoke of labor's long, often bitter, struggle for betterment. Yet, conscious as he was of labor's grievances, in this time of emergency he wanted labor to put aside its special interests and rally instantly, whole-heartedly, to the national interest. Thanks to Gompers' leadership, the conduct of labor during the war was, by and large, admirable.

He had a talent for striking to the heart of a question, which I greatly admired. One afternoon we spent a long, wearisome session trying to chart a plan of organization for our work. Everyone had talked at length, and when an attempt was made to extract a plan from the welter of discussion it seemed nearly impossible. Finally, Gompers said he had to leave to keep a dinner engagement at the White House, and asked permission to give his impression of what had been discussed. A stenographer was called in. Gompers leaned back in his chair, took a puff or two at his cigar, blew the smoke at the ceiling, and began to dictate. Without hesitating an instant, he clarified in a few minutes what had been said in hours of discussion, and put into words a plan of organization that was followed during nearly the entire life of the Commission.

He did love a good cigar. I, myself, was then a heavy cigar smoker, a pleasure I have long since given up. Once I induced him to take a few of mine. He tucked them in his vest and said, "You know, Governor, when I get a good cigar, I like to shut the door and windows and enjoy it all."

Gompers and Willard knew each other well and I could see that some feeling existed between them. Willard showed this much more than Gompers. At the beginning, both he and Julius Rosenwald would hop down Gompers' throat as soon as he opened his mouth. I soon found myself sympathizing with the labor chief. At last I felt compelled to speak up and ask that he be given a chance to express his views without interruption. In time a better understanding, and later even a kind of camaraderie, developed among the members of the Commission.

Gompers gave me an insight into labor's cause which I hadn't had previously. Largely because of him I came to sympathize with labor's problems and aspirations. I have lived long enough, however, to see the unions of Gompers' day become rich and powerful institutions which have gradually acquired some of the arrogance and some of the other evils which were once the more or less exclusive property of industry.

2

The first organizational step of the Commission took place in February, when we decided to organize ourselves into committees. Each member was to serve as chairman of one committee, with other members to be designated from government and business. This was the beginning of the system of committees and subcommittees which was eventually to bring the government into contact with every element of the nation's economy and provide the basis for its direction and control.

Each of us took the job he was best equipped to do. Willard headed the committee on transportation and communications; Coffin was in charge of munitions, manufacturing, and industrial relations; Rosenwald had dry goods, clothing, and supplies; Gompers, naturally, directed labor, including the large problem of industrial health; Godfrey began a survey of resources and engineers; Martin had the direction of medicine, surgery, and general sanitation. I was responsible for raw materials and minerals. As Executive Director of the Commission, there was named the extraordinarily able Walter Gifford, who later became president of American Telephone and Telegraph Company and Ambassador to the Court of St. James.

After this initial step was taken, I took another. From the time the problem of industrial mobilization first gripped my interest in 1915, I had recognized that victory in modern war depended upon the speed and efficiency with which the nation could convert its economy from peace and employ its resources for war. It occurred to me that one of the simplest ways to do this would be to organize into separate committees the producers of aluminum, brass, cement, chemicals—down through the industrial alphabet to steel, wool, and zinc. The membership of these committees, comprising the

industrial leaders of the country, would make available the specialized knowledge and experience required by a war effort. These men
would best know how to increase supply, speed production, prevent
hoarding, and develop substitutes for scarce materials. And so I
began to organize the basic industries in the raw materials field into
a system of advisory committees.

In time, every major industry in America was organized into
such committees. These committees, representing supply in the
supply and demand equation—an equation as crucial in the economics of war as in the economics of peace—were complemented by
corresponding commodity sections on which were represented all
interested government agencies. Thus demand was organized. This
system of industry committees and commodity sections was the distinctive feature of the War Industries Board when it was created,
and the major instrument in directing the industrial side of the war.

One of the first and most dramatic demonstrations of the effectiveness of these industrial committees came in the price negotiations with copper producers early in 1917. The price of copper
had risen from over eleven cents a pound in October, 1914, to more
than thirty-five cents in March, 1917. Anticipating that the price
would skyrocket even higher if we entered the war, I called on the
leading copper men, among them Daniel Guggenheim and John D.
Ryan, and urged them to meet the government's copper needs at a
reasonable price. In response to this appeal, the copper industry
agreed to supply over forty-five million pounds of copper to the
Army and Navy at a price of about sixteen-and-a-half cents a pound,
less than half the prevailing market price.

The armed forces were very appreciative. The Assistant Secretary
of the Navy, Franklin D. Roosevelt, wrote me on March 22nd: "I
want to congratulate you on the success of your negotiations in regard to copper, which has been a real service, not only to us, but to
the whole country."

The significance of this agreement, as I scribbled in a diary which,
unfortunately, I kept only sporadically, "was not its immediate

saving of money—about $9,000,000—but the breaking of the con-
tinuity of thought toward constantly mounting prices and the establishment of the fact that great producing interests . . . would
voluntarily reduce their prices to the government in a spirit of
service in a time of stress. . . ."

The copper incident was not an isolated one. On another occasion, one Sunday afternoon shortly after the declaration of war,
the French Ambassador, Jean J. Jusserand, informed me that ship-
ments of gasoline and other petroleum products to France were
being delayed. I immediately telephoned Alfred C. Bedford, of
Standard Oil, who was on the oil committee. He knew exactly where
the problem lay, and within forty-eight hours two tankers were
on their way to France. This was considered something marvelous,
but it was only an example of how the industry committee system
was able to cut red tape.

These first successes helped to ease my way into official Washington, and to win the confidence of my associates and the President.
Indeed, in short time Wilson was asking me to undertake assignments outside my work as Commissioner of Raw Materials.

One night at a White House reception, the President's military
aide came up to me, saluted, and said Mr. Wilson wanted to see
me. Curiously, my first reaction was to wonder what, if anything,
I had done for which I could be put on the carpet. In a moment
I stood before the President, aware that everyone's eyes were upon
us.

After the aide had saluted and backed away, the President told
me that a private syndicate had bought several Austrian ships in
anticipation of an American declaration of war. They obviously
intended to sell these vessels to our government at a handsome
profit, knowing that we would be in need of ships. The President
had assigned an official to prevent this projected profiteering at the
expense of the government, but was dissatisfied with his efforts.
Now, the President said, he was giving the job to me. "You use all

the influence you think the President has, but get those ships," he concluded.

The official whom I was to relieve was present at this reception. I asked Mr. Wilson to inform him that the task was being turned over to me. At first Wilson saw no reason to do so, but he finally agreed. He called the man to his side and told him that I would handle the ship matter. "But, Mr. President . . ." the man started to explain. "There are no more buts," Wilson snapped.

It was 9:58 P.M. when I left the White House. Arriving at the Shoreham Hotel, where I had rooms, I began telephoning the people who owned those Austrian ships. One was in Washington, the others in New York. I roused several of them out of bed that night, and managed to impress upon them the determination of the government to have the ships without profit to the syndicate. I made them see how unwise it would be to oppose the President in this affair.

Next morning I called the President. I had my watch in my hand as the White House phone rang. It was 8:58, eleven hours to the minute since I had left there, when I got Mr. Wilson on the wire. I informed him I had the Austrian ships, without profit to anyone. He was surprised, and complimented me on accomplishing a difficult task with such dispatch.

3

In spite of these early accomplishments and the able efforts of my associates, the Advisory Commission fell far short of meeting the needs of the situation. After the war, certain quarters portrayed the Advisory Commission as the most powerful and sinister agency ever to function in government. Representative William J. Graham, a corn belt mesmerizer from Illinois, charged that the Advisory Commission had been a "secret government" which had drafted a preparedness program and other war measures without any authority, even before the United States entered the conflict. He credited it with fixing prices, planning censorship, controlling food, and directing a big-business conspiracy to profiteer. I, it appeared, had been a "Super-President," running the whole show, "the most powerful man in the world."

The charges, of course, were patent nonsense and part of a campaign to smear Wilson's Administration. But as is so often the case, Graham's violent charges created the public illusion of a Commission with far more power than it ever possessed. The Commission never had the power attributed to it by Graham. What the Commission did do, though, was to chart the course for much that was accomplished later.

For example, Chairman Willard's committee on transportation and communications was the nucleus of the Railroad Administration, which was later entrusted to McAdoo. The reason this Administration was entrusted to Secretary of the Treasury McAdoo was because the major problem of the railroads, as Willard and Judge Robert S. Lovett of the Union Pacific Railroad made clear, was financing. Out of Gomper's labor committee came the War Labor Administration. Out of the committees for raw materials; munitions and manufacture; supplies; and engineering developed the War Industries Board.

In brief, our preliminary organization, working in the dark at first, became the crucible out of which was produced our entire wartime economic administration, which ultimately came to be considered the most efficient and advanced among all the warring nations. It was, for example, the Advisory Commission which recommended the creation of the Food Administration, and proposed Herbert Hoover as its Administrator. We brought to the attention of the government the need for an extensive shipbuilding program, out of which grew the Shipping Board and the Emergency Fleet Corporation. The Commission also demonstrated the necessity for the control of imports and exports, which finally resulted in the War Trade Board.

But despite this, the truth is that neither the Council of National Defense nor its Advisory Commission were suitably organized or sufficiently empowered to meet the demands made upon the national economy by the needs of the expanding Navy and the much more rapidly expanding Army. The situation grew worse when our entrance into the war brought new confusion and greater problems. In addition to supplying our own armed forces, we now had to meet the demands of our Allies and of all the other programs involved in conducting war and maintaining our domestic front.

The Advisory Commission lacked entirely the executive authority the situation required. The Commission was purely advisory, and neither the Army nor the Navy welcomed advice. The Army alone had five seperate purchasing agencies, each working at cross purposes. At the same time, it had little idea of its requirements. When, for example, Du Pont asked if we wanted toluol, the basic ingredient in TNT, the Army could not provide an answer.

When the weakness of the Advisory Commission at last became apparent to all, the Council of National Defense created the General Munitions Board under the chairmanship of Frank Scott, a young Cleveland industrialist, just as we entered the war. It was no improvement. The Board did considerable work in developing sources of supply, advising the armed forces on prices, and developing new facilities. But it, too, had no authority, and its recommendations were regularly ignored by the armed forces.

It was clear to me, at least, that a single authoritative agency was required with power centralized in one man. Consequently, in May, 1917, I urged the President to create a centralized purchasing agency with authority over prices and the closing of defense contracts. But no action was taken on this proposal.

Three months later the Munitions Board was superseded by the War Industries Board of the Council of National Defense, again under Scott's chairmanship. I was hopeful that it would be able to achieve what its predecessor had not.

On both the General Munitions Board and this first WIB, I continued in charge of raw materials. But now new faces appeared: Lieutenant Colonel Palmer Pierce represented the Army; Admiral Frank F. Fletcher, the Navy; Robert Brookings, president of Washington University of St. Louis, was put in charge of prices; Judge Robert S. Lovett took over priorities; and Hugh Frayne, of the AFL, handled labor. I served in close association with these men for the remainder of the war.

But again this new agency, lacking authority, proved inadequate to the task.

4

That fall and winter of 1917-1918 was a period of drifting and indecision in Washington, which coincided with the nadir of the Allied military fortunes in Europe. Italy had been all but knocked out of the war at Caporetto; Gallipoli had failed; the German U-boat campaign was approaching the peak of its effectiveness. The German General Ludendorff, in reviewing the war, said: "The military situation was more favorable to us at New Year's, 1918, than one would ever have expected. We could think of deciding the war by an attack on land. Numerically, we had never been so strong in comparison with our enemies."

Poor Frank Scott fell ill under the pressure of work and had to be invalided out of Washington. Willard took over the chairmanship. "Fine man," I noted in my diary, "generous and unselfish and it will be a pleasure to work with him." He, too, recognized the need for centralized authority in the WIB. But with no hope of securing it, he advised the President in January that he wished to resign and return to the B & O Railroad.

At times, it seemed to me that we risked calamity as the war reached its climax. The nitrate situation was a case in point. At a meeting of the Advisory Commission, even before we went to war, I had called attention to the urgency of stock-piling nitrate of soda—

the prime ingredient of gun-powder and fertilizer—for which we were dependent primarily upon Chilean sources. Almost a year later we were still desperately short of this critical material.

As I read over my diary with its references to the threatened crisis in nitrates, I can almost recapture the sense of dismay and frustration I felt when I wrote such entries as, "When I think how this matter has been handled I could commit murder, but I shall drive this every moment." Perhaps the intensity of this recollection is due to the fact that the President had finally made me solely responsible for solving the nitrate problem. There were a few days, during the time I wrestled with it, when I was as close to panic as I have ever been in my life. I worried constantly over the safety of the tramp steamers beating up from Chile with their priceless cargoes through submarine-infested waters. I had nightmares in which I pictured our boys going into combat using blank cartridges because we had no nitrate with which to make gunpowder. One morning while dressing, I looked at my pale, drawn face in the mirror and actually said aloud, "Why, you coward. Pull yourself together and act like a man."

What happened next made me wonder whether some special providence wasn't looking after me. When I reached my office, a Naval intelligence officer came in to show me several intercepted cables which revealed that the Chilean government was vainly trying to get its gold reserve released from Germany.

This gave me something to work on. When the Chilean Ambassador called on me soon after, and began complaining about the difficulty of controlling inflation in his country, I was prepared to make him an offer. If Chile would seize the 235,000 tons of German-owned nitrate in Chile and sell it to us, we would pay for it in gold.

So sure was I that the Chileans would act on this offer that, as soon as the Ambassador left my office, I arranged to get ships sent down to Chile so that no time would be lost in getting possession of the nitrate. The Chilean government didn't disappoint me. We got the desperately needed nitrate.

But such strokes of providence could not be relied upon to resolve all our shortcomings and mistakes, or to overcome the inadequacies of our production and mobilization programs. My diary records the frustration I felt in the last months of 1917 and early 1918 over the lack of direction and the absence of authority. "There is a tendency to too much looseness," I noted in November. "No one wants to give power to one man. This makes them less powerful; and they think it makes him too powerful. Fiddle while Rome burns."

On another day, irked by the absence of clear-cut lines of authority in our organization, I scribbled, "What is everybody's job is nobody's job."

On January 4, 1918, I noted that the Board had called a meeting to discuss a report on price fixing of nickel, but that no decision had been made. "It seems useless to have the whole board meeting and not deciding," I wrote. On January 19th: "The confusion is greater and not less here. No one has a plan and all seem too tired to do anything except criticize." On January 24th, I recorded talk of a munitions bill being drafted to overcome shortcomings in the war program. "In the meantime," this entry goes on, "the greatest disorganization is going on here and in industry. Each department is now going out and grabbing right and left . . . in order to strengthen themselves, with no thought of the thing as a whole."

But by now, although belatedly, pressure was building up in Congress for an effective administration of the war program. Senator George Chamberlain of Oregon, in particular, led an attack on Secretary of War Baker, criticizing the War Department for supply failures and its faulty supply organization.

At the height of this attack, McAdoo advised me that the President was considering me as a replacement for Baker. I admit that, aside from the honor, the prospect of such an appointment filled me with excitement. But I told McAdoo it would be a great mistake to permit Baker to resign. If the President's enemies forced

Baker out, they would redouble their attacks on other Cabinet members, and in the end disrupt the Administration and destroy the public's confidence in it. I suggested that we strengthen the warmaking agencies, and counter the Administration's critics, by re-organizing WIB.

Early in 1918, Senator Chamberlain introduced a bill to create a Cabinet post in charge of munitions, modeled after the British Ministry of Munitions. The President opposed the bill, claiming that it would take a superman to fill such a job. Secretary Baker was of the same mind. Testifying before the Senate Military Affairs Committee, he argued against the creation of a munitions ministry "because no human being could be found who could carry the burden" of deciding questions relating to the Navy Department, War Department, Shipping Board, Aircraft Board, the needs of our Allies and our civil population. Moreover, the Chamberlain bill, Baker declared, would create an industrial dictator.

Willard and I followed Baker before the Committee. Neither of us favored the Chamberlain bill, but both of us called for one-man control under the President within the framework of WIB. I disagreed explicitly with Baker. Later, as Chairman of the United States War Industries Board, the post that eventually emerged from the drive for more effective direction of the war program, I was certainly neither a superman nor yet a dictator. If it is coupled with responsibility, power does not create dictators. Nor does its effective use require supermen.

Under the pressure of the Chamberlain bill and other criticism, the President and Baker agreed at last to reconstitute WIB. Baker asked me to draft a memorandum on a proposed reorganization. This I did, repeating in essence the recommendations I had made to the President in May, 1917, and laying major emphasis on the need to centralize authority in one man under the President. Baker and I went over the memorandum, and with his impressive ability to clarify and sharpen, he rewrote it. He and I conferred at the White House with the President, on January 31st, about the proposed changes in the Board. By this time the President finally had come around to accepting the principle of one-man control.

The immediate problem was to appoint a chairman of the new WIB, since Willard had already resigned. As early as January 17th, my name had been proposed to the President by McAdoo. In a letter marked "Personal" and addressed to "Dear 'Governor,' " he wrote: "I hope sincerely you will consider Baruch for the vacancy if Mr. Willard leaves. He is by all odds the most capable man for the position."

I was favored in other quarters. Joe Tumulty, the President's secretary and one of the most devoted aides any President ever had, thought I should be appointed. So did Gompers and the influential commentator, David Lawrence. And Secretary of the Navy Josephus Daniels wrote to the President, saying he too believed I was the best man for the job. But the opposition was strong, too. The business community had been unhappy about me from the start. This fact was reflected in a letter Daniels wrote to Mr. Wilson on February 2nd, noting that a former president of the United States Chamber of Commerce had told him my appointment "would not be well received by many businessmen and would be sharply criticized." As for himself, Daniels said, "My own judgment is that in capacity to do the work and in loyalty Baruch is the best man, but whether under all the conditions and prejudices it would be wise to name him now is debatable. [Secretary of Agriculture David] Houston, whose judgment is generally good, thinks it would be a mistake. For service, in the long run it would not be, I am sure, but it would not be free from much criticism."

Wilson replied, ". . . I wish with you to follow the line of action which will bring the least criticism.

"I think you will find that members of the two Houses are learning very fast to have a very great confidence in Baruch, and after all they are our only authoritative critics."

I was, of course, conscious of the suspicion in which I was held in many places. My Wall Street reputation had preceded me to

Washington, embellished by all the rumors that Wall Street and Washington can concoct. I do not know which is the greater rumor factory.

I have noticed that unflattering rumors circulate more widely than complimentary ones. Judge Lovett told me in all seriousness that he understood I flipped a coin to determine whether or not a stock was going up. Daniel Willard, a sound and conservative businessman, was troubled by the fact that I seemed to carry all my information in my vest pocket. Both Lovett and Willard became my good friends in time, but at this point neither of them could accept the fact that a Wall Street speculator could be qualified to organize and synchronize the nation's economy.

I could understand this attitude, though I could not agree. A man of my background had experience which they could not appreciate. For one thing, I had trained myself to see the economy as a whole. My experience had not been with railroads alone, or with steel alone, but with most of the elements of our economic life and their interrelationships, which I had studied with great care. Moreover, I had one qualification which not many men shared. I did not have to go back to a job or to a business that could be affected by any of the interests I might have to antagonize.

I know that some of my associates, for all their integrity, were worried by the business enemies they were making, and one of my colleagues suffered financially after the war because of these enemies. But the only business I would go back to was under my hat. I was independent, and there is no more priceless possession.

In regard to the chairmanship of the WIB, I had none of the doubts and reluctance which I had felt in accepting the Advisory Commission appointment. I was confident I knew what had to be done, and confident I could do it.

Baker, in a letter to the President on January 24th, had suggested three names: Clarence M. Woolley, president of the American Radiator Company, then on the War Trade Board, a man with a high reputation as a business organizer; John D. Ryan; and me. However, I knew that Baker did not favor me; we had never hit it off. In fact, he told me plainly that though I had shown the best work in Washington, he did not think me qualified to head a large organization. His preference was for Ryan, as events proved.

That the President had already made up his mind by early February to name me seems clear from the letter he wrote Daniels. He reaffirmed his intention in a letter to McAdoo on February 26th, after McAdoo had inquired whether he could have me for another job.

> My dear Mac,
> I am mighty sorry but I can't let you have Baruch for the Finance Corporation. He has trained now in the War Industries Board until he is thoroughly conversant with the activities of it from top to bottom, and as soon as I can do so without risking new issues on the Hill I am going to appoint him chairman of that board.
> This is entirely confidential.

Apparently he had not told Baker of his decision, or else the Secretary was not convinced. For late in February, on a Saturday afternoon, Baker called me to his office and astounded me by asking me if I would inform Ryan that he was to be the new Chairman of WIB. I have never been able to fathom Baker's motive. It would have been a simple matter for him to have notified Ryan himself. I asked, however, what he wanted me to do after Ryan took over.

"You're expected to stay there and show Ryan how to do the job," he said.

I went to the WIB offices and tried unsuccessfully to reach Ryan, who was then in New York. I then went over to McAdoo's home. He usually went to bed on Saturday and Sunday afternoons to get some rest—he was one of the hardest working men in Washington—but he saw me immediately. I told him of my conversation with the Secretary of War. He split the air with his expletives.

A lot of men I know swear to let off nervous energy. Some men

I know never swear. Wilson would allow himself a "damn it" occasionally, but that was all. Harry Garfield never swore, and I don't believe Vance McCormick did. I never heard Cary Grayson swear or tell a vulgar story. Carter Glass usually said, "Dad bum it." I don't believe I ever heard Daniels or Baker swear, which did not make them any better than the fellows who did.

But McAdoo was a prodigious and proficient cusser. I can see him yet on that Saturday afternoon as he got out of bed in his long old-fashioned nightgown, purpling the air with his vivid vocabulary, and dressing himself as fast as he could.

If McAdoo believed in you, nothing could ever make him waver in his determination to carry through for you to the end. That afternoon I walked with him to the White House, where I left him at the gate. Every now and then on the trip over, he would wave his arms up and down, swear and make the pavement almost shake with his indignation.

Later he telephoned me and in his usual manner said, "Hell, I fixed that."

I cannot document it, but I pressume that what happened was simply that Wilson reassured him he had not changed his mind about appointing me.

I left town that night. When I returned on Sunday, I was told that Secretary Baker had been trying to reach me. When I phoned him he said, "Never mind saying anything to Ryan. We've made some other arrangements." He did not inform me what they were.

On Monday, March 4th, the President sent for me. When I arrived, he handed me a letter, naming me Chairman of the War Industries Board of the United States and outlining the new responsibilities of the Board.

In brief, the Board was charged with the duty of providing the industrial requirements of our armed forces and Allies, while meeting the needs of our civilian population. In other words, the lever of America's industrial power was being placed in its hands.

". . . The ultimate decision of all questions," the President wrote, "except the determination of prices [which was to be the function of a separate price-fixing committee of the Board], should rest always with the Chairman. . . ."

Whatever was being well done, I was to let alone. Where there was a conflict, I was to take action. From my decisions, the President himself was the only court of appeal.

By this move, it was acknowledged at last that the raising of armies and navies alone was not adequate to the demands of modern war. We had finally learned that on the home front, as well as on the battle front, discipline and control were imperative. After a year of confusing and sometimes bitter experience, we understood that if the economy were unregulated as in peace, defense production would be obstructed and profiteering would increase.

As I left the White House, with Wilson's letter in my pocket, I said to myself, "Now when you say 'no,' you must mean 'no,' and when you say 'yes,' you must mean 'yes.' Whatever you do, you must make your own decisions and never delay or wobble. You must decide."

IV

The War Industries Board

IT WOULD TAKE A VOLUME at least the size of this one to tell the full story of the War Industries Board,* how it went about the gigantic and unprecedented task of converting industrial America from peace to war, and how, in the process, it came to exercise such great control over the nation's industry that in the view of many I became a virtual dictator.

Such a view of my power is overwrought. The truth is, the eventual effectiveness of the WIB was due to our recognition of the fact that the requirements of war—of survival—demanded a drastic redirection of the nation's resources. To attempt to do this through the normal peacetime working of supply and demand would have been disastrous.

As I have said, the law of supply and demand is as vital to the economics of war as it is to the economics of peace. But there is this crucial difference. In peacetime the free working of the market place can be trusted to keep the economy in balance. The law of supply and demand has *time* in which to operate. But in

---

* It has been told in great detail in Grosvenor Clarkson's *Industrial America in the World War.*

war that equilibrium must be achieved by conscious direction—
for war, with its ravenous demands, destroys the normal balance
and denies us time. And time means lives.

This understanding of the fundamental difference between the
economics of war and peace still eludes many people. It is one of
the most tragic, single failures of economic understanding in our
time. Nothing—*nothing*—has cost this country and the rest of the
world more, except the losses and maimings of war itself, than the
failure to grasp the enormous difference in the workings of supply
and demand under conditions of war and under conditions of peace.

In 1917, the principle that a sound mobilization program must
adapt the law of supply and demand to the needs of war was considered revolutionary. Because we ignored this principle, we floundered during the first year of the war while shortages developed,
production lagged, prices rose, and many profiteered.

In the WIB we constantly sought the wartime equivalent of
supply and demand. Everything we did we tried to do in harmony
with that law. Instead of allowing prices to determine what would
be produced and where it would go, we decided, on the basis of
need, how our resources would be employed, so that first things
would come first. We regulated the demand for them by curtailing
their nonessential use, and by encouraging the use of substitutes.
We also sought to increase the supply of essential resources. And
we saved precious material and labor by standardizing and simplify-
ing production, and by encouraging conservation—by making old
things do.

Thus, when steel was in short supply we refused to permit the
building of a theater in St. Louis, saved over 2,000 tons by reducing
bicycle designs, and garnered enough metal for two warships by
taking the stays out of women's corsets. When the demand for
woolen fabric grew acute we induced the tailors to reduce the size
of their sample swatches, thus saving 450,000 yards of cloth.

How did we in WIB go about controlling the industrial output
of the United States? Actually, our specific powers were few and,

considering the scope of the task confronting us, rudimentary. However, during the first year of groping toward an effective organization, we devised and perfected methods of operation and instruments of control which, judiciously and sometimes boldly used, proved adequate to the task.

The most important instrument of control was the power to determine priority—the power to determine who gets what and when. The significance of priority was first impressed upon me in 1916 by Sir Walter Layton, the British economist. When I joined the Advisory Commission, I began to urge creation of some well-organized priority machine, to cope with the developing shortages in raw materials. A Priorities Committee was appointed in June, 1917, but it proved ineffective because it lacked authority. Finally, when I was appointed Chairman of WIB, the President vested authority in me for "the determination, wherever necessary, of priorities of production and of delivery. . . ." Thereafter, with Judge Edwin B. Parker heading the Priorities Division of WIB, this instrument of control was used with increasing effectiveness.

Through the use of priority rulings, WIB was able to direct, restrain, or stimulate war production as the ever-changing situation required. Priority enabled us to allocate scarce materials where they were needed most, to curtail less essential production, to break bottlenecks, to end reckless and chaotic competition and hoarding, to conserve fuel, to save shipping space, to pool and ration. Priority also became a potent factor in dispersal of war plants, in the regulation of transportation, and in controlling prices.

The administration of priority was a complex and delicate task. Should locomotives go to Pershing to carry his army to the front or should they go to Chile to haul nitrates needed to make ammunition for Pershing's troops? Should precedence be given to destroyers needed to fight the U-boats or to merchant ships whose numbers were being decimated by the German subs? Should nitrates be allocated to munitions or to fertilizer? Should the Railroad Administration or the Fuel Administration get the tank cars both were claiming? We were not always as wise as Solomon in deciding these questions, but we did succeed in synchronizing American industry to the needs of war through the priority power.

2

As was to be expected, our priority decisions often caused anguish and outrage in the armed services procurement agencies and even more among industrialists, neither of whom were accustomed to interference in their own affairs.

WIB had no authority over the armed forces. They were our clients and we existed to serve them. My rule as Chairman was always to provide the armed forces with whatever they needed, when they needed it, with as little dislocation as possible of the civilian population. Still, the armed forces were not overly enthused about our mission of service.

When I was appointed to head the WIB, Rear Admiral Samuel McGowan, the hard-driving sailor in charge of Navy supplies, asked Senator Claude Swanson whether the Navy need pay much attention to WIB. Swanson, Chairman of the Naval Affairs Committee, was a wise man. One of his favorite political maxims was, "When in doubt, do right." Now he advised, "We'd better find out how strong Baruch is." The Senator later told me he then went to see McAdoo and asked his opinion of the organization and about me.

"If any damn fool interferes with Baruch," McAdoo told him in his customary vivid manner, "he will get his block knocked off. The President is going to back him to the limit."

Swanson informed McGowan that it appeared I was too strong to buck. I remember McGowan coming in and inquiring cheerfully, "Well, Chief, what are the orders?"

Thereafter, relations with the Navy, whose procurement organization was superior to the Army's, went fairly smoothly. Relations with the Army were more strained. The Army's supply services were poorly organized and inefficient, and they came in for a good deal of criticism during and after the war. General Crozier, Chief of Ordnance, was a fine man and a gifted engineer, but he had no organization. Many was the night I sat with him in the War Department, working on production requirement schedules while his wife sat knitting in a corner.

Perhaps because it needed the Board more, the Army resented us more. The General Staff had little understanding of industry and production; consequently, the problems of relating supply to demand were much more complex and harassing than they might have been.

General George Goethals, the great builder of the Panama Canal, succeeded Lieutenant Colonel Pierce as the Army representative on WIB. But he didn't find the work congenial. When General Hugh Johnson began to sit in for Goethals, things improved considerably —as they always did where Johnson was involved.

General Peyton C. March, the Chief of Staff, was a cold, precise inflexible soldier of the old school who did little, at first, to hide his low opinion of WIB. He once kept me standing before his desk during an interview. General March's policy was to get as many men as possible to France, and to let others worry about supplying them. He did a tremendous job in getting more than two million soldiers overseas in one of the most prodigious efforts in military history up to that time. When someone asked him how the multitudes of soldiers being loaded into Europe-bound transports were going to get to the front, he gave an often quoted and entirely characteristic reply: "What have they got feet for?"

But when General Pershing cabled General March that this huge army could not function unless requisitions for supplies were more promptly filled, the Chief of Staff never bothered to consult WIB. I learned of Pershing's urgent request only by chance. An assistant of mine found a copy of his message on the floor in the War Department. That led to a showdown discussion between General March and me in which I made it plain that in such fundamental matters the Army would have to acknowledge the responsibility delegated to WIB by the President. We worked it out without a further row.

The tensions between the War Industries Board and the Army tended to diminish as WIB operated with increasing success in the spring and summer of 1918. We had, by this time, educated the services to what we were doing and why.

3

Although WIB acted primarily through its power over priority, we also relied on our power of persuasion to elicit the coöperation from industry which success of the war program required. When priorities and persuasion failed, we had one instrument of last resort to enforce our will—the power of commandeering—the power to seize property.

It says a great deal for the industrial leaders of America that the WIB was able to operate as effectively as it did largely on the basis of their voluntary coöperation. Many businessmen might turn apoplectic at a WIB ruling, but when they understood why it had been issued they usually did everything possible to help. I remember the Boston chemical manufacturer who came storming into my office to denounce me for taking his supply of ammonium sulphate. We had been compelled to do so because in negotiating for the purchase of fifty thousand Spanish mules, desperately needed by Pershing, the Spanish insisted on the sulphate of ammonia for their hard-pressed agriculture. When the reason for our action was explained to him, the Boston manufacturer apologized for having questioned the Board's decision.

Andrew Mellon, who controlled the giant Aluminum Company of America, sent the company's president, Arthur Davis, to me with instructions to do whatever I asked of him. As a result, the Aluminum Company was virtually placed at the disposition of the government. There were many other incidents of a similar nature which revealed the willingness of most American businessmen to do whatever was required of them when they knew why.

But it would be misleading to suggest that all industry leaders were motivated by altruism or that their coöperation was spontaneous. Had this been so, the history of WIB would not have been filled with so many instances of conflict. If some men accepted without question the intrusion of government into their affairs, others resented it and some fought it tooth and nail.

This was not from any sinister or unpatriotic motives but from the narrow perspective common among many businessmen. Some preferred to do business as usual despite the war. Some feared the extension of government authority on philosophical grounds. Not even the fact of war was sufficient to win them from their laissez-faire convictions that government intervention was somehow un-American.

The most dedicated and determined exponents of this point of view were in the two giant industries: auto and steel. WIB's struggles with these two giants illustrate some of the problems we faced and how we overcame them.

The problem of converting industry from peacetime to wartime production was always a thorny one. Contrary to widely held views, manufacturers were not always eager for war work, especially when it required them to abandon a profitable line of production. This was the case with the auto manufacturers.

WIB moved early to curtail the production of pleasure cars. We had no intention of countenancing their production while we scrounged for steel for tanks, guns, locomotives, and ships. At first we tried to rely upon voluntary agreements under which the automobile producers pledged to cut production by two-thirds. But we soon found that these agreements were not self-enforcing.

By 1918, the demand for steel, bred by the war, was more than one hundred per cent of the industry's capacity. Moreover, I knew that the demand would go higher, that great quantities of steel would be required for such programs as the one Winston Churchill, Britain's Minister of Munitions, had in mind.

Churchill had sent a special representative to advise me, in utmost secrecy, of his plan to build a great force of armored troop and weapons carriers. These tanklike vehicles, to be unveiled in the great offensive planned for the spring of 1919, would permit the attacking forces to follow close behind the artillery barrages instead of advancing on foot across no-man's land under enemy fire.

None of us could foresee that Germany's collapse would make it unnecessary to go ahead with this plan. We had to be ready to provide the steel and other resources it would require. So, in the summer of 1918, in the face of Detroit's uncoöperative attitude, we called representatives of the automobile industry to Washington.

The heads of all the great companies were present, with the exception of Henry Ford. They listened with ill-concealed impatience as we explained WIB's plans to curtail immediately the production of automobiles by seventy-five per cent, and employ the facilities thus freed for war production. Judge Parker, in charge of priorities, eloquently explained the urgent need for steel which had led us to this decision. A grave responsibility rested on us all, Parker said. It was impossible to permit production of passenger cars instead of war supplies. Reluctant as we were to check a growing industry which these men had pioneered and developed, the soldiers' needs came first.

This reasonable speech made no impression. John Dodge led the attack by giving me a personal dressing down. He did not want any white-haired, white-faced Wall Street speculator telling him how he ought to conduct his business, he said among other things. My associates, particularly Hugh Frayne, angrily rebuked Dodge. "Let him alone," I interrupted, "I'm sure that the gentleman feels better now that he's gotten that off his chest."

The other auto manufacturers, in terms less emotional than Dodge, made it equally clear that they were prepared to ignore WIB. They informed us that they had stocked all the steel and coal they needed and could proceed in spite of us. During a lull in the argument I made up my mind on what had to be done to meet this challenge to our authority.

"Just a moment, gentlemen," I said as I picked up the phone and put in a call to McAdoo at the Railroad Administration. With the auto people listening to me, I said, "Mac, I want you to take down the names of the following factories, and I want you to stop every wheel going in and going out."

The automobile men looked at me, astonished and outraged, as I read off the names of Dodge, General Motors, Ford, and other plants. This effect was heightened as I put in a call to Secretary of War Baker. "Mr. Secretary, I would like you to issue an order to commandeer all the steel in the following yards," I said. Then I called Fuel Administrator Garfield and asked him to seize the manufacturers' coal supplies.

That did it. Billy Durant, head of General Motors, said, "I quit." The others capitulated soon after, but not before some had tried to bring political pressures to bear. Henry Ford was the last to come along. I called on him at his hotel in Washington to try to explain the urgency of curtailing production of his cars. He simply could not see why this was necessary, and insisted that he could provide whatever the government needed without curtailing the output of his famous cars.

Some time after our climactic meeting with the auto men, George Peek, WIB Commissioner of Finished Products, visited Dodge in his factory in Detroit. The manufacturer expressed regret at his outburst at me and said he wanted to set it right. "Oh, hell," Peek replied, "the Chief doesn't pay any attention to that. Everybody cusses him out. If you want to square yourself, just beat your production schedule on those carriages for the 155 mm. guns." Dodge did exactly that.

Shortly after the war, I was standing in the lobby of the old Ritz-Carlton Hotel in New York when Dodge came up to me and said, "I wish you'd shake hands with me. Will you?"

"I don't know any reason why I shouldn't," I said. "I remember the job you did on those gun carriages."

Dodge went on to explain how sorry he was about the wartime incident. "Come upstairs, Baruch," he concluded, "and have a drink with me."

"Thank you, Mr. Dodge, but I'm late for an appointment," I said.

Dodge died of the impure prohibition liquor he drank that day.

4

If businessmen resented dictation over what they could and could not produce, they resented even more intensely being told what they could charge for their goods. Price controls struck the pocketbook nerve, according to some the most sensitive known to man. It also violated every principle and tradition which businessmen held dear.

In the three years before we entered the war, prices in the United States had skyrocketed as a result of frantic buying by the Allies. The average price of metals more than tripled, chemical prices had almost doubled, and food prices were up nearly fifty per cent. While these price rises reflected the traditional workings of supply and demand, it was equally clear that the war had thrown the mechanism out of kilter and that we could not continue to allow prices to go unchecked.

As I have noted earlier, one of the first things I undertook when I joined the Advisory Commission of the Council of National Defense was to negotiate price agreements with the producers of copper at prices well below the market. There were similar agreements with the producers of other raw materials. These agreements had a salutory effect on breaking the continuity of high prices, but only momentarily. Once we entered the war, the need for price controls became urgent, if runaway prices were not to swell the cost of war beyond reason and needlessly saddle the economy in the postwar period with burdensome price structures, taxes, and debts. As important as the economic considerations were the moral ones: the injustice of permitting some at home to profit—and to profiteer—while our boys were away fighting and dying, and their families were being squeezed by inflation.

But opposition to comprehensive price controls was almost unanimous. Congress refused to enact any price control legislation. It was not until the reorganization of the WIB in March, 1918, that a Price Fixing Committee, headed by Robert Brookings, was formed. This Committee was wholly independent of WIB and operated directly under the President. I was only an ex-officio member of it. But the Price Fixing Committee had very limited power. It could not arbitrarily fix prices; it could only seek agreement on prices through negotiations with producers and make recommendations to the President. Moreover, its jurisdiction extended only to raw materials—and not even to all of them but only to those in short supply.

Despite this cautious and uncertain approach to the control of prices, and despite the fact that WIB had no direct responsibility for prices, we managed to exercise a very great control over them by a broad interpretation of our duty and a judicious use of our priority power. In fact, after we entered the war prices were kept pretty well in check. Usually WIB could effect agreement on prices by negotiation. When a producer seemed bent on holding up the government, the reference to our priority order—the power to deprive him of his raw materials—was usually sufficient to encourage reasonableness. In extreme cases we threatened to wield our commandeering power.

Given the businessman's conviction of the sanctity of his right to determine the price at which he would sell his goods, it was no wonder that prices were one of the most troublesome subjects with which we had to deal. We had many conflicts over this issue, the most memorable with the steel producers.

Steel, of course, was the pivot of the war economy. Steel was needed for mines for the North Sea, for ships to replace those lost to submarines, for barbed wire on the Western front, for railroads in France, for port construction at home, and for the unending supply of weapons and ammunition that was required. Naturally the price of steel zoomed. Profits were immense.

The need to control steel prices became urgent. The first step came in the summer of 1917 when, as Chairman of the Raw Materials Committee, I went to Judge Elbert H. Gary, the redoubtable head of the United States Steel Corporation, to ask him to cut the price of ship plates ordered by the Navy and Shipping Board.

I never knew a man more devoted to anything than Gary was to the United States Steel Corporation. He seemed to think of little else. Whether you agreed with him or not—and I disagreed with him on most occasions—one had to marvel at his devotion and ability. I saw him fairly often, even socially. A quiet man, he never played cards or drank, but he would sit around until late in the evening with Mrs. Gary until the time came to go home. He was an immaculate dresser, cool and correct even on hot summer days.

Four-and-one-quarter cents was the price Gary had asked for the ship plates. I knew it to be far too high. At our meeting, my friend Tom Chadbourne was present as Gary's counsel. I had the distinct impression that Tom was uncomfortable, and perhaps less effective in his attorney's role than he might have been, because he sympathized with me and not with his client. Nevertheless, Gary would not be budged.

Troubled by this impasse, I went to see Henry C. Frick, Chairman of the Finance Committee of U.S. Steel. I found him in that splendid Fifth Avenue mansion of his. He was a very quiet man with a carefully trimmed gray beard. I told him the story of our difficulties, and explained my hope that the steel industry would set an example for the rest of the nation. To do that, I said, they would have to give the government the lowest prices possible.

Frick had a way of stroking his beard while he listened, as most men with beards do. He stroked while I talked, but I could not tell whether I was making any impression on him.

"What do you think is the right price for ship plates?" I asked at last.

"Baruch, that's not a fair question," he protested. "I'm Chairman of the Finance Committe and a director in the company."

"I know that, Mr. Frick," I replied. "But I'm asking you not as a steel man but as a citizen."

Frick didn't hesitate for an instant. "Two-and-a-half cents is enough," he said tersely.

Armed with this information, I immediately sought out Judge Gary, who was at a dinner in the Metropolitan Club. I could never enter this club's august portals as a member, and I had always felt that a man who was excluded from a club for whatever reason ought never to enter it. But I swallowed my pride and sent my name up to Judge Gary. He kept me waiting a long time before he came down, and then listened impatiently as I again appealed to him to withdraw his insistence on steel prices which I knew to be too high.

I was unable at this meeting to budge Gary, but after further negotiation a price of three-and-a-quarter cents was agreed upon. But ship plates were only one item in the iron and steel inventories whose astronomical prices had to be controlled. Connellsville coke, which had been $1.67 a ton in September, 1915, reached $12.25 by July, 1917. Basic pig iron, which was $12.59 in June, 1915, brought $52.50 a ton in June, 1917. Bessemer steel billets rose from $19.50 a ton in May, 1915, to $95 a ton in July, 1917. Structural steel shapes had been $1.20 a hundredweight in December, 1914. By July, 1917, these were $6.20.

In September, 1917, WIB moved to draw up a price schedule for coke, iron, and steel. At a meeting of the entire industry, at which sixty-five leading steel executives faced the Board, this schedule was presented. The temper of the WIB may be shown by the resolution we had agreed upon: ". . . if the steel interests should not be willing to give their full coöperation because of the prices fixed, the War Industries Board will take the necessary steps to take over the steel plants."

Judge Robert Lovett, then serving as WIB Vice-chairman, presided over this meeting. Despite his consciousness of the enemies he was making, he never faltered. He was not a bold man, but a determined one.

Lovett had an extremely dignified carriage and a leatherlike countenance which made me think there must have been some Indian in him. He listened more than he spoke, and sat in his chair like a ramrod with no expression on his face. I can see the wrinkles under his chin now as he sat erect, moving his head slowly around as he surveyed Judge Gary, Charles Schwab, Eugene Grace, and the other manufacturers present. I remember his cool, unruffled reply to Gary's opening challenge, questioning the government's legal authority to regulate prices. In his soft, drawling, Southern voice Lovett replied, "A gentleman of your eminent qualifications in law requires no information from me on that point."

The steel industry then began to unfold its carefully prepared case. A corps of experts testified on the costs of mining ore in Mesabi, transporting it to Pittsburgh mills, manufacturing coke, building furnaces—they described all the steps until the final products emerged, at the end cost. It was extremely well done.

But on our side of the table our steel expert, J. Leonard Replogle, had trouble containing himself as the steel people detailed their cost analyses. On several occasions, he interrupted indignantly to contest the claims being made by the steel representatives. After a long discussion, Judge Lovett, with no more expression than a wooden Indian, asked if there were more questions. I had been listening intently during the long meeting, and one question had been disturbing me.

"Judge Gary," I said, "I've listened with a great deal of interest to your witnesses. May I ask you if you concur in their testimony?"

"I can't see that that matters," he answered, looking me coldly in the eye.

"That is sufficient answer for the record," I replied quickly.

The meeting was a stormy one with much heated argument and impassioned oratory. In fairness to the steel industry, it should be said that its leaders were perfectly willing to fix prices on purchases by our government. They insisted, however, that the price to the public and to the Allies should continue to be determined by a free market. This was in direct conflict with the rule laid down by President Wilson that the price for the government must also be the price for the public and the Allies.

The climax occurred when I asked Judge Gary if he would be interested in a letter I possessed, and handed it to him. I have been unable to find this letter, but I can see it before me now as I write. It was a letter from the President, stating that he would commandeer the United States Steel Corporation or any other business on WIB's recommendation. Gary read the letter with an expressionless face and handed it back.

"You haven't got anybody to run the Steel Company," he said.

"Oh yes I have, Judge," I told him.

"Who?"

"Oh, we'll get a second lieutenant or somebody to run it."

That must have stung Gary to the quick.

"But that won't trouble you very much," I added. "If those mill towns find out why we've taken over, they'll present you with your mills brick by brick."

Gary rose from his seat and walked away. I could see the fingers of each hand rubbing one against the other. You could almost hear his mind turning over.

Suddenly he turned around, came back, and said, "Can't we fix this up?"

"Sure we can," I said.

The steel people went into a private conference. When they returned, one of them, long my friend, stormed over to see me.

Belligerently thrusting his face near mine, he shook his finger and shouted: "Bernie, the steel people thought you were friendly to them but they've found out you're their archenemy. They'll never forgive you as long as you live."

"Is that the steel people's message to me?" I asked him.

"It is," he shouted, apparently in a rage.

"All right," I said, "if that's the message to me, let me give you my answer." Assuming a stance as belligerent as his, I told him in unadorned language what I thought of the steel leaders, and assured him that they were not going to get away with any bluff.

That was the last shaft in the steel men's quiver. When we resumed negotiations they were more amenable to compromise. On September 24th the President proclaimed the new prices which the WIB and the steel industry had agreed upon. They were: Connellsville coke, $6 a ton; pig iron, $33 a ton; shapes, $3 a hundredweight; iron ore, $5.05 a ton; steel bars, $2.90 a hundred pounds.

The steel industry accepted these new prices in good faith and they remained almost unchanged till the end of the war. It has been estimated that this regulation of steel prices saved the government more than a billion dollars. The steel industry also did a superb job of production; but there is no question that profits, especially of the great integrated companies, were still excessive.

The government's interference with the affairs of the U.S. Steel Company always rankled Judge Gary, and he never forgave the threat I had made. After the war, he publicly charged that subversive influences in the government, meaning WIB, had sought to nationalize the steel industry as the first step in undoing America's free enterprise system. I had to set the record straight and publicly reveal the uncoöperative attitude of the steel industry in the midst of war that had compelled the government to resort to a show of force.

Ford, Gary, and Dodge typified the problem which WIB faced in educating American businessmen to the new facts of life. They had not made the transition in their thinking from Main Street to

Washington, and their values were still the values of the market place. Their pride in the achievements of industry and their mistrust of government made it difficult for them to put national interest above unenlightened self-interest.

5

In addition to serving the armed forces and regulating industrial production, another aspect of WIB's work was to act as purchasing agent for the Allies and to coödinate procurement and production programs on both sides of the ocean. Our production schedules in Washington were always geared as closely as possible to strategic and tactical needs at the front. Thus, during the great Allied drive in the fall of 1918, when word came from the French that their 75 mm. shell factories were falling idle because of a shortage in steel, we immediately assigned the Carnegie Steel Company and the Lackawanna Steel Company to meeting French requirements. Within six days the steel was en route to France.

The need for coöperation between the United States and its Allies on procurement and production became more pressing as time went on. All during the war, foreign missions were constantly coming to Washington to discuss their needs. How well I remember those early missions in particular! The overriding anxiety of these emissaries was the ever-increasing U-boat menace which was disrupting the flow of supplies. The English would relate their story plainly and unflinchingly, with typical British reserve. The French were voluble, and implicit in their words was a feeling of *"Nous sommes perdu."* The Italians were more excitable still. They were by far the most disorganized, and were very often taken advantage of before WIB began to operate effectively.

I well remember the contract for ten thousand steel billets at the exorbitant price of $140 per ton, which the Italians signed. I blocked approval, however, which left both the commission merchant who had sold the steel and the Italians very unhappy. The emissaries from Rome were on my doorstep every morning, wringing their hands, but I refused to authorize the purchase.

One day I told Price McKinney, of McKinney Steel, about the problem. McKinney spoke up in words very like these: "We've been making too much money out of the Allies. I'll provide those billets at any price you name." And he did, at a price of $45 per ton.

Two of our most vexing problems in dealing with the Allies were: first, competitive buying of such crucial materials as tin, rubber, jute, and tungsten; and second, the reluctance of the Allies to control prices on materials sold to us. To resolve these problems, I decided to send to London a mission headed by Leland Summers, one of my key assistants.

On the eve of his departure, Summers called me from New York to say that he did not have the proper authorization to draw government funds for his mission. I told him to draw upon my secretary for whatever he needed. This came to some $84,000. After the war an effort was made to secure a Congressional appropriation to reimburse me, but I refused to permit this. The money was insignificant compared with the benefit which the mission achieved and the satisfaction I derived from it. The work of the mission saved millions of dollars for America and the Allied governments. I relate this now only because it was made public, many years after the war, by James F. Byrnes.

As a result of Summers' brilliant work in London, there were created a variety of "joint executives" for tin, nitrate, wool, leather, platinum, and other commodities. These agencies became the exclusive buyers of these raw materials and allocated them among the Allies according to their need. They were the model for the combined boards of World War Two, through which the United States and Great Britain implemented their alliance in the economic field. Winston Churchill, who had returned to the Cabinet as Minister of Munitions after a short exile following the failure at Gallipoli, contributed importantly to the formation of the Nitrate Executive, as a result of which he was good-naturedly called the "Nitrate King."

Indeed, in this, as in every other Allied venture, Churchill was the model of the honorable ally, as he was again in the Second War. As my opposite number, as it were, in World War One, Churchill and I were in frequent cable communication. Those messages laid the groundwork for our subsequent close friendship.

After the war, Churchill paid this tribute to the War Industries Board:

> No British Minister had, I believe, a greater volume of intricate daily business to conduct with United States Representatives than I had during 1918. It is my duty to record that no Ally could have been given more resolute understanding and broad-minded coöperation than the Ministry of Munitions received from the War Industries Board of the United States.

As far as the question of fair prices on American purchases was concerned, Summers was able, in most instances, to get results without too much trouble. He received splendid coöperation from such men as Churchill, Austen Chamberlain, and Lord Robert Cecil. On wool alone, he secured a refund of forty million dollars on a contract which had already been signed.

But when it came to setting a reasonable price on Indian jute, it was a different story. Summers was informed, as I was by Lord Reading, the British Ambassador, that so far as jute was concerned it was a matter concerning India, over which the English suddenly had no control.

I told Lord Reading the familiar American folk tale of the hunter who one day met a ferocious-looking bear. He dropped on his knees and prayerfully called to the heavens, "Dear Lord, please help me, but if you ain't gonna help me, don't help that bear. Just stand back and watch a hell of a fight."

The point was not lost on Lord Reading, and it was further underscored when I asked McAdoo not to provide the silver which the English required for the support of the Indian currency. The

British replied in alarm that such action would cause a panic in India that would close up the Calcutta and Bombay stock exchanges. I answered through Summers: "Close them up, then." The means of influencing Indian jute prices were soon found.

6

The full warmaking potential of American industry under the direction of WIB was just reaching its peak as the war reached its end. There is no doubt that knowledge of this fact contributed materially to Germany's sudden realization of the hopelessness of her position. Not only WIB but other emergency agencies—Food, Fuel, Shipping, Transportation, all administered by able and dedicated men—were by then operating in high gear.

WIB's authority, at last recognized and accepted, was being steadily extended. We had mobilized more than three hundred and fifty industries, from asbestos through caskets to lumber and zinc. No steel, copper, cement, rubber, or other basic materials could be used without our approval. More and more of the economy was bearing some share of the war's burden. Thus, in September, WIB put non-war construction under strict control, with the very able Donald McLennan in charge. No building costing more than $2,500 could be started without WIB consent, which had direct consequences on the whole range of building trades and sub-industries. Schools and church buildings were hit especially hard. Mayor John Francis Hylan of New York, insistent on an eight-million-dollar school building program, tried unsuccessfully to bring political pressures to bear. I would not budge. Every unnecessary undertaking, I wrote him, "ties up labor, capital, materials, facilities, transportation and fuel. . . . To divert them to other ends, no matter how fine these ends may be in themselves, is at this period worse than a crime—it is a blunder that may cost us dear. . . ."

We were moving, as the war came to a close, toward controlling the whole range of consumer goods. The shoe industry was the first to be tackled. After an acrimonious fight with the manufacturers, we had worked out a plan for reducing the innumerable variety of shoe styles to a few basic ones which were to be price-fixed. In order to prevent evasion of our regulations, we planned to issue to every shoe store an insignia which would certify its compliance. This symbol of compliance was the inspiration for the Blue Eagle of the New Deal's NRA.

We had also drafted similar plans to reduce all clothing styles to a few simple patterns. If the war had lasted much longer, the civilian population would have been clothed in serviceable, if drab, apparel.

As I look back on the record which WIB helped write, I still take great satisfaction. After the war, sharp words were often spoken between America and her allies over "who won the war"—as foolish a question as ever was asked. In the outpouring of blood and agony of spirit, the Allies' ordeal was infinitely more bitter than our own. Still, there was nothing in our role in securing victory which required apology. We gave without stint of our treasure. We loaned our Allies twelve billion dollars and spent almost forty billion more on our own war costs. These were fantastic sums in 1918. But money is the least part of our contribution. Although at first our Allies did not expect—indeed did not want—us to send troops, we undertook to raise a great army. And in response to the desperate appeal from France, we sent more than two million men, three-quarters of them in the space of five months. As the German tide began to roll back the Allies, it was American man-power which stemmed it.

Nevertheless, I have always been conscious of the shortcomings in WIB's record, of the errors and inadequacies of the war effort on the home front. As a result, after 1918 I embarked on something of a one-man crusade to prevent, in any future war, a repetition of the errors which had marked our economic mobilization effort in World War One. For more than twenty years, as I shall relate in a later chapter, I preached the lessons I had learned in WIB: the importance of centralized authority over a mobilization program; the fallacy of piecemeal controls; the need to regulate not only prices, but money, man power, production—all the elements of the economy; the importance of a tax program to put the cost of war, as nearly as possible, on a pay-as-you-go basis; the necessity of preventing inflation and profiteering; and above all, the need to preserve the health of the economy so as not to run the risk of losing the peace after winning the war. These were some of the lessons I learned from my War Industries Board experience and which I tried to impart, unfortunately not very successfully.

But the lessons to be learned from WIB were not confined to questions of war. The WIB experience had a great influence upon the thinking of business and government. WIB had demonstrated the effectiveness of industrial coöperation and the advantage of government planning and direction. We helped inter the extreme dogmas of laissez faire, which had for so long molded American economic and political thought. Our experience taught that government direction of the economy need not be inefficient or undemocratic, and suggested that in time of danger it was imperative. This lesson was applied fifteen years later when the New Deal drew upon the experience of the WIB to mobilize the economic resources of the nation to meet the emergency of the great depression.

V

Some Washington Friends

FEW ADMINISTRATORS IN WASHINGTON were ever more fortunate than I in their associates. They were the most remarkable group I have ever known. The credit for the record and reputation of WIB belongs to them.

Outstanding talent can make any organization work. I have seen too many organizations fail, in business and in government, because more attention was given to tables of organization and operating handbooks than to finding the right men for the job. Consequently, as soon as President Wilson called me to Washington I began to recruit the best men I could find—and I looked for them, not among the captains of industry, but among the lieutenants on whom these captains relied.

One of the first men I enlisted was Leland Summers, a consulting engineer who was technical advisor to J.P. Morgan & Company in its capacity as purchasing agents for the Allies. They used to say that Morgan's had no use for its *Encyclopædia Britannica* as long as they had Summers. He was one of the most knowledgeable men I ever knew, expert on history, finance, science, and technology. I invited "Buster," as we called him, to my home in South Carolina to offer him, or rather to ask him, to take the job as my technical adviser. When I offered to pay him what he was earning at J.P. Morgan—about $35,000 a year—he asked, "How much are you getting?"

"Nothing," I replied.

"That's all I'll take," he said. "I'll serve as long as I can stand it." From that day until the end of the Peace Conference, he was my indispensable aide.

It was Summers, an expert in high explosives and the minerals used in munitions making, who impressed upon me the importance of building up our stocks of nitrate, toluol, platinum, and other resources in which the United States was deficient. The War Department knew very little about its requirements for toluol, the basis of TNT, but when it woke up we had an ample supply on hand, thanks to Summers.

He died, in the prime of life, a few years after the war, and never received the credit he deserved for his tremendous contribution to victory.

Summers was the one who recommended as my chief assistant Alexander Legge, vice-president of International Harvester. The more I learned about Legge, who was considered one of the greatest executives in the country, the more I was convinced that he was the man I wanted. But it was only reluctantly and under my insistant pressure that Cyrus McCormick, head of the Harvester Company, let him go.

Later I learned from Legge himself that he had done some checking on me before he agreed to come to Washington. He had asked at J.P. Morgan's for an estimate of me. It was not the place I would have sent him for a recommendation, but I learned that Morgan's considered me honest and capable although impatient and hard to control. I was, they said, largely ignorant of industry but informed about Wall Street. Also, they conceded that if I gave my word I would keep it. However one may appraise this estimate, it was not enough to keep Alec from joining me.

With his quiet smile, Legge said, "They were right about every count except your impatience. The way you let these fellows try to put things over on you before you move makes Job look like an irascible old gentleman."

When I became Chairman of WIB, Alec became Vice-chairman and head of the Requirements Division. He actually ran WIB in its day-to-day operations. He also represented me on the Allied Purchasing Commission and, as its General Manager, coördinated billions of dollars worth of Allied purchases.

Legge was a model of the shirt-sleeve executive. Tall, rawboned, broad-shouldered, with high cheekbones, freckled face, and rather small eyes which promised trouble when he narrowed them, Alec looked like the cowpuncher he had once been. He seldom smiled, preferring to appear dour. But every employee in the office adored him. He was about the most forthright man I ever knew. If he had anything to say, he said it. After the Italian debacle at Caporetto, he encountered the Italian Ambassador, who came in smiling to a meeting of the Allied Purchasing Commission.

"Say, Mr. Ambassador, when are you Italians going to stop running and begin fighting?" Alec inquired.

From any other man it would have been a mortal insult, but the Ambassador smiled on and said something diplomatic.

At times Legge would grow a little impatient with my displays of patience. Once at a meeting of the Board, after a particularly difficult discussion with the Army Chief of Staff, General March, Alec exploded into rather rough language at my failure to lay the law down to the General. There was an embarrassed silence in the room when Alec finished roasting me. As I had held my temper with March, I held it with Legge. I looked around the table and said quietly, "Gentlemen, the Board is adjourned."

As a boy I had a violent temper, but I learned to master it fairly well. I can count on the fingers of one hand the times I have lost my composure since coming to manhood, and each time I have regretted it. If a man wants to avoid mistakes in Wall Street, Washington, or anywhere else, he must learn to discipline his emotions.

Legge's office was next to mine and the door between them was never closed. But when the meeting broke up, he went out and slammed it. I sat at my desk wondering how I was going to handle Alec. But he spared me further trouble. After a while he opened the door and put his head into my room.

"Get out of here," I said, with a smile. He gave me a half-smile in return, and I knew the ice had been broken.

Later, as I stood talking to several men in the hall, I saw Alec coming toward us, leaning sideways a little, in his gait that was almost like a crab's. Reaching us he said forthrightly, "Chief, I must have made a damn fool of myself this morning, didn't I?"

"No more than usual, Alec," I said.

That was the end of it. It was his way of apologizing and I think it was the only time I ever had a serious difference with him.

After the war, Legge returned to International Harvester as president. As head of a great agricultural equipment company, he was naturally much interested in the farmer, but his concern extended far beyond commercial considerations. He was genuinely interested in agriculture as a way of life, and in the farmer as a human being. He served as Chairman of the Federal Farm Board under President Hoover, and later as head of the 4-H Clubs. When he died, he left part of his estate to establish a foundation to work for the improvement of farm life.

It was through Legge that I got George Peek, vice-president of Deere & Company, who became Commissioner of Finished Products in WIB. "He's a competitor of mine and a good man, too," Alec said. He added, with one of his rare smiles, "If I had him down here, I could watch him better."

Peek turned out to be as Legge had advertised him—able, combative, and tenacious. George never ran from a fight and he rarely lost one. In the 1920's, Peek became the farmer's chief spokesman and the acknowledged leader in the battle for farm parity. I, myself, played a part in this fight, as I shall relate later.

Immediately after I became Chairman of the WIB, I cast about for counsel. At the suggestion of Judge J. Harry Covington, to whom I first offered the job, I chose Albert C. Ritchie, then Attorney General of Maryland. I never regretted the choice. Nor did I ever forget the first legal opinion Ritchie gave me, which was to the effect that every decision I had made was *ultra vires*—that is, beyond my authority. Looking at me without blinking, he said, "You could be sued personally for a loss involved to anyone who carried out your orders."

At first this seemed a paralyzing opinion, but since I had already issued enough orders to have my fortune swallowed up many times over, there was nothing to do but go ahead as I had been doing. I will admit I thought of Ritchie's warning once in a while, but no suit was ever filed against me personally. And only one suit was ever lost in which decisions and rulings of the WIB were involved.

Ritchie was a handsome man and a delightful companion. We became the closest of friends. He went on to become Governor of Maryland for an unprecedented four terms and was often spoken of for the Presidency.

For my steel expert I recruited J. Leonard Replogle, the peppery, youthful president of the American Vanadium Company, who had been in the steel business all his life, starting as a puddler in the mills. He knew the industry from top to bottom. The steel people solicitously tried to wish on me, as candidates for this job, several men who had been put out to pasture. None of them compared with Replogle.

About forty years old when he came to Washington, he had light-blue eyes, a ruddy complexion, and dimples, which gave a somewhat erroneous impression of sweetness and softness. Sweet he may have been, but Replogle's mild and charming manner never failed to give way to the most ruthless determination when he thought someone was trying to put something over on him.

When he came to Washington he was a sturdy, stoutish fellow. When he left, he had lost his health, a good part of his fortune, and had acquired an interesting collection of enemies. All this was ample, if painful, evidence of how well he had done his job.

I had three executive assistants, or trouble-shooters. I was never one for paper work and administrative routine. I could always get more done on a park bench than at a desk. With the help of these three men, I was able to free myself of detail and keep myself mobile, as it were. These three able and extremely energetic men were Harrison Williams, who subsequently became a titan of the utility industry; Clarence Dillon, who had already made a mark as one of the keenest minds in Wall Street and was to make a much more impressive one after the war; and Herbert B. Swope, the Pulitzer-prize-winning reporter for the New York *World*. Later, Swope was the *World's* brilliant editor, presiding over a staff that included such luminaries as Heywood Broun, Alexander Woollcott, Deems Taylor, Arthur Krock, and Franklin P. Adams.

One day Swope had come to me to get a story on the lagging production of French 75 mm. guns. He backed me up against a lamp-post and poured questions at me. I don't think I gave him what he hoped to get, but I was impressed with his knowledge and with his tenacious, inquiring mind. I asked him to join me.

Herbert became my most intimate friend, and over the years my most trusted confidante. The intense feeling of loyalty and love between us made our friendship the most rewarding I have ever known. He had color, dash, and verve—to say nothing of courage and talent—a unique individual who scintillated in every gathering.

These were some of the men I recruited. There were other able men who were already on the Board when I became Chairman: among them were Judge Edwin Parker of Texas, who was in charge of Priorities; Robert Brookings, who headed the Price Fixing Committee; Hugh Frayne, representing Labor.

But these were only the men at the top. It was the men down the line, working anonymously and under great pressure, who deserved the real credit for WIB's accomplishments. We were also fortunate in having an efficient and loyal office staff. We had one particularly bright young lad—a crackerjack stenographer—named Billy Rose, who has since earned fame and fortune.

At full strength, WIB numbered seven hundred and fifty men from many walks of life. Some had left thriving law practices, such as Robert Bulkley, later United States Senator from Ohio. Some were scholars and educators, such as Dean Edwin F. Gay of Harvard, Wesley Mitchell of Columbia, and my dear friend, Alvin Johnson, who later established the much esteemed New School for Social Research. But for the most part, WIB was staffed from the ranks of business.

Men such as Charles MacDowell, Donald McLennan, Charles Otis, George Armsby, Albert Brunker, Arthur Whiteside, Charles Carroll, Everett L. Crawford, Samuel P. Bush, and others, too numerous to mention, put aside private interests—often at considerable sacrifice—to serve the government.

Arch Shaw typified the best of these men. Shaw, who owned a Chicago publishing business, headed the Conservation Division of the WIB. A man who brooked no nonsense, he was relentless in fighting waste and tireless in finding ways to save scarce resources and facilities. By standardizing models and reducing the variety of goods that had no other purpose than to satisfy fashion whims, he effected tremendous savings of precious commodities.

Everything from baby carriages to coffins was affected by Shaw's work, including ladies' fashions. When rumors arrived from France that the latest Paris designs would call for more cloth, the Conservation Division approached Jusserand, the French Ambassador, and asked him to intercede with the Paris couturiers. The Ambassador did so, and French fashions became radically slimmer and scantier.

There was never a whisper of corruption or impropriety about WIB. The quality of service which businessmen rendered in that organization was a tribute to the business community, all the more significant because there was no established tradition of public service for businessmen to follow in those days.

There was a unity and an *esprit* in the WIB which I have never seen in any other official agency. Each man knew that he had free rein to carry out his job, that he had authority equal to his responsibilities. There was a mutual confidence, and a closeness that resulted, after the war, in the formation of the WIB Associates, an informal club that for many years met annually on Armistice Day. Between meetings we kept in touch with each other, discussed the problems of the day, and exchanged information. Through these men I was able to stay in constant touch with well-informed opinion throughout the country.

The members of WIB richly deserved the tribute Woodrow Wilson paid them. These men, Wilson said, had "turned aside from every private interest of their own and devoted the whole of their trained capacity to the tasks that supplied the sinews of the whole great undertaking. The patriotism, the unselfishness, the thoroughgoing devotion and distinguished capacity that marked their toilsome labors, month after month, made them fit mates and comrades for the men in the trenches and on the sea."

2

The qualities which Wilson honored in the men of WIB were the very qualities which he so abundantly demonstrated as a war President. Wilson came to the Presidency with the ambition to improve American democracy; but history conferred on him the infinitely more difficult mission of conducting a war to preserve it. And this man, who abhorred war and tried to avoid it by every honorable means, did a superb job. He was one of the great war leaders of all time.

His prophetic vision gave the bloody business of war a meaning to those who did the fighting and dying. His messages, couched in some of the most moving and noble language to be found in state papers, communicated his own high purpose and inflexible will to the world.

In the conduct of the war on the home front, Wilson insisted on holding others to his own high ethical standards. He would not tolerate expediency or laxity, nor would he condone the slightest hint of influence peddling. Once he invited me to a White House conference to discuss a critical oil shortage which threatened to disrupt our military plans. One official proposed we seize the Mexican oil fields at Tampico. Squadrons of U.S. Marines had already been alerted. The President had only to give the word for them to push off.

President Wilson hardly waited for the conclusion of the argument. When aroused, he would speak in firm, measured tones, which left no doubt about what he had in mind.

"What you are asking me to do is exactly what we protested against when committed by Germany," he reprimanded. "You say this oil in Mexico is necessary for us. That is what the Germans said when they invaded Belgium—'It was necessary' to get to France. Gentlemen," he concluded, "you will have to fight the war with what oil you have."

On another occasion a relative of Mr. Wilson's by marriage tried to pressure WIB on behalf of a war contractor. Alec Legge complained to me that the man was making a nuisance of himself. "I'm going to throw him out by the nape of the neck, unless you say I can't."

"Chuck him out, Alec," I agreed.

Of course he didn't use physical violence, but in unmistakable language, which he knew so well how to use, Legge informed the young man that his presence in our offices could no longer be permitted. I soon learned from McAdoo that the young man had been complaining to him about WIB's attitude.

"Mac," I said, "I'm doing just what you would do and I can't do otherwise."

Shortly after this conversation, at the conclusion of a White

House meeting, the President said, "Baruch, I'd like to see you. Will you please remain?" We stood looking out the window, across the lawn toward the Potomac, in silence.

At last, referring to the young man, he said, "Baruch, I understand you've ordered him to keep away from the War Industries Board and denied him the right of coming there to find a contract."

"Yes Sir, Mr. President," I said, "but . . ."

"You don't have to give me any buts," he said. "You did exactly the right thing."

Such support from the President strengthened me, as it did others, to take summary action against the self-seekers who plagued the Administration. The politicians and influence peddlers who came around to WIB seeking contracts for the "deserving" got short shrift.

There was one aspiring influence peddler who, with his clients in tow, used to lay in wait for me mornings at my hotel. When I appeared he would buttonhole me and, for the few minutes it took me to break loose, engage me in what must have appeared to the onlookers as confidential conversation. One morning, after my secretary, Edward Corcoran, had finally put me on to him, I decided to put a stop to it. This time, when the fellow approached, I told him off in tones that carried clearly to everyone within earshot. Crushed in the presence of his clientele, he never accosted me again.

I know that my associates in the War Industry Board, and indeed in the entire wartime Administration, were inspired by Wilson's ethical standards. Yet he provided more than vision and high purpose; he provided hard, practical leadership. He understood the nature of modern war. "It is not an army that we must shape and train . . . it is a nation," he said. "The whole nation must be a team in which each man shall play a part for which he is best fitted." And again: "This is a war of resources. Men have thought of the United States as a money-getting people. Now we are going to lay all our wealth, if necessary, and spend all our blood, if need be, to show that we are not accumulating that wealth selfishly."

Wilson was the first American President to divorce politics from the conduct of war. He chose his lieutenants without regard to party, and practiced bipartisanship, about which we hear so much today, with little fanfare. Indeed, the great number of Republicans appointed to high posts in his war Administration—and the list includes such men as General Pershing, Harry Garfield, Julius Rosenwald, Alec Legge, Robert Brookings, Benedict Crowell, Herbert Hoover, Edward Stettinius, and Daniel Willard—brought the President under attack from some Democratic politicians. But he would not abandon the policy of choosing men on the basis of ability alone.

He had a leader's gift for choosing the right men, and an inspired executive talent for outlining what he expected of them. Rarest of all, he had the ability to leave his chosen lieutenants alone with their tasks, except to support them.

Once I went to him to explain a course of action I had taken. He stopped me and said, "You don't have to explain. Our minds have met and I have the utmost confidence in your judgment." His support of those he trusted was unwavering. Once, when someone referred to me disparagingly as a former speculator, Wilson retorted quickly, "Yes, and I understand he was a good one."

3

The President gave direction to the war effort and coördinated the work of the war agencies through his War Cabinet, which consisted of the Secretaries of War, Navy, and the Treasury, and the heads of special agencies, including Herbert Hoover, the Food Administrator; Harry Garfield, Fuel; Edward N. Hurley, Shipping; Vance McCormick, War Trade Board; and myself. The value of the regular Cabinet had been impaired by internal conflicts and jealousies. The President conducted very little important business at scheduled Cabinet meetings. But in the War Cabinet, as one writer put it, "the atmosphere was that of a corporate executive committee."

The War Cabinet met every Wednesday. The President was generally in good humor, and as we took our seats around the table he would exchange greetings with each of us. My place was always at his left, in a little black rocker.

Mr. Wilson would start on his right, with McAdoo, and go around the circle, each of us bringing up questions for discussion or for the President's decision. The President would usually poll the opinion of the War Cabinet, but he made the final decisions himself.

The discussions were often lively. McAdoo was never reluctant to express disagreement with the President. Although he was the President's son-in-law—he had married Wilson's daughter Eleanor, in 1914—the family relationship was never permitted to intrude into official business. I recall the heated arguments between the two over McAdoo's insistence on continuing government control of the railroads for a longer period than the President thought wise.

I worked closely and well with McAdoo, as I did with Secretary of the Navy Josephus Daniels. I must confess, however, that my first impression of Daniels had not been favorable; he struck me as a well-meaning, honest country editor out of his depth. Colonel House used to refer to him as "the man with the funny hat." But, as I learned, there were brains beneath that hat. Country editor he was, and a good one, but this solid man grew straight out of the American soil. He was loyal and devoted, firm in his convictions, and absolutely honest. I soon realized I had been wrong in my estimate of him and I grew to admire him very much.

My relations with Secretary of War Baker were correct but never very cordial. Somehow, we never struck it off. After the war, however, we came to understand each other better.

Baker was never convinced of the need for a strong WIB, and he was rather distrustful of any interference with the War Department. One of our typical disputes arose over the Board's attempt to provide a comprehensive and continuing study of the activities of the various departments engaged in the war effort. The project was undertaken after the President called me in one day and handed me the following letter:

> 24 May, 1918
>
> My dear Baruch:
>
> Do you think that it would be practicable to effect some kind of organization through which we could have a sort of picture or conspectus of all the present war activities of the Government and upon that base a periodical checking up of the actual operations and results? I think a good deal of loose talk and perhaps a good deal of loose action might be avoided if we could have such a basis of judgment and such a periodical checking up.
>
> Cordially and sincerely yours,
> Woodrow Wilson

Herbert Swope was waiting for me when I left the President's office. "Herb," I said, "what's a conspectus? I've just agreed to make one for the President."

When I was clear on what a conspectus was, I put Dean Gay, head of our Division of Planning and Statistics, in charge. Secretary Baker, however, took exception to this work and complained to the President that we seemed to be laying up material for future criticism of the War Department. But the President insisted that the work continue.

The Fuel Administrator, scholarly Harry Garfield, son of the martyred President, was a constant ally. A conflict between the War Industries Board and the Fuel Administration would have been catastrophic. Thanks to Garfield, we could almost count the Fuel Administration as a division of WIB. He was a tireless administrator, and a very proper man, which led those of us who on occasion used rough language to be more subdued in his presence.

After the war, Garfield returned to the presidency of Williams College, from which he had taken leave of absence during the war.

One day I met him on the train from Washington. As we rode along he told me of his dream to establish an Institute of Politics at Williams as a center for the study of international affairs and the encouragement of international understanding. Because the idea appealed to me and because of my personal admiration for Garfield, I offered to underwrite the venture, and did so for quite a few years. The Institute became a world-famous center, at which such prominent scholars as Lord James Bryce, Carlo Sforza, and R.H. Tawney lectured.

Edward Hurley, who headed the Shipping Board, was a dedicated man, but I had fewer official contacts with him than with any of the other members of the War Cabinet. The Shipping Board was never as closely integrated with WIB as was the War Trade Board, which was administered by the indefatigable Vance McCormick.

Herbert Hoover, the Food Administrator, was by all odds one of the ablest men in Washington. His magnificent work in administering Belgian relief led Wilson to appoint him Food Administrator when we entered the war. At first, both McAdoo and I thought the control of food ought to be entrusted to the Secretary of Agriculture, Houston. But Houston demurred. Unlike McAdoo, who ran both the Treasury and the Railroad Administration, Houston thought a Cabinet officer's regular duties were sufficient for one man.

As Food Administrator, Hoover further burnished his reputation. No man gave more to the job than he did. But I sometimes thought he took an unnecessarily dark view of situations. He was particularly pessimistic about the future of war agency administrators. "Someone has to be the first to hang on the barbed wire," was the way he put it one day to me and Goethals.

My estimate of Hoover is implicit in this exchange of letters with Wilson when the President was organizing a mission to Russia. "As Russia's greatest enemy, in my opinion, is going to be hunger and privation," I wrote to the President on July 13, 1918, "might I suggest . . . that Mr. Hoover should head the mission. If anything at all has trickled into their minds from the outside world, the Russians will realize in sending him you are sending someone to help, not to conquer."

Wilson replied: "I agree with you in your estimate of Hoover, but I cannot without dislocating some of the most important things we are handling spare him from his present functions."

To all of these men the President provided inspiration and example. Wilson has often been painted as a cold and aloof man, but I never found him so. I thought him warm and human, and I think my recollections of him in these pages will show that to me, at least, he was neither cold nor aloof. Nor was he the sober, humorless character that so many believed him to be. In the circle of his family and friends he would dance a jolly jig or recite funny limericks, often at his own expense.

But during those trying days of the war, the stern Covenanter in him was more often to the fore. He never lost courage or confidence. You always left his presence with the feeling that you could do your job, that he knew exactly what he was going to do, and that we were going to win. He always seemed to say the things that had been in my heart and mind, and which I could not say. Without his truly inspirational leadership, we could not have accomplished as much as we did.

It was a great crusade, and I count it the finest privilege of my life to have been part of it.

VI

The Paris Peace Conference

I N THE WIB, as everywhere else in the nation, we greeted the Armistice with exultation and hope. More innocent in 1918 than in 1945, many believed that the great conflict we had just fought would end war forever. Few men could have thought, amid the jubilation that swept through the country on that first Armistice Day, that the whole madness would be repeated again in a scant two decades.

We know now that there was no peace after the First World War. There was only an interlude while the European political and economic vacuum was filled by the rising tide of Fascist totalitarianism, as it was filled by the rising flood of Communist totalitarianism after the Second World War.

The truth is that the world has not known real peace since 1914. Scarcely a year since then has been free of war, its threat, or its aftermath. We have been either preparing for war, fighting it, or recovering from it throughout most of this century.

When the war ended, WIB was speedily closed out. George Peek had argued for its continuation until the transition to peace had been safely made. He was right. Had WIB been empowered

to carry on its direction of the economy, much of the waste and disorder accompanying reconversion might have been avoided. But
we had no authority to do so. I had this lesson very much in mind
after the Second World War when I urged the continuation of controls until peace was secure. But in this, as in other things, we ignored the lessons of the First War.

My resignation as Chairman of the War Industries Board became
official on the last day of 1918. I could look back on the past months
with some sense of accomplishment. We had sailed an uncharted
sea in mobilizing America's industrial forces and converting them
from peace to war. We had made a record which, with all its imperfections, would command respect.

Conscious of the inspiration that had made this possible, I sent
a note to Mr. Wilson on November 26th: ". . . I am writing to
express . . . my appreciation of what you have done. . . . Your wonderful cool judgment, Christian patience and sublime courage,
have inspired all; made the faltering steadfast and the weak strong."
In days to come, I predicted, the world would give thanks for his
leadership. As for myself, "my gratitude is greatly multiplied because of the inestimable privilege given me of serving under you.
My admiration for your wonderful achievements is sometimes, I
fear, over-shadowed by my affection for you as a man and a friend."

The President answered the next day:

27 November, 1918.

My dear Baruch:

Your letter of yesterday has given me the deepest and keenest
pleasure. I hope you have felt how entirely you have won my
confidence not only, but my affection, and how I have learned
to value your counsel and your assistance. It has been a delightful experience to know you and to work with you, and I have
learned to have the highest admiration for your ability and your
character.

But your letter sounds too much like a good bye. I do not
mean to let you go yet if I can help it, because there is much remaining to be done, and I do not like to feel that I am going

away and leaving it to be done by inexperienced hands. We will
have a talk about this.

Gratefully and faithfully yours,
Woodrow Wilson

When the President said he did not mean to let me go, I had no
idea that he was thinking of having me serve as one of his advisors
in the making of the peace. Indeed, my mind had not been on
peacemaking. In late October, when the President received the
German overture for an armistice, he called a meeting of the War
Cabinet. He read us his proposed reply from what looked to me
like stenographic notes, which he was very adept at making. Then
he asked each of us in turn to comment. McAdoo, Baker, Garfield,
and Hoover in particular, made constructive remarks. When it
came around to me, I was dumb.

"Well, what have you got to say, Dr. Facts?" Wilson inquired,
using a nickname he had coined to characterize my insistence on
presenting all the facts of a situation.

"Mr. President," I replied, "I've been thinking so much about
war, I haven't given much thought to peace."

I was to learn that war and peace cannot be compartmentalized,
that you must plan for peace while hostilities are still on, and guard
against war even when at peace.

While the war was still on, the President had begun to formulate
the principles which would form the basis of peace. This blueprint
for peace, enunciated in the Fourteen Points and elsewhere, was
endorsed by our Allies and accepted by the Germans in suing for
an armistice. Among the principles Wilson laid down were open
covenants, openly arrived at; freedom of the seas; the removal of
economic and trade barriers; limitation of armaments; adjustment
of colonial claims, with due regard to the interests of the popula-
tions concerned; evacuation and restoration of the invaded and
occupied lands; self-determination; and, above all, an association of
nations to preserve the peace.

What Wilson set out to do was to provide a new moral and legal basis for the conduct of international affairs. "What we need is the reign of law, based upon the consent of the governed and sustained by the organized opinion of mankind," he said.

There was nothing impractical in what Wilson sought. A concept of moral and legal order among nations is no more unrealistic than are the Ten Commandments as a guide to private conduct—and no less necessary, if we are to prevent anarchy in the society of nations. Yet the war-breeding issues which Wilson's charter for peace sought to resolve are for the most part still with us.

We all knew that Wilson's mind and heart were turned toward Paris, where the Peace Conference would convene. He firmly believed that the real test of his leadership would begin, and the future of the world be decided, at Paris. He hoped to forge there a peace that would open a new era—an era in which the world would be made safe from Europe's decadent old order as well as from the revolutionary new order erupting in Russia. One has only to read the last thing he ever wrote, "The Road Away from Revolution," to see how clearly he understood the appeal of that revolution to the underprivileged peoples of the world.

But I was opposed to the President's going to the Peace Conference, and told him so. I thought he should stay above the fray, that he would lose his influence if he descended into the cockpit of negotiations. General Tasker H. Bliss, on the Commission to Negotiate Peace, put it in another fashion: "Jove should not come down from Olympus." There were others close to the President who felt as I did, among them Secretary of State Lansing, Vance McCormick, Herbert Hoover, and Harry Garfield. But Wilson would not be dissuaded.

He sailed December 4th on the *George Washington*. That very night, Joe Tumulty called me to say that the President wished Vance McCormick and me to prepare to join him later. In a few days, the summons came. President Wilson, still on the high seas, sent a message asking us to proceed to Paris as soon as possible.

Vance and I quickly secured space on the *Leviathan*, scheduled to depart on New Year's Eve. But when we arrived at the pier that night, we found that the ship was not ready to sail. It needed repairs, we were told, and its passengers were to sail the next evening on the *George Washington*. I took advantage of the delay to rush over to join my wife, who was watching the New Year in with a party of friends.

There were only a handful of passengers on that crossing. Among them were Assistant Secretary of the Navy Roosevelt and Mrs. Roosevelt, Edward Hurley, and Charles Schwab. It was an extremely rough trip, and I am a notoriously bad sailor. In later years, Schwab delighted to relate how he came to see me when I was too sick to leave my cabin, and asked me how I felt about the freedom of the seas. I told him he could have all my interest in them.

At last we landed at Brest, and went at once to Paris. After getting settled, I tried to report to Colonel House. He was one of the four Peace Commissioners accompanying the President and, as always, was serving as Wilson's chief adjutant. It was not easy to see the Colonel, however, and for some days I sat around wondering why I had been called to Paris. I had the clear impression that my arrival had not occasioned unalloyed enthusiasm in the Colonel's personal entourage. Then the President learned of my presence, and I received my assignments.

I was hardly at a loss for jobs and titles. I found myself a member of the drafting committee of the Economic Section; a member of the Supreme Economic Council, and Chairman of its Raw Materials Division; a Representative on the Economics and Reparations Commission; and an Economic Adviser to the American Peace Commission.

I began to assemble my own staff. Fortunately, Leland Summers and Alec Legge were already in Paris. They had followed the path of the German Army's retreat, and knew as much as anyone about the economic situation in the devastated regions of Belgium and Northern France. With Wilson's approval, I also summoned from Washington several other assistants, including F.W. Taussig, Pierre-

pont B. Noyes, and Charles MacDowell. These men, whom I knew
and trusted, helped me to cover the large territory represented by
my official duties.

2

As the Peace Conference got under way, I could see by the view
from my own comparatively small bailiwick what an enormous task
confronted the President. When he reached Paris, Wilson had been
greeted by Europe's multitude as an evangel of peace. No man had
ever commanded such adulation nor so embodied mankind's hopes
as Wilson did in those last days of 1918. If ever there was reason
to believe in the fulfillment of these hopes, it was then. But in the
scramble for advantage, in the cry for vengeance, in the effort of
each nation to make a peace in its own image, the mood could
not be sustained. Peace, which had seemed very beautiful during
the war, began to seem almost hateful in the struggle to create it.

As soon as the war ended, Allied high purpose and unity disin-
tegrated. Wilson came to Paris with no idea of vengeance, with no
thought of spoils. The Allies came intent upon both. Long before
the war had ended, they had secretly agreed on the division of
Germany's colonies. And as the Conference convened, each had
some ambition or claim, territorial or financial, to advance.

France, dominated by fear, wanted military security above all,
and repayment for her fearful losses. Britain, too, wanted compensation, and sought as well to protect her Empire interests. Italy
coveted Fiume. Japan thought Shantung just payment for her unwanted entry into the war. The Armenians, the Koreans, the Poles,
the Swedes—every nation and every nationality was represented
by petitioners in Paris. All of them were scheming and squabbling,
seeking their own advantage at the expense of the principles upon
which Wilson hoped to create a peace. The great powers of Europe
seemed united on little else but the intention of imposing a harsh
peace on Germany and exacting enormous indemnities from her.

After four years of brutality and blood, men's veins were filled with blood-raw passions. The fierce cry for vengeance in England and France impelled their leaders to take extreme positions which, in turn, fanned the flames at home. While Wilson was making speeches about the League of Nations, Clemenceau was telling his Parliament of his unshaken faith in the old system of alliances as the sole guarantee of French security. While Wilson was calling for the assessment of reasonable reparations against Germany, Lloyd George—moved by political considerations at home—was promising to "squeeze Germany until the pips squeak." ("Heaven knows what I would have had to promise if the campaign lasted a week longer," he remarked after his bid for reëlection was over.) And while the people of Europe were acclaiming Wilson a prophet of peace, they were almost in the same voice crying for revenge.

It was not hard to understand the bitterness. Northern France had been overrun and destroyed. More than a million Frenchmen had been killed, and thrice as many wounded. The blind and the crippled were on every side. Although England's countryside had not been devastated, the Commonwealth had lost nearly a million men killed, and more than twice that number wounded. Belgium had been brutally assaulted. I remember still the shock of horror and disbelief which I felt when I saw the devastation in Belgium on a visit to the battle areas with the President.

This was one of the trips the President took to survey the battle-fields. At first he had refused to take such tours, fearful that his judgment would be affected by the emotions the scenes of destruction would call up. But he had to accommodate the insistent, even angry, demands that he witness what war had done to Europe's land and people.

We came from Paris overnight, along with Mrs. Wilson, Herbert Hoover, Norman Davis, Cary Grayson, Margaret Wilson, and a few others in the Presidential party. We were met by King Albert, dressed as always in his Army uniform, accompanied by the Queen. The tour extended over a hundred miles through the devastated areas. At Ypres we saw the "tank graveyard"—scores of Allied and German tanks, wrecked and rusting. The town itself had been leveled—only a few hastily constructed frame buildings were standing, and the countryside was all but deserted. Here and there a few refugees were trying to reclaim something from the soil.

Visits such as this one to Ypres through war-torn Europe, along with a close study of the damages resulting directly and indirectly from the war, made me conscious of the tremendous task of reconstruction facing these nations. I felt strongly America's responsibility to provide credits to our allies for this task, and I set forth my convictions in a letter to the President on May 7th:

My dear Mr. President:

German militarism has been destroyed and the peoples of the world set free from political domination not of their own choosing. The rights of self-determination and political freedom are coming to the whole world which finds itself exhausted from the struggle to attain these ends—exhausted mentally, physically and financially. It is staggering under huge debts. The consequent grave industrial problems will require the strongest and most sympathetic treatment. But unless great care is taken, military domination will be succeeded by financial domination.

All of the countries owe large debts, for the most part to the United States, England and France. Exchange has depreciated and commercial and economic life is prostrate.

In order that a government like Italy and new governments such as . . . Poland, Czechoslovakia and Jugo-Slavia . . . may establish themselves financial assistance must be given. Otherwise these people will find themselves financially shackled for years to come by a domination more severe and more difficult to throw off than was the military domination.

Permit me to say that I think it is the duty of the United States, which has done so much to free these people and to establish high purposes and ideals in the world, to complete its work of freeing these people by giving them an equal opportunity in the world.

I recommend that aid be given to stricken Europe by the United States, in cooperation with England, France and any

other country that desires to join; that the aid be not given
jointly but independently; that the United States, England and
France should each, by consultation, know what the others are
doing in order that there may be no duplication of effort.

Because I recognized that restrictive trade practices fomented
hostility between nations and that a peaceful world required economic opportunity for all, I went on to propose that a condition
of granting loans should be the removal of economic barriers,
equality of trade conditions, and the cancellation of existing pref-
erential treaties and trade agreements. I concluded by saying:

> Whatever the amount may be, it is an obligation that we cannot
> escape. It is a part of the obligation that the rich nations of the
> world, and America in particular, must carry out. America en-
> tered the war with a high purpose. It has written that purpose
> into the terms of the Peace. It must now carry through that pur-
> pose, in order that peace may be maintained by the restoration
> of normal conditions and by the granting of an equal opportunity
> to all.
> Economic inequality and barriers were among the causes of
> the war. They have not been removed; in many cases they have
> been increased. No greater use can be made of our resources and
> I know of no more fitting climax to the part that America has
> played in the war, and to your own great work, than the accom-
> plishment of this project.

Still, as sympathetic as one might feel toward Germany's victims,
one could not justify the Allies' determination to squeeze Germany
dry and to write a peace which would violate the very purposes
for which the war was fought. To prevent this, Wilson fought a
grueling battle for almost six months against tenacious and skillful
antagonists.

3

My duties in helping to write the complex economic clauses of
the Peace Treaty gave me the opportunity to participate in and

observe some of its most bitterly fought aspects. One of the more contentious issues was the economic blockade of Germany, which had been imposed when the war ended.

Contrary to American intentions, the Allies had applied the blockade to foodstuffs, medicines, and other necessities of life. For months, with Herbert Hoover taking the lead, we fought against a deliberate policy of starving Germany. The British were prepared to relent, but the French proved adamant in conference after conference—unmindful, as Vance McCormick put it in his diary, that we were "living on a volcano with two hundred million people not producing—and many hungry."

In weeks of often bitter and heated debate, the Americans and the British argued the folly and injustice of starving the Germans. At one meeting I attended, Prime Minister Lloyd George read a letter from General Plumer, "Old Plum" to his men, Commanding General of the British Occupation Forces in Germany. The General described the anger and resentment of his troops at the starvation of German women and children.

As we left the meeting, Gordon Auchincloss, Colonel House's son-in-law, whispered to me: "That was a good note the P.M. wrote himself, wasn't it?" I don't know whether this surmise was correct. But it might well have been.

The French finally agreed to a relaxation of the blockade, but they were slow to implement their agreement. We soon learned that although they were permitting silk stockings, perfume, and other luxuries of French manufacture through the lines, they were not letting food through.

At a meeting of the Supreme Economic Council, I taxed the French with this fact. Louis Loucheur, one of the French delegates to the Council, was stung, and made an impassioned speech charging me with impugning the name of Marshal Foch. But he did not refute the facts.

Still another subject of controversy was the proposal to limit the amount of raw materials that Germany might import. This, of course, would have given the Allies a heavy advantage over Germany in postwar economic development. The Allies tried to justify their proposal on the grounds that raw materials were in short supply and that they were entitled to first claim upon them. We, in the American delegation, contested this proposal; first, because it amounted to economic war against Germany, and second, because it was not true that there were not enough raw materials to go around. As a result of an investigation, we were able to show that there was actually only one item in short supply—and that far from crucial—flax. I pointed out that once the channels of trade were reopened, shipping freed, and credits arranged, there would be sufficient raw materials available for all.

On most issues, the French were especially obstinate. Although they were unquestionably entitled to compensation for the destruction of their coal resources by Germany, their demand for annexation of the coal-rich German Saar was unreasonable. The President's refusal to sanction this demand led to a bitter scene between him and Clemenceau which ended with the old Premier storming out of the President's residence.

I was opposed to a compromise proposal which would have given France ownership of the coal mines in the Saar while permitting Germany to maintain political sovereignty over the area. This would have been "a constant source of turmoil and friction," I wrote the President, and I proposed an alternate scheme whereby France would be guaranteed sufficient Saar coal to meet her needs.

The President seemed impressed by my proposal, and asked me to prepare a draft for submission to the Big Four. Leland Summers and I worked all night on the paper, but when we appeared the next morning to present it, we learned that a settlement of the issue had been reached. The French were to receive the entire output of the mines for fifteen years; a League Commission would run the Saar for that period, after which a plebiscite would be taken to determine whether France or Germany would receive the region.

As we all know, the plebiscite was overwhelmingly in favor of returning the Saar to Germany.

We were also able to moderate the French demands to separate the Rhineland from the Reich. The French agreed to a compromise whereby Allied armies would occupy the area for fifteen years. I was mindful of the humiliation and tension which might ensue from military occupation, and the deterrent effect it might have on the economic recovery of Germany, without which, I was convinced, the postwar economy of Europe could hope for little. Consequently I was among those who urged the creation of a civilian, rather than a military, commission to oversee the occupation. The efforts of John W. Davis, our Ambassador to England, were largely responsible for the acceptance of this proposal. At my suggestion, Pierrepont Noyes was appointed American representative on the Rhineland Commission.

4

But it was in the debate over reparations that the Allied effort to exact retribution from Germany was most sharply illustrated—and this was the issue that occupied me most.

My American colleagues on the Reparations Commission, on which all the member nations of the Conference were represented, were Vance McCormick and Norman Davis. Later, Thomas Lamont was named as an alternate to Davis. Our legal adviser was a young international lawyer, John Foster Dulles. The French were represented by L. L. Klotz, Albert Lebrun, and Loucheur. Lord Walter Cunliffe, Lord John Andrew Sumner, and Prime Minister William Hughes of Australia were Great Britain's representatives.

On the question of reparations, the British were as inflexible as the French, for it was Cunliffe and Sumner who dominated the British negotiations. They were motivated by a desire to eliminate Germany as far as possible as a future economic rival of Great Britain. Cunliffe was known among the delegates as "Silent" Cunliffe, a man who appeared the epitome of wisdom until he opened his mouth. Lord Sumner, a famous jurist, was a fierce Tory dedicated only to the interests of the British Empire.

It was a tribute to Lloyd George's political skill, but a handicap to the Peace Conference, that he had men like these in his camp, cheek by jowl with such liberals as Lord Robert Cecil, Jan Smuts, and John Maynard Keynes. Both groups had supported him in his election. In bringing both to the Conference, he was able to call upon either in support of whatever view he happened to be propounding at the moment. These swings on the political flying trapeze may have been helpful to Lloyd George, but they were hardly conducive to the work of the Conference, particularly the Reparations Commission.

The American position on reparations had been stated by President Wilson even before the war ended. In outlining the peace terms, he had said there would be "no contributions and no punitive damages." Of course the United States would not ask for a penny. The Allies and Germany, in accepting the peace terms, had agreed that "compensation will be made by Germany for all damages done to the civilian population of the Allies and their property by the aggression of Germany by land, by sea, and from the air." This clearly meant that German reparations would be limited, as we subsequently put it in a statement filed with the Reparations Section of the Peace Conference, to repayment for "direct physical damage to property of non-military character and direct physical injury to civilians."

But this was not the interpretation accepted by the Allies when detailed negotiations began. England and France were determined to make Germany pay to the last mark for the wealth and blood they had spent to defeat her. Lloyd George had promised his people that Germany would pay "shilling for shilling and ton for ton." The French attitude was implicit in the placards covering the walls of Paris, even as we discussed reparations: *Que L'Allemagne paye d'abord.* "Let Germany pay first." Since the Armistice, the French government had been unable to get any tax measures passed by the Chamber of Deputies, which insisted that the placards meant what they said.

At the very outset of the meetings of the Reparations Commission, the British and French tried to expand the definition of reparations to cover not only damages to civilians and their property, but all the costs of war. The British delegation, especially, championed this interpretation for the not unnatural reason that such a construction would have increased Britain's pro-rata share in the reparations.

Vance McCormick and I argued that inclusion of war costs would violate the terms of peace which Germany had accepted and, in addition, would inflate Germany's liability far beyond her capacity to pay.

President Wilson at first supported us. He refused to adopt a procedure "clearly inconsistent with what we deliberately led the enemy to expect and cannot now honorably alter simply because we have the power." In the face of Wilson's strong stand, the Allies, with Britain leading, took a new tack. They proposed to include in the definition of war damages the cost of pensions and separation allowances paid to soldiers and their families. Was it fair, Lloyd George asked, to include the cost of repairing damaged roofs in France at the expense of families that had lost a father? This kind of argument was hard to counter but I fought it as vigorously as I could. I appealed directly to the President, pointing out that the claim for separation and pension allowances was another route to the Allied goal of compelling Germany to pay English and French war costs.

But at this point a more persuasive influence was brought to bear on Wilson. The commanding figure of General Jan Smuts now gave the reparations problem a decisive turn—in the wrong direction.

Smuts represented the kind of reasoned idealism upon which Wilson hoped to build the postwar world. In his effort to be fair to

Germany, and in his support of a League of Nations, Smuts spoke for the most liberal and enlightened Allied sentiment at the Conference. The Treaty, in the end, fell short of what he had hoped for, and he signed it only under protest.

It is particularly ironic, therefore, that Smuts himself contributed to the Treaty's failure to assess fair and reasonable reparations against Germany. It was an error that was to plague the world for years.

Until the question of pensions and separation allowances came up, Smuts had favored a moderate reparations policy. Now, unexpectedly, he reversed himself and submitted a memorandum arguing that pensions and separation allowances were actually compensation to civilians for damages incurred in the war, and therefore a German liability.

I thought then, and I think now, that Smuts's argument was transparently sophistic. Nevertheless, his influence was such that President Wilson accepted his interpretation over the opposition of his own advisers. None of us could budge him. I tried several times to convince him of the mistake he was making. He usually heard me out, but once, tried by my persistence, he took me by the elbow, steered me toward the door, and said, "All right, Baruch, you've made your point." "Mr. President," I answered, "I'm going to keep on making it as long as you'll give me a hearing."

Wilson's reversal on the question of pensions and separation allowances was a serious mistake. No doubt he felt impelled to acquiesce to the British on this point, but to many of us it seemed a retreat from his principles—and an unnecessary retreat. That decision helped kill any hope of reaching agreement on the reparations question.

In time, Smuts came to regret the position he had taken. In the years following the Peace Conference, he repeatedly called for a downward revision of reparations, rightfully attributing much of the world's economic distress to that unsettled question.

I have been told by Smuts's son that the South African leader took the position he did only with great reluctance, and only because he felt that France was trying to carry off most of the reparations. When he was unable to get her to moderate her demands, he apparently felt it necessary to protect British Empire interests in the struggle for indemnity.

I was sorry to be in such complete disagreement with Smuts on this issue, and even sorrier because it seemed to me he had abandoned his high-mindedness temporarily in favor of satisfying the Commonwealth's needs.

By broadening the definition of German liability to include indirect war costs, the Allies made it virtually impossible to submit a definite bill to Germany. We in the American delegation urged that an exact sum should be levied on Germany, so that she could know the full extent of her obligations. We ourselves had drawn up careful estimates of Allied losses. But when we asked the Allies to submit their estimate of damages, they refused. Although Germany obviously did not have the capacity to pay *all* the damages assessed against her, the Allies found it impossible to agree on what she could in fact pay. And they were determined not to fix her liability short of the last mark that might actually be extracted from her.

My own study of German resources convinced me that she could meet a bill of between twelve and fifteen billion dollars. The highest figure proposed by any American was thirty-five billion by Thomas Lamont, but he qualified this in private by saying that half would be paid in real marks and half in "phony ones." John Maynard Keynes, whose views on the reparations are most celebrated, first estimated Germany's capacity at about ten billion. This, I might add, was about the only time I found myself in substantial agreement with Keynes.

However, our Allied associates in the Reparations Commission advanced figures many times this estimate. At a meeting of the Big Four, Lord Cunliffe, who was an ex-director of the Bank of England and should have known better, asserted that Germany could pay as much as one hundred twenty billion. President Wilson turned to his advisers for their reaction. "Let us all take a trip to the moon," I said.

The ironic and paradoxical fact was that the Allies seemed to consider the reparations issue in a vacuum, divorced from all the economic and political realities impinging on it. The most obvious reality was that Germany's capacity to pay reparations had been radically curtailed as a result of other provisions of the Treaty.

"Germany has been deprived of the greater part of the commercial advantages which she possessed before the war," I wrote to the President on March 29th. She was to lose her merchant marine, her colonies, Alsace-Lorraine, the coal of the Saar, as well as other sources of income. "We must therefore realize that we are dealing today with a much weaker Germany than the one we knew before the war, and we must recognize that any indemnities based on pre-war conditions would be impossible. To talk of these indemnities in exaggerated terms would result in raising false hopes in the minds of the peoples of the Allied nations that would react in a serious manner."

Neither Clemenceau nor Lloyd George would face such economic realities, if for no other reason than that they were prisoners of their political constituents. Indeed, Paris was no place for economic realities. Few places and times are, when the realities are unpleasant.

My views on reparations were governed by what I felt Germany could pay, not on what, in justice, she should pay. I was fully conscious of the terrible loss of lives and treasure which the Allies had suffered. I condemned Germany's war crimes as vigorously as anyone at the Conference. I was not concerned with mitigating Germany's treatment, except to prevent severity from developing into injustice. What I was trying to do was keep passion from usurping reason.

My own philosophy, which guided me in the Paris negotiations as elsewhere, was to seek a solution that would work. I knew that if Germany were left economically prostrate, all Europe would suffer.

I could see no wisdom in piling on Germany a reparations load so huge that in the end it would be impossible for her to pay it. This was cutting the nose to spite the face.

The reparations question was further complicated by the issues of war debts. The Allies, anxious to secure a reduction of their indebtedness to the United States, tried to link a decision on reparations to the war debt problem. They held out the promise of moderating their demands upon Germany if we would scale down the debts owed to us. But Wilson refused to discuss the question of Allied debts to the United States on the grounds that they were not a concern of the Peace Conference.

The war debts plagued us for years, and, as we know, they went largely uncollected. My own view of the issue coincided neither with those who believed in cancellation of all debts, nor with those who endorsed Calvin Coolidge's terse dictum: "They hired the money, didn't they?" I felt that the United States should have written off as a contribution to the common cause those debts incurred by the Allies in the actual prosecution of the war. But I felt that debts incurred for non-war purposes should be honored.

In the end, the impasse between the Allied point of view and ours on reparations proved to be unbridgeable. No fixed figure for reparations could be agreed upon. Its determination was left to a Reparations Commission on which America, retreating into isolationism after the war, refused even to take a seat.

Because we failed to solve the problem, reparations hung like a dark cloud over Europe. It bred discord and bitterness, leading to such incidents as the French seizure of the Ruhr in an attempt to get by force what they thought was due them. Twice, under plans formulated by Charles Dawes and Owen D. Young, efforts were made to resolve the reparations tangle and set a figure upon Germany's liability which she could meet. But in 1931, when she could no longer borrow here, Germany defaulted for the last time. In the end, she paid less than five billion in reparation, and half of that had been borrowed in the United States.

If a just reparations program could have been devised, I believe it might have led to far different consequences in Europe. A realistic plan would certainly have netted the Allies more than they actually received. At the same time, Germany would not have escaped so lightly from her obligations. Above all, the quarrels and animosities over the issue which poisoned the international atmosphere might well have been put to rest.

But it was not to be. At the meetings of the Reparations Commission, as in so many other sessions of the Peace Conference, the passions of men overrode their reason.

VII

The Big Three

Paris, in those early months of 1919, was unforgettable. In the air was a mingling of hope, excitement, and uncertain anticipation. The sense of history was all about us, and the makers of history—the Presidents, Ministers, and Plenipotentiaries—could be seen everywhere. The city was like a giant stage set on which was being played a complex, glittering drama, moving toward an historic denouement no one could foresee, but which everyone hoped would solve the problems of the world.

The chief players in this drama were Woodrow Wilson, Georges Clemenceau, and David Lloyd George. A generation later, peace was again in the hands of three statesmen: Roosevelt, Churchill, and Stalin. I knew each of them, some intimately, with the exception of Stalin. Different as all these men were in temperament and outlook, they were alike in their self-confidence and strong purpose. They were all, also, intensely human beings, not the one-dimensional figures great men often appear to be.

The Big Three at Paris were striking personalities. Clemenceau, the Tiger of France, was the oldest and, in many respects, the least complicated figure at the conference table. I can see him now, his bald head held erect over his squat, square, strong body; his short legs barely touching the floor when he sat in a chair; his hands clothed always in gray gloves to hide a skin ailment. I never saw his bare fingers.

Seventy-six years old when he was called to lead France, at a time when the Allied fortunes were blackest, Clemenceau had infused a tired and dispirited nation with his own indomitable will and courage. Like another great Frenchman, De Gaulle, a generation later, he tolerated no thought but of victory—at all costs, if need be. At the peace table, he had but one objective: security against Germany, a nation which twice in his lifetime had scourged his beloved France. He used to say to me, "Baruch, you do not understand the Germans. There is only one thing they know—that is force. A peace-loving people like the French must have security from them."

Yet, though he was the savior of France, he was shot by a would-be assassin during the Conference. And in the great riots of May, 1919, I heard Parisians shout, "Down with Clemenceau," just as Americans later turned against Wilson and as the British were to cast out Churchill in 1945.

It would be difficult to imagine a sharper contrast between two men than between Clemenceau and Wilson. Clemenceau was the peasant, as close to the soil and people as a man can be, earthy, shrewd, suspicious. Wilson was the intellectual, unable in public, for all his inner warmth, to lower the bars of reserve. He was not without humor, as those who knew him could attest, but his was not the wry, salty humor of the old Frenchman.

Once, at a Big Four meeting, Clemenceau was apparently fast asleep while a discussion droned on about the care of occupation troops in the Rhineland. There was much talk of providing barracks and recreation for the soldiers. Clemenceau opened his eyes to add slyly, "And women?" He was also fond of giving facetious names and titles to others. Because I was opposed to the cancellation of the Allied war debts, he referred to me sometimes as "Le Grand Bandit Américain."

To Clemenceau, worldly in the manner of European politicians, Wilson's fierce idealism seemed naïve. Referring to Wilson's peace principles, Clemenceau is supposed to have said, "God gave us His Ten Commandments and we broke them. Wilson gave us his Fourteen Points—We shall see!" If the story is apocryphal that Clemenceau, on rising every morning, said to himself: "Now Georges Clemenceau, you *do* believe in the League," it nonetheless represents his skepticism toward the League.

Once, on a visit to America after the war, Clemenceau fell to discussing American Presidents with me. He remarked, "George Washington—he had what you call horse sense, didn't he?" I agreed. "Wilson," he went on, "is very scholarly and erudite, but he was not like George Washington."

I couldn't agree with his estimate of Wilson as an impractical visionary, just as I couldn't agree with him on many of the major issues at Paris. Nevertheless, I could understand why Clemenceau was as he was and felt as he did toward Germany, and I conceived a warm attachment for him. I have learned in my long life that you can be friends with and admire even the people you disagree with most, if they are honest, and Clemenceau was that. Partisanship need not destroy friendship. To this day, I keep on my desk a pen-and-ink sketch of Clemenceau by Sir William Orpen, given to me by the artist.

Until his death, I visited Clemenceau at his home at 8 rue Franklin whenever I was in Paris. There the old Tiger would be sitting in his gray gloves and gray skullcap, usually wearing large gray slippers. He looked like a great, gray cat. He would always open the conversation with "Well, *mon enfant*, what is the news?" When I asked him about himself, he would give me a short account of his activities, in the third person.

I also visited Clemenceau several times at Jarde Sable d'Orlone, his country place, once in the company of André Tardieu, who was one of Clemenceau's most trusted lieutenants. During the war, Tardieu had headed the French Mission in Washington, where I came to know him well. Later he was to serve twice as Premier of France.

We arrived in time for luncheon, and found the old gentleman in his cottage, formerly a fisherman's hut, on a sandy stretch of land near the ocean. We ate from a long table in the kitchen before a huge fireplace. A stout Breton woman cooked the most delicious concoctions in iron pots that swung over the open hearth. Marvelous wines, particularly a delicious raspberry cordial, were served.

Showing us through the house, Clemenceau pointed to the wall behind his bed on which hung a stuffed crocodile. Chuckling, the old gentleman said, "Poincaré." He had no love for his political rival. The little house also contained a small study which had apparently been added on. In this room, Clemenceau worked each night on what was to be his last book, *Grandeur and Misery of Victory*. There was also another small room, as small as a compartment in a Pullman train, with water and toilet arrangements exactly as in a sleeping car. He showed this to me with great glee, saying it was "a charming American innovation built especially for me."

Cane in hand, he stumped out to show us his garden, a few green, scraggly plants trying desperately to raise their heads through sand and rock. He pointed to a mast from which was flying a bedraggled emblem that, he said, had been given him by the Chinese. They raised it, he explained, only when a strong, virile man was present, and he poked me in the ribs. "Today it is raised in your honor," he said.

Wandering about the garden, he looked up with those black, piercing eyes and said, "Baruch, tell me, what is the matter with the world?"

"Mr. Prime Minister, you tell *me*," I replied.

"I will tell you a great secret," he answered. Raising his hand to his mouth, he whispered: "I do not know."

On another visit, I accompanied him early one morning to the fish market by the sea. He was dressed in a dark blue suit, with a long coat which made his figure look squatter than ever.

Walking through the market place, Clemenceau joked with the stout wives of the fishermen and farmers, who looked with smiling and affectionate eyes at the old Tiger. He said to one, as he pinched her weather-beaten cheek, "Yes, she was beautiful when I knew her sixty years ago," and that brought shrieks of laughter. The whole market gathered around him, applauding, in great good nature.

He showed me a monument that had been erected there in his honor, depicting him in a *poilu's* helmet. I thought it a stirring thing. He showed me a piece of ground he had bought, which he planned to make into a playground, but whether he ever built it, I do not know.

When he took me to meet his friends, he introduced me as the "Prince d'Israel." He would say, "You know, Baruch, your people are a great people when they are great. They seem to rise to a finer spirit of service in the cause of humanity than any other people." I always protested earnestly and sincerely that I have never believed Jews were any better or worse than other people. I have always felt that human beings everywhere react in much the same way in similar circumstances. Human emotions are the same in all of us.

In 1922, Clemenceau visited the United States. By this time he was eighty-one, but still spry. He had a friendly reunion with Wilson, and then set out on a series of speaking engagements. I traveled with him to Chicago, where I had arranged for him to address the convention of the American Farm Bureau Federation with which I was then closely associated. I can see him now in his weather-beaten hat, welcomed everywhere with great warmth, yet failing—and knowing it—in his effort to reanimate the close war-time bonds between France and the United States.

For a long time I tried to get Clemenceau to sit for a portrait by Orpen, who had done paintings of Wilson and Smuts, both of which I owned. The Smuts portrait, which I presented to South Africa, now hangs in the Parliament building. But Clemenceau refused to have his portrait done. "Send me Rembrandt or Rubens and I will sit for him," he told me.

Finally I enlisted the help of the lovely Mrs. Charles Dana Gibson, wife of the famous illustrator, to whom Clemenceau was devoted. If she could induce Clemenceau to sit, I said, I would have Orpen paint two portraits and give her one. But not even she could persuade him. When she remonstrated, "M Clemenceau, you do not love me any more," he answered, "Ah, indeed I do. I lay at your feet all the passion of my eighty-one years, and remember, I shall love you even after death, for I shall be waiting in heaven for you. When you get there, don't go straight through but turn to the left, and in the first antechamber Clemenceau will be waiting for you."

Even in these late years of disappointments and lost hopes, he was irrepressible. I once sent him some terrapin from my plantation in South Carolina, and later asked him if he had eaten them. "No," he said, "I thought they were so amusing, I turned them loose in Sorrel's cabin," referring to the noted French artist. Clemenceau was passionately fond of grapefruit, and one of the few gifts he ever permitted me to send him was a crate of fruit now and then.

Among the mementos I prize is this letter from him. He asked that it not be published in his lifetime, a request which I have honored.

Paris, November 27, 1924

My dear Friend,

I am late in answering your good letter which touches me keenly. I could give you some excuses, but I prefer to rely upon your friendship. Do you remember the distant days of that "conference" in which we wasted so much effort without being able to come to an agreement? It was there that I began to see you talk and act as a good American, but desirous of doing for France the best you could. The American bloc was with us in sentiment, but not financially. It found itself unyielding on the famous question of the capacity of payment of Germany. America unfortunately disinterested itself in the matter and we know too well today what this cost us. You heard me ask your compatriots why they had gone to war, and whether they had achieved the ends they had proposed. They contented themselves by not answering. But that time you were at my side. With so many other excellent colleagues you always remained a sincere friend of France. If the results did not always come up to your expectations, I can well testify this was quite contrary to your intentions. How well I know that I always found you faithful to the work of fomenting the friendship of France! How many times have you honored me with your fullest confidence in this matter! What pleasure will I have in receiving you in my Vendean wine cellar if you carry out your promise for next year! I hope that this time, too, friend Tardieu will be with us.

A good handshake.

Clemenceau

2

When I think of the war's great figures who burned themselves out, using their physical and nervous energies to such an extent they were never quite the same again, Lloyd George comes immediately to mind. There never was a more amiable and ingratiating man than the Prime Minister of England. He could charm the birds from the trees with his talk.

Like Clemenceau, he had taken over a faltering war machine and provided the single-minded, driving leadership which had been lacking. He was one of the organizers of Allied victory. I only wish he had been as helpful in organizing the peace.

At Paris he was adroit, agreeable, but shifting with each tide. He was filled with sudden enthusiasms which quickly palled, bright ideas which he abruptly abandoned. At one time or another Lloyd George might be found on several sides of any given question. Domestic political considerations seemed ever in the forefront of his mind.

Politics is a legitimate factor in the decision of statesmen, but it should never, in great issues, be the determining factor. Unfortunately, it frequently is. Lloyd George came to Paris bound by his constituents to treat Germany severely. Later, when he felt different political winds blowing across the Channel, he tried, too late, to recall the harsh decisions he had helped to make.

Nothing pained me more about Lloyd George than his later references to Wilson's "halfheartedness" in the war. Indeed, this ungenerous comment did not jibe with the tribute I heard him pay the President one night. He was describing to a party of dinner guests how, at the blackest moment of the war, he had appealed to the President through the British Ambassador, Lord Reading, to send American troops to France, equipped or unequipped. Lord Reading took up the story, detailing how I had arranged for him to see the President. "I hadn't been with Mr. Wilson long," Reading said, "before he agreed to our request. 'I'll do my damndest,' Wilson exclaimed. It was a decision no potentate in the world would have dared make in such circumstances without consulting his ministers." Lloyd George added, "Those words thrilled the Allied line from the Vosges to the sea."

For me, one of the most memorable moments of the Conference was an encounter between Lloyd George and Wilson—at which I was the only witness—over Lloyd George's last minute attempt to revise the terms of the Treaty.

These terms had been presented to the Germans on May 7th in a dramatic scene at Versailles. Clemenceau, flanked by Lloyd George and Wilson, had been the Allied spokesman. How he must have savored the moment! In a few curt sentences he told the Germans they had fifteen days in which to reply. In receiving the terms, Count Brockdorff-Rantzau, the chief of the German delegation, was a model of Prussian arrogance as he denied German war guilt.

The fifteen days went by, and then seven more. Then the German reply came, sending a wave of alarm through Paris. The Germans, it appeared, would refuse to sign, and hostilities might be resumed.

At the same time, a wave of protest had developed among liberal, labor, and independent groups in the United States and Great Britain against the alleged harshness of the Treaty. The critical outburst in Britain was particularly sharp, and Lloyd George fell into what Wilson described as a "perfect funk" over the uproar.

Up to this point, Lloyd George had taken the counsel of the archconservatives in demanding a severe treaty. Now that it was attacked, Lloyd George demonstrated the agility that made him resemble, in General Bliss's words, "a greased marble spinning on a glass table top." He suddenly demanded moderation of the terms. Clemenceau, however, refused to budge. Lloyd George's only hope was to win Wilson's support.

In the midst of this crisis, I received a telephone call from the Prime Minister asking me to breakfast the next morning. I was surprised, for my rank at Paris did not entitle me to such attention, nor did I ordinarily have direct dealings with the Prime Minister.

Lloyd George was staying at the home of an Englishman not too far from Wilson's residence. When I arrived at the appointed hour, I found several other members of the British delegation in attendance. Lloyd George greeted me with a most unsettling declaration: "My Cabinet has met and unanimously informed me that unless the terms of the Treaty are changed, neither the British Army nor Fleet will move to force the Germans to sign." Then he let the cat out of the bag. "What do you think Wilson will say?"

By this time many people believed I had more influence with the President than I actually possessed, probably because Wilson had backed me in several disputes. I did not know it then, but this meeting was part of Lloyd George's campaign to win the support of the President's advisers for amelioration of the Treaty's terms.

In reply to the Prime Minister's question, I said, "I don't know, but it will be quite simple to find out. I'll go ask him." Lloyd George looked astonished; I suppose no one else had given him such a straightforward answer.

I left the room and hurried to the President's quarters, where I learned he had gone to the Crillon, headquarters of our delegation. I found him there in the corner room of his suite, overlooking the Place de la Concorde and the little street that runs between the

Crillon and where the American Embassy then stood. A young man in the outer office tried to stop me, but I brushed by him and knocked on the President's door. Colonel House let me in. In a few words I outlined to Wilson what the Prime Minister had said to me. Without a moment's hesitation, the President called for his car. In a few minutes I was riding up the Champs Elysées with him to see Lloyd George.

As we rode along, I asked the President if I might speak to him frankly. When Wilson urged me to do so, I told him I thought the Prime Minister was struggling between his campaign promises and the dictates of his conscience. It seemed to me that he had decided to assume, if belatedly, the moral leadership in the making of the Treaty—an overgenerous estimate, as it turned out. I hoped the President would permit him to do so, I added.

"I shall let the Prime Minister take the lead," Wilson replied.

On our arrival at Lloyd George's residence there was a great stir. I heard people calling, "The President!" as we went up the stairs. We entered a large room, facing the street, from which everybody disappeared but the Prime Minister, the President, and myself. I was about to leave, to wait in the anteroom, but Lloyd George said, "I'm only going to say to the President what I have said to you."

"I have no secrets from Baruch," Wilson said.

The President took a chair. I can see him now, his legs crossed, one foot tapping the floor, his hands partly clasped, twirling his thumbs one around the other. The Prime Minister, in what I thought was a truculent manner, told him what he had told me— that unless the terms of the Treaty were changed, neither the British Army nor Fleet would move to compel Germany to sign.

Wilson did not miss a beat of his foot or a twirl of his fingers. But his jaws clenched and he showed that flinty eye I had seen when the battle was aroused within him.

The two men sat looking at each other. Then the President asked quietly, "What terms?" Lloyd George spelled out his ideas, which covered changes in the Silesian settlement, the Rhineland occupation, and reparations, among others.

The President was silent for a long moment. Then he said, in words very much like these—words which revealed the anger he was trying to suppress, "Mr. Prime Minister, you make me sick! For months we have been struggling to make the terms of the Treaty exactly along the lines you now speak of, and never got the support of the English. Now, after we have finally come to agreement, and when we have to face the Germans and we need unanimity, you want to rewrite the Treaty."

The President went on to say that he would accept Lloyd George's proposals, even at this late date, if the French would agree. But he could not countenance a move to split the Allies at an hour when they had to present a united front.

In the end, after more wrangling, which drove Wilson almost to the point of desperation, some minor concessions were made to satisfy Lloyd George. Before long, however, he was again demonstrating his changeability by calling for reimposition of the blockade against Germany.

3

Winston Churchill was one of the Cabinet members Lloyd George had summoned to Paris during the crisis over the Treaty, which gave me the opportunity to meet the man for whom I had already conceived such a high regard through our wartime correspondence.

My first meeting with Churchill is as vivid in my memory as though it had occurred yesterday. I had gone to call on him at his hotel, the Villa Majestic. When I was ushered into his room I found him dressing. We immediately fell to discussing the crisis which had brought him to Paris.

I spoke, with strong feeling, of the spirit of vengeance which animated the French and the British, and of the consequences of a peace settlement based on revenge rather than reason.

I remember how he turned from the mirror, before which he was adjusting a black satin tie, and said to me earnestly: "I was all for war when it was on. Now it is over, and I'm all for peace."

Later we walked in the Bois de Boulogne. Pointing his walking stick toward the east, where the Red Revolution had erupted, he made a prophetic remark, "Russia. Russia. That's where the weather is coming from." Even then he could feel the build-up of that cold front of dictatorship which was to hold so many people in its grip.

From that time on I was privileged to have the friendship of this extraordinary man—one of the greatest in history. When he visits New York, my home is usually his headquarters; and I never fail to visit him when I am in Europe.

He used to take me around the countryside to see the sights and visit his friends. Once, in the company of Admiral Sir Roger Keyes, we inspected the fleet at Portsmouth. As we walked down the line of sailors, I heard one tar whisper: "Good old Winnie, he got us our pay raise."

More often we would sit in his home at Chartwell and talk. This was always a great treat. With what humor and color he could describe his early adventures in South Africa; with what eloquence he could discuss Macaulay and Gibbon; and with what spirit he could denounce the knaves and fools he had known!

The world is accustomed to seeing Churchill in the spotlight of public affairs. It knows him for his indomitable courage, for the strength of his leadership, and the force of his writings. But in these visits I came to know the side of Churchill he keeps well-hidden from the public. I often wish people could look in on him as he walks through his garden with his dog, pausing to admire the beauty of a rose or to lecture the goldfish in the pond as he feeds them. I wish people could read the cables I have received from this master of English prose, cables in which he expressed his enthusiasm over some development with a brisk "Oh boy!"

The years between the wars were bleak ones for Churchill, out-of-office and in disfavor even in his own party. Once, as we walked through his garden, he unburdened himself to me. His public career seemed at an end, and he wondered whether he ought not to enter some business. I tried to hearten him by pointing out that, although he might be denied political leadership for a time, he could achieve greatness with his pen. And I told him that I was sure England could not and would not go on ignoring him. Fortunately for her and for the world, England did not when the great trial began.

Although Churchill's most enduring deeds were accomplished in war, it was always peace for which he fought—peace with freedom. Some years ago we were sitting in my house in New York playing gin rummy. Outside there was a parade in honor of Greek independence. The sound of marching feet and the strains of music sifted up even to our deaf ears. We went to the window and looked down on the ranks of marchers and fluttering flags. Churchill turned to me with sparkling eyes and said: "You see Bernie, they cannot quench freedom."

They cannot indeed, as long as the world breeds men like Churchill to defend it.

Another Englishman who impressed me greatly at the Peace Conference was Lord Robert Cecil. Presiding over the Supreme Economic Council, he would sit slumped on his spine, his index fingers spired together, listening to debate. When he rose to speak, he would unfold his tall figure like a jackknife.

Cecil, descended from a great English family, son of a former Prime Minister, epitomized the best in the British aristocracy. He was a militant advocate of the League, and the American delegation always found an ally in him in our efforts to achieve a just peace. I wrote of him later ". . . He has the finest sense of justice that one can possibly imagine. He never can be much of a politician because he does not temporize nor deal in expediency. . . . He holds his head on high like a crusader preaching the gospel of truth and charity. I do not believe he ever had a mean thought or even a low idea."

John Maynard Keynes was still another personality who left his imprint on my memory. Keynes was the representative of the British Treasury at the Conference. As I have said earlier, his view on Germany's capacity to pay reparations was entirely sound. But later he had the effrontery to propose that America guarantee the payment of German reparations, and the insolence to call President Wilson "the greatest fraud on earth" after Wilson had refused to accept his plan.

When Keynes's recommendations were rejected, he burst out like a petulant and spoiled child against the whole Treaty. In his resentment he packed his bags, went home, and wrote his famous and pernicious book, *The Economic Consequences of the Peace*, which did so much to bring about the very consequences he claimed to fear.

Keynes had submitted his manuscript for comment to several men, among them Sir James A. Salter, one of the economists with the British delegation and later head of the Reparations Commission. Salter urged him to moderate his attack on Wilson, if for no other reason than that it would hurt the prospects of ratifying the Treaty in the United States. Keynes, however, preferred to use his great talents to provide ammunition for the Treaty's critics who gathered for the kill after Paris. If Keynes had had Cecil's sincerity and sense of values, he would never have attacked the Treaty as he did, and do such great injury to the League and to the cause of international coöperation.

I, too, wrote a book, *The Making of the Reparation and Economic Sections of the Treaty*, which Keynes in a review found to be a "colorless" apologia but of "significance as a human and historical document." I suppose I should have been grateful to have escaped so lightly, and not to have been subjected to a full Keynesian literary barrage. He certainly did have a marvelous facility with words. It was this very quality, however, which from the first made me wary of him at Paris. On one occasion he came to me with a statement he had drafted, and urged me to endorse it. He pointed out its virtue: "It will mean one thing to your people and another to mine."

Keynes's subsequent contributions to economics have left me singularly unenthusiastic. There is no questioning the brilliance and originality of some of his thought; but not even Keynesian theory can repeal the fundamental laws of economics. It is true that a prophet is not always responsible for the excesses of his followers. Nothing, however, has done more harm to the economic and, indeed, spiritual fiber of nations than the policies which have been inspired by Keynes's ideas.

There were other memorable figures in Paris. Here was Black Duke Michael, brother of the Czar, bitter at the destruction of the Romanoff dynasty and at a loss to explain how his own servants could join in the Revolution. He simply had no comprehension of the grievances of the Russian people.

Here was Ignace Jan Paderewski, hailed as one of the world's great pianists, pleading the cause of reborn Poland with the same fiery eloquence he displayed on the keyboard.

Once I attended a meting with this patriot and his colleague, Stanislaw Grabski. Grabski complained at great length that reports of Polish pogroms, in which many Jews had been killed and brutalized, were exaggerated. "When you stick them with a pin, they cry as if stuck with a bayonet," he said scornfully, to explain the mounting protests against these outbreaks of hate and violence.

"Why stick them at all?" I asked.

I shall never forget Paderewski's craggy head, like a sculpture in its rough-hewn lines, tossing its mane of perpetually disordered hair in vehement approval of my words.

A patriot of a different kind was Eduard Beneš, a quiet little intellectual who was destined to lead the new state of Czechoslovakia down the next two decades to the tragedy of Hitler's conquest. I frequently met him and Jan Masaryk at the President's place, where their thoughtful contributions to the discussions were always welcome.

4

But the central figure at Paris was Woodrow Wilson. Everybody wanted to meet him. An Indian maharajah asked me to arrange an audience with the President, so that he could tell his people that the "light of Wilson's countenance had shone upon him." Those were his words. Admiral Cary Grayson, Wilson's physician and Naval aide, later told me that when the maharajah entered the room he was so nervous that he did not know who the President was, although he had been accustomed all his life to pomp and important personages.

But such adulation quickly gave way to attack, and then abuse, as Wilson set himself against the demands of the Allies. A concerted campaign of raking criticism was launched in the Allied press, with the President as the primary target and with some of his advisers, including me, as secondary ones.

My position on reparations had earned me the reputation of being pro-German, which has its irony, considering what the Germans were to say about me later. I was attacked savagely in the British and French journals. One night I was introduced to the president of the Franco-American Society at a reception. He turned his back on me, murmuring audibly that I was pro-German and everyone knew it. All kinds of rumors about me were set afloat, among them that I was a Bolshevik agent.

One day, after the President had concluded an address before a plenary session of the Peace Conference at the Quai d'Orsay, someone rushed up and said he wanted to see me. I walked over to where he was conversing with a group of dignitaries. "Please wait for me, Baruch," he said. Then, linking his arm in mine, we walked out of the room. We got into his automobile, and he instructed the driver to drop me at my hotel. "I hear a great many complaints about you," he said. "You must be doing a good job. You keep at it and don't worry. You'll stay on as long as I am President."

That he should be conscious of my need for encouragement touched me. This was the kind of thoughtfulness that endeared him to me. Everybody had seen us leave the Quai d'Orsay together, and that simple act, I knew, would strengthen me in my work.

Wilson literally worked himself to the bone, and everybody else to a standstill in Paris. Most of us could find some time for rest and relaxation. I had a place outside Paris where, on week ends, I could catch a few hours of leisure. But the President had no respite. Almost every question—whether it was over the disposition of colonies, the definition of boundaries, or the establishment of the League—was hammered out in frustrating, often bitter debate. On more than one occasion it seemed the Conference would break up; once Wilson ordered the *George Washington* to make ready to take him home.

It was not only the sheer physical labor involved in these conferences, discussions, briefings, speeches—the fourteen to sixteen hours a day that he worked—that wore down his never robust health. It was the spiritual travail as well, the emotional frustration of the struggle to fulfill his conception of the peace. The violent attacks against him in the press; the bitter quarrels with Lloyd George, Clemenceau, and Orlando; the unrelenting demands from every side for some minor advantage which meant violating a major principle—the evidence on every hand of the ignoble, grasping nature of men and nations—it was all this which made the Conference, as Herbert Hoover put it in the title of his revealing, cogent book, "The Ordeal of Woodrow Wilson."

There were times when he must have come close to the breaking point. One night as the Conference neared its end, Cary Grayson and I were sitting in the Admiral's room. We were enjoying a bottle of the finest white wine I ever drank, which had been placed at the disposal of the President's suite. Unannounced, the President walked in. His eye was troubling him, he told Grayson. Would the doctor look at it? Grayson did. Then Wilson sat down and talked with us. I won't attempt to give the substance of what he said. It was one of those times when a man bares the grief and struggle in his soul. When he left, Grayson said, "He didn't have anything the matter with his eye; he just wanted to come up and be with us."

Grayson was not only the President's doctor and Naval aide, but a loyal and understanding friend, one of the very few to whom Wilson, in the crushing loneliness of the Presidency, could unburden his innermost thoughts. A President is never at a loss for aides, advisers, assistants—even sociable companions. But he is ever in need of the intellectually compatible friend who wants nothing, who represents nobody, whom he can trust implicitly. This described Grayson. A man of keen intelligence and deep religious feeling, Grayson also had a highly developed sense of humor. He was an inveterate practical joker, amiable needler, and probably the best raconteur I ever heard.

Once I made a tour of the Hindenburg Line in the company of Mme de Rougemont, the wife of my friend, Count René de Rougemont. Tardieu had assigned a French officer, who knew the terrain, to escort us. On the way we met Floyd Gibbons, the tall young war correspondent of the Chicago *Tribune*, who showed us the ground over which our boys had fought, and where he had lost an eye. The French officer explained the battle in detail. The German dead were buried in graves so shallow that corpses could be seen where the rain had washed away the earth.

We finally came into Soissons, where on this particular Sunday there was great excitement because the President and Mrs. Wilson were there. We were walking down the street when Grayson came rushing up to say that the President and Mrs. Wilson would like me to take lunch with them. I told Grayson that I had Mme de Rougemont and the young French officer with me; but he said to bring them along, which I did.

Afterward the President often told about what he thought was my embarrassment, especially when I introduced the French officer and didn't know his name. Grayson improved on the story, declaring that I was so embarrassed at finding myself invited by the President and Mrs. Wilson when I had a charming lady with me that I had grabbed the first man I met, who was a French general, and pressed him into service. The President loved to tell this story, adding to Grayson's frills himself.

Grayson never let me forget the day of one of the big races at Longchamp. I had arranged for a luncheon in the Bois and for a box at the track, and was about ready to leave when he called to say that the President wanted to see me. When I arrived at the President's residence, Grayson took in my formal attire, complete with tall silk hat, which was *de rigueur* for the occasion. I invited him to come with me to the races, but he said he had to go motoring, as usual, with the President. When Wilson saw me, he said, "Baruch, won't you stay for luncheon?" Luncheon with the President is not to be declined, so I sent word to my guests that I would not lunch with them but would meet them later at the track.

During luncheon, the President remarked to Grayson, "You ought to stay home and take care of that carbuncle on your neck. If you go motoring you'll get dust in it."

"Yes, Sir," Grayson said, looking at me with a twinkle in his eye. I knew mischief was brewing.

"Baruch will go with me, won't you?" the President went on. I could not say no, so I went motoring with Mr. Wilson.

Grayson, meanwhile, took to his room until he heard the President's automobile leave, after which his carbuncle promptly got well and he took off for my box at the races. He solemnly advised my friends how unhappy I was that I could not come, but that I had to stay away on matters of state. After the race, Grayson hurried back before the President and I returned from our ride, and pretended he had never been out.

Next day when he was out riding with the President and Mrs. Wilson, she said, "You rascal, I caught you."

"I'll throw myself on the mercy of the court," Grayson replied, "and confess that I went to the races when you, Mr. President, asked Baruch to ride with you. And I must say I had a good time." At that, the President and his wife laughed heartily, because it was some other escapade in which they had found him out. Here is a lesson for any man. Don't admit anything until you know what they have on you.

5

At last the Conference was ended. The debates were over. The compromises had been made, the boundaries redrawn, the mandates assigned. The Treaty of Versailles was ready to be signed.

On June 28th, the last act in the great drama was played in the crowded Hall of Mirrors at Versailles. In the center of that magnificent chamber, at a horseshoe table, sat Clemenceau, flanked by Wilson and Lloyd George. On a table nearby rested the document on which so much labor had been expended.

I stood in the hushed audience as the sound of bugles ushered in the two German plenipotentiaries. They signed the Treaty. Then Wilson put his name to it, followed by the long list of Allied representatives.

The Treaty fell far short of what Wilson had hoped for. He admitted it, and many of us shared his disappointment. He had been compelled to make compromises, some of which went down hard. Still, Wilson had forced the Allies to compromise too, to abandon some of their extreme demands, and to accept many of his principles which they had at first tried to reject. As Senator William Borah, who fought ratification of the Treaty, later admitted to me, the peace would have been infinitely harsher had it not been for Wilson.

Given the magnitude of his task, the forces at work in Paris, the temper of our Allies, the wonder is not that Wilson failed to accomplish all he had set out to do, but that he accomplished as much as he did.

Above all he had fulfilled his primary mission—the establishment of the League of Nations. Through this instrument of world law and order, he hoped to correct the imperfections and mistakes in the Treaty and establish the basis of enduring peace.

I shared Wilson's hope. Although I had fewer illusions when I left Paris than when I had arrived, nonetheless I believed that the Treaty enabled all to look forward with hope instead of backward with hate.

The day after the Treaty was signed, the President and Mrs. Wilson sailed for home. I was among those accompanying them on the *George Washington,* along with Tom Lamont, Vance McCormick, Norman Davis, Admiral Grayson, John D. Rockefeller, Jr., Nicholas Murray Butler, and others. The ship was packed with returning soldiers, and an escort of warships surrounded us.

Several times during the crossing I lunched with the President, and almost daily we met on deck and chatted. Once Wilson stood looking out over the calm ocean with a remote look in his eyes, and said, "You know, Baruch, only a god could perform what is expected of me." There was a quality of sadness in his voice which touched me deeply.

One day the President asked Davis, McCormick, Lamont, and me into his salon, where he read to us the message he would give Congress when he presented the Treaty to it. He asked for our comments. I made none, not wanting to be critical in the presence of others. Later, at the foot of one of the companionways, I met the President and Mrs. Wilson and made my criticism.

I thought that the message was not sufficiently forceful, I said, and that it failed to dramatize or explain the League. Most Americans had no real understanding of the League, I told the President, and he ought to seize this first occasion to tell them exactly what it was and what it would do. I felt that he must seize the initiative from his critics, and put them on the defensive from the start, otherwise they would soon have him there. But the President was never able to follow this advice. He never caught up with his critics in those last sad days that now confronted us all in Washington.

Our reception in New York on July 8th was one that none of us would ever forget. The harbor was filled with ships of every description; pennants and flags were flapping in the warm breeze; and sirens were screaming. The decks of the *George Washington* were jammed with soldiers. On the top deck stood the President, dressed in striped trousers, Prince Albert coat, and, incongruously, a golf cap. One of the reception tugs came alongside. I could make out McAdoo standing at the rail, waving frantically and leading three cheers for the President.

It was hard to believe that all Americans were not echoing the cry of the old woman who shouted at the triumphal cavalcade which carried the President through the city, "God bless Woodrow Wilson!" In Congress, a hostile band of men waited to attack.

VIII

The Fight for the League

THE HUMAN FACTOR, I have often said, is the crucial one in determining the course of events. No better example of this can be found than in the fight over ratification of the Treaty, whose outcome was decided in a clash of personalities, and by the ambitions, animosities, and prejudices of the leading actors.

When Wilson submitted the Treaty to the Senate, he was given a cold reception. He was unable to seize the offensive, as I had hoped he would, from his enemies. His chief antagonist was the patrician Bostonian, Senator Henry Cabot Lodge, who commanded a mixed crew of sincere isolationists and political hatchetmen. I could respect such men as Borah and Hiram Johnson, who stood on their principles, mistaken though I thought them to be. I could not respect men who put personal antagonism and political considerations, of the narrowest sort, before all else. And this, it seemed to me, Lodge did.

During the war he had given full support to the Administration. As far as I was concerned, I could say he always gave me unqualified coöperation. But as soon as the war ended, his one purpose seemed to be to overturn the Administration and restore the Presidency to the Republican Party, an objective made dearer by his intense personal dislike of Wilson, which Wilson fully reciprocated. The League of Nations issue gave Lodge the opportunity to achieve his purpose.

He was a shrewd and resourceful foe. He did not launch a frontal attack upon the League; many men prominent in his party, including former President William Howard Taft and Elihu Root, were committed to it in principle and there was strong public support for it too. Instead, his strategy was to wage a campaign of delay and obstruction. Thus, the enemies of the League introduced a long series of reservations and amendments to the Treaty and the League Covenant. Some of these were minor, others would have emasculated the charter. And while the Senate wrangled over these reservations, Lodge's forces were busy fomenting distrust of the League; encouraging the traditional American suspicion of foreign entanglements; playing upon the resentment of nationality groups in America to various aspects of the Treaty.

I, personally, believed deeply in the League. I had no illusions, as I have said, that the Treaty was a perfect document. Called to testify before the Foreign Affairs Committee, I defended the Treaty as severe but just, as embodying all that could have been obtained in the atmosphere of Paris. There were many things wrong with it, not least among them the reparations tangle. But I believed, with Wilson, that through the League the imperfections in the Treaty would in time be made right.

Accordingly, I threw myself into the fight for ratification of the Treaty. I followed closely the Senate debates, conferring frequently with pro-League forces on strategy and tactics. This brought me under heavy attack from the Lodge camp and the Hearst press. But I continued at every opportunity to seek to win open-minded critics to the President's side.

When, for example, the League to Enforce Peace undertook a public educational campaign on behalf of the Covenant, I guaranteed its expenditures. That organization numbered among its members many prominent Republicans, including Taft and Root. But as the fight grew more intense, many of them deserted the cause. It is a sad thing to see men of public stature put loyalty to party above their loftier principles. So many men take refuge in a group, to condone or even participate in activities which they would never sanction as individuals. One exception in the fight for the League, to his everlasting credit, was the courageous George Wickersham, Attorney General of the United States under Taft.

All through July and August the enemies of the League, including such Democrats as Senator James Reed of Missouri, pressed their attack, criticizing the terms of the peace settlement, challenging all that the President had done and left undone in Paris, and subjecting him to violent personal abuse. In the face of such opposition, many of Wilson's supporters in the Senate advised compromise, urging him to accept, as the price of ratification, some of the milder changes which had been proposed. This sentiment was expressed to me by Senator Claude Swanson when he said, "What difference does it make if the baby is tied with blue ribbons or pink ones—as long as we get the baby."

Wilson himself, contrary to the picture his critics have drawn, had not set his face unalterably against any compromise. He was determined, however, to accept no reservations which would alter the Covenant. Indeed, if the Senate would ratify the Treaty as written, he was willing to accept a corollary resolution in which the Senate set forth its own interpretation of the Treaty.

Wilson discussed this matter with me and asked me to see the Attorney General, A. Mitchell Palmer, about drafting such a resolution for submission to Senate leaders. I suggested Newton Baker as better qualified, and the President agreed. But when I told the Secretary of War what the President wanted, he was unenthusiastic. "What difference does it make whether we get one piece of paper or two?" he asked. I told him that there was nothing to be gained by arguing the point. "If this is what the President wants, let's do it," I said. Whether or not Baker himself drafted the paper, I do not know. But eventually the President gave four interpretative resolutions, which he was willing to accept, to the Democratic Senate leader, Gilbert Hitchcock.

By the end of August, after almost two months of fruitless negotiation with the opponents of the League, Wilson decided to take his case to the American people. With his unshakeable faith in the people's capacity to judge wisely if they but knew the facts, Wilson was convinced that if he could speak to them directly, they would rise to his support. Firm in this belief, he decided on his fateful whistle-stop tour of the country.

To those of us who saw him regularly, it was clear that he was in no condition to undertake such a mission. His frail constitution had been taxed to its uttermost limits by the war and the Peace Conference. He had fallen ill at Paris but somehow had found the strength to go on. Now he seemed on the brink of a total physical collapse. Cary Grayson warned him that no physician could be responsible for the outcome of such a journey. Others tried to dissuade him, too. I added my appeal.

A few days before he was scheduled to set out, I went to the White House to urge him to call off the trip. He sat at the desk in his study, his long face pale and haggard but stamped with his sense of dedication. He listened patiently to what I said. When I had concluded he said, no, he would not call off the trip. The Treaty must be ratified and there was no other way to do it but to rally the people. I pleaded with him at least to go off first to rest and prepare his speeches, which he had not yet done. No, he said, and his voice showed his utter weariness. He hadn't the time.

"Mr. President, if anything happens to you, what will we do?" I asked. There was nothing more I could say when he replied, "What is one life in a great cause?"

On September 3rd he set out on his last crusade. We were encouraged by the demonstrations of support he received as he moved across the country. Addressing great crowds in the Middle West, on the Coast, in the Pacific Northwest, he preached his mes-

sage with eloquence and passion. Again and again he warned that
the war would have been in vain if America turned its back on the
League. "I can predict with absolute certainty," Wilson declared,
"that within another generation there will be another world war
if the nations of the world do not concert the method by which to
prevent it."

But the long and exhausting trip proved too much. After an address at Pueblo, Colorado, his last reserves of strength failed. At
last, heeding the pleas of Mrs. Wilson and the warnings of Grayson,
the President agreed to cut short his punishing tour and return to
Washington. A few days later, on October 2nd, he suffered a stroke.
He lay at death's door for weeks.

                                   2

During those last months of 1919 and those early weeks of 1920,
the President slowly convalesced. Without his leadership his supporters were demoralized and confused, and the tide of public opinion could clearly be seen swinging away from him. Carter Glass,
Swanson, and others, myself included, felt that if all were not to
be lost, the President would have to accept some of the milder
reservations, especially on Article X.

Article X was the major point at issue in the ratification fight. It
bound the signatories to the Treaty "to respect and preserve as
against external aggression the territorial integrity and existing political independence of all members of the League." Wilson's opponents contended that Article X would impair our sovereignty
and involve us in foreign wars. But as Wilson put it, the League
was the "indispensable instrumentality of peace." It was necessary
to "guarantee" the peace. Article X was the guarantee, "the kingpin
of the whole structure. . . . Without it, the Covenant would mean
nothing." He would not compromise on this.

At Carter Glass's urging, I went to see the President early in

February to ask him to accept some reasonable compromises, particularly on Article X. It was not easy to do. I knew that he had almost given, and was prepared to give, his life for the cause in which he believed. I believed in it too, and would have done anything in my power to help him. But I felt it my duty to say to him that he was making a mistake in refusing to meet his opponents part way.

The President received me in his bedroom, propped up in bed against the pillows, a shawl around his shoulders, his partly paralyzed left arm hidden under it. His daughter Margaret stood on one side of the bed, Cary Grayson on the other, and Mrs. Wilson at its foot. I had not seen the President since he set out on his tour. Then I had been disturbed by his evident exhaustion; now I was shocked by his drawn and wasted appearance. Still, there was that keenness in his eyes, and I remember thinking how the look in them resembled my father's.

In asking him to compromise, I felt that I was laying my friendship on the altar of truth. Nevertheless, I begged him to accept some of the reservations proposed, saying, "If we can at least get the spirit of the Covenant ratified, we can make it work."

He stopped me; his voice was sharp. "No. They are not reservations, they are nullifications. No, I shall not accept. If I did, I would be false to every young man who lies in Flanders."

The interview was over. I walked from the room, certain that the President believed I had deserted him, and for a moment he did. Mrs. Wilson later told me that after I had gone he had murmured, "And Baruch, too."

Mrs. Wilson accompanied me to the door and wordlessly took my hand between hers in sympathy. She, too, wanted the President to compromise and at last appealed to him, as she relates in her own book:

> . . .In desperation, I went to my husband. "For my sake," I said, "won't you accept these reservations and get this awful thing settled?"

He turned his head on the pillow and stretching out his hand to take mine answered in a voice I shall never forget: "Little girl, don't you desert me; that I cannot stand. Can't you see that I have no moral right to accept any change in a paper I have signed without giving to every other signatory, even the Germans, the right to do the same thing? It is not I that will not accept; it is the Nation's honour that is at stake.

"Better a thousand times to go down fighting than to dip your colors to dishonourable compromise."

A day or two after this interview with the President, Mrs. Wilson telephoned to invite me to the White House for tea. When I arrived she told me that the President had sent for her a few hours after my visit, and told her, "You know, Baruch is true to the bone. He told me what he believed, not what he knew I wanted him to say. Tell the dear fellow that I would like him to be Secretary of the Treasury [Carter Glass had just resigned], and then that will be off my mind." This was the unforgiving, unrelenting, unsympathetic Woodrow Wilson portrayed by his enemies.

The President had entertained the thought of appointing me to the Treasury at least once before. When McAdoo retired at the end of the war, I was mentioned as his successor. At that time I told the President it would be a mistake to appoint me. My career as a speculator would not be considered qualification for the job. The President replied, "Baruch, I'm always being told it would be a mistake to appoint you to a job, and after I do, I'm told how excellent a choice you were."

Now, as Mrs. Wilson told me of the President's wish, I was inclined to accept, out of loyalty and appreciation. I asked her, however, to let me discuss it with my wife. I went home where I found her sitting before a dressing table, combing her hair. "Annie," I said, "how would you like it if we were introduced as 'Secretary of the Treasury and Mrs. Baruch?'" She looked at me in the mirror, and I was surprised to see tears welling in her eyes. My wife had never enjoyed public life. She was happiest in the privacy of her family, pursuing her interest in music and in antique furniture, quietly helping good causes. Now she said, "Bernie, please come home to me and the children."

I immediately advised Mrs. Wilson that I could not accept the offer. I cannot deny that there were times when I felt pangs of regret at not accepting the Treasury; I think I could have kept the Department from drifting as it did during that last year of the Wilson Administration. But it was a small sacrifice to make for my wife's happiness.

3

While the battle over the Treaty still raged, and the President himself lay prostrate and half-paralyzed, all sorts of fantastic stories circulated about the nature of his illness and the degree of his incapacity. These rumors led to an official visit from Senator Hitchcock and Senator Albert Fall, who was later to move from the Senate into Harding's Cabinet and thence to jail. Fall had come to see for himself, and report to his Republican colleagues, what the President's condition was. On this occasion, there occurred that often quoted exchange between the President and Fall. "We have all been praying for you, Mr. President," said the Senator in his unctuous manner. "Which way, Senator?" Wilson replied.

One of the rumors which gained particular currency during the President's illness was that a regency, consisting of Mrs. Wilson, Grayson, Tumulty, and me, or some combination of us, ruled the White House and the country. For example, in November, 1919, Senator Lawrence Sherman of Illinois was widely quoted as declaring that "the American people are living under the regency of Tumulty and Baruch." And not only was this nonsense circulated, it was believed. Senator Lodge complained to Elihu Root that the Constitution did not contemplate "a regency of Tumulty and Barney Baruch." One lady prominent in Democratic circles, an ardent admirer of the President, firmly believed that Grayson and I were running the Presidency with Mrs. Wilson's help. Even people within the Administration, people I thought I knew and who certainly should have known better, accepted the story and added such embellishments as that I was the "new Colonel House." For by this time, the once intimate and almost fraternal relationship between the President and House had ended.

A great deal has been written about the rupture between House and Wilson, and a great deal of conjecture lavished on my alleged role as House's successor as adviser to the President. In actual fact, I knew nothing of the break until it was common knowledge, regretted it, and never exercised any measure of influence with the President equal to that of Colonel House.

The Colonel's story is a fascinating one. He was a native of Houston and got into politics in Texas, a state which gave him his military title and an increasingly prominent place in its Democratic Party machinery. He came to Baltimore in 1912 and helped win the nomination for Wilson. From the first days in Washington to the last days in Paris, the President relied on and trusted him implicitly and felt a personal affection for him which he felt for few other men. I once saw Wilson pause in the middle of an address, look up at Colonel House in the gallery, and praise him in the highest terms.

Without holding any official post in the Administration, House was by far the most important and influential of Wilson's lieutenants. In many ways he was Wilson's alter ego. But there is no doubt that the Colonel, despite his calm and quiet exterior and his loyalty to Wilson, gradually became intoxicated by power.

I vividly remember calling at his home during the war, to discuss some problem. After our talk, the Colonel escorted me to the stairway. I was astonished—and chilled—to hear him exclaim, as he stood with his arms outstretched, "Isn't it a thrilling thing to deal with the forces that affect the destiny of the world!" It did thrill House, and the power which he unquestionably wielded fed his sense of importance.

Colonel House's hand was in everything. At his request I employed a man in my office in WIB. The man did his work well enough, and I paid no particular attention to him, until one day he came to me with the confession that he had been asked by the Colonel to keep tab on me. He said that he had found nothing adverse to report, and that as he came to understand the splendid spirit that prevailed in the WIB, he felt more and more guilty until he could no longer go on with the game.

The Colonel's desire to dominate appeared to grow as his responsibilities and influence increased. As soon as the war ended, the President dispatched a mission, headed by House, to make arrangements for the Peace Conference. He also named House one of the American Peace Commissioners and, as always, considered him his chief aide. But as House began the discussions with Allied spokesmen on the issues of peace, he seemed to some observers to overstep himself.

I was made aware of this even before I joined the Peace Delegation. Shortly before I sailed for Europe, the wise and faithful Joe Tumulty had asked me to see Frank I. Cobb, the able editor of the New York *World*. Cobb, who had been a member of the House mission, had quit abruptly and angrily, convinced, as he told me, that House, under British pressure, was weakening and qualifying the basis of peace which Wilson had laid down.

Mrs. Cobb told me later that as soon as her husband walked into the house upon his return from Europe, he blurted out, "Wilson hasn't got a chance. The British have House in their pocket."

Sitting in his office in the tower of the old *World* building, puffing out clouds of smoke from his corncob pipe, the shirt-sleeved Cobb bitterly assailed Colonel House for compromising the President's chances of carrying out the kind of Treaty that Wilson wanted.

When I got to Paris, where Colonel House was the major-domo of the American delegation, I was not one of his clique. Some of us resented the air of officiousness which surrounded him and his staff. Once, after a brief illness had kept House in his room, Gordon Auchincloss, his son-in-law, remarked to Vance McCormick and me that now that the Colonel was better, "Woody's batting average would improve." Vance almost bit Auchincloss' head off.

When Wilson returned briefly to the United States at the end of February, major responsibility for pushing ahead with the Treaty fell on House. Upon the President's return to Paris, although there was no public evidence of a rupture, we know now that the President was deeply disturbed and disappointed at the compromises House had made in his absence. In his zeal and self-confidence, House had gone too far on his own, making promises which Wilson felt had undercut his position.

By this time Colonel House apparently felt that he alone could save Wilson from his ideals. And this conviction is documented in his diaries, a portion of which was published after Wilson's death. The diaries record the Colonel's growing self-regard, his increasing impatience with the President, his swelling conviction that most wisdom and achievement derived mainly from his own thoughts and action. He tells the diary how wrong the President is and how wise is his own viewpoint, and the diary answers faithfully that House is indeed the real leader he is coming to think of himself as being. House was, indisputably, an invaluable adviser to Wilson, but as Herbert Hoover has put it, Wilson was no Charlie McCarthy to House.

When the diary was published, many men were simply astounded by the insight it provided into House's mind. Many others were resentful of the credit the Colonel claimed, which did not belong to him. Carter Glass, the father of the Federal Reserve System, sat down to write a history of its genesis in order to set straight the claim of authorship the Colonel put forth.

For the last few months of the Conference, Wilson and House saw each other only on business. House remained in Europe when we returned in July. He and the President never met again.

I always felt that the break between him and the President was regrettable. I once mentioned it to Mrs. Wilson. She was silent at my suggestion that it was a sad thing that two men who had been such close friends should separate at the end of brilliant careers. And when I spoke to Wilson, he started to say, "It's a terrible thing to find a man you trust . . ." and then broke off his reply. Once I told House I would try to arrange a reconciliation, if he wished. He told me, "Not now."

It always seemed to me that the Colonel was victimized by the publicity and the adulation heaped upon him, as are many men unless they are on guard. At first he was embarrassed and troubled by the attention given to him in the press. Cary Grayson told of the distress that House suffered over a series of articles written by one Arthur H. Smith, which eulogized him at the expense of the President. The Colonel was staying in the White House at this time and had to take to his bed. Grayson went to see what was wrong, and the ordinarily reserved and silent House told him, with much anguish, that he feared these articles might lose him the friendship of the President. When Grayson told the President what was troubling House, Wilson, without even putting down the pen in his hand, hurried from his study to the Colonel's bedroom. He reassured him that such a thing could never come between them.

But in Paris, extolled by the European press, which was lambasting the President at the same time, House no longer seemed troubled. There were some, in fact, who felt that House could have used his well-known influence, with the British press in particular, to protect the President from attack.

House occupied that anomalous and always controversial position which belongs to men who, as "Presidential advisers," exercise hidden power. Harry Hopkins was the Colonel House of Franklin Roosevelt's Administrations, and like House, was a trusted, tireless worker who wielded extraordinary behind-the-scenes power. In President Eisenhower's Administration, Sherman Adams occupied this position to an extent greater than either House or Hopkins achieved, as far as actual power is concerned.

Presidents have always had their Kitchen Cabinets and Brain Trusts. But the question continues to recur as to what degree of power may safely be entrusted to Presidential confidantes.

4

We all know the fate of the Treaty. Twice the Senate cast a majority vote for it, but could not muster the necessary two-thirds. The Treaty and Wilson went down to defeat, making certain the fulfillment of Wilson's prophecy of a second world war.

Although I had urged the President to compromise on Article X, I came to believe he was right in refusing to impair it. We have learned the folly of trusting to empty treaties and mere declarations to preserve peace. If we have learned anything in the last generation, it is that there can be no reign of law without the force to maintain it. That is why I have insisted, as I know Wilson would have insisted, that any agreement to which the United States is party on nuclear energy, disarmament, and the maintenance of peace must include effective guarantees for the enforcement of its terms, and for sanctions against any violation of its provisions.

Woodrow Wilson left the White House in the spring of 1921. For a while he had entertained the idea of seeking vindication by running for reëlection. None of us from whom he sought encouragement gave it to him. It would have been hopeless and suicidal. Reluctantly he recognized this and moved into his house on S Street in Washington. Rejected by the American people, in whom he had put his faith, he did not lose his faith. Broken in body, he retained his indomitable spirit. Once he wrote me a note, and asked me to overlook the typographical errors in it because he had only "the use of one hand in using the typewriter."

Through these last years, he was sustained by the love and devotion of his wife. She was a ministering angel every hour of the day, always bright and cheerful, ever present at his side. Her devotion to her husband in the last days of his life and to his memory was beautiful to see.

Mrs. Wilson and I have been friends, it seems, from our first meeting. She always called me affectionately, "My dear Baron," after the name of my plantation, Hobcaw Barony. I saw her often, of course, in Paris, but my meetings with both her and the President were more frequent in those last years in the S Street house. Whenever I visited there, I never failed to remark Mrs. Wilson's touching care and solicitude for her husband.

I recall a luncheon one day when President Wilson suddenly stopped eating his rice pudding and laid down his spoon. A bit of rice stuck to his lip, which Mrs. Wilson, who was standing behind him, wiped off. The President had laid down his spoon to emphasize words I have never forgotten.

"You know," he said, "if I had not been stricken, I would have carried through the League. But God has a mysterious way of working. Perhaps the people of the world were not ready, and it would not have worked. But someday they will go into it voluntarily and it will bring to the world what I have hoped for."

But all the love and care in the world could not further prolong the President's life. He faded before our eyes until those last hours, when he murmured to the grief-stricken Cary Grayson, who had attended him constantly, "I am ready." On February 3, 1924, he departed this world he had tried so valiantly to save from itself.

Three days later, those who were close to him gathered in the S Street house for the simple funeral. The President's body lay in state before the fireplace in the drawing room. Afterward, the cortege wound through the silent, crowded, rain-washed streets.

The President was buried in a crypt over which was then rising the massive yet graceful walls of the Washington Cathedral.

Thirty-two years after Woodrow Wilson was laid to rest, I returned to the Cathedral—on Armistice Day, 1956—to pay my respects to his memory at ceremonies commemorating the centennial anniversary of his birth. On that occasion, I tried to sum up the meaning

Woodrow Wilson gave me my first opportunity for public service. He was one of the greatest men I have ever known.

The Bettmann Archive

Wilson directed the war effort through his War Cabinet, which included (standing) Herbert Hoover, Edward Hurley, Vance McCormick, Harry Garfield, and (seated) Benedict Crowell, William Gibbs McAdoo, Josephus Daniels, and myself.

As Chairman of the War Industries Board, charged with mobilizing America's industrial strength, I was fortunate in my associates. Shown above are the members of the Board: (standing) Howard Ingels, Edwin Parker, George Peek, J. Leonard Replogle, Alexander Legge, General George W. Goethals, and Albert C. Ritchie; (seated) Admiral Frank Fletcher, Robert S. Brookings, and Hugh Frayne. At the end of the war, they presented me with a loving cup. Seated at the left is our young stenographer, Billy Rose. Standing, center rear, is Herbert Bayard Swope.

Brown Brothers

As a member of the American Peace Delegation in Paris, I came to know such statesmen as Louis Loucheur, Winston Churchill, and David Lloyd George.

The dominant figures at the Peace Conference were Lloyd George, Clemenceau, and Wilson. At Wilson's right is his doctor and naval aide, Admiral Cary Grayson.

Underwood & Underwood

On June 28, 1919, the last act in the great drama of the Peace Conference was played. In the crowded Hall of Mirrors at Versailles, Clemenceau called the German delegates forward to sign the Treaty.

The picture above, of Lloyd George, Orlando, Clemenceau, and Wilson, taken immediately after the signing of the Treaty, captures the President's hope that an enduring peace had been achieved. Four years later, his health broken by his unsuccessful effort to win America's acceptance of the Treaty, Wilson had only a few months to live.

The Democratic ticket in 1920 was headed by Governor James M. Cox of Ohio. His running mate was Franklin D. Roosevelt.

Wide World Photos

The election of Warren G. Harding symbolized America's turning away from Wilsonian idealism. Shown with Harding and Wilson, on the way to the inauguration, are Congressman Joseph Cannon, of the House, and Senator Philander C. Knox.

Underwood & Underwood

The leading contender for the Democratic nomination in 1924 was my good friend, William Gibbs McAdoo. But after one of the most turbulent political conventions in history, John W. Davis (shown left, below) received the nomination. He was defeated in the election by Calvin Coolidge, a man whom I came to like and respect.

International News Photos, Inc.

Although he had the common touch, Alfred E. Smith was one of the most uncommon men who ever aspired to the White House. He was defeated in 1928 by Herbert Hoover, with whom I have long been friends.

Brown Brothers

During the campaign of 1932, F.D.R. had imparted his own sense of confidence to the American people. Here, in his inaugural address, he tells the nation: "The only thing we have to fear is fear itself."

Wide World Photos

Two leading figures in the early days of the New Deal were (as shown above) my close friend Hugh Johnson, who headed the NRA, and Ray Moley, who headed the Brains Trust. A leading Senatorial figure in those days, who went on to fill many other high posts, was James F. Byrnes (shown below).

Wide World Photos

International News Photos, Inc.

Mrs. Roosevelt is as great and gallant a person as I have ever known. I was privileged to have her friendship, and that of the President, over the years.

Wide World Photos

Underwood & Underwood

In 1938, after returning from Europe, I reported to F.D.R. at the White House on Germany's growing military strength and our need for preparedness.

One of the men with whom I worked closely during the fight for preparedness was General George C. Marshall. As Army Chief of Staff during World War Two, he was one of the architects of victory.

During the war I played an active part in the war production program. One of the special assignments I undertook was the Rubber Report, and my associates were (above) Dr. James Conant and Dr. Karl Compton. I also worked closely with two of the ablest men in Washington, Undersecretary of War Robert Patterson and Undersecretary of the Navy James Forrestal.

When Harry Truman assumed the Presidency, he was faced with the task of concluding the war and forging the peace. One of the major problems confronting him was the control of atomic energy.

As U.S. Representative on the United Nations Atomic Energy Commission, I presented the American plan for atomic control. I was in frequent debate with Andrei Gromyko, the Russian Representative.

Ever since the Paris Peace Conference, Winston Churchill and I have been warm friends. We have often walked and talked together in his garden at Chartwell.

When Churchill visits the United States, he is frequently my guest. In January, 1952, while staying at my home, he held several conferences with President-elect Dwight D. Eisenhower.

As I look back over the years, I marvel at the changes I have seen, at the progress we have made and the perils we have survived. As I look forward, I have faith in our capacity to fulfill the promise of America's heritage.

of his life and recall his ideas and ideals which still have meaning for us today.

Freedom to him was the supreme blessing of man. Democratic government was superior to all others because it gave to men the greatest measure of individual liberty. Individual liberty—the words are inseparable. The individual, Wilson said, is the "first fact of liberty." There can be "no corporate liberty," he pointed out. "Liberty belongs to the individual or it does not exist."

This is a truth which we are in danger of forgetting in an age when, increasingly, we think and act in terms of blocs and groups. The pressure of these groups steadily erodes our individuality and independence. More and more we rely on government to solve our problems. But as much as Wilson extended the role of government, his purpose was to free the individual and never to shackle self-reliance and initiative. These are the keys to human progress. Wilson knew that only individuals, not government, can provide the sense of moral responsibility which is the basis of a just and enduring society.

Devoted as he was to liberty and the principle of self-determination for all peoples, Wilson understood that "liberty is not itself government. In the wrong hands, in hands unpracticed, undisciplined, it is incompatible with government." Democracy, he said, is more than a form of government. "It is a form of character. It follows upon the long discipline which gives a people self-possession, self-mastery, the habit of order, and peace and common counsel and a reverence for law."

That is why democracy is, as he knew, the most difficult form of government. It must be accompanied by self-discipline and the spirit of reason. It cannot be bestowed upon a people; it certainly cannot be imposed upon them. They must win it and deserve it. It cannot even be taken by them and effectively used if they are not sufficiently prepared and mature. This is a fact which nations newly come to independence and those aspiring to it should remember.

To me, the cardinal lesson of Woodrow Wilson's life is that idealism and realism are not in conflict. They are essential to each other, if humanity is to progress. The idealist, unchecked by realism, must lead people astray. The realist, without ideals, must end in cynicism and stagnation. For all his idealism and vision, for all his hopes and aspirations, Woodrow Wilson knew that the world could not be remade at one sitting, that progress comes in slow stages. He had no patience with Utopians, with theorists who sought to make a new pattern for a world they did not understand. Of one such theorist, Karl Marx, he wrote: "I know of no man who has more corrupted the thinking of the world. . . ."

Above all, Wilson understood that in this modern world, war could no longer be isolated or belligerents quarantined. "The brotherhood of mankind," he declared, could not longer be a "fair but empty phrase; it must be given a structure of force and reality." He sought to provide that structure in the League. His failure was tragic for him in personal terms, but infinitely more so for the world. Yet the failure was not his. As Field Marshal Smuts once said, "He gave the world an instrument of good will. He could not give them good will."

Someday we shall have peace in the world, I pray—as Wilson put it, "A universal domain of right by such a concert of free peoples as shall bring peace and safety to all nations and make the world itself at last free."

If we ever attain that goal, we will reach it by the path that Wilson charted.

IX

The Farmers' Plight

I LEARNED AFTER THE WAR what it meant not to be involved in some major activity. Most of the men I had worked with on the War Industries Board and at the Paris Peace Conference were either businessmen or politicians. When the historic events which had absorbed us all were mercifully ended, they returned to their careers, while I wondered what I would do next.

At the age of forty-nine, I had already enjoyed two careers— in finance and, much more briefly, in government. The war had taken me out of Wall Street, often described as a narrow alley with a graveyard at one end and a river at the other, and plunged me deeply into the broad stream of national and international affairs. Now, by comparison, the Street appeared dull.

In Washington and Paris, my horizons had been broadened. I had learned that the old "let things alone" philosophy was no longer adequate to the needs of a changed America. I had learned the hopelessness and folly of isolationism in a world which, like it or not, was interdependent. Having acquired new convictions and a desire to do something about them, I decided not to confine myself again to Wall Street but to devote as much time as I could to broader fields.

The opportunity for further participation in public affairs appealed to me, and I soon found it in connection with two of the most pressing postwar economic problems. These were labor unrest and agricultural distress—two problems which seem always to be with us.

The process of adjusting to peacetime conditions was often painful, and nowhere more so than in the labor-management sphere. The demands of labor, bottled up during wartime, had erupted when peace was restored. On his return from Paris, President Wilson had been confronted by a labor crisis. Strikes had disrupted the steel, coal, and railroad industries, as well as others. Even the police of Boston struck. The national attention which Governor Calvin Coolidge attracted by his handling of that strike eventually led him to the White House.

In an effort to restore peace between labor and management, the President convened a National Industrial Conference composed of representatives of labor, agriculture, management, and of the public. Among those he appointed were John D. Rockefeller, Jr., Judge Gary, Charles E. Russell, Lillian Wald, Ida Tarbell, John Raskob, Samuel Gompers, and John L. Lewis. He named me chairman of the public group.

We met in Washington on October 6th, sat for several weeks, and achieved nothing. Those long, tedious, quarrelsome sessions confirmed my already strong conviction that important decisions are rarely forthcoming from public conferences. A meeting of the minds is a fine thing, but I have yet to see many minds meet at the same point in a conference room, especially when the public is looking in. Conferences and committees are no substitute for decisions. It always comes down to the fact that someone must make a decision—one of the hardest things in the world to do.

As I listened to representatives of industry trying to justify their resistance to unionism and other legitimate demands of labor, I was struck by their obtuseness and stubbornness. It was clear to me, as I wrote William Jennings Bryan, that labor's "unrest, distrust and dissatisfaction have much justice, and the injustice involved must be found and eradicated. It is unthinkable that the right and . . . the generous thing should not be done toward . . . the working classes . . . [and also to], that great mass of salaried employees, private and official, who have had little opportunity to voice their difficulties."

But among industrial leaders who looked upon collective bargaining, the eight-hour day, and government mediation of disputes as dangerously radical innovations, my attitude was resented. One industry leader accused me of wrecking the conference because of what he considered my pro-labor bias. If the recognition of labor's legitimate complaints was being pro-labor, then I was guilty.

Although I sympathized with labor, I was nevertheless impressed, in those conference meetings, by the fact that labor seemed to care no more about the public interest than did industry. Of course there was a great deal of lip service, as there always is, to the "general good." But neither labor nor industry was then, or is now, overburdened with a sense of responsibility to the consumer, who alone remains unorganized; the consumers, in fact, are today one of the few groups not represented in Washington by a powerful lobby. Actually, the costs of the perennial struggle between labor and management have been passed on increasingly to the consumer.

Since that abortive attempt in 1919 to bring harmony to the industrial scene, the economic and political power of labor has grown tremendously. Its sense of responsibility, however, has not always kept pace. Labor has often abused its power to the point where it has alienated public sympathy and endangered the legislative support it worked so hard to acquire.

By abusing its powers, labor injures not only itself but the whole country. While it is the proper concern of union leaders to improve the lot of their followers, they must recognize that their demands must be economically justified. If wage and other demands are not accompanied by increased productivity, inevitably prices will be driven out-of-reach, and foreign competition encouraged, to the detriment of the entire economy. American workers will wind up as the highest paid unemployed workers in the world. At present, we are already feeling the pinch resulting from the influx of foreign cars, steel, and other products. Unless labor leaders recognize this threat, they may well wind up "unionizing" unemployment.

2

Shortly after the Industrial Conference ended, I was given a chance to examine still another basic element of our economic life—agriculture; and to participate in a small way in the never-ending effort to solve the problems of agriculture which then, as now, beset us.

During the war, farmers, responding to the appeal of Washington and to the stimulus of high prices, had increased production tremendously. For example, with the government guaranteeing the price of wheat at almost $2.50 a bushel, wheat acreage was increased more than fifty per cent. Thanks to this effort, American farmers had produced enough food not only for our own fighting men and civilian population, but for our Allies as well; and the farm belt had enjoyed unprecedented prosperity.

But the end of the war brought this prosperity to an abrupt end, as Europe, once again able to feed itself, no longer offered us a market. By 1922, our agricultural exports were half what they had been in 1919. Despite this reduced demand for our wheat and cotton and corn, agricultural production kept running at full speed, like a motor with its accelerator stuck, piling up surpluses, while prices, responding inexorably to the law of supply and demand, plummeted, and despair swept the farm land. The withdrawal of government guarantees and the general postwar deflation only added to the disruption.

Beginning in 1920, a depression of major proportion gripped agriculture—one of the worst in a long line of agricultural collapses in our history. Agriculture's plight was a frightening example of the cruel paradox we have known so often in this land—of want amidst plenty, of depression resulting from too much rather than too little wealth. This is still one of the central problems of our economy: how to avoid the alternating booms and busts, how to keep supply and demand in balance, how to distribute effectively the goods we know so well how to produce.

Early in 1920, the Kansas State Board of Agriculture, confronted by the collapse of farm prices which threatened ruin to thousands, sought advice on how to stem the decline from men in business and finance. I must confess I was surprised when I read the invitation of J.C. Mohler, Secretary of the Kansas State Board of Agriculture, asking if I could propose some suggestions to help combat the farm depression. It seemed to me odd that farmers should seek my advice. Not only was I no expert on agriculture, but I was that anathema against whom the farmers had been railing since the days of the Greenbackers and Populists—a New York financier, a Wall Street man.

Nevertheless, I did not hesitate to accept the invitation. Although I did not have a specialist's knowledge of agricultural economics, I did have a fairly thorough knowledge of the American economic system—of finance, railroads, industry, mining—which could help me to see the farm problem in broad perspective and consider it in the light of the over-all economy.

In addition, I was motivated by boyhood memories of rural, Reconstruction South Carolina, of the gaunt farmers working the skimpy fields with their worn wives and skinny children toiling beside them. At the end of the year, all their labor was represented in a precious bale or two of cotton. They would haul it into town on an ox or mule cart, all the children of the family perched possessively on top while the parents trudged alongside in the dust. At the general store, the merchant would slit open the bale, grab out a handful of cotton to sample its quality, and offer the farmer a price. No matter how fair the merchant was, he was, like everyone else, concerned to repay his own indebtedness and make a profit. And he always had the upper hand. If the price he set was unsatisfactory, the farmer—in debt, without credit, living from crop to crop—could not reject it. Perpetually indebted to the merchant, he was helpless at his hands.

I was also influenced by my recollections of my father's keen interest in the farmers' plight. There was always a pile of farm journals in our home, and Father used to experiment with new agricultural techniques in South Carolina in an effort to help the neighboring farmers improve their lot.

As a result of these growing-up experiences, and my own later observations, I had a strong feeling for agriculture as a vital part of the American way of life. To be called upon to be of some service to it, seemed to me a new and welcome opportunity.

I set out for Topeka to learn the situation at firsthand. It was a polite but suspicious group of men who met me at the State House. As one of them later put it, they weren't taking any chances with this rich city slicker: they had their watches in their shoes. Nor was their confidence bolstered when the chairman of the welcoming committee introduced me as the "Wolf of Wall Street." It was intended as a compliment, but it was a sobriquet generally applied to an unsavory Wall Street figure, and its effect was not particularly encouraging on an audience which already thought that all Wall Street men had horns and a tail, if not fangs.

As I talked to those Kansas farmers, it was evident that they wanted to hear what a man who had dealt with wholesale government requirements, as I had in WIB, thought about their problem. But I had no intention of giving them ill-prepared observations. I told them I had come to listen and learn, to study the situation, after which I would try to come up with an answer.

I talked to farmers, bankers, railroad men, warehouse men, merchants, and local politicians. I met Kansas leaders of every stripe. Senator Arthur Capper was especially helpful, and we began a friendship that proved lasting. I met William Allen White, the short, stout editor of the Emporia *Gazette* whom Mark Sullivan had called the "Peter Pan of the Prairies." He demonstrated in his perceptive remarks to me why the *Gazette* was a national institution, and why its editor held such an influential position in Republican Party councils. Later I met the other noted Kansas editor, Ed Howe, of the Atchison *Globe,* a thin, tortured man whose satiric, homely barbs were quoted everywhere in the country.

I asked a lot of questions, and did a great deal of listening. Then I went home to digest the information I had gathered and to prepare a report. This I submitted in the form of a long letter to Secretary Mohler, which was later published under the title, "Putting Farming on a Modern Business Basis."

The title expressed one of the basic problems of agriculture. Compared with industry, agriculture in the 1920's was grossly uneconomic and inefficient. This was due, in part, to its inherent nature. The farmer, unlike the manufacturer, cannot adjust production to meet market conditions. A factory owner can increase production at will by adding machines and labor to meet sudden demand, or shut down production entirely should the market fail. But the farmer cannot make the seed in the soil stand still until prices improve, or hasten the growing rate to take advantage of a favorable market. The farmer is always at the mercy of nature, which does not regulate itself in the light of market conditions.

Beyond these inherent problems, however, agriculture's troubles were compounded by its organization—or, rather, its lack of organization. Today, the family farm is being absorbed into great mechanized producing units whose efficiency rivals that of some industries. But a generation ago, agriculture was still primarily composed of small competing units, and it lacked the economic power which comes with consolidation. The thousands of farmers who came to market with their crops were competing one with another to their mutual disadvantage. The individual farmer, living from harvest to harvest, lacking credit and storage facilities, was no match for the warehousemen and processors with whom he dealt. For most farmers, every sale was a forced sale. He took the price that prevailed, whether he liked it or not, whether he made money or not. He was often victimized, in the bargain, by short weighing and undergrading.

It was clear to me, as I studied the farm situation, that here was a glaring example of the evils of unbridled competition, whose consequences are as bad, if not worse, than those of monopoly. The great corporations of America, although often eloquent in praise of competition, have nevertheless been built through coöperation, consolidation, and integration. In the WIB I had seen the beneficial results of corporate coöperation, and I was now intrigued with the idea that farmers could take this page from industry's book.

The most promising field for agricultural coöperation was in marketing. I had studied the agricultural coöperative movement, which had long flourished in Europe. I had looked into the workings of England's famous Rochdale plan, the Australian coöperative wheat pools, and various farm co-ops in the United States. The principle of coöperative marketing, it seemed to me, was the logical alternative to the destructive consequences of competitive marketing, which were so pronounced in the grain-producing Middle West.

Consequently, in my report to the Kansas farmers, my main emphasis was on coöperative marketing as an instrument for mobilizing the farmer's economic strength and improving his economic position.

As essential elements to an effective coöperative movement, I also advocated the provision of credit and warehousing facilities for the farmers. I envisaged an extensive system of warehouses, financed by public funds if necessary, but in any event under state or federal regulation. These facilities would not only assure accurate weighing and grading, and help to effect savings in transportation and insurance, but would also establish the basis for a commodity credit system. It is such a system of commodity loans against warehoused crops which is the basis of our farm support program today. I never dreamed, while I was advocating it almost four decades ago, that it would be used as uneconomically as it has been.

Although the measures I advocated would, I believed, go a long way toward removing domestic impediments to agricultural prosperity, the ultimate solution to the farm depression, I told the farmers, lay in the restoration of world trade. The loss of European markets was obviously causing the farmer to drown in his own surplus; but the loss was not irretrievable. If the Continent could regain economic stability, it would again consume American grain. The key to that stability, I believed, lay in the settlement of such issues as reparations, and the abandonment of American isolationist policies as expressed in our tariffs. If the United States hoped to sell abroad, I argued, then we would have to lower our tariff barriers, which inhibited European trade and prosperity.

In setting forth this view, I was aware that it was not popular to say in the isolationist Middle West that the well-being of the American farmer depended upon prosperity in Europe, and that America had a role in its attainment. But I had to state the facts as I saw them.

3

All in all, my report to the Kansas farmers was well received, and I soon found myself deeply involved in the agricultural movement. For the next decade I was a close student of agriculture, a champion of the farmer, a consultant to political leaders of both parties on farm questions, and an adviser to the influential American Farm Bureau Federation and other farm organizations.

At every opportunity I pressed the farmers' cause. To President Harding, I urged support of rural credit legislation. I encouraged Senator Capper in his leadership of the Senate farm bloc, and endorsed his proposal to place a "dirt farmer" on the Federal Reserve Board in order to give agriculture a voice in the direction of the nation's banking policy. I hammered away at Senator Borah and other isolationists with the proposition that the farmers had a stake in European recovery and stability. I applauded and tried to encourage the work of such men as Senator George W. Norris and former Governor Frank Lowden in their leadership of the farmers, and carried out missionary work wherever and whenever I could.

Many of my Eastern friends, especially those in business and finance, could not understand my identification with the farmer. They usually became either uncomfortable or annoyed when they heard me declaiming that the farmer must "stop dragging the chariot of the East," as I put it in one letter. They could not understand how I could support "that Socialist," Charles E. Russell, as fine a citizen as ever there was, in his fight against the "magic elevator"—a warehousing technique that cheated farmers. Nor could they fathom my readiness to aid the Nonpartisan League state officials of North Dakota. When these officials were unable to market state bonds through normal channels, because banks were reluctant to deal with so "radical" a state government, I agreed to buy them.

For many years I carried on a heavy correspondence with men who were in a position to help the farmer. One of these was Thomas A. Edison, whose interest in agriculture must have been as surprising to some people as my own. One day I received a call from Edison's secretary. Edison was on his way over to see me at my home, he told me. I had never met the "genius of Menlo Park" and could hardly fathom why he should be calling on me. When he arrived he told me that, having heard of my interest in the farm problem, he wanted my views on a plan for credit and marketing which he had drafted at the suggestion of his friend, Henry Ford. I undertook to comment on Edison's plan, and he accepted my criticism graciously. I felt highly complimented when he wrote: "You are the first man who has had imagination enough to throw off the trammels of the money religion and analyze the proposed scheme like an engineer."

My enthusiasm for the coöperative marketing movement led me

to take an active part in the affairs of several co-ops and to help launch some. One of these was the Kentucky tobacco coöperative.

By 1922, a total and tragic collapse of the tobacco market had brought Kentucky to "the verge of anarchy," in the words of Judge Robert Bingham, publisher of the Louisville *Courier-Journal* and the Louisville *Times* and later Ambassador to the Court of St. James. At the suggestion of Arthur Krock, then editor-in-chief of the Louisville *Times,* Bingham asked me to join him in organizing the Kentucky tobacco growers, which I did.

The services of Aaron Sapiro, the foremost expert in the organization and management of coöperatives, were enlisted. And under his leadership, the Kentucky tobacco co-op made rapid progress. One of the things I was able to do to help was to bring the co-op representatives in touch with the eccentric tobacco tycoon, George Washington Hill, a meeting which ended in favorable arrangements for the tobacco growers.

But my experience with the Kentucky tobacco coöperative, and with several struggling grain co-ops in the Middle West, impressed me with the difficulty of building successful co-ops from scratch. The traditional individualism of farmers, the prima donna qualities of some farm leaders, factors of geography, and the simple mechanics of organization did not exhaust the list of difficulties. Inexperience and inadequate capital were even more serious handicaps.

It seemed to me that farmers could spare themselves many trials if, instead of struggling to create an organization, they could acquire one already established, one with adequate facilities, experienced personnel, and a standing in the marketing field. With this thought in mind, I approached J. Ogden Armour, the meat-packing tycoon, in the spring of 1923. I proposed that he sell his Armour Grain Company, one of the largest grain marketing houses in the country, to several farmer organizations. This idea was not without its implicit irony. Armour was then anathema to farmers, representing all that was evil in the creation and operation

of the Chicago meat-packing empires, which Upton Sinclair had ex-
coriated in his famous book, *The Jungle*.

Armour was cool to my proposition at first, but he thawed out
after we discussed it, especially when I reminded him of the good
will that would accrue to the company's reputation through such
an act. He referred me to George Marcy, general manager of his
grain company and one of the shrewdest grain merchants of the
day. Marcy needed little persuasion. He told me that he had only
a few productive years remaining, and would be glad to devote them
to the farmers' welfare.

I suggested a plan which he readily endorsed. Under its terms,
a farmer organization would purchase the Armour Grain Company.
Its direction would be entrusted temporarily to a board comprising
the present management, representatives of the farmers, and representatives of the public. When the farmers' indebtedness to Armour
was liquidated, direction would be left entirely to the farmers.

I took pains to avoid public discussion of this plan, although
I did disclose it to a few farm leaders—Gray Silver, James R. Howard,
George Jewett, and Senator Capper. They approved of the idea
in general, but they were skeptical of its acceptance by the rank
and file of farmers. This skepticism was echoed by William Allen
White, who knew of the plan through Senator Capper. White
wrote to Capper:

June 9, 1923.

My dear Arthur:

I was glad to look over the Barney Baruch data. The whole
trouble with the application of the Baruch theory is the farmer
himself. He acts on his suspicions rather than on his information
and he generally suspects the wrong man at the wrong time.

For instance, notice Mr. Baruch says the matter has been
presented for consideration to the Farm Bureau Federation. If
by any chance the Federation should favor it, the rest of the
organizations would jump at its throat.

The farmer himself is the worst enemy of the farmer. There
is only one way to help him and that is to educate him. . . .

Personally I think Baruch's plan would have distinct advantages
even though Armour did get some credit out of it.

Sincerely yours,
W.A. White

As it turned out, White was correct. The plan was disclosed
prematurely and, true to the shrewd editor's prediction, critics
played upon the deeply felt hostility of the farmers toward Armour
and encouraged them to reject it. I was accused of trying to subvert
the farmers' interest to Armour's, and of scheming to place them
even more firmly in the grip of a grasping merchant and speculator.

Curiously enough, I was also criticized on other grounds, from
other quarters. My advocacy of the coöperative movement laid me
open to the charge of abetting a plot against the American free
enterprise system.

Many people who admired the doctrines of competition, more in
theory than in practice, professed to see in the coöperative marketing movement a violation of the anti-trust laws at the very least;
and, at the worst, a dangerous form of collectivism.

One of the loudest voices in the hostile pack was Henry Ford's,
who used his mouthpiece, the Dearborn *Independent,* to unleash
a particularly violent and bigoted attack on coöperative marketing,
labeling it the handiwork of Jews and Communists, and naming
Aaron Sapiro and me as among the alien influences responsible for
this un-American idea. I was by this time inured to Ford's attention.

Whatever genius it was that had established the great Ford Motor
Company as one of the authentic industrial phenomena of our
time, it failed Ford when he tried to formulate political and social
ideas. We have all benefited from the philanthropies which the
great Ford fortune has supported; and we can all admire the
exemplary citizenship of Henry Ford's descendents. But a good
many people who admired Ford as an industrial genius had to
agree with the estimate of Norman Hapgood, the distinguished
editor of Hearst's *International* and later of *Collier's,* that when

he was away from his own line of work, Ford's mind was "that of a child."

Beginning with the issue of May 22, 1920, and leading with a front-page editorial captioned "The International Jew: The World's Foremost Problem," the *Independent* had carried on one of the most virulent and sustained anti-Semitic attacks ever seen in this country. Its pages were filled with it for ninety-one consecutive issues. It was an operation as fantastic in its planning as in its execution. E.G. Liebold, a Ford executive, had established a detective agency in New York City to investigate the private lives of Jews and provide fodder for the *Independent*'s campaign. Many of the agency's men had numbers, like 121 X. It was this bureau that bought a translation of the spurious "Protocols of the Learned Elders of Zion," a notorious and classic anti-Semitic document, which provided the *Independent* with material for a year and a half.

One day the *Independent* appeared with a headline and story proclaiming me as the "pro-consul of Judah in America" and "a Jew of Super-Power," the head and front of a dictatorial conspiracy. If it had not been so vicious, it would have been flattering.

The press naturally picked up the story. Next morning, when I got to the office, the newspapermen were waiting for me. One of the wire service men said they had come about the story in the *Independent,* and what did I have to say about its charges.

"Now, boys," I said, "you wouldn't expect me to deny them, would you?"

That broke up the press conference. But it did not bring to an end the *Independent*'s attacks, which were renewed when I became identified with the coöperative movement. I ignored these assaults, but Sapiro was irate. He filed a million-dollar damage suit against the manufacturer, which eventually came to trial in 1927. Senator James Reed, of Missouri, was among the battery of Ford's lawyers, and his conduct of the case was in the same hammer-and-tongs vein he employed in the Senate. My friends were outraged by the nature of the slurs he made on me, but I took them in the same spirit I took the *Independent*'s vituperations. As I wrote to Joe Robinson:

It is unfortunate that Jim Reed, who is endowed with such a fine head, should have so sour a disposition. I have followed closely the conduct of the Sapiro case; but after all Reed is a lawyer and must earn his fee and some men are not particular how they earn it. His slurs upon Lowden and me do not do him any good nor his case any good so far as I can see.

Sapiro was represented by a prominent attorney from Detroit, William Henry Gallagher. On the stand, William J. Cameron, editor of the *Independent,* insisted that Ford had had nothing to do with the paper's attack and assumed full responsibility for everything with which his employer was charged. The attempts of Sapiro's counsel to get Ford on the stand were successfully frustrated by some of the most adroit maneuvering in the history of American court trials, until the case suddenly ended in a mistrial when a woman juror made out-of-court remarks about the trial to a reporter.

Before a retrial could be held, Ford suddenly did an about-face, ended his seven-year war against the Jews, settled the Sapiro case, and gave Sapiro himself a personal apology. The new Model A automobile appeared soon after.

In all this distasteful business, sparked by my interest in agriculture, I was keenly aware that I was a tempting target for narrow and vindictive men. I was a Democrat, and a Wilson Democrat at that; an advocate of the League of Nations; a Jew; a Wall Street man. These facts made me guilty of innumerable sins in the eyes of some politicians, isolationists, bigots of every stripe, plus those who cannot bear people with money. I realized that a good many of these attacks were intended to discredit causes in which I happened to be involved.

Thus, when the disclosure of the Armour plan aroused a furor,

I wrote on November 9, 1923, to President O.E. Bradfute, of the American Farm Bureau Federation:

> Please let me say to you what I . . . have said so many times before. My connection with this great movement and with the constructive results of your efforts has given me more pleasure than anything I have ever undertaken. The confidence in me of you and your associates has been a source of pride and comfort. But if at any time I become a greater liability than an asset, please frankly let me know. It is not of much importance what happens to individuals, but it is of great importance that the enemies of the farmer, by a whispering campaign, should not distract his attention from the great objectives. The cause might thus be lost. Please do not use any of your time or energy in my defense. I would not have a single unit among those charged with the responsibility of this great movement weakened because of any defense that might be made of me. When you need me, call upon me; when I become a liability, please say so, and I shall become as quiescent as I have been active. Above all, do not let them sow discord among the leaders and suspicion among your followers when the object we have striven for is so near at hand.

But the Federation, I must say, would have none of it.

4

As the farm depression worsened, it became clear that—as long as America was unable to sell her farm products in Europe, as long as she retained her tariff walls, her isolationist policies—coöperative marketing and credit programs would not rescue the farmer from his plight.

Some approach other than the one I had advocated was needed— less ideal perhaps, but more practicable in the light of all the circumstances. Such an alternative, it seemed to me, lay in a plan conceived by my old WIB colleague, George Peek.

After the war, Peek and Hugh Johnson had taken over the management of the Moline Plow Company. This farm equipment company was immediately inundated by the wave of hard times in the Middle West. Confronted at first hand with the harsh facts of the farm depression, Peek's active brain sought a solution. With Johnson's assistance, he devised a plan for "Equality for Agriculture." For the remainder of his life, Peek devoted himself to this cause.

Peek's approach to the surplus was not to seek foreign markets, but to sequester the surplus and protect the domestic market from its depressing effect on prices. He argued that the farmer could enjoy prosperity if he could get the American price for his product. As it was, the domestic price was determined by the world price—the price at which the surplus sold.

Underscoring the fact that the farmer sold in a competitive world market while he bought in one protected by tariffs, Peek proposed to give the farmer the same benefits enjoyed by industry—a tariff wall behind which prices would rise. To assure a fair price, a parity level would be established by law on the basis of a preceding ten-year average. A government corporation would also be established to buy up the surplus, and sell it abroad at whatever price it would bring. The losses involved in such sales would be met by the farmers themselves through a tax on each bushel or pound of a commodity sold. This was the much debated "equalization fee," which was designed not only to pay the cost of the program, but to discourage surplus production—since the larger the surplus to be disposed, the heavier the equalization fee to be assessed.

Peek first presented his plan to me in 1922, shortly after he had formulated it and before he submitted it to an Agricultural Conference called by Harding's Secretary of Agriculture Henry C. Wallace—the father of Roosevelt's Wallace. "I have not yet been able to punch a hole in it," I told him.

Peek's plan, differing though it did from the approach I had first taken, seemed to me to represent at least a pragmatic effort to solve the problem. There were many objections to it, primarily to its protectionist premise. I myself did not believe in high tariffs in principle. As I wrote to Senator Walter George: "The real solution . . . lies in the Democratic doctrine of a lower tariff." Still, if the farmer could not be aided by the reduction of industrial tariffs, and by a Europe rich enough to buy his produce, then he ought, in simple justice, I thought, to enjoy the same advantage enjoyed by industry under the protective system. If we were unable to knock down the old artificiality of the industrial tariff, which interfered with the normal working of supply and demand, we had to build up a new artificiality to offset it. This usually happens when we interpose man-made laws against natural law. We have to interpose another innovation to save us from the effect of the first.

An attractive feature of Peek's plan was that it was predicated on the principle of self-help. It did not require the government to make wards of the farmers, who in fact would bear all the costs of the program themselves.

The Peek plan quickly won wide support, and it was shortly incorporated into the McNary-Haugen Bill, certainly one of the most debated pieces of legislation ever to appear on the Hill. Sponsored by Senator Charles McNary, of Oregon, and Representative Gilbert Haugen, of Iowa, this bill—called by its friends "the Magna Carta of agriculture"— became a battleground in Congress and the symbol of agrarian revolt.

Although I did have reservations over the protectionist basis of the bill, my sympathy for the farmer led me to take an active part in the fight for its enactment. Peek, a man of tremendous drive and single-mindedness, was the dynamic leader of that fight.

I supported Peek in every way I could, believing that the bill should be given a test on at least one commodity. I proposed to Senator Tom Walsh, and other opponents of the bill, that it be tried on wheat. But the opponents of the McNary-Haugen Bill were as determined as its advocates. The lines were sharply drawn in this fight. The only convert I ever helped to make—and my missionary work was intensive—was Otto Kahn. My Eastern Republican associates were, almost to a man, opposed to McNary-Haugenism. I found it ironic that these staunch advocates of tariff protection for industry should fight the application of its benefits to agriculture.

But among my Democratic friends in the South, too, there was a fairly universal opposition to the bill, despite their agrarian interests. Congressman Cordell Hull expressed the free trade sentiments of most Southern Democrats, when he told me he could not support a bill which relied on the tariff to help the farmer. Senator Walter George called the bill a dole. Senator Joe Robinson and Senator Pat Harrison were alike opposed to it.

The political battle over the bill raged for most of the decade. Congress passed it twice, and twice President Coolidge vetoed it. When Mr. Hoover became President, an Agricultural Marketing Act, containing some of the ideas of the McNary-Haugen Bill, was enacted. But it lacked the crucial feature of the equalization fee. A Federal Farm Board, under Alec Legge, was established to administer the Act. I sent Legge my congratulations and my sympathy, because I was certain that the omission of the equalization fee would make it impossible for the Board to cope with the problem of the surplus. And this proved to the case.

Even before President Hoover could celebrate the first anniversary of his election, the crash occurred. Now it was not only agriculture, but the entire economy which had collapsed.

5

There is no question that the great depression had its origins, in part, in the agricultural malaise of the 1920's. A nation's economy cannot be healthy when a basic element in it is sick. Our economic life has a complicated interdependence which makes it essential for the parts to be at least in relative balance. Looking back, we can see that the so-called prosperity of those years was largely fictitious, and that there were other unhealthy symptoms beside the plight of the farmers. But if we had had the foresight to come to grips with the farm question, we might have been spared the debacle of the 1930's.

My interest in the farm problem did not end with the coming of the thirties. Although I became involved in other issues—especially those related to neutrality, preparedness, and mobilization, as the war clouds gathered—I never lost my sympathetic interest in the farmers' problems. The basic question today seems to be substantially what it was when I first became acquainted with agriculture: How, in the face of ever-increasing productivity, to maintain a balance between supply and demand; how, in other words, to restore agriculture to a sound economic basis and thus permit the farmer—through his own efforts—to reap a fair return.

Today, as in 1920, when the Kansas State Board invited my views, we are confronted with the problem of the surplus. But today, agriculture is very different from what it was four decades ago. Agriculture is now largely a subsidized industry, with all the evils that this term implies. While the nation is taxing itself heavily to support agriculture, the farmer has come to depend to such an extent on government that he seems to have lost the willingness for self-help which he has traditionally demonstrated.

As the government's role in caring for the farmer has increased year by year, it has become progressively more difficult to devise a means for him to take care of himself. And yet the farm problem, like any other problem, will never be solved until the farmer stops leaning on government, and demonstrates self-reliance and self-discipline once again. Often, as I watch my neighbors in South Carolina putting in their crops, I am struck by the thought that if they would only plant as much as they know they can sell and if they could only organize their economic strength as other groups have done, they would have no need for government price supports.

I think it entirely proper for the government to devise a method to assist family-size farms, when help is needed. It is the small farmer who needs help, not the large operators whose farms are run with an efficiency—and a profit ratio—comparable to industry. But government supports should not be used to guarantee all farm income. They should be available only on the basis of need. Above all, our objective should be steadily to reduce them and ultimately to eliminate them. For as long as government assistance programs serve as an incentive to unneeded production, we will never be able to come to grips with the problem of the surplus.

But if we can prevent new surpluses from piling up, we should be able to overcome the problems presented by those we now have.

Indeed, it is time that we stopped bemoaning their existence and recognized that, properly managed, they represent a tremendous asset whose potential for good in a hungry and imperiled world is inestimable. We wring our hands over our bulging warehouses; most nations wish they had them.

The government today is stock-piling all kinds of critical materials, in the event of an emergency. What would be more critical than foods and fibers in the event of war? Why should we not set aside a large portion of the farm surplus as a ready reserve against man-made catastrophes or natural disasters?

I have long advocated such an insurance program against emergency. I envisage the building of new, and the modernization of existing, warehouse facilities to create a scientific storage system, strategically located around the country, which would provide protection not only against the elements and pests, but against such special hazards of the twentieth century as atomic blast and radioactive fallout. If King Tut's wheat could remain alive for two-thousand years, I am sure that modern science and technology can protect our grains for as long as may be needed.

Such a stockpiling program might not only help us to face some natural or man-made disaster, but by thus permanently segregating the surplus, or a large part of it, in such a warehousing system, we would reduce its depressing effect upon prices. In addition, by pursuing an imaginative program to develop new uses for farm commodities, as well as finding ways to share them with less fortunate peoples, we would be able to transform the surplus into the priceless asset it is. But not until we put agriculture back on a sound economic basis will we have resolved a problem which has haunted our national life for so many decades.

X

Democrats in Defeat

W HEN I LOOK BACK over my correspondence of the 1920's, I am
reminded of how deeply I felt about the issues of the day.
Those were disappointing and often frustrating years for men like
myself, who felt helpless to halt the country's retreat from the high
plateau of Wilsonian idealism to the stony valley of disillusion,
cynicism, and materialism which characterized the postwar decade.

I came out of the war, as I have said, with some definite ideas.
Inevitably the strong views I entertained, about the League of
Nations, about the agricultural situation, and about other public
questions which agitated America, led me to take an active part
in politics—the forum in which great issues are debated and
resolved.

Considering my past associations and my devotion to Woodrow
Wilson, I naturally remained in the ranks of the Democratic Party.
I was, make no mistake, a very staunch Democrat. Time and
fading party lines have somewhat dulled my partisan spirits, and
at times I have even found myself so unhappy with my own party
that I could not, in good conscience, support its candidates. Nevertheless, I still try to hold to my Democratic allegiance.

Despite my intense interest in politics, especially in the years after the First War, I have never had any desire for political office. On several occasions I have declined high appointive posts, and I have reason to believe I could have had some support for elective office. In fact, in the 1920's there was a move to enlist bipartisan support for me for the Senate. The response was flattering, but I insisted that it be stopped.

Some men have been kind enough—and foolish enough—to assert that I could have aspired to the Presidency. To most men, I suppose, such a suggestion would be a heady thing. The possibility of being President, however remote in reality, generates a fever more virulent than any known to medical science. Nor is it a rare disease; it is easily acquired. Let a man be assured a few times, by his subordinates and admirers, "You know, they could do worse than nominate you," and the symptoms become evident. I have known men who would rise from their coffins to announce their candidacy if it were no more than hinted that the White House might be within their reach.

But leaving aside the kind of considerations that defeated Al Smith in 1928, I never had the least ambition to be Alderman, let alone President. Such ambition, of course, is essential in the game of politics. Consequently, Presidential dreams never disturbed my slumber.

Some people have criticized me for my indifference to political preferment, among them my good friend Lord Beaverbrook, who took me gently to task in his memoirs for shirking what he felt was my responsibility for service. Quite apart from the fact that there are many ways in which a man may serve, I myself have always felt that I could contribute more as an independent private citizen than as a public officeholder. By maintaining my independence, free of the obligations which so often accompany office-seeking, I felt I could best fulfill my conception of public service.

2

In the Presidential election of 1920, my dearest wish was to see Wilson's principles vindicated.

For a time, indeed until the Democratic convention met, Wilson, despite his broken health, seemed intent on seeking the nomination himself. Those of us who knew this were naturally distressed. We knew that he could not be renominated, and we wanted to spare him both the effort and the disappointment that would almost certainly have cost him his life. Carter Glass, Homer Cummings, and other of his devoted friends prevented his name from being offered to the convention.

The President's son-in-law, McAdoo, was the leading candidate for the nomination, and I was his enthusiastic supporter. Besides my personal affection for this peppery, courageous fighter for good causes, I believed he deserved the Democratic nomination on the basis of ability and past performance. He had been one of the original Wilson campaigners, responsible for getting him nominated in 1912. Later he had taken over the Democratic National Committee leadership from the failing hands of Billy McCombs and done much to ensure the President's election. As Secretary of the Treasury, he had been one of the outstanding figures in Wilson's Cabinet, and he had done a superb job as Director General of the Railroad Administration during the war.

He had other excellent qualifications. This Georgian educated in Tennessee had begun his career as a Chattanooga lawyer, and later had played a leading part in the construction of the Hudson tubes connecting New York and New Jersey. He understood finance and the economic structure of the country; he had a solid background of political experience; and he was unswervingly true to the principles of Wilsonian democracy.

Because of his relationship to the President, McAdoo was often called the "crown prince" and the "heir apparent." Had he been that in Wilson's eyes, the nomination would almost certainly have been his. But Wilson refused to endorse him.

Nevertheless, when the convention met in San Francisco, McAdoo led the field. His chief adversaries were A. Mitchell Palmer, who had made a name for himself as Attorney General during the great Red scare of 1919, and Governor James M. Cox, of Ohio, a colorful newspaper publisher and Party stalwart. After a long and rancorous fight, in which the League and Prohibition issues threatened to split the Party, the convention chose Cox on the forty-fourth ballot. As his running mate, the delegates nominated Franklin Delano Roosevelt.

I was not very enthusiastic about this Democratic ticket or its prospects for victory. But my reservations about Cox himself disappeared after he and F.D.R. came to pay their respects to Wilson. The new standard-bearer was under heavy pressure to soft-pedal the League issue; and, of course, it would have been the expedient thing to do. But if Cox ever had any intention of bowing to this pressure, his visit with the haggard President drove it from his mind. He sat down immediately after leaving Wilson, and drafted a forthright statement making the League the major issue in the campaign. This was an example of political courage and principle seldom duplicated. I knew then that, win or lose, Cox would do, and I never had reason to change my opinion.

I was active at headquarters during the campaign, but almost from the beginning it was clear that defeat was certain. The amiable Warren G. Harding straddled all issues, while his Party capitalized on the inevitable postwar reaction which had been setting in since 1918. The Democrats were buried under an avalanche of seven million votes, the worst defeat a major party ever suffered up to that time.

There seems to be a pendulum in the life of nations that swings from idealism to cynicism. In 1920, we were on the wrong end of the swing. The disillusioned turning away from Wilsonian idealism was a disheartening forecast of the decade to come. Thus began the bleak years for the Democratic national organization. For the next twelve years, that organization floundered to regain its purpose and power—a goal made all the more difficult by the fact that the Party was financially destitute.

In politics, as in any other endeavor, adequate financing is required. A political organization can no more operate sucessfully on a shoestring than can a business organization. And the Democrats were reduced to shoestrings in the 1920's. Deeply in debt, with campaign contributions dried up as a result of political hard times, the Party was literally on the verge of bankruptcy.

A competent and conscientious man like Cordell Hull, who served as Chairman of the National Committee in those days, was forever scrounging to meet bills. His troubles were evident in this excerpt from a letter he wrote to me on November 12, 1923:

> I am still writing my own checks for more or less substantial amounts every week in order to squeeze by the weekend. This, of course, has crucified me in my efforts to do the real things that I should have been doing on as nearly a hundred per cent basis as possible during past months. I shall continue to hold on with a death grasp, however, and do the maximum amount of work possible on a shoestring.

Time and again Hull and other leaders appealed to me for financial support, as the Party came to rely more and more upon a few Democrats to carry the burden.

I was one of the small group who helped to carry the Party in those hard times. This I did without embarrassment or any attempt to hide the fact. Giving financial support to the party of your choice is a privilege too few Americans exercise.

Still, it is traditional in America to believe that if a rich man gives to political causes, he must have ulterior motives and probably sinister ones at that. Too often this has been the case, I must admit. But most men contribute to political causes out of conviction and a sense of responsibility.

Nevertheless, it is clearly undesirable for political parties to rely primarily on individuals of great wealth for support. Rather, such support should be as widely spread as possible. In fact, I have sometimes declined to contribute more even though I could afford to, because I felt so strongly that one man should not be the chief support of any movement.

If a party is in financial difficulties, as both our major parties are from time to time, it is not the fault of the party itself nor of the rich men who have supported it, but of the people who claim to be enrolled under its banner. If the public is concerned about the question of the influence of great wealth, and pressure groups, on politics—as indeed it should be—it must understand that the remedy lies in its own hands, as do the remedies for most of our problems. With the cost of campaigns what they are today, candidates and parties are more than ever dependent on so-called "fat cats," corporate and individual. But if every registered voter contributed only a dollar or two to the party of his choice, this dependence would be ended. If enough voters did this, it would not only greatly mitigate the danger of undue influence, it would mean a most salutary change in American politics. The parties would then truly belong to their supporters.

Although I helped support the Democratic Party in the years after Cox's defeat, I was often at odds with its leadership, and disappointed in its failure to give the Party imaginative and able direction. For, far worse than the defeat of 1920, the Party had lost its way. Wracked by factionalism, torn by disunity, often in the control of men of small vision, it seemed to lose its purpose and vitality, except for internecine fighting.

This seems to be the fate of parties deprived of power. Adversity in politics does not encourage cohesiveness, it seems. Deprived of the fruits of power, a national political party seems to break down into regional or other factions. Unity can only be regained by victory—yet victory is forestalled by disunity. Such was the situation of the Democratic Party after the great defeat of 1920, as it was for the Republican Party after 1932, until General Eisenhower led it to victory.

My disappointment in those days may be gauged by the letter I wrote Mark Sullivan in January, 1923:

> The Democratic Bloc has got to purge itself from many of its men and many of its methods before it can succeed. Before men like myself can go before the American people and ask them to cast the franchise for a Democratic President, we are going to require calm and steadfast men for the times that are now before us. Above all we want clean and honest men, honest in thought as well as honest in action.

There were others who shared my dissatisfaction with the Party. From time to time, rumblings of insurrection were heard. On more than one occasion, earnest Democrats urged me to go after the Party chairmanship, so as to undertake a vigorous house cleaning. But I did not feel equipped for this task.

Nor did I pay heed to talk of a third party. I have always felt that, in the American system, third party movements are usually devisive and misleading. Adherents to third parties are generally people who cannot make a choice between two practical alternatives, who insist on all or nothing and frequently get the latter. To be effective, a citizen must choose one of the two major parties as the instrument through which he will try to work.

He may be unhappy with that party, and if so, then he must try as hard as he can to change it. Failing that, and being sufficiently unhappy, his most effective move is to punish and perhaps enlighten the party by joining temporarily—or even permanently—with the major opposition. The creation of splinter parties, however, is not only politically ineffective, but a danger to the democratic system. To all talk of third party movements, I have always given the answer I gave in 1922 to Josephus Daniels:

> This talk about a third party is ridiculous. It is only another way of cheating the people out of what they are entitled to. . . . I

propose staying in the Democratic party and trying to make it the progressive, liberal, constructive party. I don't believe in running away from your crowd simply because they don't happen to agree with you or you with them for the moment. I believe my people are pretty good people; and my people happen to be Democratic people.

3

The death of President Harding in 1923, and the revelations of scandals as Coolidge took command, made the coming election all the more crucial. I was still for McAdoo. He was, as I wrote former Senator Charles Thomas, of Colorado, "head and shoulders above every man who has been talked about." If he were elected, "there will be no more shillying and shallying," I predicted.

McAdoo was prepared now to fight to the bitter end for the prize. Well before the convention, he and I discussed his plans. As early as February, 1923, he had confided to me his decision to enter the race. From then on, I was deeply involved in his unfolding campaign.

We were in constant touch. As I look back over our voluminous correspondence, he emerges from it alive, vital, and full of fight. His letters are filled with defiance for his enemies, and conviction and confidence in himself. On one occasion, he wrote to denounce "the weak-kneed Democrats" who feared to support him. On another: "I am glad to throw the gage of battle down to my enemies, and I am absolutely confident of the outcome."

McAdoo's pugnaciousness and his colorful manner of speech were not to everyone's taste. A good many people were put off by these qualities—Mark Sullivan for one. Sullivan was one of the most able and upright figures the world of journalism has seen in my time. We did not share political allegiances—Mark was a rock-ribbed Republican—but that did not impair our mutual affection. He was a frequent visitor to my home, and one of the most delightful of the company of political and journalistic figures who convened regularly at Hobcaw.

Mark was not given to verbal excesses, and some of McAdoo's pronouncements made him wince. He wrote me once, after one of McAdoo's typical fighting speeches:

> McAdoo's whole manner of speech sounds more like an adventurer making a raid on the Presidency than a statesman making a dignified campaign for it . . . . Some of McAdoo's friends who are trying to make him President ought to tell him that old story which ended with the saying "All we want out of you is silence, and damned little of that."

I myself tried to restrain McAdoo at times, especially from making his move in the nominating race too soon. "This is a time for the jockey to sit down and let his horse rate along in the last bunch," I cautioned him early in 1923. "Some time in the early part of next year is the time to give the horse his head." Later in the year I warned him: "As your friend, there are certain things I am going to suggest that you guard against. I think that no promises should be made that can't be fulfilled. . . . I would rather lose in the right than win in the wrong and be unable to make good our promises."

As the pre-convention maneuvering grew more intense, my role as an adviser to McAdoo expanded. I don't know how many people appreciated the paradox. Here was I, a Wall Street man and an Easterner, firmly in the camp of a man who represented the Western wing of the Party and against whom the East, particularly New York and Tammany, were irrevocably opposed. Al Smith was their man.

Smith had long been my friend, as I have written earlier; I had the warmest personal feelings for him. But I was unequivocally behind McAdoo. As I wrote to Bryan in March, 1924, " We have a great chance, but the chance will disappear unless we nominate a progressive and a dry"—which described McAdoo exactly.

The principal issue between the two men was Prohibition, one of the most emotion-packed issues of this century. I was a militant dry. My feelings about Prohibition were something like my father's about pistols. He was convinced that the sale of pistols encouraged crime, and he spent a good deal of effort trying to get legislation passed to prohibit their sale. Similarly, I believed that you could legislate against the abuses of liquor. Wilson was wiser. He had vetoed a prohibition bill, predicting what would ensue if it were enacted.

Even as I write these words, I have trouble believing that I advocated Prohibition. It was a blight which permeated our national life. I can only say, like the late Fiorello La Guardia, "When I make a mistake, it's a beaut."

As the election year opened, McAdoo was clearly out front in the race for the Democratic nomination. But then, the very day following Woodrow Wilson's funeral, McAdoo's chances were dealt a crushing blow. In the midst of the great storm over Teapot Dome—a storm which seemed certain to sweep the Republicans from office—McAdoo's name was dragged into the scandal. It was disclosed, with full blown innuendoes, that he had been legal counsel for Edward L. Doheny, one of the oil men accused of bribing Cabinet officers in order to gain control of government oil lands.

Although McAdoo's legal services to Doheny were entirely proper and were unrelated to Teapot Dome, he was inevitably tarred. I could not help recalling the last conversation we had had before he moved to California. We had talked about clients, and I told him he would have to be very careful which ones he accepted. He said he knew that, and I also told him his clients ought not to be rich.

"Well, do I have to remain poor all my life?" he asked.

"If you want to be President," I replied, "you'll have to remain poor and maybe your wife will have to take in washing."

McAdoo, an honest and brave fellow, grinned at me. "I think I know how to conduct myself," he said.

Yet now he was being smeared from every direction, not only from the Republicans but from the Smith camp, which coined such slogans as "There ain't no oil on Al."

McAdoo came to Washington to testify before Senator Tom Walsh's committee investigating the scandal. Several nights before his scheduled appearance, he met with some of his friends and advisers in the old Shoreham Hotel. Dan Roper, Tom Chadbourne, Tom Love, David Rockwell, and several other of his supporters were there. It was a gloomy assemblage, except for McAdoo, who was his usual fighting, confident self.

"What did you fellows think you were doing when you started out to nominate me for President?" he said. "Did you think you were going on a honeymoon?" Then he told us the story about the Union volunteer in the Civil War who couldn't wait to shoot up the Johnny Rebs, until he got into his first battle and saw the man next to him fall, hit by a bullet. Whereupon, throwing down his rifle, he exclaimed, "By God, those fellows are shooting real bullets." None of us, he hoped, was going to run now that the fight was hot.

Later, McAdoo followed me down to my room. He was suddenly very grave. "Now, Bernie," he said, "you and I have been friends for a long time. If you so much as bat an eye, these fellows are going to run out on me."

"Mac," I said, "you always stood by me; now I'll stand by you. I wouldn't do it, though, unless I felt that you would make a great President. But let me tell you that even though I'll stick, I don't think you have a chance unless you follow a plan I've got in mind."

I then unfolded my suggestion to counter the political capital his enemies were making at his expense. At the suggestion and with the help of the astute Arthur Krock, I had drafted a statement which I wanted McAdoo to read before the Walsh Committee. This statement vigorously defended his good name against the false and sinister charges which had been made. It accused those responsible for the slander with deliberately seeking to injure not only him but the Democratic Party. And it announced that, in order to prevent such injury to the Party, he was withdrawing from the race for the Democratic nomination and stepping back into the ranks.

I believed that such a statement would gain sympathy for Mc-Adoo, help to overcome his opposition within the Party, and lead to a general revulsion of feeling against his detractors. I felt that, by offering to withdraw, he would create a sentiment that ultimately would lead to his nomination.

McAdoo, however, did not agree with this strategy, and refused to make the statement. I believe it cost him the nomination.

He spent the following month touring the country, waging primary campaigns, and rounding up delegates. I have a bulky file of telegrams and letters from him simply exuding confidence that he would win. And when the convention gathered in Madison Square Garden in June, he did have impressive strength. But so did Al Smith.

Never has there been such a convention as the Democratic convention of 1924. It was, as Frank Kent wrote, "the longest, wildest, most turbulent political gathering in the history of the country." It was also the first political convention to be broadcast by radio, and for two weeks millions tuned in on the clash and clamor.

From the moment the convention came to order on June 24th, acrimonious debate filled the hot and smoky Garden. An uproarious floor fight took place over a motion to denounce the Ku Klux Klan by name. It lost by exactly one vote out of almost eleven hundred cast. An equally dramatic fight, but nothing so close, took place over the motion to get an unequivocal declaration for the League. It was defeated despite the inspired appeal made by Newton Baker in the most magnificent address I have ever heard.

But the platform fight was only preliminary to the main contest for the nomination. Seventeen men were nominated; and when the first ballot was taken, McAdoo led the field by far, with Smith second. But then, as ballot after ballot was counted in the sodden heat, it became all too evident that the expected break to McAdoo would not take place. He and Smith were deadlocked. Day after day the incredible and hopeless struggle went on. Over and over the roll was called while, on the floor and behind the scenes, candidates and their managers scurried and pleaded and fought for delegates.

On the sixty-ninth ballot, McAdoo reached his high point of five hundred and thirty votes. But it was clear by this time that he could not win. I admired his never-say-die spirit, but I told him that his cause was hopeless, and urged him, as did other supporters, to withdraw from a conflict which threatened to destroy the Party. He insisted, however, that the fight go on. Not until the one hundredth ballot, with his support steadily dwindling, did he concede defeat.

The convention then wearily turned toward a compromise candidate, the former Ambassador to London and distinguished lawyer from West Virginia, John W. Davis. He was nominated on the one hundred and third ballot. The exhausted and dispirited delegates chose William Jennings Bryan's brother, Charles, as his running mate.

I came away from the Garden disappointed and discouraged. I had little hope that we could win. Still, I was prepared to help Davis make a fight of it. Immediately after the convention, I laid before him several campaign proposals. They were ambitious and, I thought, useful, and I offered to underwrite the cost of implementing them. Davis' managers, however, brushed them aside, and made it clear that all they wanted from me was free access to my checkbook. This I wasn't prepared to grant, which seemed unreasonable of me to some of the men at Party headquarters. Jesse Jones, then finance director of the National Committee, angered at my refusal to abandon my own judgment or surrender my independence to his demands, penned me a long and rancorous letter charging me with running out on the Party.

I replied with some heat, informing Jones that I would not

be bound by his judgment of my responsibilities. In all the many years in which I have been active in politics, there have been but two instances that I can recall when differences of opinion involved me in personal controversy. This exchange with Jones was the first. Later, Jones apologized and we patched things up.

During the campaign, I tried to win farm support for Davis. But farm leaders to whom I appealed were cool. I tried particularly to get George Peek to come out for the Democratic ticket. His was the first influence among farmers, and since he was a Republican, I felt certain that a great many farmers would follow him if he could be won over. But in 1924, Peek was still willing to trust to Republican promises.

The election was no contest. President Coolidge did nothing to alienate his own followers, while his opposition was splintered by the independent ticket headed by Senator Robert M. La Follette. Davis, an able and courageous man, could not overcome the odds he faced.

I learned a lesson from the frustrating events of 1924. I made up my mind never again to take part in the internecine fighting for the Presidential nomination. I would support the Party's candidates if I could. I would take my stand on issues. But I was determined that, from this point forward, I would have nothing to do with divisive and destructive political warfare between personalities. I have clung to that resolve to this day.

XI

The Harding-Coolidge Years

FOR MANY YEARS I have been referred to as an "Adviser to Presidents," a title first bestowed upon me in a citation accompanying an honorary degree from Johns Hopkins University.

I realize that "Adviser to Presidents" sounds terribly important. It somehow suggests a measure of power or influence, which in my case, at least, never existed. Moreover, it is not so unusual a distinction as it seems. Every President has a legion of advisers. It is true that my advice has been asked by Presidents, but it must be confessed that my recommendations have been honored as much in the breach as in the observance. Arthur Krock once remarked: "Either Baruch gives lousy advice or nobody takes it." I won't admit to the first part of that observation, but I cannot deny the latter.

I have known all of our Presidents since Woodrow Wilson; and I have had the privilege of serving under some of them. Still, my opportunities for service during the administrations of Presidents Harding, Coolidge, and Hoover were not very great, and the fate of the recommendations I made to them from time to time hardly qualifies me as a Presidential adviser.

I had known Warren G. Harding casually when he was in the Senate. He had always given me his full support when I headed the WIB. But he was, of course, not qualified for the position of great trust and responsibility to which he was elected in 1920. A man easily preyed upon by his friends, he was a shining mark for the opportunist and self-seeker, of which there are always a plenitude in Washington. I gave the following estimate of Harding in 1922 to Mark Sullivan, who tried hard to see something commendable in him:

> Yes, I believe the country is disappointed in Harding. . . . I like your making excuses for Harding; Harding makes a lot for himself. But he is not afraid of the danger that lies "in the executive taking action outside the constitution and without the authority of Congress;" he is afraid of making any decision at all. He is a kind, companionable fellow to go with on a fishing expedition or play cards with; but he is not the man to have as President or leader. You spoke of his being "sure-footed" and "conservative." He is neither in my opinion. I had hoped for him but he is nothing.

It is often said of the Presidency that the office makes the man, but Harding was a notable exception. However, it is also said that a President reflects the temper of his times, and this was indubitably true of the former Senator from Ohio. His election symbolized the state of cynicism and disillusion into which our Republic fell after the war, as Woodrow Wilson had symbolized the idealism of the New Freedom and the war years.

I know that the present generation thinks of the twenties as the Jazz Age, a time of joy unconfined, of stimulating literary ferment; a period of prosperity, gay parties, and lighthearted flaunting of the law. It may have been all these things to some people, but to those who thought about the character of national life, it was a decade that could only be viewed with indignation and dismay.

One could only be incensed at the spectacle of America, under Harding, turning on itself and denouncing the very goals and sacrifices which had made the Wilson years a high point in our national life. One could only be outraged to be told that the war which we had fought for great ideals had been undertaken to advance sinister and alien causes, and that graft, corruption, and profiteering had been the real aim of those who directed the effort.

In view of the prevailing cynicism and suspicion of the Harding years, it is not surprising that a plague like the Ku Klux Klan could infect the nation and serve as a focus for every kind of bigotry. From its center in Indianapolis, there radiated an organization able to summon demonstrations at will in thousands of American cities. Those parades of white-robed, white-hooded men through curiously silent streets, and the subsequent ominous glow of crosses burning against the night sky, were symptomatic of the sickness that gripped the land.

Yet, if the pillow slips and false faces of the Klan were offensive, we ought not to have been surprised by the existence of such a phenomenon. How could it be otherwise, I asked William Allen White in June, 1923:

> . . . when the community was so persistently taught that the country was inefficiently and dishonestly managed, that the business interests of the country were profiteering, that the farmers were profiteering, that labor was profiteering, that the war was made for the "interests," that the Catholics and Jews controlled the government, that we had sold out to the foreigners, and that no one in authority could be trusted because he was either a fool or a knave? With this teaching, and with the bootlegger enthroned, what can be expected of a confused people . . . ?

To this, White replied:

> Your letter was a joy to me. I have been fighting greed and suspicion and fear now four years—in the Ku Klux, in the hundred percenters, in the narrow-guage partisans and fanatical pro-leaguers; in the dam [sic] fool anti-leaguers and in the bigotry of Henry Ford and the stupidity of Cabot Lodge so that

I feel like a man on a raft with nothing left to eat but his toe nails when a friendly ship hoves in sight.

But what shook the nation in those years—and what came to epitomize the Harding Administration—was the scandal of Teapot Dome, the revelations of which were not made public until the unfortunate President was in his grave. When Senator Tom Walsh, who exploded the case, got his first leads, he came to ask my opinion of the course he should follow. Naturally, I encouraged him to drive his investigation relentlessly. But I must admit that, as he unfolded the facts of bribery and betrayal, I found it difficult to believe that men could be as grasping as Harry Sinclair and Edward Doheny and as faithless as Attornel General Daugherty and Secretary of the Interior Fall.

Teapot Dome was a Republican scandal out of which partisan Democrats made much political capital, but I could take no partisan joy. It seemed to me that the scandal reflected not on Republicans alone, but on all Americans. I suggested to Senator Joe Robinson that, in any speeches he might make, he stress the point that "despite the fact that the wrongs were committed by Republicans during a Republican administration, it is nothing to speak of in a partisan spirit, because it is something that all Americans, Republicans and Democrats alike, should hang their heads in shame about." I urged him to "let it go at that rather than make too much of it."

Perhaps I can characterize the moral tone of the Harding era by describing an incident which occurred at Friendship, the country home of publisher Ned McLean. There I was confronted one evening by Daugherty, shortly before his involvement in the Teapot Dome scandal was revealed. The Attorney General, some-what in his cups, came up to me and said mockingly, in reference to my wartime service in Washington, "Baruch, you're an honest so-and-so."

He seemed to be so amused by the idea of honesty, that I could feel my temper rise, and I'm afraid I answered with the distaste I felt: "Mr. Daugherty, you just can't understand how a man in my position could have refrained from lining his pocket."

Paradoxically enough, men of such integrity and ability as Hoover and Hughes and Mellon had sat in Harding's Cabinet alongside Daugherty and Fall. But it was the latter two and their entourage who left their imprint on the Administration.

Somehow the tragedy of Warren Harding is summed up for me in one sentence, from a letter he wrote to me on January 24, 1922. He was thanking me for some ducks I had sent from Hobcaw. He closed his letter with these words: "I do not think the Presidency ought to deny one the contact with his personal friends or make him insensible to the very agreeable amenities of life."

If he was partial to his friends and indiscriminating in his choice of them, if he was more concerned with the amenities of life than the burdens of his office, Harding was nonetheless not an evil man. He was an amiable, agreeable fellow who would not countenance injustice or dishonesty, when he knew about it. Once, Congressman William E. Mason, of Illinois, charged in the House that I had profiteered to the tune of twenty million in copper alone during my wartime service. I was so incensed by this attack that I planned to erect a sign near the Capitol with the legend in bold letters: "Mr. Mason, Make Good Your Charges."

But the reputation with which Daugherty in his peculiar way had credited me, saved me the trouble of challenging Mason. For President Harding, I was told, called Mason in and said, in effect, "Lay off. Baruch is an honest man, and an able one, too."

Harding also showed an admirable sense of fairness when some of the Wilson-haters around him, in resentment at President Wilson's promotion of Cary Grayson, out of line, to Rear Admiral, planned to have Grayson transferred to the Philippines. I happened to learn of this plot, and protested vigorously against it to Senator Jim Watson of Indiana. Watson immediately went to the White

House, and within an hour came to my hotel to say that Harding had put a stop to this vindictive scheme.

2

An entirely different kind of man took over in the White House after Harding's death.

I had often heard my friend Dwight Morrow speak affectionately of his classmate and friend, Calvin Coolidge. But Coolidge had not stood out among the more vivid personalities who thronged Washington. In fact, one day when I was lunching at Friendship at the same table with a quiet little man, I had to ask the lady sitting between us who he was. I recall my surprise when she whispered back, "He's the Vice-president."

Coolidge appeared much younger than his pictures; he was the kind of man who would always look less than his years. He did not engage in the luncheon conversation, but his eyes held an amused look that was not reflected in the rest of his countenance.

I saw President Coolidge more often than I had seen Harding. Occasionally he asked me for my views on various public questions. My files contain memoranda I gave him on such issues as agricultural relief, industrial mobilization, tariff revision, and foreign debt settlements. More often than not, however, I found myself in disagreement with his policies and critical of his Administration. Despite this, there developed a degree of friendship between us, which grew warm after he left office.

The first time Coolidge invited me to the White House was just after he was elected to a full term in 1924. I was one of his guests at a small dinner. At first, he seemed preoccupied, but when his big collie appeared on the scene he brightened up. He amused us all by addressing a good many witty remarks to the dog about the political situation in Congress.

After dinner, while I stood talking to Mrs. Coolidge, she

glanced over my shoulder and remarked that the President wanted to see me. I turned and looked down the hall. The President was standing there, with a box of cigars under one arm, beckoning with his head for me to follow him. We went into his study, where he motioned me to a seat, lit the fire himself, and asked me to take a "see-gar."

I looked around the room and remarked that it was familiar to me. I pointed to the little black rocker I had occupied when I sat with President Wilson's War Cabinet. "You're just as welcome here now and in that chair as you were then," Coolidge told me. I was unprepared for his warm and friendly spirit, which I had not expected to encounter in a man widely thought to be cool and reserved.

Coolidge settled back in his chair. "I want to talk to you about the railroad situation," he said. He did just that, at some length. Then he went on to discuss the farm problem, the tariff, and taxes. Although I can do my share of talking, I wasn't given much of a chance. From time to time I tried to interrupt to make my own views clear. Mr. Coolidge would listen attentively but would then take over the conversation again.

When I had stayed as long as I thought I should, I got up to leave, but the President wanted to talk on. I was delighted to hear his views, and to know this man who was so much more human and so much more of a companion than I had any conception of from the stories I had heard.

As I was leaving, I got an insight into why Calvin Coolidge was known as "Silent Cal." As he walked with me from his study, I said that he ought to reserve the time and attention he had given me for some of his prima donnas who felt they ought to be recognized. He chuckled—it was more of a dry New England cackle. I went on to thank him for the long and interesting talk; and, with a smile, added, "You know, Mr. President, everybody says you never say anything."

"Well, Baruch," he said, "many times I only say 'yes' or 'no' and even that winds them up for twenty minutes more."

There was a frankness about Coolidge which I found appealing. Once, at his request, I accepted an appointment to the George Washington Bicentennial Commission. I'm afraid I didn't pay much attention to the very limited duties of this body; on one occasion I neglected to attend a meeting that had been called at the White House. Some time later I met the President at some function in Speaker Nicholas Longworth's room in the Capitol. All he said to me was, "Why didn't you come to that last meeting at the White House?"

It was a surprisingly direct question, and I had no adequate reply. I made up my mind to attend the next Commission meeting, which turned out to be a very large affair at the White House. The President sat at a little table, listening to speaker after speaker. After considerable time had elapsed, his attention began to wander. His eyes moved over the semicircle of listeners sitting facing him. When his gaze rested on me, he gave an almost imperceptible wink. At first I thought it was involuntary, but every time he looked at me I could see that little crinkle in the corner of his eye. Later he remarked wryly, "That meeting had some speakers, didn't it?"

Although Coolidge was not given to philosophizing, he had an understanding of human nature. Once we were sitting in a large room overlooking the White House grounds, discussing the subject of disarmament. In the course of his remarks, Coolidge fell silent. He stared into the fire, puffed on his cigar, and then said, ruefully, "If people want to fight, they'll fight with broomsticks if they can't find anything else."

Coolidge never seemed to resent the fact that I was frequently critical of his Administration's policies. In fact, he once complimented me on my interest in political affairs. When I explained why I was a Democrat, he said that that pleased him too, because we needed a two-party system.

On occasion, I was able to help him politically. When he had to muster Democratic support to settle the Italian war debts, I was able to persuade several Democratic legislators to give the President their votes.

I nearly went on a foreign mission for Coolidge. He intended to send Dwight Morrow and me to parley with the young Chinese Republic of Sun Yat-sen. But the plan did not come to fruition because, as Morrow later told me, the President concluded that there was no stable government with which to deal.

I had a better opportunity to know Calvin Coolidge after he left the White House, for we worked together closely on the National Transportation Committee in 1932. The Committee also included Al Smith, Clark Howell, and Alec Legge. It had been convened by an association of banks and insurance companies with heavy financial interests in depressed railroad securities, to study and recommend a national policy which might help restore the railroads to economic health. Coolidge was Chairman, and I was Vice-chairman of this Committee.

The report we issued contained far-reaching recommendations, which were then largely ignored but which are still pertinent to an industry which remains weak. Our major recommendation proposed the elimination of excess and obsolete lines, advocated the consolidation of railroads wherever feasible, and envisaged the ultimate creation of a national railroad system.

Consolidation was then, and is now, the major reform required for an inefficient railroad system plagued by overlapping lines and profitless competition. There is presently much talk of railroad consolidation, and several important mergers are being planned. One can only hope they will be carried out. In the past, railroad leaders have endorsed the objective of consolidation; but when it came to acting, no railroad executive was anxious—in the words of Daniel Willard—"to consolidate himself out of a job." Railroad consolidation, long overdue, would serve the best interests of the railroads, their investors, and the communities they serve.

Coolidge presided over the National Transportation Committee with such good taste and judgment, with so much consideration for everybody, that he won the affection and respect of us all.

He and Al Smith held each other in the highest regard, but there was occasionally a little good-natured chaffing. One day Smith said jokingly, "Mr. President, did you know that the rooms you are occupying now were once used by the Association Against the Prohibition Amendment?"

"Well, I guess we can fumigate them," Coolidge replied.

His dry humor was constantly in evidence, as in this letter written to me on October 27, 1932:

> I shall go to New York on Tuesday afternoon of Election Day and could attend a meeting Wednesday morning from nine to eleven, or in the afternoon from two o'clock to nine o'clock. I mistrust that you and Governor Smith will be rather tired on Wednesday morning, at which time I shall be glad to extend to both of you my sincere sympathy.

It was, of course, congratulations, not sympathy, which he extended that day.

When I wanted to include in the Committee report a provision on reorganizing bankrupt railroads, Coolidge didn't much favor the idea. "People who've had a hanging in the family don't like to talk about a rope," he explained.

He did have positive ideas, however, particularly about thrift and the value of money. He worried about the Committee's expenditures, and once wrote to me characteristically:

> It is necessary to watch people in Washington all the time to keep them from unnecessary expenditure of money. They have lived off the national government so long in that city that they are inclined to regard any sort of employment as a Christmas tree and if we are not careful they will run up a big expense bill on us.

Before the Committee completed its work, Calvin Coolidge died, leaving us all with a very real sense of loss.

During my association with him he emerged as far more attractive than the silent, reserved, laconic, even somewhat comic figure that the public saw while he was in the White House. Campaign pictures of Coolidge in an Indian war dress, or involved in others of the silly poses that are the unfortunate lot of Presidential candidates, detracted considerably from the genuine charm he possessed. His characteristic thrift, and other New England attributes, made him appear to many as a small man in nature as well as stature, which again was in opposition to the truth.

3

Curiously enough, the most intriguing invitation to undertake a large task during the twenties came to me not from the White House but from a most unlikely source—the Kremlin.

Like most Americans, I had been appalled by the brutality which had accompanied the Russian Revolution. And it goes without saying that I rejected out-of-hand its philosophy of government. Yet it seems to be in the nature of revolutions to commit excesses; and the Czarist autocracy had certainly sowed the seeds of its own destruction by its neglect and oppression of the Russian people. In the early years of the Revolution, before Stalin fastened his grip on the country, I had been hopeful that somehow a system of government would emerge, and a standard of living be achieved, which would justify the sufferings the Russian people had endured. I still hope so.

Strangely enough, I was asked to help the struggling regime. The first time the idea was broached was in the spring of 1919. I was sitting for the sculptor, Jo Davidson, in his Paris studio one afternoon when Lincoln Steffens, the famous journalist, came in. He was just back from the Bullitt Mission to Russia and, bursting with enthusiasm for what he had seen, uttered his often quoted declaration, "I have seen the future and it works."

Steffens, it turned out, had been discussing me with Lenin. The Premier, confronted with the formidable problem of industrializing Russia's primitive economy, had compared the task with that faced by America in mobilizing her economy during the war. For that reason, according to Steffens, Lenin was keenly interested in me.

Steffens quoted the Premier as saying that he knew I was not interested in money (a strange admission for a Communist to make about a Capitalist), but that he was ready to pay me a million dollars a year if I would undertake to help revamp the Russian economy.

I was, of course, intrigued by what Steffens reported, but the matter did not develop further—at least not for several years. Then, in 1925, when I was again in Paris, William Reswick, an American newspaperman who had been stationed in Moscow, reopened the matter.

Reswick was on close personal terms with Alexei Rykov, Lenin's successor, and with other members of the Soviet Politburo. He gave me a graphic account of conditions in Russia, particularly of the economic problems still besetting the regime. The "New Economic Policy" of Lenin had failed to create a strong industrial base, and the moderate Bolsheviks in control of the Kremlin were willing to relax dogma in order to attract foreign capital and know-how into Russia. Premier Rykov, after telling Reswick of Lenin's idea of enlisting my help, admitted ruefully, "Here is one capitalist who has played havoc with our Marxist concept of the profit urge. We were willing to let him name his own terms but he didn't come."

Leonid Krassin, Commissar for Foreign Trade, was another who had spoken to Reswick about me. According to Reswick, Krassin was convinced that only a man with the experience I had acquired in WIB could direct the task of mobilizing the untapped economic wealth of Russia. And Leon Trotsky was still another, according to Reswick, who had told him that Russia needed an industrial strategist such as they considered me to be.

Accordingly, the Kremlin now wanted to approach me directly.

Premier Rykov had asked Reswick to arrange a meeting between Krassin and me. I readily agreed to meet Krassin, who was then in Paris. But because the United States did not then recognize the Soviet Union, I refused to visit the Soviet Embassy. Krassin was equally reluctant to call on me at my hotel. So we met at an out-of-the-way hotel at Versailles.

Over tea, Krassin, with a wealth of detail at his command, unfolded a concessionary plan which the Soviet was then contemplating. It embraced a vast network of industrial projects: oil in Baku; iron, coal, and steel in the Donets basin; tractor and machine plants at Tsaritsyn (Stalingrad); as well as railroad, highway, and power developments. All of this, Krassin pointed out, was part of a grand design aimed at laying the foundation for heavy industry on which the edifice of a new Russia was to be built. Its success, he went on, was imperative. If this concession plan failed, not only would Russia fail to meet her economic goals, but the political moderates—whose idea it was—would be doomed. Krassin summed up by saying that the Kremlin was ready to give me any of the concessions I wanted—steel, oil, coal, copper—if I would help them to carry out their plan. "We have been counting on you, Mr. Baruch," he said, "to do for us in peace what you did for your own country in war."

It was as exciting an offer as I have ever heard. I was impressed with Krassin and felt that if he represented the new Russia, there was hope. Still, I could not agree with the basic premise of his plan.

"I will come," I told Krassin, in words very much like these, "and stay in Russia at my own expense, without accepting any remuneration or concessions for myself—but only if your government agrees to put first things first." By that, I meant that heavy industry could not be given priority over the more pressing needs of the people. Agriculture had to be modernized to feed and clothe them, I said, and housing, hygiene, and transportation had to take precedence over foundries and dams. "I would want to bend everything toward improving the standard of living of the people," I went on. "If I understand it correctly, that was what your Revolution was all about, and I am convinced that the peace of the world depends on this kind of effort in every country."

I pointed out the consequences likely to follow the intolerable strains of building up heavy industry by a people still convalescing from the ravages of war and revolution. The price exacted from the Russian people would be fearful, I warned, if they attempted to do in a few years what was the normal work of decades.

Krassin shook his head slowly, and appeared depressed by what I had said. Our conversation ended on this fundamental difference of view.

A few years later Stalin came to power, and the forced draft on the Russian people began in earnest. Under his ruthless drive, and the demands of survival in the war against Germany, Russia did create, within a generation, a modern industrial, scientific, and technological order. In this, their achievements have been remarkable. But the instrument of this success has been terror—and the price, freedom. And, one must ask, is it necessary to use this instrument and pay this price? I believe not, and many of the nations newly come to independence are proving it, as they build their economies, practically from scratch, under democratic systems.

Since Khrushchev's elevation to power, the Kremlin seems finally to be concentrating on raising living standards of the Russian people. Some observers have felt that the Kremlin had no option —that for all its power over the masses, the people were no longer willing to slave for dams and hydroelectric plants.

Also, some of the worst features of Stalin's police state have been removed. The Russians, if we can believe reports, seem even to have recognized the advantages of individual initiative, and are rewarding personal enterprise. This could have momentous meaning for the future. I remember Franklin Roosevelt's prediction that, with maturity, the Soviet Union might move away from totalitarianism and adapt many features of capitalism to their economic system. Whether or not this prediction is justified, the Russians seem to be learning that the profit motive, which they once sought to repeal, represents a fundamental fact of human nature.

The profit motive has been assailed even in our own country, where many people have come to believe that there is something immoral and even wicked in it. Yet, if we examine the origins of the profit motive, we will find that it was born of idealism and nourished by freedom.

The belief that the community would prosper if each man were permitted to pursue his own gain reflected a conviction in the essential goodness of the natural order. If all the many conflicting forces in the world were left alone, it was believed, they would find a natural balance which would come closer to serving the general good than any that governments might decree.

We know, of course, that men's greeds and grievances are not necessarily self-correcting. We have seen too many examples of how the desire for gain by some individual or group or nation has hurt —not benefited—the general good. Yet private profit and community interest are nonetheless interdependent in a free society. Only if men's labors show a profit can society and each member of it have the means for material progress. To produce at a loss must leave less to share. Put me down as old-fashioned, if you will, but I still believe that a profitable enterprise contributes more to civic virtue than an unprofitable one.

True, the profits of men's enterprise may often be shared unjustly and even stupidly. But such abuses will hardly be corrected by shackling the profit motive.

What are the alternatives to the profit system? What incentives for work can be put in its place? One alternative would be to have men work for the love of their labors, or out of a sense of service to others. Some persons do find happiness in living altruistically. But I know of no community which has ever been able to hold together for long behind this ideal.

The other alternative to the incentive of profit is to force men to work by order of some higher authority, as in the Soviet Union.

Wherever it has been applied, it has meant a loss of some freedom. At times, it has reduced men to slavery.

The profit motive, however, offers a form of incentive that does not rest on coercion. In this respect, it is a vital mechanism of personal freedom. That the profit system emerged as part of a revolt against excessive governmental authority was no accident. Nor was it accidental that there has flourished along with it a degree of personal freedom never seen before.

I have never believed that the abuses of profit-making should be permitted to go unchecked. There is a difference between freedom and license. But I do believe that the profit system has proven itself too valuable a social tool to justify being discarded because of some abuse. It is well within our capacity to minimize any abuse, and still preserve the material and spiritual benefits of profitable enterprise and of a system of incentives that does not require coercion.

It is instructive to consider the paths that America and Russia have followed since 1920. Russia had broken sharply with her past, in a revolution ostensibly aimed at a Utopian society. The United States, in 1920, was turning from idealism toward a concept of frank materialism, whether publicly acknowledged or not. On the surface, at least, Russia and the United States seemed headed in opposite directions. Yet we have totally reversed our positions since then.

Why have we emerged as the better society, by any objective measurement of humanity and history? I believe the answer lies in the single word "freedom." Here we have been free to emerge from our errors, as we did after the 1920's, when we survived the depression and pulled ourselves together for the greatest war effort in history. Since then, whatever our faults, we have been the leaders of the world in an effort to make a better human society.

By sharp contrast, Russia's original errors were not only perpetuated, but multiplied by a regime which abolished freedom and imposed from above a way of life which had to be followed without the opportunity of choice. It ought to be clear to everyone who cherishes freedom that democracy creates enlightenment, no matter what dark periods it may traverse, while the totalitarian state can only produce the absolute materialism of which America is so often falsely accused.

The Soviet Union has long had its dams and hydroelectric plants, and a great deal more; technologically, Russia has made enormous, incredible strides. But the cost has been that of human freedom, not only in Russia but wherever her power reached.

XII

The Defeat of Al Smith

WHEN I RETURNED HOME from the European trip which had been highlighted by the talk with Krassin, I had little opportunity to dwell on Soviet economic problems. There were issues closer to hand which absorbed all my interest. During the last months of 1925, and the early months of '26, I was engaged in the fight for the McNary-Haugen Bill; working on a plan for the settlement of reparations and war debts, which I submitted to Secretary of the Treasury Mellon; lecturing and writing on industrial mobilization; and, of course, taking an active part in Democratic Party affairs.

I must admit that after the Democratic debacle of 1924, I was very dispirited. My state of mind can be judged by a note I sent McAdoo at that time: "As far as politics is concerned," I wrote, "I don't even let anybody come into my office and talk about it to me."

But this was only a momentary reaction. James R. Keene used to sigh, after some bruising encounter with the stock market, "I get awful tired but I come again." That's very much the way I felt as I resumed my interest in the Democratic Party after the election.

Determined to take no further role in the incessant struggle between Presidential contenders, and convinced that the Party's future depended upon its legislative record, I now devoted most of my political activity toward helping to strengthen the Democratic representation in Congress and toward achieving unity within our ranks.

I developed close political and personal ties with leaders in both houses, and took an active part in the work of the Democratic Congressional and Senatorial Campaign Committees. I met frequently with Party leaders to map strategy and discuss issues. My home in South Carolina became the scene of many political get togethers, which were lightened by the pleasures of duck shooting and good conversation for which Hobcaw was famous. In the process, I got a clear insight into the problems of Congressional office holding.

We Americans pay far too little attention to the selection of our Senators and Representatives. Even in a Presidential election, democracy's most impressive rite, it is unusual for more than half the electorate to vote. In off-year elections, when only Congressional and local offices are at stake, an even smaller portion of the public bothers to take part in the decision. Underlying this apathy is the deep-seated disdain of Americans for professional politicians and for politics as a career. This attitude, so widely held, is regrettable. For politics—"the art of the possible," as it has been called—is a profession which deserves the public's respect.

For nearly fifty years I have known many of the men prominent in political life. A few were, unquestionably, men of no great talent or principle, whose only concern was to stay alive politically. Once, after I had testified in favor of a measure to prevent inflation before a Congressional committee, an unfortunate legislator came to me with an embarrassed apology. "I'm sorry, Baruch. I know I ought to vote for this bill," he said. "It's good for the country. But if I do, they'll throw me out. I've got to vote against it." But men such as this were far outnumbered, in my experience, by those who stood by their convictions.

This conflict of expediency *versus* principle is the daily fare of politicians. Still, most men find honorable compromises—and let us not sneer at politicians and their compromises. Compromise is the essence of politics in a democracy, the solvent in which divergent interests are broken down and fused into a common purpose. Compromise, as Edmund Burke said, is the foundation of all government. Without it, government would be paralyzed; no decisions would be possible if everyone insisted on all-or-nothing. As with all general propositions, however, it is the application of the rule that counts. There is a great difference between compromise and surrender.

In politics, the pressure to win is probably greater than in any other line of endeavor. There is nothing so dead as a defeated politician. An office seeker may be endowed with intelligence, ideals, courage, and a dozen other primary attributes, but he must win the election before he can bring his talents to bear on the problems of his time. Yet, despite the pressure to win, the level of integrity in politics is certainly as high, and perhaps higher, than in other competitive fields.

I have known many men in politics whose abilities would have earned them large fortunes in business or the professions. A good many have remained politicians at considerable sacrifice, and have endured, as well, attack and ridicule when their views happened to offend some important segment of the electorate. Yet they have remained in politics out of conviction.

Some of the men I have admired most, men whose friendship meant much to me over the years, were professional politicians. I think of Carter Glass, as strong in spirit as he was frail in body. Glass could have been Secretary of the Treasury under Roosevelt had he been willing to forget his principles, which it was impossible for him to do. Then there was the "Veep," Alben Barkley, a shrewd, amiable, and uncommonly tough gentleman, whose Senatorial career I was fortunate enough to help launch. In 1926, the Democratic party in Kentucky had been badly split over the selection of a Senatorial nominee. At the request of Party leaders in Congress, I undertook to harmonize the feuding Kentucky factions, and succeeded in uniting them behind Barkley.

I think of James F. Byrnes, one of my closest political and personal friends, whose abilities first caught my attention when he was a young Congressman. In 1924, I wrote to former Governor Richard Manning of South Carolina: "What do you think about Byrnes' chance for Senator? He certainly looks very good to me. . . . I have a very high regard for him." In the following decades, no man in public life grew in stature as Byrnes did.

The roster of my politician friends, whose character and abilities I have admired, is long: Pat Harrison, of Mississippi; Key Pittman, of Nevada; Peter Gerry, of Rhode Island; Robert F. Wagner, of New York; Cordell Hull, of Tennessee; Ollie James, of Kentucky; John Garner, of Texas; and most beloved of all, Joe Robinson, of Arkansas, for so many years the Senate's Democratic Majority Leader. These are only a few of the men I knew who brought distinction to politics. Nor were all of them Democrats, by any means. On the other side of the aisle, I was on warm terms with such men as Borah, Capper, Watson, and McNary.

2

The mid-term elections of 1926 resulted in substantial Democratic gains, and almost immediately the lines began to be drawn for the impending national convention. The prospect loomed for another knockdown, no-holds-barred struggle between McAdoo and Smith. This would make a great public spectacle, I knew, but would leave the party exhausted and easy picking for the Republican opposition when election time came.

"If we give up fighting for candidates and turn our attention to fighting the enemy," I wrote Josephus Daniels, "we should make a great deal of headway. David Reed's holding up the Senate for the purpose of hiding a dishonest ballot box, the veto of the McNary-Haugen Bill while giving an advance in the tariff on pig iron, our international policy, and the various other things that will occur to you are the matters we ought to talk about—not about Smith and McAdoo."

For myself, I was determined to hold fast to the vow I had taken in 1924, never again to participate in a pre-convention fight. As the campaign drums began to beat, the pressure from both the Smith and McAdoo forces on uncommitted Democrats began to mount. I had been one of McAdoo's closest advisers in 1924. It was taken for granted by many, and the idea was encouraged by some, that I would once again take a place in the McAdoo inner circle. I tried to explain to McAdoo why I would not, and wrote to him early in 1927:

> I devoted a great deal of time and much money to the last Congressional and Senatorial elections. I am going to start now to get ready for the Congressional and Senatorial elections of 1928 because I think much can be gained if those things are early organized. . . . I wanted to get clearly in your mind exactly where I stand on the political situation. You know, of course, of my affection for you and of my admiration for your sterling personal qualities, your fine business and executive qualifications, and your broad view of life and of other people. Nothing that anybody could do, or that you could do, would ever change me in that respect. But I am going to hold to the position as to which I made up my mind from the beginning that I am not going to enter into any primary fights. We Democrats spend most of our time killing one another off before the final battle, with the result that we are left exhausted and the Republicans walk away with the candy.

Some men might have resented the position I took, but McAdoo did not. He quickly replied that he understood and respected my feelings.

Such is the nature of politics, however, that avowals of neutrality are rarely given credence. My absence from the McAdoo camp was

generally construed as a sign that I had deserted him to join the
Smith forces. These conjectures were as painful to me as they
must have been to McAdoo. The fact was that if McAdoo could
win the nomination, I would have been delighted, and would have
done everything in my power to help him win the election. Consequently, I tried to reassure him that I had not jumped into the
Smith camp.

> A lot of things the newspapers say in reference to me, especially
> when they discuss you and Smith, try to make it appear that
> there has been a wedge driven in between you and me. They
> base it upon the fact that I am not taking any position and am
> not actively getting delegates for you. As I have told every-
> body, I have not been for any candidate. . . . All this talk about
> my supporting Smith is bunk. I want you to know that if you
> are ever nominated for the Presidency, there will be nobody
> who will do more and work harder and more enthusiastically for
> you than I.

But McAdoo was not to have the nomination. His Presidential
chances were over, although in the Democratic sweep of 1932 he
was elected Senator from California.

At the Democratic convention in Houston in 1928, the Smith
forces were in complete command, and "The Happy Warrior" was
nominated on the first ballot. By this time I had come to recognize
the folly of Prohibition and could endorse Smith's clear-cut position on its repeal. I felt he was a worthy candidate in every way,
and was glad to support him.

I had known Smith, as I have said before, since the days when he
was Sheriff of New York County. I had supported him for Governor
and greatly admired his achievements in that post. In 1923, he had
talked me into accepting an appointment to a committee to study
the development of Saratoga Springs. "Your old daddy would have
wanted you to do it," was Al's clinching argument, referring to my
father's pioneering interest in spa therapy. True, we had been on
opposite sides in 1924, but that circumstance did not diminish my

affection or respect for his remarkable personality, his warm heart, and his great ability.

Smith's life is an inspiration to all people of humble origins who aspire to great things. He used to say that his only diploma was from FFM—the Fulton Fish Market. A product of Tammany ward politics, he rose far above its petty provincial limitations, yet his simple, homely character remained the same. He could always produce some apt story to illustrate a point, and he was seldom without his highly developed sense of humor.

He sometimes talked about the problem of getting jobs for Party regulars, who took it as a matter of course that he would look after them. As he climbed higher, these requests grew progressively more ambitious and more difficult to meet. When he got to be President of the Board of Aldermen, one of his stories went, an old associate came in one day and greeted him warmly: "Good mornin' to ye, Mr. President."

"Good morning to you, Mike," Smith said, "and what can I do for you?"

"Well, Al," Mike said forthrightly, "it's a job I'm after and I know just the one it is—inspector of elevators."

"I'm afraid I can't get you that particular job," Smith told him. "That's civil service. You have to take a test."

Mike assured him that that would be no handicap, and inquired what he would have to know. Smith explained that he would have to pass an examination on such matters as hydraulics and motor maintenance, and—but before he could go on with the list, Mike cut him short.

"Don't hand me that stuff, Al," he protested. "It may be good enough for these other fellows, but I went to school with you."

This common touch of Smith—the feeling of so many people that they went to school with him—was one of his great assets, but a major liability as well; the common man is not always Everyman's choice for the Presidency. If more people had only known it, however, Alfred E. Smith was one of the most uncommon men who ever aspired to the White House.

In organizing his campaign, Smith asked me to serve as Chairman of the Party's Finance Committee. I declined, explaining my preference for working in an unofficial capacity. Smith readily appreciated my position. On a later occasion, another Presidential nominee was to be less understanding when I declined a similar request.

I was, however, very active at Smith's headquarters, providing ammunition to refute Republican claims that their economic policies had brought a golden age of prosperity. But most of my effort was concentrated on the agricultural issues of the campaign.

For eight years I had been a militant advocate of "equality for agriculture." My concern for the farmers had no partisan bias. I had consistently urged them to punish their enemies and reward their friends without regard to party. But it was clear to me, and to an increasing number of farmers too, that as long as the Republican Party remained wedded to the doctrines it then professed— and as long as it continued to take the farm vote for granted —agriculture could expect little at its hands.

It was equally clear that the Democratic Party could not regain power without winning that farm vote. As I wrote to Clemenceau, who sought my views on the domestic political scene: "The balance of power is held by the farmers, the so-called farm bloc, but unfortunately they do not know how to use their own power either for their own benefit or for the benefit of the country generally." Their situation is much the same today. They are largely unorganized and victimized by empty promises.

Thus my interests in agriculture and in the Democratic Party were allied. I was convinced that the farmers could secure their rights only by supporting the Democrats, and that the Democrats could succeed only by helping to redress the farmers' grievances.

At the 1924 convention, I had tried and failed to get a farm plank adopted which would be satisfactory to George Peek, the

farmers' chief spokesman. In the ensuing campaign, Peek had resisted all my efforts to get him to support John Davis. But now,
after two Coolidge vetoes of the McNary-Haugen Bill, he was ready
to lead a political revolt in the Middle West. Together we had
gone down to Houston and, this time, succeeded in getting the convention to endorse the principles of McNary-Haugen. Then Peek
turned, with all the energy and ability that so distinguished him,
to rallying the rank and file of farmers in support of Smith.

The Smith Independent Organization Committee, which he
headed, kept up a continuous barrage against the Republicans and
their candidate, Herbert Hoover, for their stand on agriculture.
In the three months of the canvass, Peek conducted a vast and
complicated campaign in the farm belt. He spent half-a-million
dollars, distributed more than three million pamphlets, and made
many converts—but, as it turned out, not enough.

While Peek was directing the fight for the farm vote on the
firing line, Hugh Johnson—who had been working with me on
many of the economic studies I had been carrying on—and I were
advising Smith in New York. But although Smith was entirely
sympathetic to the farmers, he did not think the farm issue was as
politically important as we did.

Johnson and I, working day and night on this issue, were anxious
for Smith to treat the farm question in several carefully prepared
speeches. But he insisted that he would give only one major address to it—one subject, one speech was his rule.

He made this clear, early in the campaign, to a group of advisers
who had been pressing him to increase the number of addresses he
had planned. "This ain't a circus," he protested. "I can make five
or at the most six speeches. After that they are sure to be flops. I
don't have any more in me." Moreover, he would give them in his
own way. "I suppose I could make a lot of speeches in the 'court-
of-appeals language' of Charlie Hughes," he said—and he delivered
a series of well-rounded sentences, without any trace of his cus-

tomary accent or reliance on the vernacular—"I can do it, but that's not Al Smith."

I insisted, however, that the complexity of the farm problem, and the need to dispel the notion that he was neither familiar nor interested in it, required Smith to deliver his one major address from a carefully prepared manuscript. Smith refused, agreeing only to read a few paragraphs which dealt with the specific prescription he intended to apply to solve the farm problem.

Smith went out to Omaha and delivered a masterly farm address. At headquarters, we were convinced that he had captured the farm belt. Peek, Johnson, and I were jubilant until Senator Borah, in a brilliant forensic display at the Twin Cities, quelled the incipient farm rebellion against the Republicans. Forgetting his earlier denunciations of Hoover as a foe of agriculture, Borah pulled out all the stops in portraying him as a patron saint of the farmer. There were few men who could match the emotional appeal of Borah's eloquence. I have always believed he took the farm vote away from Smith.

Still, the bid for the farm vote was not entirely disappointing. Smith did much better in the Middle West than Davis had done four years before. He would have done even better had it not been for other political handicaps. For there were far more potent forces at work to defeat him than the traditional Republicanism of farmers.

3

Smith went into the election fight with a burden of liabilities which, in retrospect, made his bid all the more remarkable. He was running against a candidate who symbolized the prosperity which Republicans claimed as their handiwork. Moreover, he was Wet, he was Tammany, he was Catholic—all dirty words in the semantic jungle of politics, and all contributing to Democratic divisiveness.

After the convention, I did what I could to rally disaffected Democrats—primarily, McAdoo men—behind Smith. Some whom I thought I had persuaded—men like Dan Roper—didn't stay persuaded. Others—such as George Fort Milton, the Democratic editor —couldn't be budged, openly fought Smith, and bolted to Hoover. McAdoo himself offered nothing but silence. I appealed to him to support the Party's choice, and tried to find some way to bridge the differences between him and Smith. But McAdoo's price was a statement from Smith on Prohibition which would satisfy McAdoo's own scruples. He sent me a draft of the statement which he wanted Smith to issue. But it clearly violated Smith's conviction, and was impossible for him to accept. This was one instance where compromise was not possible.

As I have indicated, I could no longer agree with McAdoo and other Drys on Prohibition. Smith's advocacy of repeal was not a real issue—indeed, by this time, Prohibition itself was a false issue. We never did have Prohibition in this country; the law was on the books but was simply ignored. I once asked William Jennings Bryan why the Prohibition law did not punish the buyer as well as the seller. That would have involved search and seizure, he replied, and would have violated the individual's rights. That may have been so, but the law as it stood was worse than useless. I couldn't see how any Dry could continue to favor a statute and support an Administration which had made such a farce out of law.

Nor was the talk of Smith's Tammany ties anything but a red herring, in my view. Tammany is a handy word to swing around in political campaigns. It makes people whose own political organizations are not so notorious feel self-righteous. Without apologizing for Tammany, whose sins are considerable, I knew that it was Smith who dominated Tammany, not the reverse. During his terms in Albany, there had not been the slightest evidence of Tammany influence in the Governor's efficient and progressive administration of the state's business.

What it came down to, then, was that the principle issue in the campaign of 1928, and the decisive factor in Al Smith's defeat, was religion. As I wrote to McAdoo, shortly before the election: "There is one issue in this campaign and that is religion. Whoever put it there, no matter how it got there, it is there and the filth and dirt is enough to make one boil!"

Nothing more ugly has happened in American politics than the campaign of hate that was waged against Smith. He was fair game for bigots of every stripe, including some in high places. I was outraged by the spectacle of Senators and Bishops resorting to crude and unabashed appeals to prejudice. Once, after Senator Tom Heflin had delivered one of his anti-Catholic tirades, I wrote to McAdoo:

> I am surprised that somebody did not call Tom Heflin down for his narrow-minded attacks upon the Catholics. If there was anything we came to this country for, it was to have religious liberty, and intolerance in religion is hateful to me whether expressed by Catholic, Protestant, or Jew.

Bishop James Cannon of Virginia was another who abused his place and calling by his attacks on Smith. One man he couldn't intimidate was Carter Glass, in spite of threats to drive the Senator from office. When the Bishop injected himself into the campaign battle, I wrote to Glass: "This is one of the times I wish I was a Methodist so I could trim the good bishop who is attempting to dictate politics instead of being a sky pilot directing sinning souls like myself in the direction of a higher life and a better world."

Glass's contempt for Bishop Cannon was complete. He once said to me, "I'm a religious man, Bernie. I try to lead a good life and I expect to go to Heaven. But I'd give a lot to have the pleasure of seeing the Devil burn the robes off that old Bishop."

Time blurs memories and dilutes emotions. But as I read through my correspondence of 1928, the intensity of my feelings about the religious issue comes back with much force. Perhaps I felt it so keenly because I had known the barbs of prejudice myself. Although I never heard him complain, I could appreciate what Smith was being subjected to, and understand how his spirit must have been lacerated. Then, too, I was filled with distress and shame because so much of the bigotry was emanating from my native and much-loved South.

Campaigns such as that waged against Smith always breed similar tactics. In certain Democratic circles, a campaign of vilification was waged against Herbert Hoover, which I resented in equal degree. One day I got a call from a Hoover aide, protesting against a most offensive charge which was about to be aired against the Republican candidate by a former Republican Senator who had defected. The aide thought the speech ought to be squelched, and when I was told of its nature, I agreed.

I called John Raskob, Chairman of the Democratic National Committee, and then George Peek, in an effort to bring pressure to bear on the speaker. Unfortunately, the man would not be deterred. He made his charges, which were immediately and forthrightly repudiated by Democratic headquarters.

I informed Hoover of my effort to have the speech suppressed, and went on to say that:

> . . . so far as I am concerned I will not be a party to any attacks upon your personal integrity or personal life. We seem to have different views regarding the philosophy of government and on that alone am I willing to contend against you. I believe contentions of that kind result in better goverment for all.

To this, Hoover replied:

> . . . I thoroughly agree with you that the only basis for political party controversies should be the principles to which we adhere in the matter of Government. . . .
>
> I have done my best to keep this [religious] issue entirely out of national politics as no one abhors it more than I do. However, there is no controlling the extremists on either side. It is my

impression that if we could stop discussion on the whole question of tolerance by speakers on both sides and thus discourage
the engendering of further feeling on the subject, it would be
infinitely better both for your side and for the future of the
country.

As the campaign neared its climax, I wrote to Winston Churchill
and attempted to sum up the situation as I saw it:

> The principal issue in the campaign is Governor Smith's re-
> ligion. I say this because it is being used more effectively than
> anything else. In the South the most scurrilous statements re-
> garding Governor Smith's religion, his personal habits, the Pope,
> have had a widespread currency since his nomination. . . .
> No one, of course, can measure the extent to which religious
> prejudices can be roused. The history of the world has shown
> that it can rouse people to the highest pitch and to the most in-
> human acts. The preachers of the South are spreading Anti-
> Catholicism most actively. . . .
> This is the bitterest and most strenuous campaign that America
> has entered into in many a day. Personalities are flying back and
> forth; statements are being made regardless of the truth; and
> prominent people are publicly leaving their parties to vote for
> the other side. . . .

Despite the formidable obstacles placed in Smith's path, up until
the very end I thought that he could win. But, although he polled
over fifteen million popular votes, in the Electoral College he won
only eighty-seven—and the traditionally Solid South was overwhelmingly against him.

The exploitation of religious prejudice in the campaign of 1928
was a grievous departure from American ideals. Happily, the barriers of religious and racial prejudice have been largely dismantled
during the past generation. We must hope that in the future our
votes, for or against any man, will never again be determined by
considerations of religion or race.

XIII

The Great Crash

THE 1920's WAS, among other things, the era of the New Economics, which could best be described as a system in which everything on the charts of business activity was supposed to go up and nothing was supposed to come down. Experience, as well as common sense, showed that this could not be. Yet, in the overheated atmosphere of the great boom, few questioned it seriously. Indeed, it was difficult not to be caught up in the whirl.

It was as though the whole nation had been seized by a money madness. Everyone worshiped at the shrine of business. "There seems to be something sacrosanct about big business," I wrote George R. James of the Federal Reserve Board. Anyone who doubted the sanctity of business, or questioned the government's policies toward it, was made to feel rather like a subversive.

Looking out over world affairs in those years, I could see where a new surge of prosperity might be touched off if we could solve such problems as the farm collapse, reparations, and war debts. But while these problems remained unresolved, there seemed to be no justification for the prices people were willing to pay for securities. Stock prices may have been booming, but if one took the trouble to study the business situation carefully, he could find reasons for being uneasy. A full three years before the crash I wrote to Mark Sullivan:

> Now let me make a prediction to you. Business has undoubtedly reached its zenith, and what we see in motors, steel, and railroad statements, is evidence of what has gone by and not of what is before us. There has been a stimulation of business by high-power salesmanship on the partial payment plan of homes, radios, automobiles, etc. Whereas it is wise to buy things on the partial payment plan that will result in time in increased economies and better living, at the same time it can be overdone. I am afraid it has now been overdone.

A year later, in December, 1927, I was holding to my suspicions about our much-trumpeted prosperity. I wrote to Churchill:

> Business conditions in this country are not as good as the newspapers make them appear. Old corporations and large businesses are making less net money than a year ago. The so-called mail order and chain store businesses show great increases, but that is due primarily to the elimination of a large number of small concerns.

But there was not much of an audience for those of us who felt uneasy about the state of our economy. To most people, from financier to laborer, it seemed as though prosperity would never stop, that everyone would simply go on making, and spending, more and more money.

Now the concern for money is a very human thing. It might be said to reflect a primeval instinct. The acquisitive urge is more or less present in most men, whether they live in so-called primitive societies where wealth is measured in cows or cocoanuts, wampum or wives, or in so-called complex cultures where it is measured in gold or securities. Indeed, this acquisitive instinct can even be found in lower animals, where it functions as a mechanism of survival.

There is not much difference, really, between the squirrel laying up nuts and the man laying up money. Like the squirrel, the man—at least at the start—is trying to provide for his basic needs. I don't know much about squirrels, but I think they know when they have enough nuts, and I'm sure they don't gamble away what they've accumulated. In this, they are superior to men, who often don't know when they have enough, and frequently gamble away what they do have in the empty hope of getting more.

Never before had there been such gambling as there was in those last turbulent years of the twenties; but few people realized they were gambling—they thought they had a sure thing.

Some of the wildest gambling of the decade took place in the Florida land boom. On the assumption that every American would soon settle in Florida, or at least vacation there, people fought to buy land, usually unimproved and often uninhabitable, at ever-spiraling prices. In the space of months, land values doubled, tripled, quadrupled. Building lots which once sold for a few hundred dollars were selling for as high as $20,000. It was a speculative mania in the classic tradition.

At the height of the boom I visited Palm Beach with Cary Grayson. We rode in an automobile from Palm Beach to Miami, past the ornate residences of the new multimillionaires and the newest golf course, so exclusive it would not permit ordinary folks like me to join. We passed through Boca Raton, where lavish developments were being carried out, and on to Coral Gables, where still more developments were under way. As we drove along the beautiful asphalt road that ran beside the ocean, I gazed out at the miles and miles of property with nothing on it but shrubs and scattered trees. I began to wonder where the people were who had money enough to buy and build at the astronomical prices then being asked. Where would the money come from?

My Florida visit was cut short by a summons from Secretary of the Treasury Mellon, who wanted to discuss with me the pending negotiations on settlement of foreign debts. Consequently, I didn't have time to investigate further what my brief observation had told me was a dangerously unhealthy situation in Florida. Yet I had seen enough to start selling my Florida county and municipal bonds. But I didn't act quickly enough. When the Florida bubble burst, I was left with many seemingly worthless bonds.

2

People should have been warned by the collapse of the Florida boom in 1926, but they were not. Few could resist the mad scramble for wealth, led by some of the greatest names in finance. Gambling in stocks—I hesitate to call it speculation—was made fashionable and respectable as never before in the climactic years of the twenties.

In every bank and brokerage house, in business places, on street corners, and in elevators and restaurants—wherever people met—one could hear the familiar phrases "what I heard" and "the tip I got." Token margin requirements enabled anybody to test his luck in the market. Taxi drivers told you what to buy. The shoeshine boy could give you a summary of the day's financial news as he worked with rag and polish. An old beggar, who regularly patrolled the street in front of my office, now gave me tips—and, I suppose, spent the money I and others gave him in the market. My cook had a brokerage account, and followed the ticker closely. Her paper profits were quickly blown away in the gale of 1929, and she had to be rescued from being sold out entirely.

Whenever some cool, calm voice like Carter Glass's was raised against this madness, it was jeered. Whenever the market fell back—and there were some sharp setbacks on occasion—from every quarter would come the chorus that all was well. Unfailingly, the prophets of the New Economics in government and finance promoted the boom and nourished public confidence in it. From the White House itself came President Coolidge's soothing statement, about the mounting loans on Stock Exchange collateral, that "five billion isn't very much." In those days it was; we are less impressed with billions now.

Nothing did more to spur the boom in stocks than the decision made by the New York Federal Reserve Bank, in the spring of 1927, to cut the rediscount rate. Benjamin Strong, Governor of the bank, was chief advocate of this unwise measure, which was taken largely at the behest of Montagu Norman of the Bank of England. Ostensibly, this easy-money policy was designed to stop the flow of gold out of England. Its primary effect, however, was to cause a re-evaluation of all securities, and to further inflate our already inflationary credit system by making large sums of money available for financing stock speculation.

From this point on, the market got completely out-of-hand. I do not make this criticism as the result of hindsight, which is so often the case with criticism. At the time of the Bank's action I warned of its consequences, and six months before the crash, I wrote to Senator William H. King, of Utah, about the soaring prices on the Stock Exchange:

> The original difficulty started in 1927 when the Federal Reserve System reduced its rate to $3\frac{1}{2}\%$ either for the purpose of forcing gold out or stimulating our exports. Whether that was wise or not, they evidently had in mind the accomplishment of some definite, constructive purpose. But they overlooked the fact that when they artificially reduced the rate . . . there would be a re-evaluation of securities and an artificial stimulus to business. Whatever their purpose was, they should have acted very promptly in raising the rate and that would have stopped the things they are now objecting to and which they directly caused.

In spite of the feverish quotations on the Stock Exchange, I felt that sooner or later the market had to break. Eugene Meyer put it wryly one day, as he watched a stock favored by speculators bid up from one high to another. "What will happen when they forget to bid?" he asked. The answer was inevitable. The higher they went, the farther they would have to fall. All this was in the normal, inevitable course of economic events. The history of all markets, from the day of their founding, has been a record of cyclical rise and fall.

There were some who believed that prices would never descend and others who thought that, if they did, it would still be possible to get out in time. But of those who remained aware of the market's nature, who realized that the boom had to end, none knew when the expected break would come.

Hugh Johnson was associated with me in various business ventures at this time, and I remember telling him to keep close watch on automobile sales and on construction statistics. These were the segments of the economy primarily dependent on the credit-inflation boom. When they began to slip, we would know that the whole structure was in danger.

I shared my apprehension about the state of the market with others. I remember a weekend in Atlantic City with Alexander Woollcott, Arthur Krock, Heywood Broun, and a few other delightful companions. As we strolled the boardwalk, the conversation got around to the market, as it usually did. My opinion was asked. My advice was to pull out of speculative situations, get out of debt, and put one's funds into sound bonds. I don't think my advice was well-regarded.

I, myself, was doing as I advised. By 1928, I had begun to liquidate my stock holdings and to put my money into bonds and into a cash reserve. I am very old-fashioned in this respect. I always like to have some hard cash around, especially in times of trouble. I also bought gold, which at that time was still the last repository of man's monetary faith. It is illegal to possess gold today, but before we went off the gold standard in 1934, I made regular purchases of the metal from the Alaska Juneau Gold Mines, in which I was interested. I paid the full assayed value of the gold and had the bars shipped and stored for me in America. This was the basis of the stories which circulated about the huge cache of gold I secretly possessed. The amount was not very large, and there was nothing secret about it. When the government decreed private ownership of gold to be illegal, every last ounce of it was turned over to the Treasury.

One of the men who sought my advice on the market was Will Rogers. Rogers was much more than a fellow who could twirl a lariat and wisecrack; he was a shrewd and original commentator who illuminated the serious with his humor. The only time I ever heard him put aside his sharp wit occurred when I took General Pershing to see the Ziegfeld Follies, in which Rogers starred. I had a slight cold and had kept on my overcoat. Will spotted me, turned to the line of chorus girls, and remarked, "Girls, you're not warming things up tonight. I see Barney Baruch next to General Pershing, and he's sitting in his overcoat." Then, in an unexpectedly serious tone, he asked the General to stand, and paid him a generous and heartfelt tribute as the theater shook with applause.

In the spring of 1929, Rogers told me that he had a contract which would bring him a very large sum of money, almost a million dollars, within the next three years, and he wanted to invest it. I asked him if he had any debts. He said he owed money on some property in the West in which he had great faith. When I advised him to pay it off before he did anything else, Rogers tried to explain the wisdom of having a mortgage on property, since it made it easier to sell. Besides, he admitted, rather than pay off his mortgage, he wanted to get into the market.

I looked at him and said, "What you want to do is gamble. But I want to tell you that you're sitting on a volcano. That's all right for professional volcano sitters, like myself, but an amateur like you ought to take to the tall timber and get as far away as you can. There may come a time when the man who holds your mortgage will want his money and you may not have it, and your friends won't have it either."

Rogers slumped down in his chair, scratched his head, and chewed his gum as I lectured him. About two years later, after the volcano had erupted, I met Will in a corridor of the Capitol. I backed him against a wall and asked him, "Will, how did you come out of this?"

"I did what you told me," Rogers said, shifting his gum, "and you saved my life."

3

In the summer of 1929, I went abroad. I met Churchill in Deauville, and then went on to Scotland, where I went each year to a lovely old castle to hunt grouse on the moors. While I was away I received highly optimistic messages from home concerning the economic situation.

In August, I received an invitation to participate in the formation of two new investment trusts. Investment trusts were then the rage; huge amounts of stock, much of it watered, were being offered to the public through them. The Shenandoah and Blue Ridge corporations, whose stock I was being offered, were among the largest and, as events were to prove, not very solid.

On receipt of this invitation, I cabled to three leading financiers more or less as follows: "The formation of these companies looks like financial whoopee. What is your opinion of the general situation?" Two of the men sent me noncommittal replies. The third, a man holding one of the highest positions in the banking world, cabled back that the market is "like a weather vane pointing into a gale of prosperity."

After I got this cable I went for a walk with General Pershing, who was my guest. We talked at length about the state of affairs in America, and I expressed my growing concern over the danger signs in the market. As we strolled along, I went over all the factors involved in the Shenandoah and Blue Ridge issues; even at a distance of three thousand miles, I could see that these and many other enterprises were foolhardy. My intuition, which after all is only the accumulated force of experience, was sending out warning signals.

I decided to shorten my stay in Scotland and depart for home. But in London, waiting to embark, I thought of that message about the "gale of prosperity" and several times cabled my office orders to buy stocks, only to follow them with orders to sell.

On the boat was a brokerage office, operated by a charming young man who solicited my business. I gave him several orders to sell. I think he felt I was favoring him, rather than expressing an opinion of my own.

Immediately after arriving in New York, I began to sell everything I could, in anticipation of the break I now felt to be imminent. This was near the end of September. The condition of the market could be measured by its wild fluctuations, followed by assurances from every direction that all was well. But I had heard this lullaby before. I knew that the continuity of confidence was beginning to break.

The market continued to fall and rally. Then, suddenly, there were no more rallies. There was, instead, a final, cataclysmic break that began on Wednesday, October 23rd, when a premonitory plunge sent a shudder of apprehension through Wall Street. On the next day, Black Thursday, the plunge became a descent so terrifying that panic swept the floor of the Exchange, by that time a frantic madhouse. Winston Churchill, who was here on a lecture tour, witnessed the scene from the visitor's gallery before the governors prudently ordered it closed for the day. There was an incredible interval that day when stocks went begging without buyers, no matter what the price.

The descent continued that week and next, when on Tuesday sixteen million shares changed hands in one record-breaking day. But still the plunge continued—deeper and deeper. Thomas Lamont and Thomas Cochran appealed to me to join a pool which Morgan & Company was forming to try to stem the collapse. I declined;

I did not think their plan would work. The day was past when the House of Morgan could rally Wall Street in such a crisis.

At last, in mid-November, the results could begin to be assessed. They were almost unbelievable. Only a few months before, averages on the Exchange had been at an all-time peak. General Electric had been at 396; A.T. & T. at 310; brokers' loans, by which margin buying could be judged, had been almost eight billion. Yet now, in a space of time so brief that men could hardly grasp what had occurred, the bottom had fallen out. G.E. was 168, A.T. & T., 197. The stock of the Shenandoah Corporation, which had opened at $17.50 per share, and had sold almost immediately for $36, would eventually reach an abysmal bottom of 50¢. The value of stocks had declined by more than thirty per cent; the paper loss was a staggering twenty-six billion. And this was only the beginning—worse was to come.

The human toll was far worse. Close at hand I could see my son, a young broker who had shrewdly avoided the crowd madness, coming home exhausted and depressed by the scenes of despair and desperation at the Stock Exchange. Many of my friends, who had ridden the waves of the boom, now found themselves swamped, and needed help to keep from being sold out. Many people I had known for years, professionals in Wall Street as well as amateurs, were wiped out.

I remember the plight of a man who had headed a distinguished firm specializing in government bonds, and who was known for his generous philanthropies. I can still see him as he appeared in the days before the crash, in his shining top hat and morning coat, walking up the steps of Morgan & Company.

After the crash, he came in to see me. I hardly recognized him, so changed was his appearance. He had come to borrow some money. I asked him why he had not gone to the Morgans, with whom he had done so much business. He gave me several excuses which suggested that he had worn out his welcome there, although the Morgans were generous people.

I gave him a few hundred dollars that day, but soon he was back again. He told me he was seventy-eight years old, and that he still had hopes for the future. After that he came in several times, gradually asking for smaller amounts. By this time there was not the slightest resemblance between the broken man in my office and the banker in shining top hat who had once given large sums of money to charities.

Who and what were to blame for the collapse of the tinsel structure of our prosperity? Rarely has there been so much blame to share among so many. Government leaders, for one, were to blame for a long series of erroneous policies: the high tariff bills of the preceding twenty years, beginning with Payne-Aldrich and ending with Hawley-Smoot; the unwise policies of the Federal Reserve Board; the neglect of agriculture. Along with these could be listed the failure to resolve the question of German reparations and foreign debts, the encouragement of public as well as private debt, and the attempt to bolster our export trade by indiscriminately lending money abroad.

Bankers and brokers were responsible for the collapse, too. Many of them had become mere purveyors of securities, freely and ruthlessly abusing the machinery of the Stock Exchange to take advantage of the speculative mania. The stereotype of bankers as conservative, careful, prudent, responsible individuals was shattered in 1929. Some bankers were shown to be incompetent to handle other people's money, and others turned out to be unworthy. It took the public a long time to get over some of these revelations.

Yet, in the last analysis, it was the public which was chiefly responsible for its own undoing. The stock market boom was a classic example of the madness of crowds. History records some of the most notorious of these mass movements—the Mississippi Bubble, the South Sea Bubble, the Tulip Mania—and the madness of the twenties must certainly be added to the list.

Many years ago I came across a remarkable book by Charles Mackay, *Extraordinary Popular Delusions and the Madness of*

Crowds. Mackay's book, first published in 1841, documented some of the unbelievable crazes that have swept mankind. In a foreword to a reissue of this volume, and in reference to the stock market frenzy preceding the 1929 crash, I wrote the following:

> All economic movements, by their very nature, are motivated by crowd psychology. Graphs and business ratios are, of course, indispensable in our groping efforts to find dependable rules to guide us in our present world of alarms. Yet I never see a brilliant economic thesis expounding, as though they were geometrical theorems, the mathematics of price movements, that I do not recall Schiller's dictum: "Anyone taken as an individual, is tolerably sensible and reasonable—as a member of a crowd, he at once becomes a blockhead," . . . Without due recognition of crowd-thinking (which often seems crowd-madness) our theories of economics leave much to be desired. It is a force wholly impalpable—perhaps little amenable to analysis and less to guidance —and yet, knowledge of it is necessary to right judgments on passing events.

The prehistoric tribal eruptions from Central Asia, the Crusades, the medieval dance crazes, witch burnings, all these—right down to the Florida boom and the 1929 market madness—were phenomena of mass action under impulses which no science has explored. Such impulses have power unexpectedly to affect any static condition or so-called normal trend. For that reason, they have a place in the considerations of thoughtful students of economic affairs.

It has always seemed to me that the periodic madnesses which afflict mankind must reflect some deeply rooted trait in human nature—a trait akin to the force that motivates the migration of birds or the rush of lemmings to the sea. In economics there seems to be a cyclical rhythm to these movements. A bull market will be galloping along and then, suddenly, something will occur— trivial or important—to break the continuity of thought. And then panic sets in.

One curious thing about these crowd madnesses is that no nation or people is exempt. Nor does education or rank provide immunity.

The market madness of 1927 to 1929 certainly affected every level of society.

Although there is no scientific cure for these madnesses, still there may be potent incantations. I have always thought that if, in the lamentable era of the New Economics culminating in 1929, even in the very presence of dizzily spiraling prices, we had all continuously repeated that "two and two still make four," much of the evil might have been averted. And I think it would be a salutary thing in the present situation, which in many respects so resembles the twenties, if we reminded ourselves of that immutable fact.

4

Shattering as were the effects of the crash, its full implications did not come at once.

I had expected some adverse reaction in the general economy to the market collapse. In fact, I thought the government ought to be prepared to counter any significant rise in unemployment. Within two weeks of that memorable Black Thursday, I wired Senator Joe Robinson: "Think it would be good idea for you to suggest that the United States government get a program ready for . . . [public] improvements to be put into effect as soon as unemployment commences to show itself. . . ."

But I never imagined, in those last months of 1929, that the collapse of stock prices was the prelude to the great depression. Anyone who knew the potentialities of the American economic system, as I had come to know them, could not help but believe that the market break would just as inevitably be followed by an even greater prosperity. In the long run, of course, that has happened. By and large, the value of securities today—and even of Florida land—is greater than it was in the days of the boom.

But I certainly did not know, and I doubt that any man in 1929 knew, how deep and terrible the depression would be, or how long it would take before the great forces of the American economy could reassert themselves. As the months went by, my initial confidence that the country would quickly right itself waned. From time to time in that first year after the crash, I thought the bottom had been reached. I was wrong. The economic indices kept falling lower still.

The present generation cannot, I think, grasp what the depression meant to those who lived through it. Millions of older Americans, however, must still recall with a shudder those dreary years of the early thirties, when as many as thirteen million people were unemployed; when crowds followed garbage collectors; when thousands of homeless men slept on the grass of Grant Park in Chicago, well within sight of the gaiety and glitter of the world's fair; when other thousands subsisted in makeshift shacks; when nagging fear shared the bed and board of most citizens; and when sound observers such as Hugh Johnson found such depths of desperation among the American people as to raise the specter of revolution.

I saw the effects of the depression up close in South Carolina, where a decade of agricultural depression had preceded the ultimate collapse and made it even worse. At Hobcaw, the people were taken care of, but some farmers in the area were utterly impoverished. My neighbor, Tom Yawkey, owner of the Boston Red Sox, and I helped provide food for them. But private charity could not make a ripple in the ocean of destitution.

Even in the darkest days of the depression, however, I never lost sight of the fundamental strength and wealth of America. Down in South Carolina I had seen storm and hurricane lay waste the land, leaving homes and farms and towns utterly shattered, the people dazed amid the remnants of their belongings. Yet no matter how hopeless the outlook, the people had always reclaimed and rebuilt when given the right kind of encouragement. I was sure that, with proper encouragement and help, we could recoup the grievous losses of the depression if the people's belief in themselves and their country could be restored.

But this was no easy thing to do. As the depression spread across the land, a black and brooding pessimism accompanied it. Worse, in many ways, than the joblessness and privation was the loss of will, the seeming hopelessness which gripped the country. The unreasoning optimism of the Coolidge years was replaced by the equally unreasoning defeatism of the Hoover years.

"Today fear, the most corroding of influences, is the moving cause . . ." I wrote in 1930. It was this feeling which President Roosevelt would recognize in his rallying cry for courage: "The only thing we have to fear is fear itself."

"Never have I witnessed such despair and hopelessness," I wrote Frank Kent on June 1, 1931. "Everybody is chucking it. You would think that the efforts of civilized man were going to drift back to the condition where cobwebs will cover the railroads, factories and mills. Where, oh, where are the brave leaders of 1929?"

Those leaders were resorting to the optimistic forecasts and cheery incantations that had worked during the boom years. But these could not work now to dispel fear and disillusion. As I told a group of distinguished financiers who, at President Hoover's request, asked me to join a movement to help restore confidence in Wall Street: "You can no more stop this liquidation with words than Al Smith could stop the cataract at Niagara with his brown derby."

The situation required far more than words. It required, for one thing, measures to alleviate the suffering of the unemployed. This could not be done through private charity or local aid as the Administration contended.

Those who argued that relief was not a responsibility of the federal government were not callous men. They were captives of economic theories. They had been brought up to think of government as having no role in economics, and not even the great emergency seemed to them sufficient reason to amend their views. In their concern with economic abstractions, they were largely unconscious of the "human equation," of the fundamental fact that all theories of economics and government come back at last to the individual and his fate.

But the unemployed were entitled to more than relief. "The unemployed have rights that are above charity—they have the right to work," I told a WIB reunion in November, 1931. And it was the responsibility of government to pursue policies which would permit men to exercise that right, policies which would also re-establish the confidence so essential to the restoration of business and employment.

But this, President Hoover was unable to do—and it was not for lack of ability or compassion. I have often said that if I were given some great responsibility and were allowed to choose the most able men I could find, Herbert Hoover would be among the first I would select—and I say this as one who did not always agree with him, as one who fought hard against him in some political and economic battles. But Mr. Hoover, who had so brilliantly mastered such great problems as Belgian and postwar relief, who had distinguished himself as a forceful and imaginative Secretary of Commerce, was unable to cope with the great depression.

I think most people have come to realize that President Hoover did not invent the depression; indeed, he was as much a victim of it as anyone. Nor were his efforts to combat it as meager as his detractors have claimed. The Reconstruction Finance Corporation, for example, was a constructive idea which the Roosevelt Administration continued. Yet Mr. Hoover was assailed as few Presidents have been; this shy, sensitive man was spiritually lacerated not only by unmerciful and often unfair attacks, but by the nation's suffering he was powerless to stop.

In recent years, the American public has shown Mr. Hoover some of the regard and affection which he deserves; and he has continued to serve his country well. The several commissions on government reorganization he has headed have done important and valuable work.

Although I believed that the policies pursued by Republican

Administrations during the twenties had contributed to the disaster,
I naturally felt that such an emergency as we now faced required
nonpartisan coöperation. Yet it must be admitted that many
Democrats were eager to take partisan advantage of the situation.

Shortly after the collapse, Garet Garrett called to say that he
wanted to see me urgently. I told him I was taking the train to
Albany to see Governor Roosevelt and that he could ride along
with me. He came as far as Poughkeepsie, and on the way talked
at length about the economic situation. We were old friends, and
could talk freely, but I could see that Garet was holding something
back.

As the conversation went on, I kept looking at him questioningly.
Finally he flushed and said, "All right, I'll tell you the truth.
Hoover asked me to get your thoughts." I told him I'd be glad to
give the President any help I could; he had only to ask.

The President did ask, and I was able to be of some help. In the
summer of 1931, for example, when he needed Democratic support
for a moratorium on war debts, he phoned from his Rapidan camp
and told me of his plans. I told him I thought it would be a
temporarily helpful measure, but that it would not alter the basic
situation. He asked me, nonetheless, to use my influence with
Democratic leaders in Congress to support the proposal.

It did not take long for these leaders to make their reaction
known. They were generally hostile. But I urged them not to tie
the President's hands when he was trying to do something constructive, and eventually I prevailed on them to give Mr. Hoover
the support he asked.

While the plans for the moratorium were getting under way,
I went to Europe. On the ship I met Ivar Kreuger, whose fabulous
juggling had resulted in a seemingly great financial empire. It
was soon to be shown as a gigantic fraud, and led to Kreuger's
suicide. On the ship, however, he gave no evidence of what was
impending.

When I got to Paris, Ambassador Walter Edge, acting on Mr.

Hoover's instructions, consulted with me on the moratorium discussions he was holding with the French. As a result of my help in
this matter, President Hoover cabled me: "I wish to thank you for
a real national service."

There were other occasions, however, when I could not respond
to requests from Mr. Hoover. When he appointed the Organization
on Unemployment Relief, Walter Gifford, who headed it, called
me at the Ritz Hotel in London, where I was staying. Speaking
from the White House, Gifford told me that the President wanted
me to join the committee. I told him that I could not accept, because it seemed clear to me that the unemployment committee
was inadequate to the task.

Also, despite the urging of friends, I declined appointment to
the Reconstruction Finance Corporation. I felt that I might be
better able to serve as a free agent than as a member of an
organization whose policies I would be required to support whether
or not I felt them right.

I was then asked to suggest some other Democrat—"one as smart
as Eugene Meyer," was the stipulation. I recommended Jesse Jones,
as smart as any man I have ever met. When F.D.R. became President, Jones became Chairman of the RFC and established a remarkable record there.

5

When one recalls the boom of the twenties and the ensuing crash,
one is haunted by the question: Can it happen again?

From time to time, most recently in 1958, our economy has
faltered badly, and a shudder of fear that we were about to plunge
into another depression has spread through the land. But each
time, with the help of safeguards built into our economy since
1929, we have regained our equilibrium. Such programs as unemployment insurance, bank deposit insurance, social security, and

a host of regulatory measures to prevent economic abuses, have helped maintain stability in time of stress. The investor in the stock market is protected today, as he was not in 1929, by a watchful SEC. He has the benefit of a vast amount of information that companies are required to divulge. He can also seek the advice of professional, disinterested investment analysts.

Nevertheless, the measures have not yet been devised which can permanently protect men from their folly.

There are many danger signals flying today, and many disturbing points of comparison with the boom of the 1920's. Our government owes an astronomical debt; private indebtedness is also at a record high. We are enjoying the good life on the installment plan. Public participation in the stock market exceeds anything we have ever known. True, speculation is not as unbridled as it was in the 1920's, but it is still dangerously prevalent. Taxes are huge, yet it is a rare occurrence when government, at any level, can balance its budget.

But added to all this, our economy of today operates in a world atmosphere of instability and uncertain peace. It will continue to be subjected to tremendous strains and pressures as long as the cold war continues.

Above all, the American economy is also laboring under the imbalances caused by a generation of inflation. And it is this inflation, more than anything else, which undermines our economic strength. If we are to maintain a healthy economy, we must learn to control this cancer.

Depths and heights are inevitable in any economy, and they are of course in direct ratio to each other. If we wish to escape the pit of depression, we must stay off the inflationary heights. We must learn to scale down the mountain of boom and fill in the valley of bust, so that economic progress can be achieved at a sure and steady pace. But if, for whatever reason, we succumb to some economic madness, we will surely let ourselves in for trouble. And, as in 1929, we shall have only ourselves to blame.

XIV

F.D.R. and the New Deal

AFTER THREE YEARS of grinding depression, the election of a Democratic President in 1932 was all but inevitable; with the prize so obviously to be had, there was no shortage of candidates.

Three men who had run before were ready to run again: James Cox, John W. Davis, and Al Smith. Newton D. Baker was prominently mentioned; so were Albert Ritchie, John Garner, and Owen D. Young. But, from the first, the leading candidate was Governor Franklin D. Roosevelt of New York.

Among the ambitious hopefuls and their friends, ever on the lookout for allies—and enemies—there was a pronounced interest in where I stood. All sorts of reports circulated, identifying me first with one candidate and then another. In the course of lauding some of my old associates at a WIB reunion in 1931, I had praised Bert Ritchie. This was taken as a sign that he was my choice for the nomination. Jim Farley, among others, was convinced that I was backing the drive for Ritchie.

It was a mistaken belief that died hard, persisting even into the convention. I was closer to Ritchie personally than to any other candidate, and thought he would have made a fine President. But I was determined not to break the resolve I had made in 1924 never again to participate in the nominating battles. As I wrote to Mc-Adoo a few months before the convention: "I haven't opposed anybody and I haven't advanced anybody's candidacy. Bert Ritchie could get the South Carolina delegation if I tried to help him, I believe, but I am not going to do anything to help him or anybody else just now. . . ."

In some quarters I was identified as favoring Al Smith. Another rumor had it that I really preferred Newton Baker. James F. Byrnes, to judge from his memoirs, still seems to be under that impression, but this report was no more true than the others. In fact, Baker would have been my last choice. Far more likely was another imaginary recipient of my support, the able Owen D. Young, then Chairman of the General Electric Company and an outstanding citizen. Young knew he was a potential dark horse, and gave me a letter authorizing me to speak for him if his name came before the convention; but that situation never arose.

In the months before the convention, Franklin Roosevelt's friends were particularly active on his behalf. W. Forbes Morgan, Jesse Straus, and others tried to smoke me out on the subject of the front runner. Some, not giving credence to my neutrality, felt I must be part of a stop-F.D.R. cabal, on the theory that if I wasn't for him I had to be against him. This attitude persisted in Farley and other F.D.R. lieutenants long after the election.

I must confess I was no Roosevelt enthusiast, but I was emphatically not part of any stop-Roosevelt movement. So many false stories were circulating about my pre-convention attitude, however, that I decided to set the record straight. I wrote to Roosevelt on December 8, 1931:

Many people are asking me about my views politically. Some have even wanted to know how I stood in reference to you, apparently coming from you. I always felt if you had any interest in my views that our relations are so close that you would personally make the inquiry, as our long-standing friendship requires no intermediary. I also feel that you know that if I had any opinions in the matter that I would express them frankly so that everybody would know where I stood. I am not interested in any candidate for the nomination by the party. I feel it is unwise to have these contentions as it may result in killing off some most desirable candidates. We will have trouble enough battling our opponents without battling with ourselves. . . .

I want you to know—and I am sure you do—that I would not engage in any surreptitious, underhand methods affecting anything that interests you. Your services to the nation, to the party and to the state certainly deserves better of a good citizen than that. Sometimes one's friends injure him more than one's enemies.

In my opinion the question that is going to be uppermost in the mind of any citizen when he faces the ballot box is, "Which one of these men is going to give me the better conditions under which to work out my existence and that of those dependent upon me?" Issues will be more economic than anything else. . . .

Governor Roosevelt replied, somewhat disingenuously, on December 19th:

> . . . In regard to the national political situation, I am much in the position of one who sits on the side lines and has little personal interest but a great deal of concern as a Democrat and a citizen. A sense of humor and a sense of proportion are both of assistance, especially because of the rather constant association with national and party problems since 1912.
>
> I do not need to tell you that I know you yourself would not engage in any surreptitious methods because you, too, realize that the situation from the national and the party viewpoint is too serious to engage in such tactics—and also because you personally are above them. But I cannot, of course, help knowing of the conversations of some people who profess friendship but nevertheless emit innuendoes and false statements behind my back with the blissful assumption that they will never be repeated to me.
>
> I am glad that you believe with me that issues this coming year will be more economic than anything else. It is not enough for us to say "the times are out of joint;" a more definite leadership is demanded; and at the same time this leadership can be success-

ful only through the greatest amount of party harmony during the coming year. . . .

I went to the Chicago convention ready, as I told Carter Glass, "to back the candidate whosoever he may be." Accompanying me were Hugh Johnson, and a party of friends including Mrs. Woodrow Wilson and her brother, John Randolph Bolling; Cary Grayson, Morton Schwartz and their wives; the publisher, Condé Nast; and the talented and charming Clare Boothe, now Luce, then an editor with the Nast publications. Although there was a difference of opinion among us over who the nominee would be, we were alike in believing that the Democratic convention would pick the next President.

Two days after we arrived, the convention opened and the really serious business of horse trading got under way. Throughout the convention I maintained my attitude of neutrality, taking a position only on the question of abolishing the two-thirds rule. Some Roosevelt lieutenants, fearful that the combined strength of Smith, Ritchie, Garner, and others would block F.D.R., began to urge a change in the rules in order to permit nomination by a simple majority. I was opposed to revising the rules once the convention was under way. I also felt that the two-thirds rule protected the South. Roosevelt, when he learned of the proposal, urged his supporters to withdraw it.

When the balloting began, Roosevelt quickly took a commanding lead. But he was still short of victory, and his drive seemed in danger of stalling. The astute Jim Farley, masterminding F.D.R.'s campaign, then came to me with an offer to deliver the Vice-presidential nomination to Ritchie if I could switch the Ritchie forces to Roosevelt. I told Jim he would have to woo the Ritchie camp himself.

Meanwhile, the old enmity between McAdoo and Smith flared again. Each came to me with charges against the other. McAdoo, who was supporting Garner, thought that Smith intended to swing to Newton Baker, whom he opposed. There were, in fact, many reasons to believe this might occur. Determined not to be caught, McAdoo planned to move before Smith did.

Smith, meanwhile, sent a man to me to find out if McAdoo intended to throw his support to Roosevelt. I didn't know McAdoo's intentions—but when California finally did switch to Roosevelt, it was not McAdoo's decision. The California delegation was controlled by William Randolph Hearst, who also was behind the Texas delegation through his support of John Garner. After the third ballot, when the going did indeed get rough, Hearst swung these two states behind F.D.R., which assured him the nomination, with second place going to Garner.

Once the Party had made its choice, I prepared to support our nominee. With Hugh Johnson, I went in search of Farley and Louis Howe. When I found them I said, "What are the orders?" I also telephoned Jimmy Byrnes, at the Roosevelt headquarters, to offer my help. Although Byrnes was eager to get me to participate in the campaign, my offer did not evoke any demonstration of enthusiasm on the part of others around headquarters. This reflected a resentment at my hands-off attitude during the nominating contest. It was a perfectly understandable reaction on the part of partisans, who had fought for their man and were naturally hostile to those who hadn't carried their flag. I could understand how they felt and harbored no resentment, nor did I intend to force my services on them. I simply let them know I was available, if wanted.

While the convention waited for Governor Roosevelt to make his dramatic flight to Chicago—the first time any nominee had ever appeared before a convention to accept a nomination—W. Forbes Morgan asked me to look over F.D.R.'s acceptance speech. A row had developed between Louis Howe, who had prepared one version, and Raymond Moley, the Columbia professor who headed the famous Brains Trust, who had been largely responsible for another draft which had been prepared even before the convention.

Howe had no objection to showing me his draft; but Moley did. He and I were soon to become good friends and co-workers, and I came to have the highest regard for his ability. But at the time, as he himself has described, he was resentful and suspicious of me. When Jesse Straus suggested that Moley show me the speech he had prepared, he exploded in fury, convinced that my influence would be used against it.

Moley, as he later admitted, misjudged my reaction. His speech, as I told him, was much better than the one Howe had prepared. F.D.R. thought so too. In deference to Howe's sensitive ego, however, Roosevelt used the first page of Howe's draft—but the remainder of his acceptance speech was the one Moley had worked on.

2

Surveying the divided condition of the Roosevelt camp, and aware of the mixed attitude toward me, I concluded that the best thing I could do was go home, which I did before F.D.R. arrived at the convention.

A few days after my return to New York, Roosevelt asked me to come to Hyde Park to attend a conference. I drove up to that sprawling, comfortable old house on the Hudson the next day. It was full of children and dogs, and the clutter which always gave F.D.R.'s surroundings that "lived-in" quality, whether it was the White House or his cottage in Warm Springs. I found the nominee highly confident; he was as certain as the rest of us that he would be the next President of the United States.

As I sat with him that night I could not help reflecting on how far he had come since I had first met him, a youthful State Senator taking on Tammany Hall in his fight against "Blue-eyed Billy" Sheehan. Later, during the First World War, I had known him even better as the able and sometimes brash assistant to Josephus Daniels. His driving energy in that job had resulted in a small flurry with me, when he tried to raise the Navy's copper requisitions after I had induced the producers to cut prices. I had to hold F.D.R. to his original figures, and in later years he often reminded me of our little hassle.

I could remember him, too, at the 1924 convention, clumping up to the podium on his crutches, making the huge hall forget his crippling handicap as he placed "The Happy Warrior" in nomination. I could remember his campaign for Governor in 1928 when, in the face of Republican landslides throughout the country, he had won. His four years as Governor had exceeded my expectations; I had not hoped for as much as he had achieved.

While he was in Albany, I had served as Chairman of the Saratoga Springs Commission, whose possibilities as a medical-therapeutic center interested us both. From time to time, he also sought my views on economic matters. Thus, on March 22, 1932, he had written me:

> I am getting on well with the nine hundred and some odd bills passed by the late lamented Legislature, and am so close to seeing daylight that I am wondering if you could not run up here some night soon or else to Hyde Park Saturday or Monday next, for the very good reason that I am most anxious to talk with you about the situation in general and about the economics of it in particular.
>
> As you know, I have had a tremendously busy three months but at the same time I have tried to read everything I could in regard to the fundamentals that lie beyond the control of this state. You have such clear thinking processes and such a fund of information that I should much like to get your slant on things.

Now he wanted my help in the coming campaign, and of course I was glad to give it. That night at Hyde Park was the first of the sessions I was to join during the campaign. Next morning, F.D.R. presided at a meeting of his chief advisers. Gathered around the table were Ray Moley, Louis Howe, Forbes Morgan, Adolf Berle, Jr., Hugh Johnson, and others I do not now recall. (Some of these men were soon to become known as part of the Brains Trust. I remember the first time I heard that phrase; as I joined a circle of his advisers one day, F.D.R. waved his hand and said: "Bernie, this is my Brains Trust, and you are the professor emeritus.")

We spent several hours discussing the issues and strategy of the campaign. Although he was later to alter his course, at this point my views and Roosevelt's were in accord, especially on the fundamentals of recovery.

Essentially, I believed that the many measures which government would have to undertake to help speed recovery would have to be based on sound economic principles. I did not believe in deficit financing, nor in tinkering with the currency or other inflationary panaceas. I did believe in refraining from spending money we didn't have, in sacrificing for frugality and revenue, in cutting unnecessary governmental spending, and in paying for everything we undertook out of taxation.

I believed then, as I do now, that the keystone in the arch of a sound economy is a balanced budget, and that preservation of the nation's credit is the first imperative for economic health. A balanced budget need not foreclose expenditures for relief. Indeed, I favored government building programs of a self-liquidating character—roads, bridges, and other public works—which would in time provide revenue. The only condition I attached to borrowing for such purposes was that sufficient taxes be levied to cover interest and amortization on these projects.

In some quarters today these views are considered hopelessly old-fashioned, but I know of no experience which invalidates them. Although I believe that the government has a vital role to play in regulating the economy, and although I reject the outworn dogmas of laissez faire, I do not believe that government can decree prosperity or legislate us out of the consequences of our folly.

After that first Hyde Park meeting, I gave Roosevelt a lengthy memorandum which Hugh Johnson had helped me prepare. It summarized the economic studies I had been making for the past three or four years, analyzed the budget and fiscal policies of the Hoover Administration, and capsuled my economic recommendations. In connection with this memo, Moley wrote to Roosevelt on July 16, 1932:

> Tugwell, Berle and I have had a number of conferences with Mr. Baruch and General Johnson and have discussed with them at some length the memorandum which Mr. Baruch has handed to you by now. It is a most excellent document.
>
> It seems to me that at the outset it would be wise for you to introduce your series of campaign speeches with a general indictment of the Hoover "New Economics," giving in detail much of the specific material in the first part of the Baruch memorandum.
>
> Following that, the subjects he treats might in large part be amplified into speeches. For the most part, his policies with regard to Tariff, National Budget and Foreign Debts are approximately in agreement with what Tugwell, Berle and I believe. With regard to Agriculture, the difference is not great. With regard to Taxation, we had no discussion.
>
> In my opinion, Mr. Baruch's memorandum is a distinctly valuable contribution to the campaign.

Throughout the campaign, I continued to provide a steady stream of memos, on economic and financial subjects, to F.D.R. and his staff. Roosevelt's program, at least as it was forecast in his campaign speeches, was one to which I could whole-heartedly subscribe, adhering as it did to tried and true economic principles.

In addition to contributing ideas to Roosevelt's campaign, I was able also to render service by helping enlist Al Smith in the fight. Smith had been bitterly disappointed by his failure to get the nomination, which he thought rightfully belonged to him. He had no intention of taking the stump for the man he felt had betrayed him and usurped his right. I could understand his disappointment, but I was not content to see him sit out the election. Neither the Party nor his own reputation would be served by such a course.

For three months he resisted every pressure to speak out for Roosevelt. Finally Felix Frankfurter, Herbert Swope, and I, in a last effort to persuade him, took him to lunch. We all had a turn at it, and Felix gave him a particularly stirring speech. Smith listened silently, and I could see the conflicting emotions rising within him as his face flushed red and the perspiration stood out.

When Frankfurter finished, Smith surrendered. "Well, you're right," he admitted, "and that's that." He turned to me: "But Barney," he said, "you've got to come with me when I make my speeches." I promised to accompany him on his first speaking trip.

All along the route, crowds were gathered at the stations to greet him. Some people thought his Newark speech was bitter because he attacked the people who had attacked him. But to all his old friends, it was as though he had reached out and taken them to his bosom and warmed their hearts by the fierceness of his assault upon his enemies, which was what his friends wanted to hear.

At Providence, Senator Peter Gerry and his wife headed the welcoming crowd. Local politicians were on hand to take the usual advantage of such occasions by making themselves seen and heard, but the crowd would have none of them. "We want Al," they chanted. I had seldom seen such a magnificent tribute before.

But the climax came in Boston. It did not seem possible to get through the huge crowd. I was torn away from Smith briefly, but he stopped and said, "I'm not moving until Barney Baruch gets with me."

The police succeeded in getting us together again. As we faced the surging, singing audience, Smith was visibly stirred. And when he rose, the great assemblage went wild.

Finally the tumult quieted. At first, he could not speak. He held out his hands to the audience in a simple, affecting gesture and said, "Home again!" With that, they broke loose once more; it sounded as if the roof would come off. Massachusetts had been true to him in 1928; and he was still their man.

Mayor James Curley, sitting next to me, shouted into my ear, "And this is the man I tried to take the state delegation from!"

referring to his attempt to swing the Massachusetts delegation from Smith to Roosevelt in the convention.

In his speech, Smith took these faithful followers and plunked them down for Franklin Roosevelt, proving how wrong his critics at headquarters had been when they said he would have no effect on the voters. "I know my people," Smith told me.

At last the campaign was over. This time, George Peek helped deliver the farm vote en bloc, and this time all but six states were in the Democratic column—reversing almost exactly the figures of 1928. The voters had paid little heed to Mr. Hoover's gloomy prediction, in his final speech of the campaign, that if Roosevelt won, grass would grow in the streets of a hundred cities and weeds would overrun millions of farms.

It was a Republican stalwart, William Allen White, who accurately assessed what the election meant—"a firm desire on the part of the American people to use government as an agency for human welfare." Another veteran politician, Winston Churchill, cabled me: ". . . Accept my congratulations on a grand slam in doubles no trumps."

3

As the nation waited for the new President to take over in the White House, an air of hopeful expectancy could be felt everywhere. During the campaign, F.D.R. had given a strong sample of the massive dose of confidence which he was to administer to the sick nation when he moved into the White House. This proved to be one of the President's distinguishing qualities—his ability to instill confidence in the people through all the ups and downs the nation experienced while he was in office.

Along with the surge of confidence that swept the country, there was endless speculation about personalities, new and old, who might be brought into Washington by the new Administration. Part of this conjecture was on the role I might be expected to play. The speculation was heightened when F.D.R. called me down to Warm Springs, where he was resting after the election.

During this visit, the President-elect and I, along with Hugh Johnson, who had played a vital role in the campaign, discussed the economic problems confronting the incoming Administration. F.D.R. asked me to continue to work with Moley, Rex Tugwell, and other of his advisers. He particularly wanted me to discuss with Henry Morgenthau, Jr., the plans which were being formulated for agricultural relief. This I did, and in the following weeks I devoted much time to consulting with these men.

These activities seemed to give credence to reports that I would be appointed to a post in the Administration. In fact, there seemed to be some sentiment in various Democratic quarters for me to be given a place in the Cabinet. Hearst, who had once been a vitriolic critic of mine, now urged Roosevelt, through McAdoo, to give me the State Department portfolio. So did Carter Glass. There were others, I was told, who urged the President to include me in his official family. But by the same token, I knew there were influential persons around the President who were most unhappy at the prospect of my being included in the Administration.

Shortly after the election, I had gone to see F.D.R. at his house on 65th Street in New York. Harold Ickes was there. It was the first time we met, and Ickes told me later how much he distrusted me then, and how concerned he was that I might join him in the Cabinet. Ickes had no cause for fear, because F.D.R. never offered me a Cabinet post, which makes it almost superfluous for me to add that I would not have accepted one.

My feelings about the talk of a Cabinet appointment were summed up in a letter I wrote McAdoo on November 21, 1932:

> I feel exactly about all the kindly suggestions that have been made about me as I did when you offered me my first opportunity for a Cabinet position in 1918. There are so many people who want these things that I would not want to stand in anyone's

way. I have never received a political preferment from the hands
of my friends and that is the way I would like [it] to be to the end
of my days.

Despite the fact that I held no place in the new Administration,
the rumors of my influence would not down. The appointments of
Hugh Johnson to head NRA and of George Peek to head the AAA
were widely interpreted as a tribute to my authority within the
Administration. These "Baruch men," so-called, were supposed to
be levers by which I exercised power. Intriguing though such notions may have been to Sunday supplement analysts, they were
without substance. Both men were the logical and obvious choices
for their respective posts. I was never even consulted about Johnson's appointment.

The rumors became even more outlandish through an incident
which occurred in June, 1933, at the time of the London Economic
Conference. The President had called me in, and I was working
closely with Secretary of the Treasury William Woodin and his
assistant, Dean Acheson. I was also in close touch with Moley,
who, as Assistant Secretary of State, was playing a leading role in
advising the President on the London negotiations. At a crucial
moment, when the Conference seemed about to collapse, Moley
dramatically left for London in hopes of saving the situation.

Before leaving, he asked me to stop in at his office and to keep
him advised of developments here at home. He mentioned this
fact to newspapermen at the time of his departure. I was astounded
when a great fanfare broke out in the press. Since the President
was vacationing at sea, and both Moley and his superior, Secretary
of State Hull, were in London, Moley's remark was interpreted
to mean that the nation's affairs had been placed in my hands.
News stories had me serving as "Acting Secretary of State" and as
"Assistant President."

Some of the men around the President were incensed by these
stories. A few may even have believed them. In any event, in a city

where the suggestion of power and influence is often taken for the substance, the story aroused a good deal of jealousy.

Far from being a power behind the scenes, my role during the New Deal was largely that of observer and critic. There was much in the New Deal that I applauded. But there was also much that disturbed me, and moved me to protest.

4

Washington has never seen anything like those first three months of F.D.R.'s Administration. A steady flood of ideas emanated from the White House, and were quickly translated into legislation during the famous Hundred Days. Among the measures enacted were the Emergency Banking Act, to reopen the banks and prevent the hoarding of gold; the Economy Act, to reduce government expenditures; the creation of TVA and CCC; the abandonment of the gold standard; the Emergency Farm Mortgage Act and Farm Credit Act; the Securities Act, requiring full disclosure on issue of new securities; and the AAA and NRA.

It was in the fate of these latter two New Deal experiments— the Agricultural Adjustment Act and the National Industrial Recovery Act—that I was particularly interested.

After more than a decade of fighting for farm equality, I was hopeful that the Roosevelt Administration would be able to alleviate farm distress, which had reached appalling proportions. Farm prices had plummeted fifty per cent in the three years since 1929 alone. Foreclosures were driving men from their land and violence was breaking out.

During and after the campaign, I had discussed the Administration's farm plans frequently with Morgenthau, Tugwell, Secretary of Agriculture Henry Wallace, and Wallace's estimable though over-academic adviser, Dr. Mordecai Ezekiel, as well as with the President himself. The program which the Administration formulated was embodied in the AAA, which sought to raise farm prices by adopting a policy of subsidizing farmers in order to control production—a policy which I seriously questioned.

When the bill was passed, Wallace called me to Washington and asked me to administer it. Present at this meeting were representatives of the processors, whose coöperation was essential if the bill were to succeed. They promised to sign on the dotted line if I accepted. I asked Wallace for a few days to consider. During that time, Wallace, evidently anxious for me to accept, asked George Peek whether he thought the President could induce me to do so.

"Nobody can do anything with the old boy if he doesn't believe in it himself," Peek said.

After restudying the bill, my misgivings were still so strong that I advised Wallace I could not accept responsibility for a measure which I thought unworkable. Peek was then offered the post. He took it on, with considerable misgivings himself. After a short and stormy tenure, during which he found himself increasingly at odds with the Administration, he resigned. Needless to say, the AAA did not solve the farm problem, which still remains to be solved. In 1935, the Agricultural Adjustment Act was declared unconstitutional.

As the AAA was designed to revive agriculture, so the NRA was conceived to restore industry. By exempting industry from anti-trust laws, by encouraging coöperation through trade associations, and by guaranteeing wages, hours, and working conditions for labor, the government hoped to revitalize business.

I was especially interested in the National Industrial Recovery Act because its central idea—of industrial coöperation under government controls for the public good—had its origins in the War Industries Board. It was no accident that among the chief contributors to the conception of NRA were WIB alumni, such as Hugh Johnson and Gerard Swope. Even the idea for an NRA insignia—the famous Blue Eagle—was taken from WIB. I had suggested such a symbol in a speech delivered in May, 1933, and as early as 1930

I had called for the suspension of anti-trust laws in order to permit industrial coöperation. I had also urged the application of WIB'S experience, in mobilizing the nation's economy, to the emergency created by the depression. Naturally my close relations with Hugh Johnson, who had played a major role in drafting the NRA statute and who was chosen by F.D.R. to run it, heightened my interest in the experiment.

If ever a man gave heart, mind, and soul to his work, Hugh did to the NRA. But that, of course, was how he devoted himself to every position he ever held. As a general in the First World War, he had done a superb job in the difficult task of running the draft. Later, he had ably represented the Army on WIB. After the war, he became my associate in business and public affairs; there were few in whom I put so much trust.

This talented man, a tireless worker, could dig out facts and organize them with extraordinary skill. As a human being he was colorful, vivid, and outspoken, with a command of racy, forthright language—a hearty, zestful man whose big laugh and rough voice filled a room. Some people wrote him off as "Old Iron Pants," a hard-living professional Army type. But he was gentle and literate beneath that bluster and conviviality, and he was a warm and loyal friend. His concern for those he loved was almost a legend with those who knew him well. General Jonathan "Skinny" Wainwright, the hero of Bataan, was one of his particular friends. I sat beside Johnson as he lay dying in Walter Reed Hospital, and the last words I heard him speak were: "Take care of Skinny Wainwright."

For all Johnson's efforts, however, the NRA fell far short of its goal. The public, which had at first rallied to the experiment, turned against it as the urgency of the crisis waned and its excesses and abuses appeared. There were not many who were overly upset when the Supreme Court declared it unconstitutional.

Although I attempted, as far as possible, to help Johnson in the herculean task he had undertaken, I was often unhappy with the measures adopted by NRA. On more than one occasion, I warned

Johnson that he was trying to do too much. In his zeal to combat the depression, he was forgetting the wisdom of Wilson's admonition to me when I was appointed Chairman of WIB: " . . . let alone what is being successfully done and interfere as little as possible with . . . normal processes."

This prescription of moderation is not easy to follow in times of stress. Many men in the new Administration seemed to think that recovery could be decreed. Unquestionably, the times required the government to intercede, and forcefully, in the nation's economic life. But the authority of government alone is never sufficient, as so many seemed to think, to force recovery. Social and economic problems do not automatically yield to government intervention.

"I have seen a lot of fiat measures," I wrote Josephus Daniels about the prevailing notion that the depression would yield to legislation. "I don't think any of them will ever work until we pass a fiat changing the law of supply and demand, and the workings of human nature."

For the fact is that although agencies proliferated and regulations abounded during the New Deal, we often worked against, rather than in harmony with, the natural curative processes inherent in our economic system. And while I was frankly dismayed at some of the fiscal policies of the New Deal, it was not the costs of the New Deal experiments which disturbed me. "The loss of money is not so very important," I wrote Joe Robinson in January, 1934. "It is important only to those who have permitted it to possess their souls." The important point, I went on to say, was whether the New Deal had "broken down the morale and character of our people and whether when it is all finished, they will be able again to fend for themselves."

This is what concerned me most. To extreme New Dealers, government seemed to be a great mother to whom we could run whenever we were in trouble, who would wipe our tears, calm our fears, keep us from harm, and tell us to go off and play when we got into trouble. But this is not the role of government in a democracy.

When mature men rely on government to take care of them, they renounce their independence. The thing that bothered me most about certain aspects of the New Deal was its tendency to dampen initiative and incentive in our people.

I was so often reminded of the story about the two frogs who jumped into separate cans of milk, which were sealed and put on a freight train. One frog called out, "Help! Help! Help!" The other cried, "Hustle! Hustle! Hustle!" When the cans were opened, the first frog was dead. But the second had hustled so hard that he had made a cake of butter on which he was sitting safely. Much of the New Deal, despite its good intentions, discouraged people from hustling for themselves.

An illustration of the failure of good intentions and experimentation in the New Deal was the Subsistence Homestead program, in which I took an active interest at the behest of Mrs. Roosevelt. I will pause here to say that Mrs. Roosevelt is as great and gallant a person as I have ever known. No good cause has ever been too modest, and no decent person too humble, for her to help. She has an admirable sense of humor, with the blessed ability to laugh at herself. Warmhearted as she is, however, she is tough-minded.

She has earned universal admiration, even from her critics. Clare Luce, who has often disagreed with Mrs. Roosevelt, remarked in a letter to me on her "honesty, integrity and good will. . . . Even though I do not agree with her in politics, I think she is a great lady. I could only wish I had half her patience, compassion, inflexibility of purpose and . . . physical durability."

The Subsistence Homestead program was a genuine back-to-the-soil movement which aimed to relieve population congestion in industrial centers and to assist farm families living on submarginal land. Because of its undeniable humanitarian character, it became a favorite project of Mrs. Roosevelt and, curiously enough, of hardbitten Louis Howe. Their dream, and that of others, was to see tidy little villages established where refugees from the poverty of both city and country could raise their own food in their own gardens, engage in light manufacturing, or take up hand weaving and woodworking.

Reedsville, in the terribly depressed coal-mining region of West Virginia, was selected as the first homestead site. But planners in Washington, with no conception of local needs and problems, soon made chaos out of this venture. The houses provided for the home-steaders were too flimsy for the severe West Virginia winters. They had to be redesigned and rebuilt at mounting costs which soon exceeded the homesteaders' ability to pay. There was not sufficient light industry in the area to provide employment, and there were no plans to recruit any. There was not even sufficient arable land available to support the family gardens.

Even while the Reedsville project was getting under way, I warned Mrs. Roosevelt of the mistakes that were being made. "Placing people in homes or in circumstances in which they cannot carry on, would be tragedy," I wrote. "The blame would rest entirely upon our shoulders. That is one thing I fear in connection with many of the things we are trying to do for people—that they may be left in circumstances where we have not helped them but have hurt them. . . ."

There were a good many aspects of the New Deal which were, like the Subsistence Homestead program, noble in purpose but hope-lessly inept in execution.

But if I was critical at times of New Deal measures, I was equally critical of the business community whose excesses and follies had helped bring on the depression and whose stubbornness helped prolong it. As I wrote to my old WIB associate, J. Leonard Replogle, on March 2, 1938:

No one knows better than you that the fault is not entirely on the side of government or in the laws that have been enacted. Many of these laws have been enacted for the purpose of doing away with injustices, whether they be in working conditions, wages or unfair competition. You and I know that business has not done its share first of all, in trying to keep its workers satisfied, and second, in joining with government in making regulations which we know are quite necessary.

I believe that if we had been wise and given better cooperation, we would have had better laws and a better administration of them.

Complain, as anyone may, about Roosevelt, he has at least awakened from its lethargy our consciousness of the need of those who are generally termed "the under-privileged."

If we do not go to sleep again and will do the right thing, everything will be all right. But no change in tax laws or any other laws will do us any good unless the great masses of people feel that they have been justly dealt with.

To Joseph E. Davies, then our Ambassador to Moscow, I wrote:

> There is not enough tolerance on either side. I think the business men have been fighting for silly, losing, rear-guard actions all the time. Roosevelt has awakened the consciousness of the people of this country to the necessity of an attitude of helpfulness towards the underprivileged . . . and it is well for us not to be lulled to sleep again. The wisdom with which we meet that problem will mark the progress of the world, because the world is looking to us for leadership. There is more in this country to divide, and it ought to be divided wisely and tolerantly. The extreme ends ought to be taken in hand. Both are unwise, intolerant and bigoted.

Nevertheless, there were times when I found some of the New Deal experiments pretty strong medicine to take. I was no more happy with "do-everything" government than I had been with "do-nothing" government of earlier years. I recognized and appreciated, of course, the many constructive aspects of the New Deal. The enactment of minimum wage and maximum hour legislation, which I heartily supported, the development of the Tennessee Valley, the adoption of Social Security—these and other measures were enduring achievements. But the fact remains that the New Deal did

not end the depression, and one of the reasons was that we tried
to spend our way rather than work our way out.

5

A great deal of what I felt to be wrong in the New Deal I attributed to the men around the President, rather than to F.D.R.
himself. By and large, Roosevelt was a shrewd, practical, and pragmatic politician. He once complained to me, "Rex Tugwell wants
me to do in a day what it would take many years to do." I have
no doubt, on the other hand, that he might well have complained
to Tugwell, "Bernie wants to go too slowly. But we've got to keep
the old fellow in line."

The mistakes of the New Deal no doubt mirrored certain qualities in the President—laudable qualities in themselves. One was
his compassion, his concern for people; another was his fascination
with new ideas. I can illustrate the first with a small episode which
occurred when I visited him in Warm Springs before the first
inaugural.

He took Hugh Johnson and me for a drive in his car, which
had been specially built so that he could drive it himself. We
meandered around the country roads for a while, and came at last
to a high ridge, where we could look down on a village nestling in
the valley below.

"There's a bank in that town," the President said, "and it holds
the mortgages and notes of all those people living there. Now
what I want to know, Bernie—are we going to get recovery by
squeezing these people out through the wringer by natural processes, or are we going to help them? I don't think we can put them
through the wringer." I agreed, but I warned that we must help
them to help themselves, and not make them dependent on government.

Roosevelt's remark exemplified his compassion. In spite of his errors of commission and omission, there was always in his decisions an essential concern for humanity.

But one can depart only so far from the lessons of experience and the natural laws of economics. Whatever government does must be in consonance with those laws; they can't be circumvented or ignored. The collision of this fact with Roosevelt's humanitarianism explains some of the shortcomings of the New Deal.

His fascination with new ideas was almost legendary. Ray Moley loved to tell the story of the crackpot who began to propound some very esoteric monetary ideas to F.D.R. The President seemed rapt as the man droned on and on. Finally, F.D.R. sent him off in a blaze of enthusiasm. When someone asked why he had given this eccentric so much time, the President looked ingenuous and said, "Well, he might have had something, you know."

Although I tried to support the President whenever possible, the gulf between the Administration's views and mine gradually widened. Increasingly I found myself in the role of critic, and unable to support him. One instance was in the Supreme Court fight in 1937. When he launched his court-packing plan, he invited me to the White House and asked for my support. I disagreed profoundly with him on this attempt to control the judiciary. I told him that "the best you can expect from me is silence."

There were other times when I could not give him even that, and fought him directly, as when he undertook his "purge" of the Senate in the following year.

Angered by the mounting resistance of many Democratic Senators, F.D.R. decided to seek their defeat in the election of 1938. Prominent on his blacklist were Senators Millard Tydings, Walter George, Guy Gillette, and "Cotton" Ed Smith. The President had expressed his resentment against these and other Senate Democrats to me, complaining that men such as Borah and Johnson gave him more support than some of the Democrats did.

I told him he ought to try to solidify his Party following, rather than alienate it. When I learned that he planned to add Alben

Barkley's name to his purge list, by supporting Albert Chandler's bid for the Senate nomination in Kentucky, I went to him to protest. Barkley was certainly one of the most able and loyal men in the Senate, I argued, and the President would be doing Barkley an injustice and himself a disservice by opposing him. F.D.R. agreed. He also told me he would not oppose Walter George, an assurance which I reported to the Senator. Shortly afterward, however, the President shared a platform with George in his home state, and to the amazement of all, asked the people of Georgia not to return him to the Senate. After that, the fight was on.

I contributed actively to the election campaigns of several of the men whom the President had marked for defeat. I felt that the President had no right to try to dictate the choice of candidates in the states. Furthermore, some of the men he sought to unseat shared my basic philosophy and were my personal friends. The President knew exactly where I stood in this fight, which he decisively lost. Whether I was for or against Roosevelt, I never failed to speak my mind to him.

You could disagree with F.D.R., but you couldn't stay angry—at least not for long. When charm was given out, I am sure he was first in line. He loved to talk, and he was always a wonderful companion. I attended many a "children's hour" when F.D.R. would relax, mixing very potent cocktails—"two fingers," he would grin, measuring the distance between his index and little fingers.

He could listen when he wanted to, and he had the knack of making the person doing the talking feel important. He concentrated on his visitor, and he seldom disagreed. While listening, the President had a habit of smiling and nodding his head. The uninitiated naturally took this to mean that the President was in full agreement with what they were saying, that he was nodding to confirm the wisdom of their opinions and the value of their suggestions. It was nothing of the kind. It was simply a Roosevelt mannerism. But many a man left F.D.R.'s office certain that the

President had endorsed whatever it was they were discussing, only to find out quite the opposite. The shock was often severe.

This geniality had another aspect. Mr. Roosevelt hated personal unpleasantness as a rule, though he could be acid and biting on occasion. Generally, when there were unpleasant decisions to impart, when someone had to be fired or reprimanded, he liked to delegate the job.

Once he tried to get me to lecture Jimmy Byrnes on the need for greater Senate coöperation with the White House. This was just a day or two after the funeral of the much-loved Joe Robinson. It was hardly the time to tell Senate Democrats that the President was dissatisfied with their support and expected them to work harder for his program. Many of Joe's friends believed he had literally worked himself to death on behalf of the President's Court plan—not because he favored it, but out of loyalty to F.D.R. I told the President: "No, sir, Mr. President, if you've got anything to say to Jimmy, you tell him."

There were other times when F.D.R. found me equally uncoöperative. Once, when he was trying to get me to agree to go along with him on a certain course of action and I failed to see it his way, he remarked, "Bernie, you know you're the most stubborn man in the world." I looked at him, smiled, and said, "Yes, Mr. President." He threw back his head and laughed uproariously, knowing that I had the same idea about him.

Despite my concern over some of the measures of the New Deal, my disagreement was submerged in my growing awareness of an imminent danger as the troubled thirties drew to a close. I refer to the prospect of war. It took no clairvoyance to discern the trend of events in Germany and Italy, and I was alarmed by the complacence with which the people of Britain, France, and America watched what was taking place. The dangers of unpreparedness, which I had been preaching for two decades, now assumed a more ominous shape than ever before, and I was more deeply concerned every day with the continuing public apathy about it.

In the light of this situation, I knew where the real test of both the President and the nation would come. I was determined to permit nothing—not my own doubts and disappointments over domestic policy; not the criticisms of me by others; and least of all not my own feelings, which at times were severely hurt—to keep me from helping wherever I could to prepare for the crisis that lay ahead.

XV

The Fight for Preparedness

A NEW ERA BEGAN with the year 1933, one which would reveal the heights and depths of which humanity is capable. President Roosevelt was inaugurated at the beginning of March; a month before, Hitler had become Chancellor of the Third Reich. While the President began mobilizing America for war against depression, Hitler started marshaling the resources of Germany for war against freedom.

I never had the slightest illusion about Hitler. At a time when most people were inclined to dismiss his boasts and threats as the hollow rantings of an excitable demagogue, I was one of that small minority in the democracies, of whom Churchill was the most prominent, who took Hitler seriously. By 1935 I was saying in public speeches: "Hitler and peace! The very terms are antithetical. He is today the greatest menace to world safety."

The free world, chronically apathetic, was unwilling to face this fact until too late. But for me, the rise of Hitler gave added urgency to the campaign for preparedness for war, which I had been waging for almost two decades.

From the end of World War One, the problems of preparedness, particularly those of its economic and industrial aspects, had been foremost in my mind. As a somewhat lonely realist in the deceptively halcyon twenties, I realized that war was an ever-present consideration in our national existence, that America could never again afford to be caught—as it had been in 1917—inadequately armed, and without any plan for mobilizing her resources or any blueprint for regulating her economy to the requirements of war.

In any future war, I knew, the delay and improvisation which had characterized our early World War One efforts would be costly and could be fatal. Consequently, year in and year out, in lectures before the Army's War College and Industrial College; in newspaper and magazine articles; in speeches; in discussions and correspondence with businessmen, labor leaders, generals, Congressmen, Cabinet Officers, and Presidents, I tried to impart the lessons I had learned in World War One.

Among these lessons were the need, in the event of war, for stringent taxes—to put the costs of war, as far as possible, on a pay-as-you-go basis; for control over prices, wages, and credit; for an effective priority system; and for centralized control over the entire mobilization program. I advocated the enactment of legislation which would, at a moment's notice, "mobilize effectively the resources of the nation . . . eliminate war profiteering; prevent wartime inflation and equalize wartime burdens." And I urged that this legislation be on the books *before* a crisis occurred. This we have never done. Even today, when we are again enveloped by the danger of war, we do not have a statute on the books which would provide for control of the economy in the event of war.

In this fight, as in others I have undertaken, I was espousing an unpopular cause. Among the few who shared my convictions were Congressman J.J. McSwain, of South Carolina, and Senator Capper, both of whom introduced bills on the subject. Pat Hurley and, later, Louis Johnson, when they were in the War Department, were also strong advocates of this cause. And the Army Industrial College undertook some studies and training programs. But these were only small islands of concern in a sea of indifference. For the most part, there was not much of a congregation for the gospel I preached.

In 1931, President Hoover appointed a Joint Congressional and Cabinet Commission to review America's mobilization plans. I testified before this Commission on behalf of a statute that would embody comprehensive economic controls in the event of war. But men of such standing as Army Chief of Staff Douglas MacArthur and former Secretary of War Baker challenged my views. General MacArthur was later to change his mind. But before the Commission, he and Baker argued against the need for over-all controls, especially over prices. They were willing to rely upon the methods of improvisation and voluntary coöperation which had carried us through World War One. So was the Commission; so was Congress.

As for the public, it simply mirrored the official attitudes toward preparedness—or perhaps it was the other way around. In any event, it was either apathetic or hostile. It is not hard to understand why, in view of the notions about war and peace which prevailed in those days.

The time between the wars was an era of naïveté about world affairs, studded with such well-meaning but ineffectual attempts to prevent war as the Washington Conference of 1921-22, the Kellogg-Briand Pact of 1929, and the London Naval Conference of 1930. These empty promises of peace fed the general conviction that war would never come again, and naturally bred apathy toward any discussion which presumed the possibility of international conflict.

I myself have never placed any faith in renunciations of war, or in disarmament agreements as a means of preserving peace. My views on this subject are implicit in a comment I wrote Arthur Krock in regard to the London Naval Conference in February, 1931:

> There is a great deal of nonsensical talk about this disarmament conference, [and] the outlawry of war. . . . I don't know of any greater nonsense than what is going on in London just now.

I believe the people are just as muddle-minded on this subject as they were on finance a few months ago. I should call this "international whoopee" instead of "financial whoopee."

In the past, disarmament treaties—lacking, as they always have, the provisions for enforcement—have actually been detrimental to peace. They have lulled peace-loving nations into a false sense of security, while potential aggressors went ahead unhindered with preparations for war.

Certainly, disarmament today is a goal we must pursue relentlessly and in good faith. We must try to lighten the costly burden of arms and diminish the danger of loaded guns, if at all possible. But let us not delude ourselves. *Peace does not follow disarmament; disarmament follows peace.*

We must remember, too, that disarmament agreements which rest on nothing more than treaty pledges are meaningless. They are worse; they are invitations to disaster. Only when disarmament can be effectively supervised and enforced by international authority —only when we have devised a reliable system of inspection and control—only then can we safely ground our arms. This principle was crucial in my thinking when, in 1946, I was given the task of drafting a plan for the control of nuclear energy, the most lethal weapon man has yet devised. Inspection, control, and punishment of violators were the cardinal tenets upon which the plan was based.

2

But the cause of preparedness was obstructed in those years between the wars, not only by a misplaced faith in pledges of disarmament, but by the militant opposition of those who believed that preparedness actually bred war. In its exaggerated form, the idea held that wars were made by "munitions makers." This myth, an article of faith with isolationists, was widely propagated by the activities of the Senate Committee to Investigate the Munitions Industry.

The Committee, established in 1934, was headed by Senator Gerald Nye, and included such well known and respected Senatorial figures as Arthur Vandenberg, Walter George, and Bennett Clark. Assistant counsel for the Committee was a rising young government lawyer named Alger Hiss.

Today, I suppose, the Committee's hearings are often remembered for the grotesque stunt perpetrated by a circus press agent who contrived to seat a midget in the lap of J.P. Morgan, one of several prominent bankers who testified. The picture that resulted became famous, although it was scarcely a contribution to the vital questions the Committee raised.

The blunt and naked purpose of the Nye Committee, as James F. Byrnes has phrased it, was to prove "the simple theory that war was the result of munitions makers' thirst for profits," and that these men were "merchants of death." As the theory had it, they were controlled by "international bankers." I was one of these, according to the charges made repeatedly against me by such men as Senator Huey Long and Father Charles Coughlin.

I might digress for a moment to say something about the Senator from Louisiana, who was in a class by himself as a demagogue. I was one of his favorite whipping boys; on more than one occasion, the Senate chamber echoed to his denunciations of me.

Just as the Nye Committee turned its attention to the emotion-charged subject of war profiteering, in December, 1934, President Roosevelt announced the appointment of a committee, under my chairmanship, to formulate plans for mobilization legislation. I had been after the President for some time to take such a step. At a White House meeting, he finally agreed to do so. Among those whom he named to the committee were Secretary of State Hull, Secretary of War George Dern, Army Chief of Staff MacArthur, Secretary of the Navy Swanson, Secretary of the Treasury Morgenthau, Secretary of Agriculture Wallace, George Peek, and Hugh Johnson. F.D.R.

dismissed my remonstration that it would be out-of-place for me, a private citizen, to preside over such a group.

The President's announcement was greeted with an outcry by Nye and his supporters, who saw it as a maneuver to check their investigation. Nye's adherents evidently feared that enactment of a mobilization bill, which would prevent profiteering in war, would make their inquiry superfluous. Whether this consideration was in the President's mind, I do not know; he certainly never discussed it with me.

As far as I was concerned, his decision to push for legislation in this field was necessary and proper. Such legislation was part of what I had been advocating in my campaign for preparedness—a goal far removed, of course, from that of the Nye Committee. But the furor which greeted his announcement made F.D.R. retreat.

In a meeting with Nye, the President assured him that he wanted the Senate munitions hearings to continue. As for the committee I headed, I don't believe there were more than two meetings. Hugh Johnson and I prepared some recommendations, but they were quickly filed and forgotten.

Having killed off this opportunity to get stand-by mobilization legislation on the books, the Nye Committee then invited me to testify. At the same time, Committee sources leaked the report that my tax returns for the war years were missing from government files. The implication of dirty work was clear; the innuendo was cultivated that I had connived at their destruction in order to conceal my wartime profits. The returns were missing, of course, but only because the government had thrown them away with countless others no longer needed.

Stale stories of my alleged wartime profits again went the rounds. I immediately offered to provide the Nye Committee with all the information I had, relating to my personal finances and wartime business transactions. I was angered by the smear attempt; more important, I knew that witch hunts such as Nye's could only weaken America's will and understanding on matters of defense at a time when it was becoming more and more important to face up to the impending storm. With the aid of my incomparably efficient secretary, Mary Boyle, I reconstructed my financial records for the war years; and with Herbert Swope at my side, I went down to testify before the Committee.

I laid before it all the facts they claimed were missing. I made all my records available, disclosing how I had divested myself of interest in any company manufacturing munitions of war. I showed that my income for 1917, the first year of America's entrance into the war, had been seventy per cent less than in previous years; that, in 1918 and 1919, I had received not a single dollar of taxable income, and had actually incurred net losses in both those years.

By the time I had completed my testimony, the Committee was denying that any invidious suggestions about my record had originated with or emanated from them. I remained on the witness stand for several days, being interrogated on the problems of mobilization and controlling wartime profits. Most of the questioning was done by Hiss, who struck me then as bright but dogmatic.

Out of these unpleasant proceedings, one happy experience was the way in which my friends rallied. James F. Byrnes appeared unannounced before the Committee to speak for me. Carter Glass also came to the hearings, to observe and comment on the Committee proceedings. To the vast delight of those sitting near him, he would mutter: "Never heard such dad bum fool questions in all my bo'n days."

Looking back on the Nye Committee almost fifteen years later, President Truman gave this opinion in a letter written to me on May 5, 1948:

I think the Nye Committee did more damage to the morale and welfare of this country than any other Committee that held Hearings in the Senate. It was fundamentally the cause of our continued isolationist program and contributed more than any other one thing to our complete unpreparedness when World War Two broke. I happened to be in the Senate while those Hearings were going on and I know what I am talking about.

3

While the Nye Committee was still holding its hearings, Hitler denounced the Versailles Treaty and Italy invaded Ethiopia. The following year, 1936, German troops were to march back into the Rhineland, and bloody civil war was to erupt in Spain.

The war clouds were gathering fast, but America—under the illusion, fostered by such as Nye, that we had been seduced into the First World War—withdrew into an isolationist shell, and sought to escape involvement in Europe's conflicts by adopting a doctrine of neutrality. The Neutrality Act of 1935 forebade the shipment of arms to belligerents. When the Act was extended, the following year, the granting of loans was also prohibited.

"We must not mumble, jumble, fumble or tumble into war," I told the South Carolina Press Association in January, 1936. These words expressed my hope that we might stay out of the conflict brewing in Europe; but they did not reflect my doubts that we could. I knew that declarations of neutrality and embargoes were no guarantees of peace. They had not succeeded in Jefferson's time; they would not, I feared, succeed now. Indeed, in this shrunken world in which we live today, no nation can take refuge in neutrality.

In the modern world, neutrality is a delusion. Carried to its ultimate end of refusing commercial intercourse with belligerents, it can amount to economic sanctions—which are, in effect, acts of war.

As for the embargo of lethal weapons—despite the idealism which may motivate it—it is often devoid of real justice. It serves the advantage of the stronger powers engaged in conflict, as it was to the advantage of Italy in her violation of Ethiopia, of Japan in her war on China. Moreover, everything is lethal in modern war, cotton as well as guns. To be consistent, an embargo would have to include not only guns and ammunition, but sealing wax and cabbages.

Today, there are no so-called "non-strategic" materials. In a recent appearance before a Presidential committee studying this subject, I challenged the members to name a commodity which could be said to have no military significance. There was a long silence broken finally when the Chairman suggested, "Bubble gum!" I would not be surprised to learn that even bubble gum has an important use in modern war.

These were some of the arguments I advanced before the Senate Foreign Relations Committee in 1939, in advocating the repeal of the Neutrality Act. I favored the more realistic "cash and carry" policy, which permitted nations to buy whatever they desired from us, including war goods, as long as they took title to their purchases in this country and carried them home in their own ships. To the extent that cash and carry favored a belligerent in control of the seas, I was ready to admit that "this is not neutrality—not by twenty sea miles." But if cash and carry, which Congress eventually adopted after war in Europe had erupted, helped Japan in her war with China, it also aided France and England to withstand the Germans.

If America hoped to stay out of war, I argued, it would not be through proclamations of neutrality, and not through a policy of weakness—but through a policy of strength. "If we want peace we must be prepared. If we are forced into war, we must be prepared." This was my insistent theme during those climactic years preceding World War Two.

In 1937, I came back from a trip abroad convinced of Hitler's purpose. I told reporters who met me at the ship that Europe was a tinderbox. The threat to peace was so clear that I could not understand why the nation was not alive to it.

For the following years, until Japan's attack upon Pearl Harbor, I kept sounding the tocsin of impending war. To those who would listen, and to some who wouldn't, I preached the urgency of rearmament, of stock-piling strategic raw materials, of enacting legislation for economic controls, and of establishing a mobilization organization to do the job WIB had done in 1918.

But there were few in Congress, in business, or in the press who shared my sense of urgency. I remember vainly trying to impress the journalist, John Chamberlain, with the inadequacy of the government's defense program. He was doing a piece on this subject for *Fortune* magazine. But, as he wrote me recently, ". . . nobody around the shop—whether they were editors, researchers, or writers —could see spending billions for armament at the time."

In the summer of 1938, before I went off on another trip to Europe, I visited F.D.R. at the White House. Hitler had invaded Austria that spring, and was then waging his war of nerves against Czechoslovakia. The need for mobilization planning had grown more compelling, and I had been pressing the President to appoint a group such as he had appointed in 1934 to draft mobilization legislation. I pointed out to him what it would mean, not only in terms of getting America's home front in order, but in encouraging the European democracies and perhaps giving Germany something to worry about. They'd be thinking: *Die Amerikaner kommen wieder!* "The Americans are coming again!" The President agreed, and said that he again wanted me to head the group. But first, he said, he wanted me to inquire into the defense situations abroad and report to him upon my return.

As I got up to leave, the President jotted down the following memo:

> DEFENSE COORDINATION BOARD
> To start Sept 1 and study
> & report to Pres. by Dec. 1st
> Chairman—B M Baruch

I spent several weeks in Europe gathering information on the French, English, and German armament situation. What I saw hardly reassured me that the Allies were equipped to call Hitler's bluff on Czechoslovakia—if, indeed, he were bluffing. Everyone had been talking about the splendid French Army. To me, it seemed just a shell; its purported Air Force was particularly inadequate. England's defenses were sketchier still. "Where are you going to get your shells and ammunition and guns?" I asked Sir Thomas Inskip, Minister for the Co-ordination of Defense. "From France," he replied. "You won't get anything," I said. Meanwhile, I learned something of German aircraft production and of the impressive build-up of the Luftwaffe through James Kindelberger, the aviation expert.

More disturbed than ever, I telephoned F.D.R. from Scotland on my birthday, August 19th, and said in effect that the democracies had nothing with which to stop Hitler. I suggested that I come home at once so that he could convene the Defense Coördination Board without further delay. I tried to impress upon him again that this action would hearten and encourage England and France and might give Germany pause. Above all, it would help get the defense wheels turning in America. But the President was noncommittal.

Winston Churchill came down to see me off when I left Europe. He was then out-of-office and in general disfavor because of his insistent warnings of war. He remarked a bit wistfully: "Well, the big show is going to be on pretty soon. You'll be in the forefront of it over there, and I'll be on the sidelines here." Fortunately, his reputation for foresight does not rest upon that prediction.

The trip left me disturbed not only by the relative state of preparedness between the democracies and Germany, but by the plight of Hitler's victims. I had many relatives who had felt the Nazi lash in Germany, my father's homeland. I had helped some of them to flee, but not all could get out. When Hitler instituted his "final solution" of the "Jewish question"—the gas chambers and ovens of the concentration camps—some of my relatives were among his victims.

I was profoundly conscious of the need for a place of refuge, not only for Jews but for others of all faiths and nationalities whom Hitler had marked for destruction. Regrettably, refugees had few places to go; the democracies found many excuses for not opening their doors.

During the trip abroad, I had discussed the refugee problem with King Leopold of Belgium, who had invited me to Brussels. The King told me that he did not know how to cope with the problems created by refugees who were streaming into his country. I asked him why Belgium couldn't throw open her African colonies and make welcome there all who would come. King Leopold said he could not do that because the land belonged to the natives. "You see," I said, "no one wants them."

During the next few years, I continued to think about the idea of establishing a sanctuary in Africa, financed by private funds and open to all refugees. With modern science, technology, and engineering, it would be possible, I believed, to create a refuge for all those who had lost their homes. There were a million and one reasons why such a plan was impracticable. Still, the desperate plight of hundreds of thousands of people could not be shrugged off because better solutions were not available.

I thought such a project might be realized under the leadership of Herbert Hoover. Hoover expressed sympathy with the idea when I presented it to him. So did President Roosevelt. As I explained my idea, F.D.R. sketched a map of Africa on a scratch pad, outlining the temperate, largely unpopulated areas where such a scheme might be put into effect.

The outbreak of war, however, relegated this hope to the scrap heap. Yet how many lives might have been saved could such a scheme have been adopted.

Shortly after I arrived home from my European trip, the President asked me to a private dinner at the White House to give him a full report. I summarized my observations of Germany's hell-bent progress toward war, and of the unpreparedness of Western Europe to withstand the impending assault.

I told him that we were running out of time, that we had to expand, modernize, and mechanize our Army, create a two-ocean

Navy, and build airplanes and still more airplanes—all of which should be paid for out of increased taxes. I emphasized the need of establishing better cultural and economic relations with Latin America, where German economic penetration could bring that continent under her control without a shot being fired. Finally, I urged the President to proceed with the appointment of the Defense Coördination Board and to ask for necessary mobilization legislation, as he had planned on doing before I had gone to Europe.

But he had abandoned that idea. I am sure that F.D.R. agreed in principle with everything I said. But he apparently felt that the public would not yet support an all-out commitment to mobilization. It still needed educating. In order to probe public sentiment and perhaps help educate it, he asked me, as our meeting broke up, to come back and give out a statement to the White House press corps on what I thought our defense program ought to be. "And then I'll back you up at my press conference," he said. Of course I agreed.

It was late at night when I left. I walked across Lafayette Park to my hotel. I was troubled and unhappy at what I thought was the President's excessive caution. But the next morning I went back to the White House to see Steve Early, the President's able and devoted press secretary. I told him what Roosevelt wanted me to do.

"Before you go out," Steve said, "I'll tip off the reporters that you have something to say."

When I emerged, the White House correspondents gathered around and asked me to comment on my visit with the President. I repeated what I had told Roosevelt—that we could not defend our own borders; that our armed forces ought to be increased to at least 400,000 men, equipped with modern weapons; that we should have a two-ocean Navy and a vastly increased Air Force; and that we should gear our industry to provide all the guns, planes, ships, and tanks we needed, all to be paid for out of increased taxes. I concluded with the point I had been hammering away at for so long—that we ought to place industry on a mobilized basis at once.

But, although the President did endorse almost all the points I made, he still failed to declare himself for all-out mobilization. He was silent, too, on the need for increased taxes.

The fact that my appeal for rearmament was issued from the White House steps naturally attracted much attention to my words —much of it critical. At home, the isolationist press and the lunatic fringe castigated me in terms only a little less rabid than those employed by the Nazi propaganda machine. It was not particularly pleasant to be cast in the role of Cassandra, but the fury I aroused in the Reichschancellory gave me at least some satisfaction.

My friend from World War One days, Samuel R. Fuller, Jr., acting as an unofficial emissary for the President, had gone on a trip to Germany. While there, he was taken by Hjalmar Schacht to visit Hitler. During that meeting, Fuller referred to me. As he later told me, the mention of my name sent Hitler into a paroxysm; he almost foamed at the mouth.

4

In a way I must have seemed obsessed on the subject of preparedness. Jimmy Byrnes once said to me, "Bernie, why does a man of your age want to get into a thing like this?" (I was then only sixty-eight.) Knowing how defenseless we were, I had no choice.

I knew that while we were ignoring the lessons of the last war, Germany was basing her mobilization plans on the experience of WIB, a fact which had been reported by our military attaché in Germany, Colonel Truman Smith. I knew, too, some of the distressing facts which could not be made public. For example, for lack of a minor appropriation of three million dollars, the War Department was unable to proceed with developing badly needed gunpowder facilities. As Louis Johnson has since revealed, I offered to advance these funds, but he was unable to accept my offer.

But above all, I knew just how defenseless we were. In 1940, our defense program called for only 2,710 .50 caliber anti-aircraft guns—yet we had only 728 on hand or contracted for. The plans called for 120 105 mm. howitzers, but only 48 were on hand or contracted for; 1,181,000 75 mm. shells, and not a single one in the stock pile; 578 Flying Fortresses required for hemisphere defense, and only 178 available.

There were, of course, men who shared my alarm, and who fought the battle for preparedness, though strangely enough Secretary of War Harry Woodring was not one of them. His Assistant Secretary, Louis Johnson, was. General Marshall once told me that "Germany would never have gotten off the ground" if America had had the full complement of B-17's which Johnson had requested before the war.

When he was Secretary of Defense in the Truman Administration, Johnson was blamed for stripping our forces so that we were unprepared for the Korean War. But he had been an excellent Assistant Secretary of War in the Roosevelt Administration, and F.D.R. had promised to appoint him Secretary when that post became vacant. When Woodring resigned in 1940, however, Roosevelt felt it necessary to bring Republicans into the Administration, and he named Henry L. Stimson Secretary of War.

I was in the President's office when Johnson, having learned of Stimson's appointment, sat in flushed and indignant silence while F.D.R. tried to explain the "reasons of state" which made it necessary for him to break his promise. After a while, Johnson could no longer contain himself. "But, Mr. President, you promised me not once but many times . . ." he began to protest, his face flushed and his voice unsteady. I recognized the danger signs on both sides. Reaching over with my foot, I gave Louis a gentle kick to tell him to shut up. He did.

General George Catlett Marshall, that great organizer of victory, was another with whom I worked closely in the campaign to build our defenses. I had known him since the time when he was General Pershing's aide. I remember the day Pershing told me at luncheon: "I have just done a great thing for our country. I have recommended to F.D.R. that he appoint Marshall as Chief of Staff." Pershing certainly did not exaggerate when he characterized Marshall as the greatest organizer in the Army and MacArthur as the greatest leader of troops. Marshall's contributions to America in war and peace, and his qualities of character, placed him among the foremost of our soldier-statesmen.

In those years, when he was trying to build up the Army, Marshall and I became warm friends. He used to explain his ideas to me. Once, he told me how he trained his commanders to handle large bodies of troops in mobile fashion, for he foresaw that the impending war would be fought very differently from World War One. On several occasions, he invited me to attend maneuvers and arranged for me to visit Army camps.

Several times, Marshall asked my help in his efforts to win Congressional support for his plans. Once I was able to help save an Alaskan defense appropriation, which was being stricken from the budget, by doing missionary work among certain Congressmen. On another occasion, I was asked to attend a dinner which Jimmy Byrnes gave for the purpose of having some of his Senatorial colleagues hear General Marshall and me discuss the military budget.

Marshall had asked me to lay before the guests some of the facts about the state of our preparedness. As I outlined the weaknesses of our program, the usually contained Marshall suddenly interrupted: "Let me take over, Baruch," he said, and then—with as much emotion as I have ever seen him display—he pleaded eloquently for the funds the Army needed. This meeting was a turning point in convincing such critics of preparedness as Senator Alva Adams of the urgent need for speeding the rebuilding of our defenses.

No one was more conscious of the inadequacy of these defenses than President Roosevelt. From the very first, he had recognized the aggressive designs of the dictatorships and reproved the weakness of the democracies, which invited these designs. Speaking in Chicago, in October, 1937, he had warned the nation that if agression succeeded abroad, " . . . let no one imagine that America will escape, that America may expect mercy, that this Western Hemisphere will not be attacked." His task was to shake America loose from its isolationist delusions before it was too late.

I realized what a formidable task this was. I realized, too, that it was an easy thing for me to preach re-arming, to call for increased military appropriations, to advocate all-out mobilization. I had no office, no formal responsibility, no political opposition, no need to accommodate conflicting policies and requirements, as did the President. I was fully conscious of the many threads he had to weave into the fabric of national unity. And I could understand why he felt the need for caution.

"Why is it," he complained to me, while his critics were still fuming over his call to "quarantine" the aggressors, "that you can talk like a Dutch uncle to the public, and if I do the same all hell breaks loose?"

On another of the many occasions when I was pressing him to take more decisive preparedness measures, he remarked, "A good leader can't get too far ahead of his followers."

But having said all this, I still believe that the President, on the issue of preparedness, moved too slowly. I believe that if he had laid it on the line to the American people, and provided on this issue the kind of dramatic leadership he had provided on others, the nation would have followed him.

Certainly, on the question of economic mobilization, there was an excess of caution, and undue procrastination. This was not a matter which involved the drafting of hundreds of thousands of men or the appropriation of billions of dollars. This was a subject on which the President could have acted on his own authority, to initiate plans and prepare an organization. It was not as if Roosevelt did not understand the importance of economic mobilization. Indeed, he had once shared my views. In March, 1931, after I had testified before President Hoover's Joint Congressional and Cabinet

Commission, F.D.R. had written me a warm letter, congratulating
me on my statement:

> I do hope that something will come of it for it is not either
> right or worthy of this country to lie back and get into the same
> kind of a jam as we had in 1917 in the event of another war.

Yet, we did find ourselves in such a jam. Not until the eve of
Germany's invasion of Poland did the President take his first step
toward mobilizing the economy. As he had planned to do in 1934
and 1938, only to change his mind on both occasions, now, in
August, 1939, he authorized the creation of the War Resources
Board. The Board was headed by the conscientious Edward Stet-
tinius, and included John Pratt, director of General Motors; Dr.
Harold Moulton, president of Brookings Institution; Dr. Karl
Compton, president of the Massachusetts Institute of Technology;
Walter Gifford, president of A.T. & T.; and General Robert Wood,
chairman of Sears, Roebuck. My close friend and associate, John
Hancock, was added later.

There was a good deal of speculation in Washington and in the
press over the fact that I was not included, and a good deal of conjecture over what the omission implied. I did not bother with
any speculation of my own; I simply offered my services and coöp-
erated with Stettinius in the course of his work.

The report made by the War Resources Board, in November,
followed closely the lines I had been advocating for twenty years.
A central provision was that in the event of war, the WRB would
assume the functions of the old WIB—that is, provide centralized
control over the emergency economic agencies and their activities.
But the President proved unwilling to accept this concept, unwilling to sanction centralized authority until the stumbling war
effort compelled him to do so. The report of the War Resources
Board was simply shelved; it was never even made public. The War
Resources Board itself was permitted to expire.

How does one explain the suppression of the War Resources

Board recommendations? How does one explain the President's apparent refusal to accept—until events were to compel him—the principles of mobilization which experience proved to be essential?

First of all, F.D.R. almost instinctively rejected the concept of a mobilization "czar." He never willingly entrusted great authority to a single subordinate. He liked to keep the reins in his own hands.

A second factor, and this was related to his reluctance to delegate power, was the President's belief that war and war mobilization might give industry the opportunity to dominate the economy. Suspicious of big business, of "Economic Royalists," he and many of the men around him feared that the leaders of big business—who would necessarily play a vital role in a defense production program—might create an industrial oligarchy. This fear was, in my judgment, without foundation. Still, it was widely accepted that one reason why F.D.R. permitted the War Resources Board to expire was because he would not entrust power over the defense program to a group under the supposed domination of "the Morgan interests."

A third factor in F.D.R.'s approach to the mobilization question was politics. In announcing that the report of the WRB would not be published, the President explained that the public was not interested in plans for war. The politically sophisticated would have said that, with the 1940 elections impending, it was preferable not to provoke the voters with talk of the danger of war and the need for unpleasant controls and restrictions. The issue of a third term would be exacerbating enough.

This issue was, indeed, agitating a great many people as the election year began. For myself, I was not pleased with the idea of breaking the two-term tradition. But the question was academic. The Democrats had nobody else to offer, and there was never any doubt in my mind that F.D.R. would run.

I remember a dinner I had with the President early that year. He had just hammered back the cork into a bottle of sherry and was discoursing on the British appreciation of that wine. Then, turning the conversation to politics, he said, "Who do you think would make a good candidate for the Presidency?" I answered, "Mr. President, are you trying to kid me or kid yourself?" F.D.R. threw back his head and laughed, in his characteristic way. Then he went on to say that he would like to have Hull for his running mate, and asked me if I would use my influence to persuade Hull to accept. I spoke to my old friend, but he told me that he did not wish to be considered for the Vice-presidency. The President finally chose Henry Wallace.

5

It was not until May, 1940, when Europe had already been at war for more than six months, that the President created the first of the many organizations which were to grapple with the mobilization effort. With defense production just getting under way, he resurrected from World War One days the Council of National Defense and its Advisory Commission. To the Commission he appointed Stettinius, Sidney Hillman, William Knudsen, Leon Henderson, Ralph Budd, Chester Davis, and Harriet Elliott.

But this was merely repeating the errors of the past. The Advisory Commission had been ineffective in 1916; it was ineffective now. This was soon recognized, and after the 1940 elections, the President established the Office of Price Administration and Civilian Supply, under the direction of Leon Henderson, an energetic, cigar-smoking, dynamo of a man. At the same time, he created the Office of Production Management.

The creation of these agencies was scarcely an improvement. For one thing, it violated the fundamental principle that all control—allocation, priority, price-fixing—should be centralized in one agency. Not even OPM functioned under the authority of one man. Ostensibly to preserve a balance between labor and industry, the President had named Knudsen and Hillman to preside jointly over it.

My relations with Hillman were never very close; I found him doctrinaire. He had no experience in production and economic mobilization, but was acting in OPM as a guardian of labor during an emergency. Like some other Presidential advisers, Hillman seemed convinced that the lessons of 1917-18 were no longer applicable. For me, there has always seemed to be little hope for the future unless we are able to learn from the past. Hillman's view of me, and of the lessons I was trying to impart, was summed up by a blunt remark he made when we were discussing the problems of the OPM: "I don't want to hear about that old World War One stuff."

Knudsen was a different type, a great Dane of a man, a production genius who was happy only at his work. The intrigues of Washington, the demands of politics, and the formalized rituals of government were not for him. Before he took over his OPM job, Knudsen came to New York to see me. We had lunch together and discussed the Washington scene and defense production problems. He remarked, in his still strong accent, "I don't understand this political nonsense. I'll work for you or the President, but nobody else."

Knudsen was miscast in OPM. Telling me about his adventures there, he once remarked that he felt like an old cat trying to make progress on a highly polished floor. When that agency was, inevitably, superseded, he became the Army's production chief, a job I had originally recommended him for. In that position, he performed an invaluable service to the nation.

For almost a year, OPM struggled manfully but inadequately to give force and direction to the accelerating defense effort. But its shortcomings, particularly the breakdown of its priority system, finally compelled the President, in August, 1941, to create yet another organization. This was SPAB—the Supply, Priorities and Allocation Board—another alphabetical mistake.

SPAB was, in effect, an enlargement of the existing board of

OPM, which consisted of Knudsen and Hillman and the two service secretaries, Stimson and Frank Knox. SPAB comprised these
men and three others: Henderson, then head of OPACS; Hopkins,
in charge of Lend-Lease; and Wallace, serving as Chairman of the
Board of Economic Warfare. Donald M. Nelson was named Executive Director. But all that SPAB actually did was to bring around
the table all the agencies with a responsibility for distributing
available supply. It did not put the priority power where it belonged—in the hands of one responsible official. SPAB was fine
as a high-level general staff, but it lacked a commander.

The President, it seemed to me, was going from one mistake to
another with the creation of these successive agencies, and making
the same basic mistake with each of them. As one observer later
put it, "Control by no one was the plan and the result during the
year that culminated in Pearl Harbor."

On the day Roosevelt announced the creation of SPAB, he
called me down to the White House. I suppose he knew that I
was going to be unhappy, and perhaps he was a little concerned
about my reaction, since he was trying to get my support for this
step. He was right; I was unhappy—and had been for a long time.
Still, I had done my best to go along, and to help wherever possible.

I know my constant insistence on one-man control of the defense
effort had annoyed and even angered the President at times. Once,
at a news conference, when he was asked about the "Baruch plan,"
he retorted with impatience that he had never heard of it. On another occasion, he had burst out irritably that he was sick and
tired of hearing that he would have to appoint another Baruch to
do the mobilization job.

When the President told me about SPAB, I told him plainly that
it fell far short of what the situation required. As I left the White
House, I was stopped on the steps by reporters who asked what
I thought of the new defense setup. I was so upset by the course
of events that I could think of nothing more charitable to say than
that I considered it "a faltering step forward."

When I got back to the Carlton Hotel, where I was staying, my statement had already reached the Presidential sanctum. General Edwin "Pa" Watson, the President's secretary, was on the phone, asking me to modify what I had said. I told Watson, "Pa, I'll be glad to change my statement. But if I do, I'll have to say that SPAB is a faltering step backward."

I amplified my feelings in the following letter, written on September 10th, to General Watson:

> You cannot doubt my affectionate loyalty to the President and to you. But, loyalty does not mean subservience or no honest criticism.
>
> When cleared of all the verbiage, what I said the other day is what I have said and repeated for twenty years. I was irked by the unnecessary delays in reaching the present formula.
>
> Don't forget this last action is the third setup. Regarding each one of them I made the same remark. I said the same thing about price-fixing. If you will look back to the memoranda, recommendations and objections I made to the President—all frank and in detail—you will find that many of the things accomplished have been along the lines of my suggestions. They were not my ideas alone. They were culled from a number of people and from the experiences of myself and many others. There is hardly a thing that has been done in the way of industrial mobilization that has not come out of the experience of the past. Where that experience has been ignored, we have faltered.
>
> I called the President's attention to all these things in 1937, 1938, 1939 and 1940 and down to the present time.
>
> However, there is no good going into "I told you so" because that only makes for bitterness and I have nothing of that in my soul. I only wish I had been wrong!
>
> I have but one object and I never talk about but one subject and that is to get the production which the President needs so badly to carry out the hopes we all have of beating Hitler and making a better world for us all to live in.
>
> It burns me up when I see men advising the President to do things in which they do not believe themselves. However, I feel quite calm and only hope that the present change will succeed. They have already asked for suggestions which I have made. It

will command my interest and effort, as every part of the national program has done.

I know of your affectionate regard for me but I do not want you for one single moment, ever to defend me or my actions. You have one job, and one job alone (and you are doing it well),—to help the President. I have tried to help him. I shall continue to do what I think is right. You may rest assured I will never do anything mean or dishonorable.

I am sorry if I have caused you or him any distress but I have acted, as I must, according to my lights.

Another moment of friction came in October, when William Randolph Hearst published a letter I had written him endorsing the militant stand he had taken in the preparedness fight. The Hearst papers had long been ardent advocates of preparedness, and were far more critical than I of the President's failure to go far enough and fast enough. Hearst used my letter on the front pages of his newspaper. Reading it in Hyde Park, F.D.R. was angered—by the letter itself and by the fact that I seemed to be giving aid and comfort to the "enemy." But rather than approach me directly, he instructed Steve Early to ask me for an explanation.

There was an affectionate bond between Early and me. But when he approached me on this matter, I knew he was speaking as the President's aide. I had no intention of being intimidated—or, for that matter, offended. But I intended to stick by my principles—and I told Early so.

If such organizations as OPM and SPAB were handicapped by the President's failure to centralize authority, OPACS was similarly handicapped by the failure of Congress to enact a strong price-control bill. True, the outbreak of war in Europe had induced Congress to approve large sums of money for defense. But it did not take the corollary step of providing controls that would curb inflation, hold down the costs of the defense program, and prevent profiteering.

In the fall of 1941, Congress belatedly took up a price-control bill, and I was called to testify before the House Banking and Currency Committee. Appearing on September 19th, I told the Committee:

> I do not believe in piecemeal price fixing. I think you have first to put a ceiling over the whole price structure, including wages, rents, and farm prices up to the parity level—and no higher—and then to adjust separate price schedules upward or downward, if necessary, where justice or governmental policy so requires.
>
> I do not believe that you can treat price control as a separate effort. It must be intimately tied up and move in step with all other war controls, wage and rent control, priorities, conservation, commandeering, war trade, war finance, and so forth. They are like the fingers of a hand. Without all together, the job cannot be done satisfactorily. . . .
>
> The control of prices is essential for the successful conduct of our national defense, for avoiding social and economic aftermaths of war, for taking the profits out of war, for the maintenance of morale, the stoppage of inflation, and the placing of America in the dominating place at the peace table. . . . With such great stakes we cannot afford an ineffective program of price control. . . .

There were men in Congress ready to support an effective price-control bill, including Albert Gore of Tennessee, who introduced one, and Clinton Anderson, Mike Monroney, and Jerry Voorhis. These men were willing to do the right thing, even though it was unpopular. Evidently, it didn't hurt them, either. Gore, Anderson, and Monroney, at least, have moved up the political ladder. Marriner Eccles, of the Federal Reserve System, was also one of the few who favored over-all controls.

But there were not enough in Congress or the Administration who shared the views of these men. Henderson, Hillman, Nelson, Morgenthau, and Hopkins were among those who thought we could make piece-meal controls effective. During the fight over the price-control bill, I wrote to my friend, Joseph Pulitzer, of the St. Louis *Post-Dispatch:*

The price control bill as now before Congress, if carried out, will be an inflationary bill and in the end will do only harm to those it seeks to benefit. And when peace comes, with the high price structure we are now fastening upon ourselves, we will pay the cost of the peace. . . . A low price structure is the only thing that will help us and the world. The selfish interests—farmers, laborers, and all the other segments of society struggling to better themselves at the expense of one another—will find that they have hurt themselves and injured the whole social and economic structure of America.

This is exactly what came to pass. Pressure groups got to work. Each could advance cogent and compelling reasons why it should be exempt from controls, or should be given a privileged position. When the price-control bill was finally enacted, the farmers got special dispensation, as did labor. In addition, taxes were never really high enough. All in all, no segment of our economy was asked to bear the load it should have borne.

6

I was sitting in my hotel room in Washington on Tuesday, December 2, 1941, when I received a call from Ray Moley. He asked if I would see a Mr. Raoul Desvernine, an attorney for the Japanese Mitsui interests, on a matter of great importance. I agreed, of course, and when Desvernine came in he asked me to meet with Japanese special envoy Kurusu—then engaged, with his compatriot, Ambassador Nomura, in fateful discussions with our State Department.

These conversations had been going on since mid-November as the United States sought some just *modus vivendi* with the Japanese, under which Tokyo would abandon its aggressive designs. The Japanese had, at this time, invaded Indo-China, and were poised to move on Thailand. The Nomura-Kurusu-Hull discussions were now at an impasse, for we found it impossible to accept Japanese demands. War seemed imminent.

Desvernine explained that Kurusu wanted to get a message directly to the President, without going through the State Department, and hoped that I might help. I told Desvernine that I could not see the Japanese envoy for so irregular a reason, and at so delicate a moment, without consulting the White House. I then called General Watson and told him of the strange request. After consulting the President, Watson advised me that the President would not meet Kurusu without Hull, but had no objection to my seeing the Japanese to find out what message he wished to transmit.

Accordingly, I met with Kurusu and Desvernine at the Mayflower Hotel on Wednesday, December 3rd. What Kurusu had to say was truly extraordinary.

He assured me that he himself wanted peace, that the Japanese people and the Emperor wanted peace, but that the war lords were sitting with a loaded gun in each hand, as he put it, determined to shoot. He thought, however, that such a calamity might still be averted. It was imperative, he said, that he see the President privately; Secretary Hull, he claimed, was hostile and untrusting. If the President would set aside protocol and receive him without Hull's presence, Kurusu was sure that the proposals he would put before him would prove acceptable.

When I asked Kurusu what exactly were his proposals, he replied that it was paramount that President Roosevelt appeal directly and personally to the Emperor—which Kurusu felt would immobilize the military. He further proposed that the President act as intermediary in the war between Japan and China. He assured me that Japan would accept such an offer and that she was prepared to negotiate with Chiang Kai-shek on a general settlement. He stressed the need to keep the conversations going between his government and ours, and suggested that this could be done if the President sent a personal representative, such as Hopkins, to Japan, as Japan had sent Kurusu here.

At my request, Kurusu then dictated the substance of his proposals to Desvernine, who took them down in longhand. I reproduce Desvernine's notes:

> The following idea must come from President not from Government and is based upon the the expression of the President of his being the "introducer."
>
> That they [Japan] will accept introduction and good offices of President in Chinese situation and that they will agree to confer with Chinese Government (Chiang Kai-shek) as to a general settlement with China. They only have in mind keeping troops on Mongolian border with Russia & 1 or 2 garrison in North China all to be agreed to by military experts of Japan, China & U.S. All other troops in China to be slowly evacuated as military experts shall agree—this refers to only question of time.
>
> Southern troops to be withdrawn upon complete settlement.
>
> 2. Pending such conference, Japan agrees no further military advances—will freeze existing military situation & possibly have a general military truce.
> 3. Indo-China question entirely dependent upon settlement of Chinese incident.
> 4. If President desires he can secure commitment confidentially in advance of any announcement.
> 5. State Dept. will only represent Chinese cause & requires full agreements on all points in advance, whereas they [Japan] are willing to settle questions in course of conversations under President's introduction, thereby avoiding appearance of capitulation.
> 6. Axis treaty can be settled by formula.
> 7. Non-discrimatory trade purely matter of establishing details in a treaty to be negotiated and principle admitted.
> 8. Breaking down attitudes—peace possible.
> 9. Keep open.

I did not then know enough about the situation to be able to judge the merit of Kurusu's proposals. I did feel, as I wrote in a memo at the time, that they "did not seem to me to be anything into which anybody could put their teeth." Certainly, China could not be expected to accept the continued presence of Japanese troops on her territory as a precondition to a general settlement, nor could the United States endorse such a proposal. We know now that Hull distrusted Kurusu, and felt that the envoy's role was to lull the United States until Japan was ready to strike. I do not know whether such was the case, though I must say that Kurusu seemed entirely sincere to me.

Before Kurusu left, I promised him I would convey his message to the White House. I told him, too, with emphasis, that if Japan went to war with us, she would surely be crushed.

I immediately telephoned General Watson, who came over with a White House stenographer to whom I dictated a summary of my conversation with Kurusu. On December 6th, the President did, in fact, appeal directly to the Emperor. Such an appeal had been under discussion for several days in the White House. But, of course, it was now too late to stay Tojo. On December 7th, the war lords struck.

XVI

War Production Problems

P EARL HARBOR, in one horrifying, shattering Sunday afternoon,
stripped America of the illusion we had so long nurtured—
that we were exempt from aggression. On that bleak and bitter day,
we were at last compelled to face the truth that we were unprepared
to fight a war in our own defense.

As is so often the case when calamity strikes, a search for scape-
goats began. There was a plentiful supply on hand in both the
armed forces and in the government. But while our leaders may
have been much at fault, in the last analysis it was the people themselves who were to blame. If there had been official apathy or inefficiency in the face of grave danger, it was only a reflection of the
national attitude in the decades since the First War.

Still, that fateful afternoon in the Pacific galvanized the country.
As it always has, crisis brought out the best in the American people. Even during that dark winter of 1941-42—with Europe overrun, Britain under siege, our arsenal all but empty, and our Naval
shield lying on the ocean floor—even then, America seemed never
to doubt the final outcome.

For me, the years of sounding the alarm were over. Now the task was to help fight the fire. For more than a year before Pearl Harbor, I had been serving as an adviser and trouble-shooter in the defense program. Now I was to be involved almost full-time in the war effort. I had no office, no title, but functioned, in effect, as an unofficial free-lance, helping wherever I could, taking emergency assignments from the President and his assistants in the production and procurement programs.

In January, 1942, President Roosevelt finally placed authority for war production in one man's hands when he appointed Donald Nelson as Chairman of the War Production Board. Such a step was one I had been urging for years. Had it come earlier, we would have been spared the consequences of trial and error which inevitably accompanied the WPB's early efforts.

These trials and errors were many—too many. It took almost two years for the WPB to get our war production program into high gear. Our failure to mobilize properly, and in time, cost us billions of dollars. But infinitely more important, it added months to the conflict and names to the casualty lists.

Nelson's appointment had come as a surprise to me. Sometime before he took this step, Roosevelt had asked my opinion on whom he might appoint to recommend changes in the war production organization. I had suggested five top-flight men: James Byrnes, William O. Douglas, Wendell Willkie, John Hancock, and Charles E. Wilson. "In no circumstances should it include me," I wrote Pa Watson, "as I would be looked upon as a 'prejudiced' investigator." Either Byrnes or Douglas, I added, would make an excellent choice to head a new war production setup.

Subsequently, the President told me that he had decided to name Douglas, and he asked me to be present when he discussed the matter with him. F.D.R. did offer the post to Douglas. But at the last minute—in a maneuver which was to become common—he switched to Nelson, whom Harry Hopkins enthusiastically favored.

Nevertheless, I was delighted that the President had appointed a man as qualified as Nelson seemed to be. He had made an enviable reputation for himself at Sears, Roebuck, and had been called early into the defense production program, where his ability had attracted much attention.

At the President's request, I sat in with Nelson and tried to help him in every possible way. Some men might have resented me, with the rather strange position I occupied in official Washington as a free-lancer without portfolio. Nelson did not. He told me that he wanted my assistance and wished to take advantage of the experience I had. The press and the public looked to me as the expert in the field, he said, and he hoped for my support. I was glad to give it.

At Nelson's request, I came down to Washington to speak before influential groups of industrial leaders—the men who, in effect, were going to have to carry out Nelson's programs and orders—and I besought their coöperation for WPB.

I worked closely with Nelson, and with Jim Knowlson, William Batt, Charles E. Wilson, Sidney Weinberg, and other top associates in WPB. Nelson and I would usually have dinner together on Wednesday evenings, and we would go over WPB problems. Looking over my memos to Nelson of that period, I see that in February, 1942, I sent him a report on the raw materials situation. A month later, at his request, I was investigating the role of small business in war production. In May, the job was to help break the bottlenecks in shipbuilding.

I tried to support Nelson on every occasion. My attitude toward him and his task is reflected in the following memo I sent him on July 6th:

. . . You must be the boss and when you say anything . . . it just has to go. You may make some wrong decisions but I would not let anyone question any decision you make. Everyone must make good on them after you have made them. Otherwise the authority you have been given will be worthless. . . .

You have always been very kind and courteous to me. I have tried to be helpful and I want you to know that I will be with you at all times. We have just got to pull this thing out. The tougher it is and the worse it looks, the more certain we must be and the harder we must work. If the home front becomes dissatisfied, the appeasers will get in their fine work. . . . You must see that the Army, the Navy, the Marines and the Air Force . . . get what they want with the least exploitation of the civilians. I am sure, as you are, that the American people will take what they have to take, if they are certain it is necessary.

2

In addition to working with Nelson and the WPB, I was privileged to assist the men running other war agencies: Leon Henderson, and later Chester Bowles, in the Office of Price Administration; Admiral Emory Land, the peppery, driving sailor in the Maritime Commission; Milo Perkins, on the Board of Economic Warfare; Robert A. Lovett, Assistant Secretary of War for Air, and the distinguished son of my WIB colleague; Robert Patterson, Undersecretary of War; James Forrestal, Undersecretary of the Navy; General Lucius Clay; General Brehon Somervell; General Levin Campbell; and General "Hap" Arnold.

Of all the men in wartime Washington, Bob Patterson and Jim Forrestal were among those I admired most. Patterson had enjoyed a distinguished career on the bench, having been appointed first by Hoover to the District Court and then by Roosevelt to the Circuit Court of Appeals. The fact that he was a Republican may have served the cause of bipartisanship in the Administration, but his ability and patriotism served an even more important purpose —winning the war. When Stimson brought Patterson to Washington to take over the major responsibility of procuring the Army's requirements, the President asked me to help him.

What I liked most about Patterson was his absolute concentration on the job of winning the war. He tolerated no compromises, no frills. When it was proposed to exempt any part of the population from its full share of the burden, he could be counted upon to oppose it. He came to be known affectionately, and somewhat ruefully in some quarters, as "Seven-Up" Patterson, because, after noticing a truck carrying that beverage during the early days of the war, he had demanded to know where such nonessential carriers were getting scarce gas and tires. This was the kind of situation he fought constantly to eliminate.

Something of the closeness of our relationship is implicit in this letter, written to me by Patterson on August 17, 1945:

> Now that the war has been won, I am going to tell you what your steady support has meant to me over the past five years.
>
> I came to the War Department in July 1940. I was convinced that events beyond our control would sweep us into the war and that we would be in need of all the weapons and supplies that could be produced. At the same time I was without knowledge of how to go about production of the things needed by a large army, and there were certainly no stocks on hand. To get the utmost in the way of information I read everything that you had written in the 1920s and 1930s, and I lost no time in meeting you and going over the many points that were perplexing me.
>
> Ever since those days in the summer of 1940 I have looked to you for guidance. You came to Washington over and over again at my asking, never sparing yourself and never wavering in your strong support. I have always felt your hand on my shoulder. I owe you more than I can express in words.
>
> On the personal side I have the warmest attachment for you. You have seen me do foolish things and heard me say foolish things, but you bore with me none the less. I shall never forget the sincerity and cordiality of your friendship.

Forrestal had much the same character as Patterson. Perhaps more sensitive, and certainly a more tortured man, these very characteristics made him the highly conscientious, single-minded public servant that he was. I have noticed that outstanding success in every arena is related to this quality of single-mindedness. I myself have always believed it impossible to do two things well at the same time. Patterson, Forrestal, and others who made major contributions to victory were men with a single purpose.

The average citizen cannot fully understand the grinding pressure under which the men who ran the war on the home front labored. Wartime Washington was not, contrary to popular impression, one long round of cocktail parties. Men such as Forrestal and Patterson spent every day—every hour, almost—wrestling with critical questions, making crucial decisions, fighting for their convictions against men equally sincere and equally determined.

Knowing this, I was all the more ready to respond to any call for help at any time. I remember one Sunday afternoon when General Clay telephoned me about a particularly tough production problem. We decided during our conversation that my presence in Washington might be helpful. I put on my coat immediately, went out to the airport, caught a plane, and in a few hours was sitting in Clay's Pentagon office. When I left the meeting that night, we had the problem in hand.

Another man with whom I worked closely was General Campbell. While investigating the ordnance situation for the President at the beginning of the war, I had been impressed by Campbell's understanding of production problems. When the President sought a new Chief of Ordnance in 1942, I recommended him.

I served on Campbell's advisory committee, along with Lewis Brown, of Johns-Manville; Fowler McCormick, of International Harvester; and General Robert Wood. One day, at a meeting of this committee, General Campbell told us of a move to relieve the regional ordnance headquarters of their procurement responsibilities, which were to be taken over by Army area commanders. I said I couldn't believe such a move would be contemplated; the system of ordnance regions was working too well. Nevertheless it was true, Campbell replied, and he was willing to bet me a new fifty-cent piece on it.

I left the meeting at once, and went to see Patterson and then General Marshall. Both professed not to know anything about the impending change, so I went directly to the White House and told Pa Watson I wanted to see the President. Always genial but firm, Pa said it was impossible; the President was too busy to be interrupted. But I insisted. "If you don't let me in the front door, Pa, I'll go around the back way," I said.

Watson finally relented and took me into the President's office. I told the President about the reported revision in the ordnance procurement organization, and told him too that, in my view, it would be a serious mistake. F.D.R. agreed, and immediately dispatched a note to Secretary Stimson. A day or two later, the President sent me a copy of Stimson's assurance that the plan would not go through. Several days after that, a new fifty-cent piece arrived in the mail from General Campbell.

3

Throughout the war, President Roosevelt called on me for assistance in the war production program. One of my first assignments was to study the ordnance production situation. There were then many bottlenecks impeding the flow of arms; a synchronized, balanced flow of all the interdependent elements in the munitions program had not yet been achieved. I found, for example, that while tanks were rolling off the assembly line in great numbers, we were not producing the necessary guns and ammunition to go with them. Harry Hopkins had been anxious to promise the Army tank delivery for the North African invasion, which was then in the planning stage. At my insistence, however, this commitment was held up until the kinks in the tank program were ironed out and we could be certain that when they were delivered, they would be ready for combat.

Hopkins, no mean driver himself, used to complain that I was never satisfied with the war production program, which was largely true. Production, I often said, was the alpha and omega of the war effort at home, and I was constantly driving to improve it. At luncheon one day, during Winston Churchill's visit to the White House in the late spring of 1943, Harry remarked that I was always complaining. He said it not without a touch of annoyance. The President agreed, but added: "Every time Bernie sticks his nose into anything, production increases." Turning to Churchill, he went on: "You know, Bernie is my burr—the burr I stick under the tails of these boys. I'm going to give him a golden burr."

One of the most important assignments the President asked me to undertake was in connection with the rubber program. To understand the importance and magnitude of the problem, one need only recall that foreign sources, which supplied the rubber upon which our industrial and military machines rolled, had been cut off by the Japanese. It was not difficult to picture the catastrophe that might result if we could not develop another source of rubber.

My own awareness of our dependence on foreign rubber antedated the war by some four decades. As far back as the turn of the century, the rapid rise of the auto industry and the absence of a domestic supply of rubber had led me to investigate the possibilities of creating a source nearer home.

In 1903, I had learned that an inventor, William A. Lawrence, had succeeded in extracting rubber from guayule, a silver-leafed shrub indigenous to northern Mexico. Going to Mexico to see for myself, I found the shrub growing wild over millions of acres, and learned that the simplest methods were all that were necessary to cultivate a crop which would mature in about three years. Here, it seemed to me, was a source of rubber at our doorstep. I set about helping to establish a company to develop the guayule rubber industry. But various difficulties, capped by the Madero revolution of 1910, put an end to the venture, although it was by that time on a dividend-paying basis.

For many years after that, especially as the threat of war loomed, I tried in vain to introduce guayule into this country. I was still trying on the eve of our entry into World War Two, when the long-range rubber situation was beginning to alarm everyone. Guayule, of course, would not have solved our problem, but it would have eased it. I believed, as I wrote Stettinius on August 12, 1940, that "if guayule production had been undertaken in this country within the last six years, we would now be producing on American soil about one fifth of our total needs."

But long before the war had erupted, I had also been pressing the government to stockpile crude rubber. I had brought to Secretary of Agriculture Wallace a plan to exchange surplus American cotton for surplus British rubber, to the advantage of both countries. Wallace saw merit in the proposal, but Secretary Hull, who opposed bartering in principle, at first objected. At my urging, however, he finally relented. As a result of negotiations carried out by Ambassador Joseph Kennedy in London, we did acquire some rubber through this proposal, but not nearly as much as could have been gotten.

In 1940, through the Rubber Reserve Corporation headed by Jesse Jones, Congress had finally authorized a rubber stockpiling program. Regrettably, Jones demonstrated no great sense of urgency, either in stockpiling natural rubber or in pushing the development of the synthetic rubber industry. I wrote to Arthur Krock six months before Pearl Harbor: "All of Jesse's . . . rubber factories should have been built and in operation by now. If we had a sufficient supply of rubber and rubber substitutes, the Dutch Indies would not look like such a prize to the Japanese. . . ."

When we were at last drawn into the war, our rubber stockpile was sufficient to meet just one year's normal demand. By this time, the only solution to the problem lay in rapid development of synthetic rubber. But the synthetic rubber program then existed largely on paper, and its development was hampered by conflict over whether grain alcohol or petroleum should be used as the basic raw material. It was also hindered by inter-agency squabbles, the absence of centralized authority, and the failure of WPB to provide the driving force required. In particular, the incompatibility of Jones and Ickes, each of whom had a voice in the rubber program, was legendary in Washington. But their private feuds, amusing as they might be to discuss at dinner parties, distracted energy and attention from the problem of getting rubber.

During the first six months of the war, the rubber shortage grew more perilous, and dissension over proposed solutions mounted. The issue of gas rationing was particularly thorny, although it was clear that such rationing was essential if existing rubber supplies were to be conserved. With the rubber question getting more involved every day, I sent a suggestion to the President through Steve Early. Early summarized it in a "Very Confidential" memorandum to F.D.R. on June 6th:

> Dear "Boss":
>   Baruch called me on the telephone this morning to offer what I think is an excellent suggestion. He points out that the rubber-gas rationing question has gotten into a badly muddled condition. He contends that the men you have appointed—such as Nelson, Henderson, Ickes and Eastman—should have made the decision themselves and NOT laid the responsibility on your doorstep. And here is his suggestion: That you appoint Jimmy Byrnes or Douglas or some one of their caliber to investigate the rubber-gas situation—that the investigator report and make his recommendation to you.

Shortly after this proposal went to the President, Congress moved to take command of this tangled issue. It passed a bill to create a rubber czar independent of WPB. At the insistence of the farm bloc, the bill also made it mandatory that special plants be built for the manufacture of synthetic rubber out of grain alcohol.

The President wisely vetoed this bill. He then asked Chief Justice Harlan Stone to investigate the rubber situation. Stone's unassailable position, the President felt, would permit him to lift the rubber controversy above politics. The public could expect to get an unbiased report from the Chief Justice, a report which would command support even from those whom it might hurt. But Justice Stone felt that his judicial position precluded his taking this assignment.

The concern which many men in the government felt at this point over the rubber problem was implicit in a long, gloomy letter written to me on July 29th by Petroleum Administrator Harold Ickes: "I have to weep on someone's shoulder and I don't know of any better one than yours," Ickes began.

Then, in his blunt yet highly articulate fashion, Ickes reviewed the long, dismal history of the rubber problem. Of course, he blamed the whole "worst possible mess" on his favorite enemy, Jesse Jones. Jones, he said, "had been betting with himself that the war would be over shortly and that we might not even be involved, particularly in the Far Pacific. He hadn't built up a stock pile of rubber that he had been instructed to build up, and for which he had been given plenty of money. He had even slept peacefully on the synthetic rubber program. So we were hit in a vital spot."

Ickes then went on to describe his own efforts to prod the President and Donald Nelson into taking positive steps. He concluded:

> The President has shown that he has a just appraisal of the public state of mind when he asked Chief Justice Stone to determine the facts as to rubber. In refusing to do so, especially in so curt a manner, the Chief Justice has done a distinct disservice to his Country. To whom now can the President turn who can go into the facts and make a statement that the people will accept? I doubt if there is a public official in Washington who can persuade the people of the facts even if they are all rock-ribbed.
>
> You are one of the wisest men that I have ever known—perhaps the wisest. There is no more important task for any of us than to get the people of the United States in a sane and sure state of mind about rubber. Here is a job worthy even of you.

Whether Ickes had some foreknowledge, whether he was sending up a trial balloon, or whether it was simple coincidence, no more than a week elapsed before I got this handwritten, undated note from the President on August 4th:

Dear Bernie:
  Because you are "an ever present help in time of trouble" will you "do it again?" You would be better than all the Supreme Court put together! Sam [Rosenman] will tell you & I'll see you later.

As ever
FDR

Rosenman briefed me on what the President wished me to do. He told me that I was to survey the entire rubber question and recommend the methods best designed to produce the synthetic rubber required for the war effort. Some suggestions were made as to who would be associated with me in this task, but I picked Dr. James B. Conant, then President of Harvard University, and Dr. Karl T. Compton, President of M.I.T.

I was glad to accept the task, and particularly happy to be associated with Presidents Conant and Compton. My acquaintance with them proved to be much more than a pleasure. It was a rewarding and invaluable experience for me. I had never before been exposed to scientific minds, and I came away from this association with my own horizons broadened. I developed the highest admiration for both Conant and Compton, not only as scientists but as men. Both distinguished themselves not only in their originally chosen fields of science and education, but as citizens and public servants.

Our staff, including some twenty-five technicians and engineers, was quickly assembled. Secretary to the committee was Samuel Lubell, whose capacity for work was infinite, and who was to become one of America's most perceptive and respected political analysts. In this and many other tasks, Lubell was always a loyal and tireless aide upon whom I could depend.

The President had urged speed. Accordingly, we plunged into

our work even before we had office space. One day Conant, Compton, and I went out to Lafayette Park, and sat down on the grass to confer. A reporter came along, recognized us, and wanted to know what was going on. "We're just having a meeting of the Rubber Committee," I said. He hurried away and soon came back with a photographer. The pictures in the papers next day added to the legend about me and park benches, even though the Committee was actually sitting on the ground.

The complexities of the various synthetic rubber processes, I am quick to admit, went far over my head. I left it to my scientific colleagues to determine the relative merits of the grain-alcohol process, which the farm interests so vociferously championed, and the petroleum process, which the oil industry advocated with equal force. When technical matters were discussed at our meetings, I always turned the chair over to Conant. "All I want to know," I told the scholarly President of Harvard, "is what process will produce rubber the quickest."

This proved, in the judgment of Conant, Compton, and other scientists, to be the process which used butadiene derived from oil. When Conant unfolded a huge chart depicting this process and spread it before me, I said, "Doc, all I want to know is, does it work?" He assured me it did, and I said, "Well, fold it up. That's what we're going to do."

After five weeks of hearings and intensive study, we issued our report. Our recommendations included, first of all, the endorsement of the petroleum process. We also proposed the expansion of the synthetic rubber program based upon it, and called for a capacity of three hundred thousand tons.

We had tried to see the whole spectrum of the rubber problem. Thus we recommended, "as the only way to save rubber," a gas-rationing program which would limit nonessential motoring to an annual average of five-thousand miles per vehicle. We also recommended the imposition of a maximum speed limit of thirty-five miles per hour, to save wear and tear on tires.

Confronting the problem of conflicting authority and agency vendettas, we recommended that the President clarify the WPB's authority to provide direction of the war economy. But in order to assure unified direction of the rubber program, we also recommended the appointment of a Rubber Administrator, who would operate within the general framework of WPB. To him would be delegated full authority over all phases of the program, including research, development, plant construction and operation.

On this point, there had been some disagreement within the Committee. Both Conant and Compton had favored excluding Nelson entirely from the rubber program. They had urged that the Rubber Administrator, with autonomous power of priority, be completely independent of WPB.

I resisted any proposal to divide authority, which violated the principle of unified control I had preached for so long. I insisted that Nelson's power to decide priorities must not be infringed. After a complete airing of our respective views, my associates agreed to go along with me; they never qualified their support.

The report was well-received in the nation. The President called it excellent, and took immediate steps to carry it out. There were some, of course, who objected, particularly farm spokesmen such as Senator Gillette and Senator Norris. One newspaper publisher, championing the grain-alcohol process, came to me in solicitous concern that the oil interests were pulling the wool over my eyes. I assured him that I had both eyes open, whereupon, in an effort to discredit our report, he publicly—and falsely—asserted that one of our staff was in the pay of the oil interests.

When we presented our report to the President, we said that the rubber problem could be overcome by "bulling through the present synthetic program and by safeguarding jealously every ounce of rubber in the country." We also suggested a candidate for the difficult job of Rubber Administrator—William Jeffers, who had first been suggested to us by Averell Harriman.

Roosevelt acted on our nomination. He couldn't have chosen

a better man to "bull it through." Jeffers, who was, in fact, called "Bull" Jeffers, had worked his way up from water boy to president of the Union Pacific Railroad. He was a tough railroader who didn't mince words or try to mollify those who obstructed him. The ultimate success of the rubber program was due to his forceful leadership.

And the success of the synthetic rubber program was one of the brilliant achievements of the war. In our report we had called for increasing capacity by 300,000 tons. By 1944, production had soared to 800,000 tons. By the end of the war, a billion dollar industry had been built from scratch.

4

Shortly after the rubber report was completed, I received the first of several bids to join the war administration. Although I had been working full-time in the defense program on an unofficial basis, there was, I knew, some sentiment for me to take an official role. This sentiment emanated, in part, from those who believed I might contribute more in an administrative capacity than in an advisory one. One of these men was Harold Ickes, who had written to F.D.R. only four days after Pearl Harbor:

> I wish that you could be persuaded to recall Bernie Baruch and give him the authority that he so well carried out twenty years ago. I believe that this would be particularly reassuring to the country at this time, and in all frankness I don't believe anyone can do the job as well as he.

Of course it was gratifying to know of the confidence that Ickes and others had in me. F.D.R. himself, it was reported to me, wanted to have me in the government. But there were also some who thought that I might be disbarred, or at least inhibited, from acting as goad and critic, could I be brought into the Administration.

There is no surer way to silence a critic, which was essentially my role—a constructive critic, I hope—than to elect him to the team.

The first time I was asked to join the Administration was in the fall of 1942. While Congress was debating the Economic Stabilization Act, F.D.R. sent Sam Rosenman to ask if I would take the post of Economic Stabilizer—the "super-duper" job, as Rosenman called it.

The Stabilization Act, authorizing the control of all prices, wages, and rents, was signed into law early in October. It was a long overdue attempt to grab the reins on the inflationary forces which had been galloping through the economy since before our entry into the war. As in the genesis of the WPB, we had moved step by faltering step in the matter of inflation control. In January, 1942, Congress had enacted a so-called price control act. But OPA's authority to fix prices was made subject to the condition that farm price ceilings would be set at 110 per cent of parity—a special concession to the farming interests. And in May, when OPA issued its price regulations, both farm prices and wages were left uncontrolled. Not until July was a wage-control policy devised through the Little Steel Formula.

By the time the Stabilization Act was passed, the cost-of-living index had risen about twenty-five per cent above prewar levels. Inflation was not finally checked until the President issued his "hold the line" order the following April. But by this time, the damage had been done. We are still paying for it.

Although I welcomed the Stabilization Act, I was not especially enthusiastic about the opportunity to administer it. I was, first of all, perfectly satisfied to retain my unofficial and independent status which in many ways added to whatever effectiveness I had. Moreover, I was not willing to accept a job unless I were given the tools to do it. In the case of economic stabilization, I felt that the determination of tax policy was vital. I told Rosenman that I could not accept the post of Economic Stabilizer unless I could have some assurance that I would be consulted on the government's tax program. This would have required the concurrence of Secretary of the Treasury Morgenthau, which he was not likely to grant.

He was jealous of his prerogatives. I remember that, when he was appointed to the Treasury in 1934, F.D.R. had asked me to help him. At that time, the President had explained that with Morgenthau in the Treasury, Wall Street would never get the keys to its back door. And this was true, for Morgenthau served with complete dedication and integrity.

At the President's request, I met with the new Secretary. I remember urging that he take advantage of favorable interest rates to refinance part of the government's debt. But I had the clear impression that Morgenthau did not welcome my views, and I quickly discontinued giving them.

I now discussed with Rosenman my doubts over accepting the Economic Stabilization post. He agreed that I would not be given a voice in tax policy. I decided to decline the offer.

A few days later, however, another Presidential emissary came to my apartment at the Carlton Hotel. This time it was Harry Hopkins. Hopkins told me that I was still the President's choice—and his, too (though this I doubted)—for Economic Stabilizer.

Again I declined, for the reason I had given Judge Rosenman. Hopkins then asked if I had any candidates for the post. As always, when an important and difficult job was to be done, I suggested James F. Byrnes. At that very moment, Byrnes walked in. I can still see him, his head cocked birdlike on one side in a characteristic Byrnes attitude. Hopkins and I explained our conversation, and Byrnes said, "If the Commander in Chief asks me, I'll accept." Contrary to what has been suggested elsewhere, Hopkins did *not* offer Byrnes the post. He had not the authority to do so; nor would he have presumed.

Byrnes was then on the Supreme Court. I think I had been one of the first to recommend him for the Court. In 1940, he had told me that, because of illness, he was thinking of leaving the Senate. Would he be remiss in his duty to the Party, he asked, if he did so and took a seat on the Federal bench? I told him I thought he would not only be justified, but wise to do so. I also said that I thought he was qualified to sit on the High Court. Byrnes was skeptical that the President would offer him such an exalted appointment.

Not long after that conversation, I spent an evening with the President. This was the occasion, previously mentioned, when F.D.R. had asked whom I thought would make a good candidate to succeed him. During our talk that night, I raised the question of elevating Byrnes to the Supreme Court. I pointed out that he was qualified by reason of ability and service, and that the Senate would look with particular favor on this appointment. When I had concluded, the President, although expressing his reluctance to lose Byrnes from the Senate, said, "I'll do it at the first opening." He went on to discuss Byrnes as a potential Vice-presidential nominee—a subject I shall revert to again. When there was a vacancy on the Court in the summer of 1941, the President—true to his word—named Byrnes.

Now, when the President offered Byrnes the Economic Stabilization appointment, he resigned from the bench. With his wide experience, his standing with Congress, and his great talents, Byrnes proved to be an excellent choice for the job.

5

By the beginning of 1943, the war production program was entering its critical phase. We had been at war for over a year. We had launched our first invasion, in North Africa, and the rough going there suggested what lay ahead.

The armed forces were beginning their big build-up. But the war production program was still not operating in high gear. Working with Patterson, Forrestal, and their subordinates on procurement problems, and with Nelson and his WPB associates on production problems, I could witness the growing struggle between the military and civilian agencies.

Quite properly, Patterson, Forrestal, Somervell, Clay, and all the other representatives of the armed forces were concerned with one objective: to obtain for the military whatever it required to fight the war. The WPB's responsibility was much broader. It had to meet the needs not only of the armed forces, but of the civilian population and the Allies as well. In a sense, conflicts were inevitable, though wise leadership and effective administration would have kept them in bounds.

The conflict between the Army and WPB, over the allocation of resources and matériel, was sharp enough in itself. But there were also numerous abrasions of personality to complicate the situation. It was the old story of the human equation. Plans and procedures may be formulated *ad infinitum;* but, in the end, men must implement them—and human ambitions and sensitivities then come into play.

Disagreement between Patterson and Nelson had erupted almost at once. Patterson insisted that the Army's needs were not being met; Nelson, that the Army was demanding more than it required. Because I was working with both men, and was trusted by both, I tried to act as mediator in their dispute. Early in their quarrel, I did manage to bring them together, and was able to report to the President that they had reached an agreement. But this was only a temporary truce, which evaporated as the tempo of war and pressures on the home front increased.

The Army had come to feel that Nelson was hostile to their needs, and that he ought to be replaced. They argued that he had neither the stature nor the ability for so crucial a job. Nelson, and others in the WPB, meanwhile, felt that the Army was indifferent to the needs of the civilian population.

To some in WPB, disagreement with the Army—in itself, perhaps, a necessary, proper, and unavoidable difference, given the differing responsibilities of each party involved in the quarrel—

was improperly translated into a fight against "militarism." It was even charged that the Army was using the war to secure domination over the economy of the country, which it would perpetuate in peacetime. General Somervell, in charge of the Army's Service of Supply, was a particular target for such criticism. Attacks on him went so far as to characterize him as a Fascist. Some highly placed people actually urged me to ask the President to dismiss the General. Naturally, I refused.

Patterson came to me, one day, in some concern over the attacks against Somervell. "Bob," I said, "pay no attention to them. He's a free-running horse. When the gate goes up you don't have to hit him. You don't even have to cluck to him. He's ready to run. Let him alone."

My philosophy in the Army-WPB dispute was simple enough. I believed that the armed forces must have what they wanted, when they wanted it, with the least possible dislocation to the civilian economy. In any conflict between civilian and military needs, the military would have to have priority. Despite the inconveniences at home—and I felt they could hardly be called more than that—no one could say the home front suffered seriously in terms of material things. Guns *and* butter were fine, if possible; but if not, guns had always to come *before* butter—simply because the lives of our youth and the survival of our nation were at stake.

I had no sympathy with the groaners who complained of small deprivations, and who, it sometimes seemed to me, could not understand why they could not eat as much, wear as much, drive their cars as much, or carry on as though the war did not exist. Yet, there were people like this, and I am sorry to say that some of them were in official Washington.

Nor had I any patience with the numerous shabby evasions of wartime restrictions I could see going on around me, whether in or out of Washington. And I had nothing but contempt for those who, under the guise of free enterprise, profiteered during the war.

The struggle between WPB and the Army was coming to a head

in the first weeks of 1943. Not only was the Army at odds with the War Production Board, but WPB itself was riven by dissension and distrust between supposedly pro-Army and anti-Army factions. The Board had become a tunnel of whispers, and operated in a climate of scarcely suppressed animosities. Between Nelson and some of his chief lieutenants there developed a gulf of suspicion and conflict. Nelson was particularly resentful of Ferd Eberstadt, who held a key position directing priorities in WPB. Nelson considered Eberstadt to be an Army Trojan horse in his camp.

Eberstadt was no one's man, but his own. Combining tenacity with imagination, he had no other purpose than to win the war as quickly as possible. It was he who conceived the Controlled Materials Plan, through which WPB so effectively controlled priorities. Eberstadt was absolutely unyielding on principles. On one occasion, pressure was brought on him to fire an aide who had incurred the wrath of the White House. Eberstadt refused to do so. He grimly told the President: "If he goes, I go too." They both stayed.

The strife within WPB was eliciting much criticism in the press—and in Congress, too, where there was a sustained attack against Nelson's administration of the agency. This discord in WPB, and the damaging vendetta between it and the Army, greatly troubled me. I rejected as nonsense the WPB's talk of militarism, but I nevertheless believed that the Army had to acknowledge and abide by the Board's authority. I had gone through such battles myself. Despite much talk that I was supporting the Army in its fight with Nelson, I was actually trying to resolve their differences.

On Wednesday evening, February 3, 1943, Nelson and I had dinner together and canvassed frankly the subject of his quarrel with the Army. I reminded him of my own conception of the role of WPB—that it was to provide central authority over the entire war production program. I reaffirmed my belief in one-man control, and pledged to support him to the hilt in the proper exercise of his authority.

I tried to impress upon him, too, the importance of ending his dispute with the Army, a dispute fraught with danger to the country. I pointed out the need for ending the intrigues within his agency, and I particularly stressed the need for better relations between him and Eberstadt. When we parted that night, I felt our minds had met. I was convinced that Nelson would seek to end the breach within WPB and the quarrel with the Army.

Two nights later, James Byrnes called on me at my hotel. Without previous warning or consultation, he handed me a letter signed by President Roosevelt asking me to accept the chairmanship of WPB. The letter read:

February 5, 1943

Dear Bernie:

For a long time I have been calling upon you for assistance in questions affecting our war production. You have given unsparingly of your time and energy and your advice has been exceedingly valuable. I know that you have preferred to serve in an advisory capacity and have benn [sic] disinclined to accept an appointment that would require you to devote all of your time to an administrative position. However, I deem it wise to make a change in the direction of war production and I am coming back to the elder statesmen for assistance. I want to appoint you as Chairman of War Production Board with power to direct the activities of the organization.

With your knowledge of the subject and your knowledge of the organization, I am sure you can arrange so that it will not require you to work day and night. I would not want you to do that, but I am confident you will accept because of your willingness to make any sacrifice you believe will aid in the prosecution of the war.

Sincerely yours,
Franklin D. Roosevelt

This was the first act in a strange and, for everyone concerned, disagreeable little drama.

I did not learn the background of this letter until much later. As he relates in his memoirs, Byrnes had discussed the growing complaints against Nelson with the President, who was so disturbed about the situation that he was contemplating replacing Nelson with Charles E. Wilson. On February 5th, Byrnes wrote and handed a letter to the President advising him that he thought it would be a mistake to appoint Wilson—because Nelson's supporters within WPB would be bitterly resentful, and harmony at this point was essential. Byrnes went on, in his letter, to propose that I be appointed to replace Nelson:

> You would be taking no chances. He knows that organization better than anybody in it. For the past year he has spent four or five days each week in Washington, and the heads of the various divisions have taken their problems to him. Without any power he has accomplished miracles in straightening out controversies and in securing the cooperation of manufacturers. Mr. Wilson, Mr. Eberstadt, and every other leader in the organization would welcome the appointment of Baruch.
>
> You and I know his appointment would be welcomed by the Congress. Mr. Hill telephoned me today that the agitation for the Pepper bill was due entirely to their belief that War Production Board was not performing; Truman is of the same opinion. They believe the appointment of a strong man would kill the Pepper bill. When they say "strong man" they do not mention Baruch, but I know they would throw up their hats for his appointment. The press would welcome it. . . .
>
> Last but not least, he is loyal to you. For a year he has worked as hard as if he were on the payroll and had the honor of an appointment from you. You would be appointing not only the best man for the place, but appointing one of your best friends.

Byrnes and the President discussed this recommendation. The President, according to Byrnes, expressed his affection for me and his respect for my ability. But Roosevelt was afraid, Byrnes thought, that I might carry my criticisms to the public. As Byrnes put it, "President Roosevelt did not want advice—publicly." Finally, F.D.R. told Byrnes to draft the letter, quoted above, offering me the appointment.

Back in his office, Byrnes wrote the letter—hastily, as the typographical error in it indicates. He took it back to the White House at once for the President's signature, and it was this document he had handed to me that night.

The proposal came as a bolt from the blue. Byrnes—much less the President—had never so much as hinted, much less asked me directly, whether I would accept the WPB post.

When I recovered a little from my astonishment at F.D.R.'s letter, I considered what I should say. Should I give up my work as an independent trouble-shooter, where I felt so strongly that my very independence enabled me to be of the most value? Should I do what I preferred not do, and accept an official position that would at once by its nature bind me in ways that I preferred not to be bound and perhaps diminish my usefulness?

Plainly, it was not a question to be decided in a moment. "I can't answer you now," I told Byrnes. "I'm going to New York tonight. I'll give you my answer tomorrow."

Byrnes was obviously disappointed that I did not accept on the spot; he was somewhat insistent. But I told Byrnes I would have to consult my doctor first, to see if I could undertake a job that was already wearing out Nelson physically. I also wanted to talk with John Hancock, and find out whether I could count on his help if I took the position.

Hancock and I had been friends and associates since the First War. Bluff and hearty, Hancock had more the manner of a rancher from North Dakota, where he was born, than of an investment banker and specialist in corporate re-organization, which he was. He had a remarkable ability to master detail, and possessed one of the most independent minds I ever met. I was once asked how I managed to do so many things apparently so well. "It is quite simple," I said, "John Hancock is the answer." If I took the WPB job, I wanted him at my right hand.

I got as far as Philadelphia that night on my way home when I began to feel feverish. When I arrived home I sent for the doctor, who examined me and put me to bed. I was rather sick for several days, and the doctors seemed unable to agree on a diagnosis. There was a frightening moment when they thought I might have a very serious liver disorder, perhaps even a cancer.

My illness, whatever it was, proved to be nothing so serious. Within a week, I was ready to return to Washington. I had by this time decided that I was duty bound to take the WPB job. John Hancock had agreed to come with me as my deputy.

In Washington, I went at once to the White House to advise the President of my acceptance. In the hall outside the President's office, I met Sam Rosenman and Pa Watson. They took me aside hurriedly and said, "The President has changed his mind." They had no chance to explain further before I was summoned inside.

As I walked in, my mind was turning over rapidly. I understood what Rosenman and Watson had meant: The President was withdrawing his offer of the WPB chairmanship. But how was I to act? What should I do? Should I let F.D.R. know that I was aware of his change of heart? Should I make it hard for him—demand an explanation and have it out with him? There flashed through my mind the memory of that painful episode when the President had withdrawn his promise to appoint Louis Johnson Secretary of War, and of how I had kicked my rejected friend's leg to keep him from losing his temper. As I entered F.D.R.'s room, I knew that I was not going to lose mine.

The President leaned back in his chair, and puffed on a cigarette stuck in an uptilted holder. He greeted me in his customary genial fashion. He showed no sign of embarrassment or uneasiness.

"Mr. President, I'm here to report for duty," I said. My salutation went unacknowledged. It was as though he had not heard me.

"Let me tell you about Ibn Saud, Bernie," he said confidentially. And he launched into some general observations about that Middle Eastern monarch. Then he suddenly interrupted himself. "Forgive me, I have to go to a Cabinet meeting," he said, and rolled off.

That was the end of it; neither he nor I ever mentioned the WPB chairmanship—then or later.

Jimmy Byrnes says of this incident in his memoirs: ". . . It was evident that for some reason the President did not want to appoint Baruch, and equally apparent that Baruch did not want to assume the responsibility of the office. . . ."

The latter conclusion is entirely wrong. Although I had not sought the WPB post, I had decided to accept it in view of the President's urgent request and Byrnes's insistence. I had gone so far as to recruit John Hancock to assist me, and had indeed reported for duty to the President.

At the time, I had the feeling Byrnes was angry because I did not force the issue with F.D.R. Secretary Stimson, too, felt that I should have fought with the President, but that would have been foolish. It was useless to quarrel with him after he had so clearly changed his mind. The post was not mine to have by arguing. A quarrel would have been productive only of discord and recrimination, and might have made it impossible for me to continue doing what I had been trying to do to help the war effort. I will not deny that I was disappointed and hurt, that my anger could have flared had I let it. But I had spent a lifetime learning to curb my temper, and I did not intend to let any personal feelings stand in the way of any service I could render. My pride went down hard, but I swallowed it.

But why had F.D.R. changed his mind? I soon learned the answer. While I had been ill in New York, word of the President's decision to replace him had reached Nelson, despite Byrnes's precautions to keep it secret. Nelson's first reaction was to fire Eberstadt, who, he erroneously believed, was to be named my deputy. Then, it appears, he went directly to Harry Hopkins, and Hopkins persuaded the President to retain Nelson at the head of WPB.

This was not the first time Hopkins used his influence against me. As Judge Rosenman has written: Hopkins "was chiefly responsible for Baruch's absence from several situations where his services would have helped tremendously."

Although Hopkins was filled with that suspicion and jealousy of place that afflict men so close to the throne, he could, however, be a delightful companion when he relaxed. He visited Hobcaw several times. During one visit before the war, I remember he was trying to decide whether to enter the Cabinet as Secretary of Commerce or of War. He remarked that if he took the Commerce post he would champion the interests of businessmen as vigorously as he had championed the interests of workingmen in other posts he had held. I urged him to take the War Department because, with what the future seemed to hold, I thought it would offer far greater opportunity for service and achievement. He did not agree with me on that, but this was not uncommon. Hopkins and I rarely saw eye to eye.

For all that, I admired his ability, loyalty, and drive, which never diminished despite his precarious health and the pain that dogged him so much of the time. I sympathized, too, with the pounding Hopkins took from the anti-Roosevelt press. Few men were abused as he was.

I'm afraid I was guilty for one unfair broadside directed at him. When he remarried I asked his bride what she wanted for a wedding present, and she said she would like a party. I gave a dinner for the newlyweds at a Washington hotel. Any patron could have ordered the same dinner any night of the week, but the Hearst and McCormick-Patterson papers immediately raised a great cry over what was naturally termed a Roman extravagance in wartime, perpetrated by those hated New Dealers who were so busy selling austerity to everyone else. And poor Hopkins bore the brunt, even though he was only a guest.

Nelson remained as the head of the War Production Board for another eighteen months. But the dissension in that agency continued to grow, and the conflict between it and the Army did not abate. Nelson grew more and more suspicious; and more time than ever was spent on vendettas. The intrigue and bitterness reached the stage where, Nelson told me in the summer of 1943, he intended to appoint three men to important posts in WPB: a whisperer, a big talker, and the best conniver he could find. Those were the talents he said he needed to run his agency.

Such a situation could not continue. By the beginning of 1944, it was clear that Nelson had to be relieved. In many ways, he was a casualty of the war in Washington, I told the President. Stimson and others continued to insist upon his replacement. Finally, the President felt called upon to make the change. He asked Nelson to undertake a mission to China, and replaced him in WPB with Julius Krug.

There was one final effort to enlist me officially in the war mobilization program. A few months after the WPB incident, Byrnes was named to head the newly created Office of War Mobilization. He became, in effect, the czar of the entire war effort on the home front—the Assistant President for domestic affairs. Thus far had the President been compelled to move from his original opposition to one-man control of the mobilization program.

When he took over in OWM, Byrnes told me that he had F.D.R.'s approval to offer me the post of Economic Stabilizer he was vacating. Once again I declined it. Byrnes then asked Fred Vinson, who accepted.

A temporary peace of a kind had come to the troubled agency front. As 1943 moved on to midyear, war production began to hit full stride. But there were still many problems to overcome. With some of these, I was asked to help.

XVII

Plans for Reconversion

ONE OF THE THORNIEST problems of the war was manpower, particularly the control of labor. This was so because, first, the effective use of manpower is one of the crucial factors in the conduct of war; and, second, manpower is not nearly as susceptible to clear-cut control as are other economic elements, such as raw materials, transportation, money, and credit.

Here, again, one comes up hard against the human equation. Because manpower decisions affect immediately, and directly, the lives of countless human beings, it is an emotion-charged issue. Every decision in war, of course, affects human lives. But a ruling to give high-octane gas priority over steam valves is essentially impersonal, and of a very different kind from a decision on conscription quotas, or collective bargaining principles, or labor controls. Moreover, manpower issues usually involve philosophical as well as purely practical considerations, which serve to complicate them.

The fundamental question in manpower, as in every other basic problem of war, was how to equate supply wtih demand, how to divide our available human resources among the armed services, the factories and farms, the professions and services. At the root of this problem was the sensitive issue of whether or not the civilian working force ought to be subjected to compulsion; in short, whether labor ought to be subject to conscription. This was a proposition to which I was unalterably opposed, and which—despite overwhelming official support for it—I helped to defeat.

Throughout the war, F.D.R. sought my views on the manpower question. On November 7, 1942, for example, I sent him at his request a long memo setting the manpower problem in perspective against the over-all problem of mobilization. The memo said, in part:

> Our first problem is to determine the size of the army required. In determining this we must take into consideration how many can be trained and made mobile wherever it is desired, and what volume of weapons and other supplies can be provided for their use—while we are engaged at the same time in producing and transporting the lend-lease requirements of our allies; and in taking care of civilian necessities. To the extent our Army is enlarged, our difficulties multiply; to the extent our Army is held down in size our problems are made easier.
>
> Next, we must decide in what fields our available workers are to be used—
>
> How many to provide the total needs of our armed forces, and the promised supplies for our allies?
>
> How many to produce irreducible civilian needs?
>
> How many required on the farms, in the factories, in the mines, in the transportation and distribution services, and in all the professional services, such as medicine and hygiene, nursing, teaching, etc.

I went on to point out that the pressure on manpower could be eased, and our war production program accelerated at the same time, if we could "simplify American life by taking away the bigger and better frills. . . . Simplification and standardization will result, not only in manpower savings, but also will reduce prices and make it easier to regulate them."

In conclusion, I wrote:

1. We need no further laws. Our problem can be handled by executive action.

2. We should rely on voluntary cooperation instead of compulsion—except, perhaps, in stopping the pirating of labor, and this can be handled by requiring that all transfers pass through the central employment agency.

3. Selective Service, United States Employment Service, and the whole manpower problem of assigning and shifting workers should be under the direction of one central authority.

4. There should be no further enlistments. Airplane factories and other essential industries are losing too many trained men by enlistments.

5. Improved administration in all war agencies, to attain a better flow of materials and a fuller use of manpower, is imperative. And we must put a stop to the jurisdictional fights between agencies, which have assumed proportions almost equal to the previous jurisdictional fights between labor, and with greater deterring effect on the war effort.

6. Consideration will have to be given to the length of the work week—with maximum productivity our primary aim. Too long hours will result in inefficiency. Experience dictates that a 48 hour week of real work is the best over a long period of time.

And in final summation: Rather than strive to get all we want, let us concentrate on getting all of the things possible to obtain in a full-rounded program—although some elements in that program may be smaller than we would like to have.

At the time I wrote this memo, there was an already visible sentiment to conscript labor. This sentiment was to grow stronger as the war progressed and manpower problems became more acute.

But at this point, the President and I were in accord on this subject. He responded to the recommendations in my memo with a note of his own, sent to Rosenman, Byrnes, and me on November 11th:

I like B.M.B.'s conclusions:
1. No further laws.
2. Voluntary cooperation.
3. Central authority.

4. No further enlistments. (I question this)
5. Improved administration.
6. Length of work week.

But on this latter I call attention to the fact that this whole hullabaloo is not aimed at long hours. It is aimed solely at time-and-a-half for overtime. I am convinced that the most efficient production standard is forty-eight hours a week (except in a few exceptional cases where that is over-long, and a few other exceptional cases where fifty-two or fifty-four hours can be used effectively).

Shortly thereafter, the President ordered a forty-eight-hour minimum work week in areas of labor shortage.

As 1943 moved on, however, labor shortages and dislocations began seriously to impede production schedules, posing a threat to the fulfillment of our war plans. This was particularly true on the West Coast where, in the summer of that year, airplane production fell off sharply. General "Hap" Arnold, Air Force Chief of Staff, seeking my assistance, told me of the potentially disastrous consequences which would follow our failure to meet airplane production schedules. At the request of Byrnes, in charge of OWM, John Hancock and I agreed to study the West Coast manpower situation and to recommend a program to meet the problem.

What Hancock and I found was not only an acute labor shortage, aggravated by the labor hoarding practices of certain defense plants, but—even more serious—a total failure to organize and regulate the existing labor supply to meet the demand. It was the same old story of supply and demand. Once again, the vital factor of priority had been neglected. As we said in our report: "The first and greatest gap in our manpower program is the failure, thus far, to apply any system of priorities to labor."

Moreover, the West Coast labor crisis reflected the failure, evident in so many other sectors of our defense, to take an over-all view of the war program and to coördinate all the elements in the production picture. Manpower problems could not be solved by thinking solely in terms of labor controls. Control over production was equally important, because the fundamental objective of any sound manpower program was to bring production demands and labor supply into balance.

To bring order to the confused West Coast manpower situation, Hancock and I proposed a "labor budget plan" for each critical labor community on the Coast—Seattle, San Diego, Los Angeles, San Francisco, Portland. Under this plan, labor would be budgeted; employers could draw upon existing labor supplies on the basis of priorities determined by the War Manpower Commission. At the same time, the War Production Board and other procurement agencies would be responsible for keeping production demands in balance with the available labor supply. No new contracts would be let in the area unless other production demands were commensurately reduced so as to maintain the budget in balance.

Hancock and I submitted our report to Byrnes in mid-August. There was an immediate demand in Congress for its publication, and a corresponding effort to keep it from public view. I was never told why an attempt should be made to suppress the report, but it may well have been because of our criticism of manpower policies, or our failure to advocate the conscription of labor which was then increasingly favored by the Administration. Whatever the reason, Byrnes made the report public only after heavy Senate pressure was brought to bear, particularly by Senator Arthur Vandenberg.

Byrnes soon put the "labor budget plan" into effect with salutary results. There was no breakdown in airplane production on the Coast. When the war ended, General Arnold, in appreciation for what he said was my service to the Air Force in this matter, presented his silver aviator's wings to me.

2

In making our West Coast Manpower Report, Hancock and I had written: "We have always felt that the American people will do voluntarily what is expected of them as long as they know what is wanted and why—and feel that they are being treated fairly." If we were wrong in this assumption, we went on, the only alternative would be a National Service Act—that is, the conscription of labor.

There were many, as I have said, who had hoped we would recommend such a measure in our report. The pressure for it was being fed by the growing number of strikes during 1943, especially since the President's "hold-the-line" order on wages that April. The strike of coal miners and railroad workers, both of which ended only after the President had seized the mines and the railroads, were only two of the more dramatic labor outbreaks which seriously threatened the war program.

Although I could not condone strikes while the nation was at war, and although I favored a "work or fight" bill, I was opposed, without qualification, to the conscription of labor. I had argued the case back in the twenties and thirties in what were then academic discussions of mobilization. I remember tackling President Coolidge on the subject, after he had endorsed the idea of conscripting labor in the event of war. Now that the issue was real, I was one of the very few men close to the President, and not officially identified with labor, to take this position.

Among those most insistent upon subjecting labor to the compulsions of a draft were Secretaries Stimson and Knox. Byrnes, Hopkins, Rosenman, and Admiral William Leahy were also proponents of such a measure. I served with these four on a special advisory committee to the President.

This Clearance Committee was Rosenman's idea. It was intended to provide the President with a small group of trusted advisers to serve as something of a War Cabinet. As it worked out, however, the Clearance Committee dealt only with the manpower issue, and in it I found myself a minority of one on the subject of conscripting labor.

I remember a meeting in the President's office at which were present more than a score of top Administration figures. I was the only one in the room who was not in the official family. Secretary Stimson set forth the case for conscripting labor in eloquent and powerful words, and apparently everyone in the room agreed with him. I was the only one who spoke against the proposal. I argued that conscription of labor violated the most basic American liberties—that it was unconstitutional to compel one man to work for another's profit. How could you conscript labor, I asked, without imposing similar compulsions on every other aspect of our society—without, indeed, conscripting industry as well, not to mention every man's wealth? How could you justify the conscription of labor, I wanted to know, when the government was granting agriculture 110 per cent of parity, and when it failed to tax private and corporate incomes to the absolute limit? Finally, I concluded, conscripting labor seemed to me not only unjust, but clearly impractical. We could go through the motions of drafting a man to work, but unless we were prepared to resort to the lash and the knout, we could not compel him to produce.

As the meeting in the President's office broke up, I said to F.D.R.: "This is one time I won't remain silent. I'm going to make a fight." Thus, he knew exactly where I stood; and he was correct when he told an associate: "Bernie will join the labor leaders on the Hill and help beat hell out of us."

In order not to alert opponents, the President instructed Rosenman—under the injunction of strictest secrecy—to draft a National Service legislation. Rosenman was the right man to keep a secret. He was, in many ways, the ideal Presidential assistant—able, loyal, with a "passion for anonymity," which F.D.R. sought in his aides. His book, *Working with Roosevelt,* is the most objective account to come from those who were part of the President's inner circle.

There was no leak from Rosenman, and consequently it surprised —and even annoyed—proponents of labor conscription when F.D.R. called for such a bill in his annual message to Congress in January, 1944. Both Stimson and Byrnes, among others, were put out because the President had kept them in the dark.

In the ensuing debate over the bill, I was not silent. The situation was not without its irony. Here was the President, the great champion of labor, advocating a measure which many New Dealers were sworn to fight. And here I was, hitherto considered suspect by these same New Dealers, but one of the few men outside labor's camp to defend their viewpoint. In the end, the effort to conscript labor was defeated.

3

One of the things that impressed me most from my study of manpower was the frightening number of men incapacitated for military service because of physical or emotional disability. Nearly four million men and women were rejected, or separated from service as unfit, during the war. This represented an appalling waste of manpower, not only in terms of fighting the war but in terms of the nation's future growth. Human beings are the nation's most valuable asset; it came as a shock to discover that in this land, with the world's highest standards of living and the most modern medical facilities, so many of our young people were below par.

I knew that after the war the number of these disabled citizens would be swelled by returning servicemen, who had been scarred in mind and body during the conflict. The rehabilitation of these men—the 4-F's and the veterans— seemed to me to be one of our major responsibilities; and studies I had carried on into existing standards of veterans' care had shown much to be desired. My concern over the problem was reflected in a letter written to the President on November 29, 1944, in which I expressed my concern for the rehabilitation of wounded servicemen. I suggested that F.D.R. send the following letter to the Secretary of War:

I am deeply concerned over the physical and emotional condition of disabled men returning from the war. I feel, as I am sure you do, that the ultimate ought to be done for them to return them as useful citizens—useful not alone to themselves but to the community.

I wish you would issue instructions to the effect that it should be the responsibility of the military authorities to insure that no overseas casualty is discharged from the armed service until he has received the maximum benefits of hospitalization and convalescent facilities which must include physical and psychological rehabilitation, vocational guidance, pre-vocational training and resocialization.

I was much pleased by the President's reaction. On December 4th, he replied:

Dear Bernie:

I think that is an excellent idea of yours about the men returning from combat and I have sent a copy of your proposed letter to the Secretary of War. I will let you know what he says.

Always sincerely,

FDR

My interest in rehabilitation, whether of veterans or those rejected for service, or indeed of all those who were handicapped in any way, was not suddenly acquired. It has been one of the major concerns of my life, inherited, so to speak, from my father, who had pioneered in physical medicine and rehabilitation at a time when these branches of medicine had been looked upon as semi-quackery.

When Al Smith was Governor of New York, I had become interested in Saratoga Springs, and had envisioned making that spa, with its therapeutic waters, a center for the practice and teaching of physical medicine and rehabilitation. Later, as Chairman of the Saratoga Springs Commission, appointed by Roosevelt when he was Governor, I had supervised extensive studies and had formulated ambitious plans for developing the spa into such a center. When the depression foreclosed public financing of the project, I offered to endow it myself. But the plan foundered when the doctors whom I hoped would head the project—all of them eminent physicians—were rejected because they were "foreigners," even though no native Americans of comparable caliber could be found in their stead.

Now, in the midst of war, and in anticipation of the problems which would confront us at the war's end, I tried again to encourage the concept of medical rehabilitation. Through the good offices of Herbert Hoover, I was able to induce the late Dr. Ray Lyman Wilbur, president of Stanford University, to direct a comprehensive study by a group of distinguished physicians on the subject of physiotherapy. Among those who served with Dr. Wilbur were Dr. Frank Krusen, of the Mayo Clinic; Dr. William Sanger, of the Medical College of Virginia; Dr. Carl Comstock, of Saratoga Springs; Captain Charles F. Behrens, of the United States Navy; Dr. John S. Coulter and Dr. Kristian G. Hansson; and Lt. Col. Benjamin A. Strickland, Jr., of the United States Army.

Acting on the recommendations of this Committee on Physical Medicine and Rehabilitation, I was pleased to establish programs of research and training, as a memorial to my father, at such institutions as Columbia University, the Medical College of Virginia, and the New York University-Bellevue Medical Center.

Nothing has given me greater satisfaction in life than the knowledge that I have been able to encourage and support a branch of medicine which has helped restore thousands of disabled people to constructive, rewarding lives.

4

The fact that I was thinking about the subject of rehabilitation at the end of 1943 indicated that I, like most Americans, was thinking ahead to the peace. But, unfortunately, in anticipating victory, many Americans were slackening up on the war effort. As

1943 came to a close, peace jitters began to sweep the country—prematurely, to say the least. We were still beset by manpower problems, production bottlenecks, shortages of every kind and description; Hitler's Europe was still unbreached and the Pacific had still to be rewon. Yet the country was being distracted by thoughts of peace. Workers were reluctant to take war jobs; manufacturers were hesitant to take war contracts. Many people were beginning to jockey for position, planning to get in first on peacetime opportunities.

The preoccupation with reconversion and production cutbacks posed a serious threat to military plans. I agreed with General Marshall that this was a "vicious business." I had warned in the report on West Coast Manpower that "the surest way to lengthen the war and increase our toll of casualties is to act as if the war were already won."

In that report, I had also suggested that it might be possible to minimize the harmful effects of the reconversion fever, if the public knew that the government had plans to permit a quick and orderly return to peace.

Byrnes, to whom this report was addressed, was thinking along the same lines. He had asked various agency heads to begin drafting programs for the discharge of servicemen, the disposal of surplus stocks, and the termination of contracts, among other things. When the President asked him to appoint a special unit in OWM to coördinate these policies, Byrnes asked John Hancock and me to undertake this task.

Both Hancock and I were ready to respond, but we wanted to have our responsibilities clearly defined. We wanted no repetition of the attempt to suppress our views, as with the West Coast Manpower Report.

Byrnes assured us that we would be free to go about our task in our own way, with our own staff, providing we used no one embarrassing to the President. He particularly had in mind Will Clayton and Jesse Jones—both of whom, I was told, were then *persona non grata* at the White House. He also assured us that, unless it were a question of basic policy, he would expect us to make and announce our own decisions.

With this understanding, Hancock and I went ahead. An old Negro woman, who had been in my service for forty years, said, when she heard of my new job, "The boss must be going to make a powerful lot of money, or he wouldn't work so hard at his age." When she was told that I was working for the government, she answered fervently, "May Jesus prop him up."

There was, at this time, much bleak talk among economists, businessmen, and government officials that hard times—and perhaps a depression of major proportions—were sure to follow the end of the war. Despite the charts and graphs with which this forecast was documented, it seemed to me false. Common sense alone told me that peace would unleash a tremendous demand for cars, homes, clothing, refrigerators—goods and services of every kind. Half the world would need rebuilding.

Unquestionably, the task of reconverting from war to peace would be difficult—in many ways more difficult than converting from peace to war. Yet I was convinced that, for at least five to seven years, there would be work for all American hands and minds willing to work—which proved a conservative estimate. And I was confident, too, that our adjustment to peace, if wisely handled, could be an "adventure in prosperity," as I put it.

Hancock and I issued our report, "War and Postwar Adjustment Policies," in February, 1944. It won the complete support of Byrnes, and was generally approved by the press and the public. At its heart were proposals designed to permit the speediest transition of industry from war to peacetime production.

"Speed in shifting . . . from war to peace is our most effective attack against . . . unemployment and inflation," we wrote. To permit this rapid shift, we recommended "quick, fair and final settlement of terminated war contracts," with adequate safeguards to prevent fraud or abuse of the government. Some people, prominent among them Lindsay Warren, the Controller General of the United States, opposed final settlement until a painstaking audit of every contract had been made. Such a procedure, we pointed out, might "quibble the nation into panic" by creating "unemployment by audit."

We also recommended a system of "termination loans" to assist manufacturers in converting their facilities from defense to peacetime production. These and other contract termination proposals were soon adopted, and, as a result, billions of dollars worth of war contracts were quickly and quietly settled.

Another of our major recommendations called for the creation of a Surplus Property Administration to sell off the government's surplus property, under terms which would assure the widest and most useful distribution. All transactions, we warned, would have to be "in a goldfish bowl" and open to all.

Our report underscored a point which I have made before, and which is worth repeating: Our surpluses are too precious to be dumped. "Let no one feel," we said, "that precious surpluses will bear down upon us and destroy us; that vast amounts of metals, raw materials, ships and airplanes will smother us and engulf us. These are assets of tremendous value. They will have a real force not alone in making the peace but in opening to the whole world, and therefore to us, vast opportunities." We would do well to remember this today, when there is much hand-wringing over farm and other surpluses.

Our recommendations on surplus property were adopted. Although Will Clayton was supposed to be outside the pale, I urged his appointment as Surplus Administrator. Byrnes agreed that he was right for the job, and got the President to name him to the post. There were a great many objections to Clayton from extreme liberals. But knowing Clayton's uncompromising integrity and independence, I meant it as a compliment when I predicted to Mark Sullivan that "before he is finished the Right Wingers will not like him either."

Other recommendations in our report on "War and Postwar Adjustment Policies" called for special attention to the problems of small business, and the encouragement of education and scientific research. We also advocated the continuation of wartime controls until inflation was absolutely licked (a proposal which was generally ignored); and the immediate preparation of plans to reduce taxes when and if conditions warranted.

Mindful always that demobilization and reconversion were primarily problems of people, our report laid special emphasis upon the human factor. We urged the best possible medical care for our disabled veterans, and proposed a vocational training program for all servicemen and workers. We advocated, as well, unemployment insurance and a job-placement program.

In order to provide centralized direction over the entire field of human demobilization, we proposed the appointment of a "Work Director"—a man of such outstanding caliber as to command the confidence of the country. Our choice for this job was William Jeffers. This was one recommendation which was not carried out. Instead, General Frank T. Hines of the Veterans Administration was appointed Retraining and Re-employment Administrator.

Our report was designed to help prepare for peace. But in February, 1944, there were still many arduous months—and many bitter trials to face—before reconversion could become a reality.

XVIII

Mission to London

A s THE THIRD YEAR of the war unfolded, it became increasingly evident to those around the President that he was badly in need of a rest. He was carrying an inhuman burden, and it was wearing down even his remarkable constitution and spirit.

It is difficult for the ordinary citizen to comprehend the load a President must carry even in the best of times, much less the awful responsibilities he must bear in time of war. President Roosevelt was called upon to make fateful decisions daily; the problems of the world flowed across his desk in a never-ending stream. The lives of millions, the very survival of the Republic, were his constant concern.

After a decade of day-by-day crises, he was beginning to falter. In the winter of 1944, he developed a hacking, persistent cough. Several press conferences had to be canceled, and rumors began circulating about his health. The President's doctors urged him to take a vacation in a warm climate—Guantánamo Bay was mentioned. When I learned of this, I offered him my South Carolina plantation, Hobcaw, as a Presidential retreat. He gladly accepted.

There are few better places to rest than Hobcaw. It has no an-

335

noying distractions of any kind, not even a telephone. The big brick house, situated on a knoll overlooking the Waccamaw River, is surrounded by a broad expanse of fields, woods, and streams. The gardens would be in bloom when the President was there, and then it would be one of the loveliest places on earth. For forty years I had retreated to Hobcaw when I was tired, and I invariably came away refreshed in mind and body.

President Roosevelt's arrival, on Easter Sunday, was cloaked in wartime security. But the secret was not kept for long from the surrounding countryside as the Presidential entourage—camouflaged Marines, Secret Service men, White House correspondents, and various aides—moved in. There was, too, a constant coming and going of distinguished visitors.

At Hobcaw, the President enjoyed more rest than he had in years. He fished and cruised the Pee Dee and Waccamaw Rivers, visited some of the show-place gardens in the neighborhood, sat in the sun, and managed to sleep ten to twelve hours every night. He had intended to stay only two weeks, but he enjoyed his visit so much that he extended it to a month.

The President was, of course, in hourly contact with the progress of the war. One day he received a Naval report on Japanese plane losses. He remarked to me that he had trouble believing its accuracy; it seemed so inflated. Actually, as we were to learn, Japan was already being forced to scrape the bottom of the barrel to sustain its air forces.

I spent many hours with F.D.R. during that sojourn, though I left for Washington or New York whenever he had important visitors or conferences. On those warm April days, only a year from the end of Roosevelt's life, I felt that our friendship—which had survived many disagreements—was closer than it had ever been.

On his return from Hobcaw, F.D.R. looked rested and tanned. But he was tiring, to be sure, and functioned best early in the day, when he was fresh. I recall telling Byrnes that he should try to discuss all important questions with the President in the morning, and try to keep him from working much in the afternoon. But, of course, no one could keep Franklin Roosevelt from his man-killing task.

When he returned to Washington, he was faced not only with the climactic phases of the war, but with the impending Presidential elections. Although the war's end was still many months away, 1944 was a Presidential year, and the great game of politics was being played almost as usual. Not since Lincoln's time had there been a Presidential election during war. And though one might resent the distraction of elections at such a time, it was nevertheless a source of pride that even in such circumstances the democratic process went on.

In 1940, F.D.R. himself had had doubts for a while whether he ought to seek a third term. But in 1944, there was no doubt in his mind. He was determined to finish the job of war and to help forge the peace. As for the Democratic Party, clearly no other candidate was possible.

If there was no question that Roosevelt would again be the Party's nominee at the Chicago convention, there were many questions about who his running mate would be. It was the general consensus that Henry Wallace could not be renominated for the Vice-presidency, although he was the favorite of labor and the liberals. The convention had accepted him in 1940 only under F.D.R.'s threat to withdraw his own name, if Wallace were rejected.

The most likely Vice-presidential candidate was James F. Byrnes; and he was the man Roosevelt at first preferred. Indeed, F.D.R. had even considered him as a running mate in 1940. On the night when he had told me that he would appoint Byrnes to the Supreme Court, he had also mentioned him as a possible Vice-presidential candidate. Byrnes himself, despite his earlier refusal to have his name put before the convention in 1940, had wavered momentarily. With the delegates in angry uproar over Wallace, he had phoned me and proposed that I ask the President to accept him for second place on the ticket. This I declined to do; for, as I told Byrnes, I knew that the President was determined to have Wallace.

As the 1944 convention approached, Donald Russell and Walter Brown, close associates of Byrnes, consulted me about Byrnes's Vice-presidential chances. As far as I was concerned, he was eminently qualified. He had unquestioned ability and incomparable experience; even his enemies admitted these. He had served in the House, in the Senate, on the Supreme Court—and as "czar" of the home front, as "Assistant President." It was true, however, that he would have to overcome serious political obstacles, not the least of which was the fact that, in administering OES and OWM, he had been the Administration's "no" man and had, in consequence, made many enemies.

Sometime*before the convention, after Roosevelt had assured Byrnes that he wanted him for the Vice-presidency, Byrnes asked for my help in securing the nomination. I found a strong sentiment for him among many Democratic leaders. Bob Hannegan, the National Chairman, was particularly enthusiastic. But the powerful New York boss, Ed Flynn, was not. He told me that Byrnes would hurt the ticket because of his Southern origins and labor's hostility to him. But, Flynn said, he would do "whatever the Boss wanted." He was being less than frank in giving that assurance, for he had every intention of blocking Byrnes—and he succeeded. In the end, the "Boss" apparently did what Flynn wanted.

Byrnes has recounted frankly, in his autobiography, how this happened. The essence of the story is that on the eve of the convention, Flynn and Sidney Hillman convinced Roosevelt that Byrnes would alienate both the Negro and labor vote. They prevailed upon the President to drop his support of Byrnes, and to endorse Harry Truman and William Douglas. Hillman's role in blackballing Byrnes gave birth to the phrase: "Clear it with Sidney" —the instructions Roosevelt is said to have given after approving both Truman and Douglas as acceptable nominees.

Hillman later telephoned me to assure me that he had not opposed Byrnes's nomination! When I told Byrnes of this call, he expressed himself in unmistakably lively terms.

After the convention, Harold Ickes wrote a letter to me which came close to expressing my own views:

> I don't feel too happy about what has happened here in Chicago. I don't object to Truman, but I react strongly against the method of his nomination and the seeming dominating position that the corrupt city bosses now have in the Democratic National organization.
>
> I didn't see Jimmy Byrnes while he was here. I put in several calls, one or two of them personally, but I can understand it if Jimmy felt too bruised in spirit not to want to be bothered to talk even with one who sympathized deeply with him and whose only object was to tell him so.

It was true that Byrnes felt his rejection deeply. It was a terrible disappointment to him. But he did not permit it to embitter him, as he resumed his vital work in OWM. I believe that if Byrnes had been nominated and had succeeded to the Presidency, he would have filled that high office with the same distinction with which he filled every other office he has held. But this can only be speculation. Harry Truman received the nomination to run with F.D.R. Fortunately, Mr. Truman proved equal to the task he was suddenly compelled to assume.

The Vice-presidential nomination, so often used in the past to reward party regularity or as a sop to dissident elements, has assumed increasing importance in recent years. And this is as it should be. In these times, no man should be selected for the Vice-presidency who is not thoroughly qualified for the Presidency itself.

2

The long awaited Second Front was launched shortly before the nominating conventions. By the time Roosevelt and Truman had decisively defeated Thomas Dewey and John Bricker in the elections, the Allied forces were striking toward the German heartland, while the Russians were crushing the Nazis in the east. Despite the bitter setback in the Ardennes at the end of the year, the end of the war in Europe was now visible. The growing hope was expressed in the following message from Winston Churchill to me, dated January 13, 1945. The credit he so generously accords America is typical of this appreciative ally.

> I agree with you that brighter days are before us. The great American victory in the salient may well have broken Rundstedt's teeth. The brilliant successes of MacArthur in the Philippines and such work as we British have been able to do here and there from time to time, together with the continued stamina and relentless will-power of our two peoples will, I believe, reap their reward in Europe in 1945. We have only to stand together and fight down harsh, premature judgments of each other's solutions of war problems to bring the whole world out if its misery and secure our children from a renewal of these torments.
>
> In all this you and I think and have long worked together.

The Allies were now preparing for the conference at Yalta. On January 21st, the day before his departure for the Crimea, I had a meeting with the President. He was in good form as he discussed his impending meeting with Churchill and Stalin, and he expressed confidence that they would succeed in laying the foundation of peace.

As always, he was throwing out ideas and seeking reactions to them. One idea he discussed with me was of creating a United States of Europe—a federal union which, he thought, might be the answer to many of Europe's age-old political and economic problems. He asked me what I thought. I felt that there were too many barriers to such a union in the immediate postwar world, and that our best prospects lay in an effective international organization designed to maintain world order.

Before I went in to see the President that day, I had scribbled

down some of my hopes and fears over the impending conference
which, I felt, could be decisive to the future peace of the world. I
gave the President this letter, which read in part:

> The bible and history are filled with missions upon which
> countless men have set forth to help their fellowmen.
> Never has one been fraught with such possibilities as the one
> upon which you are about to embark.
> You carry not only the hopes of the world, but you have an
> opportunity to make successful all previous attempts by making
> a peace in which their efforts can bear fruit. . . .

The letter went on to recall Wilson's tragic failure in 1919, and
to underscore the urgency of heeding the lessons of experience.
"We can learn from the mistakes of the past," I wrote. "Your mission
must succeed. Above all go my hopes and prayers for all who look
to you and I know you will not fail them."

As he read the letter, I could see that the President appeared
suddenly to be deeply affected. He said that he would keep the letter
and have Pa Watson read it to him before he went into a conference. He said he was counting upon me to help him solve some of
the economic problems of the peace, and explained that he was not
taking me to Yalta because these problems would not be discussed
there.

"Mr. President," I said, "you don't have to make any explanation
to me."

I went on to urge him to accept no proposal, and to make no
agreement, until every possible precaution against misunderstanding had been taken. The President nodded. "And remember," I
said, putting my arm on his shoulder (the only time, I believe, I
ever permitted myself this familiarity), "wherever you sit is the
head of the table."

Whether he was moved by my affectionate words and gesture,
or was suddenly overcome by the weight of his burdens and the
realization of the trials that still lay ahead—whether it was any or
all of these things, I do not know—but, as I finished speaking, I

saw tears well up in the President's eyes. He dropped his head on his chest to hide them, and sat thus for a long moment. Then, regaining his composure, he looked up and thanked me again and said good-bye.

But the next day, when the President set out for Yalta, his resilient spirit had banished the momentary dejection I had seen, and restored his confidence and good cheer. With all that he had on his mind, he still found time, before sailing, to write me the following letter, acknowledging some books I had sent:

January 22, 1945.

Dear Bernie:—

I am thrilled by those lovely books. That is a grand copy of "Mahan" and I am awfully glad to have it.

But that copy of the "Royal Palaces" is the most beautiful thing I have ever seen—the plates, etc. I do not want anyone to know that I have a copy of the "Royal Palaces" because some Hearst or Patterson newspaperman will write a story that I am considering myself at least the equal of King George III, and that the White House is going to be made to cover about four times as much land as it occupies now.

All these plates are a joy and are reminiscent of the previous era before we lost the art of doing the same thing. If we had not lost that art they could have done an aquatint of you and me sitting on a throne in the East Room. I have only had a chance to look through them but I am going to do it again as soon as I get back.

With my warm regards,
As ever yours,
Franklin D. Roosevelt

The Yalta Conference has been grist for the mill of many special pleaders, but those who condemn it seem to have been blessed more with hindsight than with foresight. I myself have never subscribed to the thesis that America was sold out to the Russians at Yalta, or that Stalin pulled the wool over the eyes of a failing President. If Russia had kept the pledges she made at Yalta, the alliance which had won the war would have been able to devise a just peace.

When I saw President Roosevelt on his return from Yalta, he showed the destructive physical effects of his difficult trip. He was deeply depressed, too, by the loss of Pa Watson, who had died on the voyage back.

The President told me about some of the agreements reached at Yalta, including the decision to give the Soviet three votes in the United Nations General Assembly. I thought this a mistake and told the President that if this secret leaked out, he could expect a howl from his opponents and a strong public reaction generally. I urged him to have Sam Rosenman draft a statement in which the United States would claim two additional votes, to which Stalin was prepared to agree. But the President did not think the matter important.

During the course of our conversation, the President suddenly asked: "Bernie, how long do you think it will be before we have real peace in the world?"

"Five or ten years," I ventured to forecast.

"Good God, no!" he exclaimed.

But I thought this a reasonable estimate. If we were to have peace, I went on, we would have to find men who knew how to wage peace, and who knew how to "get people back to work at jobs of their own choosing." F.D.R. liked that phrase—"Yes, that's what we have to do," he agreed.

Shortly after this talk with the President in mid-March, I was asked to undertake a mission to London for him. The immediate origin of this assignment was a visit from Harry Hopkins, who talked rather vaguely of difficulties the President was having with Churchill. Hopkins complained that neither he nor Ambassador John Winant had been able to get anywhere with the Prime Minister. Because of my close friendship with Churchill, the President wanted me to go over and confer with him.

A few days later the President called me in. Our appointment was in the afternoon, and he appeared very tired. When I entered, the President began the conversation by telling me of Field Marshall Kesselring's offer to surrender the German forces in Italy and of Russia's insistence that the negotiations be held up until Soviet representatives could attend. I told the President I hoped he wouldn't delay, which, of course, he had no intentions of doing.

His refusal to accede to Soviet demands in this matter precipitated a rude and angry outburst from Stalin. He accused the President of promising Germany easier peace terms in exchange for the capitulation of their forces in Italy; and he charged that, as a result of this surrender, German troops had been shifted to the Russian front. Later, when I was in London, Churchill showed me a copy of Roosevelt's reply. There was nothing tired or vacillating in the President's denial of Stalin's false charges, or in his denunciation of the "vile misrepresentations" of those who had persuaded Stalin to believe the President guilty of bad faith.

In asking me to go to London, the President explained that he wished me to explore with Churchill various problems relating to the peace. I could not, however, elicit any detailed instructions from him; I had the impression he was almost too weary to make decisions. He specified only one point he wished me to raise—that it would be a grand gesture if the British restored Hong Kong to China. This was no new idea with the President. His frequent needling of Churchill over the question of Britain's colonies sometimes got under the Prime Minister's skin. I told the President that I myself disagreed with him, but that I would, of course, deliver his message.

Before departing, I undertook a round of briefing sessions. Among those with whom I conferred were Secretary of State Stettinius and his aides, Berle, Clayton, and Acheson; General Arnold, and Admirals Leahy and King. Stettinius and Acheson advised me on the state of negotiations relating to UNESCO. Clayton filled me in on British applications for loans. Admiral King asked me to sound out the British on American retention of Naval bases in the Pacific. General Arnold was similarly concerned to maintain, though not exclusively for military use, the network of air bases that we and the British had built around the world.

The President had cabled Churchill on March 19th: "I would very much appreciate it if you would see Bernie Baruch as soon as convenient to you, and also appreciate it if you could wire him as he counts you one of his oldest friends and would much prefer having your approval before he goes." Churchill replied at once, asking me to come over immediately. On March 28th, I left for London in the President's plane, the *Sacred Cow*.

3

The sight of bombed and battered London, a city which I knew so well, hit me hard. It is one thing to read about the effects of air raids in the papers; it is quite another to walk among the ruins.

I have often wished that delegations of American citizens could have been taken on tours of wartime London or Coventry, and of Auschwitz or Buchenwald, too. I think such an experience could only have had a beneficial effect on the attitude of those who knew war only at a distance of three thousand miles.

I was, naturally, looking forward to seeing my old friend, Churchill, again. I had seen him briefly on several of his wartime visits to the United States; and we had been in touch throughout the war, though his communications were understandably very brief.

I was barely installed in my hotel room when the Prime Minister and Brendan Bracken, his Minister of Information, were ushered in. I was reminded instantly of that first meeting with Churchill in the Villa Majestic during the Paris Peace Conference. Here we were, discussing the problems of peace again.

I found the Churchillian vigor undiminished. He was so eager to begin conversations that he was all for bundling me into his car and carrying me down to Chequers that very night. But the long flight over the Atlantic had tired me, and I did not want to do any serious talking, even with friends, while I was fatigued. It is much too easy to make mistakes and engender misunderstandings. But I agreed to go down to the Prime Minister's country home next day.

As we drove through the English countryside on the following morning, Churchill talked with admiration about the President, and about Harry Hopkins of whom he was also very fond. To a great extent, the Anglo-American alliance was based on the uniquely personal relationship which existed between Churchill and F.D.R.

In a way, the ride down to Chequers illustrates how such personal relations can often accomplish what formal representations cannot. "What's all this talk about the boys having difficulties with you?" I asked, referring to British opposition to UNESCO.

Churchill explained that he didn't think that such an organization as UNESCO would prove effective.

"Will it do any harm?" I asked.

"No," he acknowledged, "but it won't do any good."

"Well, if it won't do any harm, why not give the President what he wants." By the time we reached Chequers, Churchill had agreed to support the UNESCO plans.

A few days later, he told me that he had received Cabinet approval. I asked him to communicate this to Washington through Ambassador Winant, not through me, as I was not an official representative of the government.

The following days were filled with conversations of the most intimate sort with Churchill. I spent two weekends with him at Chequers. It was a great treat to sit again at table with him, and to hear him hold forth—with his inimitable verve and eloquence—on a host of subjects, great and small.

In addition, he arranged for me to attend several Cabinet sessions at No. 10 Downing Street, and to confer with members of his government and other important British figures. Among those

I saw were Foreign Secretary Anthony Eden; Deputy Prime Minister Clement Attlee; Sir John Anderson, the Chancellor of the Exchequer; the Labour Party leaders, Herbert Morrison and Ernest Bevin; Lords Camrose, Kemsley, and Beaverbrook, influential lords of the press; Prime Minister Smuts, of South Africa and Prime Minister Fraser, of New Zealand; Foreign Secretary Evatt, of Australia; leading bankers and industrialists; and Churchill's Army, Air, and Navy staffs.

The major subject of these conversations was Britain's economic future and the question of American financial aid. I found almost everyone bemoaning England's economic outlook and fearing the worst when the war should end. This pessimism, it seemed to me, was both unrealistic and dangerous. It threatened to rob Britons of their native self-reliance, and impelled them to lean upon the United States.

In all my discussions I sought to dispel this gloom. As I later wrote in the report on my mission: "I, for one, refuse to accept the depressed valuation some place on the Empire." Although I realized the tremendous battering Britain had taken in the war, I felt confident that the same fortitude which had sustained the British through the blitz would enable them to recover from their sufferings and loss, and reach new heights in peacetime.

For one thing, as I pointed out to my British friends, and as I had emphasized in my report on "War and Postwar Adjustment Policies," the sound basis for prosperity lay in the accumulated wartime savings of the people and in the long pent-up demand for peacetime goods. This idea seemed to impress Churchill. On several occasions I heard him ask whether "through the savings of her people, hasn't Britain already paid off part of the cost of war?"

Another factor I emphasized was that the defeat of Germany and Japan, and their elimination from world trade, would give Britain a tremendous opportunity to swell her foreign commerce in both volume and profit.

Although I had confidence in Britain's future, I knew that she would need financial assistance to make the transition to peace, and I believed America should give it. It was a responsibility we could not evade. But I did not believe that America was required to provide massive financial gifts; I thought it would be sufficient to provide what I called a "cylinder head loan."

"You know," I said to Churchill, "in the old days when you used to crank an automobile, if it didn't start you would put a little gasoline in the cylinder and it would fire up. That's what you need to start your economic machine." This analogy struck Churchill's imagination. He later quoted it to leaders of the Commonwealth in reminding them that Britain might not need as much help as some anticipated. Indeed, as I later reported, Churchill seemed to be using me to break down the gloom within his own government and to invigorate the outlook of those around him.

It was natural for the proud and self-reliant Churchill to respond to my confidence in his country, and to reject any notion of its dependency upon America. American aid would be required, he felt, but Britain would and could make her way in the postwar world only through the efforts of her own people. "Sweat and thrift," he said to me, would restore Britain's depleted wealth as "blood, sweat and tears" had brought victory in war.

But Churchill's view that only a modest amount of assistance was required from America—a view shared by Beaverbrook and Bracken—was not the prevailing view in Whitehall. Throughout the government, there was a strong sentiment that the United States should provide financial assistance on a major scale.

One of my discussions on this subject took place in the underground dining room at 10 Downing Street, where Churchill put me, figuratively, "into the ring" with his Cabinet. At this meeting, I held up what I considered Britain's bright future if she would modernize and improve her industry and seize her opportunities in foreign trade. America, I went on, would be glad to aid Britain; but she could not rely upon us to carry her. When I asked Sir John Anderson, Chancellor of the Exchequer, how much money England wanted from us, he replied, "I just can't say." To which Churchill retorted sharply, "If you don't tell our friends what you want and why, how can you expect them to help us?"

It developed that Lord Keynes and the Bank of England really wanted between five and eight billion dollars—as a loan, if necessary, but preferably as a gift, though "honeyed up not to appear so," as I later wrote. When I pointed out that the United States, rich as it was, could not go about distributing such huge sums, Keynes, impervious to such a point of view, spoke up. "What we need is some kind of a brain wave, like Lend-Lease," he said airily. Lord Thomas Catto, governor of the Bank of England, went on to paint a dismal picture of England's indebtedness to her dominions and colonies, and the need to meet their demands for repayment.

"Well, they're your own people," I replied somewhat abruptly. "It's been Lend-Lease with us right along. Why can't it be Lend-Lease with them?"

Many British officials talked of seeking some new monetary measure of value as a way out of their difficulties. Gold no longer served, it seemed, because they didn't have any, although Field Marshall Smuts remarked in my presence that rich new gold reefs had been discovered in the South African Rand. (The potentialities of this new strike were so impressive that I jokingly offered to swap the almost twenty-one billions in Fort Knox for what lay underground there.) But some of the British were serious in asserting that, since America had all the chips, they had to devise some new kind of game.

This is often the case; when the rules of the game no longer serve our advantage, we try to change the rules, if not the game. I didn't get into any argument over this except to say that, if they could devise some other financial instrument that would meet my definition of good money—that which people would voluntarily take for their goods and services—I would be glad to advocate it.

According to Ambassador Winant, the effect of my talks with the British was very beneficial. He felt that I had helped dispel

some of the gloom in financial and official circles. When I left
London, the Churchill government was prepared to do more for
themselves and to ask less of us. Unfortunately, this attitude of self-
reliance was not followed by the successor government. Moreover,
instead of devoting herself to rehabilitating, renovating, and mod-
ernizing her obsolescent industrial machine, England, under the
Labour government, diverted much of her energy and resources
from the task of recovery to a program of economic experimentation.

My conversations with Churchill and his associates ranged over
a wide variety of subjects. I took up with the Prime Minister, as
the President had directed, the question of ceding Hong Kong back
to China. His silence was more eloquent than anything he might
have said. As for the Pacific islands we had wrested from the Japanese, which the Navy wanted as bases, Churchill declared unequivocally: "You can take the whole Pacific Ocean. Whatever America wants to do there will satisfy us."

The future of Germany occupied a substantial portion of our
talks. I found the British torn between a fear of a resurgent Germany, capable of again waging war, and a desire to rebuild her as
a buffer aginst an aggressive Russia. At this point, as I shall relate
later, I favored the strictest control of Germany.

In one discussion at Chequers, the subject of German war crimes
and punishment came up. There were some original and unique
suggestions on what ought to be done with Hitler, if he fell into
our hands alive. But Churchill, I recall, thought it would be much
simpler if he were to perish with the evil he had created.

Churchill also spoke to me about the possibility of an Anglo-
American defense alliance, a project dear to his heart. I told him
I did not think the American people would accept it, but that I
did feel they would join in a world organization to fight for peace.
I knew that America had outgrown the narrowness which had led
her to reject the League. Churchill agreed, reluctantly, that a pro-

posal for an alliance between our two countries would not fare well.

At the time of my visit, England was looking forward to an election. Churchill appeared quite confident about the impending test. He had good reason, considering the magnificent leadership he had provided during the war and the whole-hearted way in which his people had rallied to him. He talked of the possibility of the President paying him a visit in London sometime before the election, which would have been a feather in his campaign hat.

Yet, despite Churchill's optimism, I had intimations that he might be defeated. Sam Rosenman, who was then in London making preparations for the Nuremberg trials, told me that Harold Laski had shown him figures which indicated the trend was away from Churchill. When I asked the Prime Minister about this, however, he dismissed it. Actually, Churchill was only a few months away from losing his tenure. In July, England voted him out of office. It was a shattering surprise to all the world, but a useful reminder of the fickleness of electorates.

As an interlude in my London talks, I flew to General Eisenhower's headquarters at Rheims. To my disappointment, Eisenhower was away, but I had a good reunion with my old friend, General Walter Bedell Smith, Eisenhower's Chief of Staff. Smith arranged for me to fly into Frankfurt to see General George Patton.

The city was a smoking ruin. I was driven to Patton's headquarters in an armored car, with outriders to the front, rear, and on the flanks. Such precautions seemed absurd to me, but they were occasioned, I was told, by broadcasts on the German radio that Nazi "werewolves" were out after me.

Patton was certainly a great soldier and an unforgettable personality. During luncheon, he recounted some of the exploits of his famous Third Army, and spoke caustically of the orders which had compelled him to slow his drive across Germany. "If they'd given me the gasoline, Baruch, I'd have been in Berlin long ago," he declared. He remarked, with appropriately lurid adjectives, that his troops had driven the Germans back eleven miles that morning and were going to give them more of the same that afternoon.

At about this point, with lunch still unfinished, I stood up and said: "General, this is no place for a visiting fireman. You've got business with the Germans, and I'm not going to take up your time."

Before leaving Frankfurt, I visited a military hospital and talked with several badly wounded boys. It was a grim experience and it left me shaken. When I left the hospital, I sat for a long while in a nearby park, thinking of those boys in the hospital and the boys who would yet be brought in. I thought of the two wars which had seared the world in my own lifetime, and the countless convulsions which had gone before. I remember trying to come to grips in my mind with what it was in men which makes them capable of such incredible folly. I couldn't understand it then, nor can I now.

4

Upon my return to London, I wound up my talks and prepared to return home. On April 12th, I sent a cable to the President:

> Arriving Saturday and will hold myself subject your wishes. I have been deeply impressed by the foresight and courage which have characterized this great military achievement and by your patience and wisdom in handling the many delicate and intricate international problems. Affectionate good wishes. Bernie.

I do not know whether this message ever reached the President.

That night, I attended a dinner with Churchill. It was a gay occasion with much toasting of the bright future beckoning. After it was over, I returned to my rooms at Claridge's. Sam Rosenman, who was also staying there, stopped by to chat for a few minutes. I was preparing for bed when the telephone rang. It was Brendan Bracken.

"Have you heard about the President?" he asked, his voice hushed and trembling.

"No. What's happened?" I asked.

"He's dead."

I could hardly believe what I heard.

When I recovered from the initial shock, I sent for Rosenman and told him the terrible news. From the radio, we soon learned some of the details. The President had been at Warm Springs when he suddenly collapsed. "I have a terrific headache," he had said as he lost consciousness. He died a few hours later.

Rosenman decided to return home with me the next day. Elliott Roosevelt and Ed Flynn were then in London, and I asked them to fly back with us in the *Sacred Cow*.

Meanwhile, Churchill called; he was deeply grieved. "Do you think I ought to go to Washington?" he asked.

"No, Winston," I replied, "I think you ought to stay here on the job." We talked for a few minutes, and he agreed.

"Come by and see me before you leave tomorrow," he said before hanging up.

He was still in bed when I went in to see him the next morning; he looked greatly upset. "Do you think I ought to go?" he asked again. I assured him that it would be wiser if he remained at home.

At noon, my companions and I took off on the long and gloomy flight to Washington. None of us felt much like talking. We were all occupied with our own thoughts and memories of the President.

I recalled once again the first time I met him in Albany in 1911, when as a State Senator he was attracting attention by his audacious attack on Tammany. He was young and somewhat haughty then, but beneath the youth and hauteur, one could sense determination and confidence. I remember telling Thomas F. Ryan that here was no upstart who could be easily intimidated.

I thought of him in Washington during World War One, pushing the Navy's cause with energy—too much energy to the taste of some who dealt with him.

A man's character can be measured by his reaction to adversity. And no one can fail to be moved and inspired by the courage and will power with which Roosevelt faced up to his personal ordeal. I remembered the admiration which I felt, along with everyone present in the hall, as he swung on crutches up to the podium, to make his "Happy Warrior" speech at the 1924 convention.

I never heard him complain about his handicap; he mentioned his legs only once in my presence, and then jokingly. I had come to see him at his house in New York. As I came up in the elevator, F.D.R. greeted me cheerfully: "Well, you see Bernie, with these elevators and things a man doesn't need legs."

Random memories such as these flowed through my mind as we winged home to the funeral. I recalled a Christmas Day when Roosevelt, an expression of affection and amused tolerance on his face, sat listening dutifully while his mother gave him a vigorous lecture against the soldiers' bonus. As she turned away he winked at me, just as she spun around to shake a warning finger at him and say, "And Franklin, don't you wink at Mr. Baruch!"

He was devoted to his mother, as she was to him. One day I was with him in his office, discussing the German attack on the destroyer *Greer*, when the telephone rang. He picked it up, and his face suddenly went grave. He said, "Yes. Yes. Yes." When he put down the phone, he said to me: "That was Ma's physician. She's very sick. But I don't think I can go up to Hyde Park until her birthday. I've got to attend to this matter of the *Greer*."

"Mr. President," I said, "I am a much older man than you but I have never ceased regretting the days I could have spent with my mother and didn't. You can just as well handle this matter from Hyde Park."

He didn't say a word, but pushed a button on his desk. General Watson came in, and the President said: "Pa, get the train ready. I'm going up to see Ma tonight." He got there just in time for her to recognize him in her last moments. Several times later he referred to this incident, saying: "Bernie, I'll never forget your making me go up to see Ma."

Now that the President himself was dead, I remembered with particular force his zest for living. He used to enjoy the pleasures of the "children's hour," with its ritual of cocktail-making and the convivial conversation of his friends. He enjoyed betting on horse races, and enjoyed winning them even more. When he once won a bet on Bold Venture in the Kentucky Derby, his delight was uninhibited.

His sense of humor was always evident. I recalled many of the amusing messages he had sent me, such as the one I received when I turned seventy-three. "Keep right at it," he wired. "Someday you will grow up."

Thinking back across the years, I also recalled the times we had been annoyed and angry with each other—the times we had fought and argued—over the Senate purge, and SPAB, and National Service legislation. But no disagreement over public issues could impair my genuine affection for F.D.R. or sever our friendship.

I arrived in the mourning capital in time to attend the White House funeral services for the President. Only two of the President's children were present—Anna and Elliott; his other three sons were away at war. Mrs. Roosevelt, pale but composed, provided strength for others.

Later, the body of the Commander in Chief was borne on a flag-draped caisson past hundreds of thousands of sorrowing citizens. Some stood in silent grief; many wept openly. I rode on the funeral train which carried the President back to Hyde Park and his final resting place in the rose garden of his home.

Franklin Roosevelt's place in the front rank of history's great men is assured. To have been elected four times to the Presidency; to have instituted a series of far-reaching social and economic reforms; to have led the nation through a shattering domestic crisis, and then through a terrible war; to have set up a framework on which a durable peace might have been built—this is only part of the record of greatness he wrote.

But what were the qualities which enabled him to write this record—to meet and make so many great occasions? For one thing, he had courage; adversity never fazed him. He had, too, confidence in himself and faith in the causes he championed. He had vision and imagination. And he had the rare gift of leadership—the ability to share his courage and confidence, his vision and imagination with others. Like Woodrow Wilson, he had the capacity to raise men's hopes, strengthen their wills, and call forth the best that was within them.

Whatever his defects and errors, Roosevelt believed deeply in the ideas and ideals of democracy. He thought of liberty, justice, equality of opportunity not in abstract terms, but in terms of human beings. And because he dedicated himself to helping men realize these ideals—and because he succeeded in such great measure—his place in history and in the memory of the people will endure.

XIX

Control of Atomic Energy

WITHIN A WEEK after President Harry Truman had taken office, I called on him, accompanied by Secretary of State Stettinius, to present my report on my London mission. I knew how overwhelmed the President must have been in those first hectic days of his Presidency, but he gave no evidence of being ruffled or uncertain. Before taking up my report, Truman and Stettinius engaged in a brief discussion of Argentina's bid to enter the war against the Axis, a move which Truman characterized as an effort "to get in on the gravy train."

Then, turning to me, the President said, "Mr. Baruch, I would like to read this carefully. I'm a very slow reader."

"That's all right," I said, "I have all day and all night."

So the three of us sat there while President Truman read, nodding his head in evident agreement as he went along. The report summarized my conversations with the British, and contained various recommendations on the problems of the impending peace. Briefly, I favored aid to Britain on condition that they "do more for themselves and . . . ask less of us." I proposed strict control of Germany, a policy of friendly firmness toward the Russians, and a revamping of our peace-making machinery. About all this, I will have more to say later.

When he had finished reading the report, President Truman said: "I don't want anyone to see this document. It is going to be the basis of my policies." I was, of course, gratified by the President's reaction, though puzzled by his injunction about secrecy. There was nothing of a security nature in the report.

Before our meeting broke up, I asked, "Don't you think Will Clayton ought to see this report?" I was thinking of the references in it to trade and commerce, duties and Lend-Lease, which came under Clayton's jurisdiction in the State Department. The President agreed. But the next day I received this letter from Stettinius:

> On second thought I believe it is much better not to show the report to anyone, not even Will. It has been put in my vault in the Department of State. I have reported this to the President.
>
> I am asking Will to call on you some time next week and I hope that at that time you will be good enough to tell him about a few of the economic matters you discussed about which you feel he should be informed.
>
> I am confident that as a result of your visit things between us and the British will be much easier. It was of tremendous value to this Government for you to have made the trip at the time you did, and I am personally grateful to you for your great contribution in ironing out many of our difficulties.

That was the beginning of an inexplicable secrecy about my report. Not even James Byrnes saw it after he succeeded Stettinius as Secretary of State. More recently the State Department was unable to secure Truman's permission to publish it in a volume of official documents. To this day, I cannot understand why it was suppressed.

When Truman assumed the Presidency, the war was coming to its crashing climax. Three weeks after he took over, the "thousand-year-Reich" unconditionally surrendered. Four months later, as we braced for the final, dreaded assault on Japan, she was brought to her knees—suddenly, dramatically—by two mighty blasts that awesomely punctuated the end of the most violent war in history.

2

I have never forgotten the sense of awe I felt when I learned the meaning and implication of those gigantic and terrifying clouds which spread in evil splendor over Hiroshima and Nagasaki. I am still overwhelmed by the thought of this power which men have torn from nature—a power which can make the deserts bloom or incinerate the globe.

When I learned some of the facts about the atomic bomb, I realized that I had been given two earlier intimations of nuclear energy development, though I had not recognized them as such at the time. As far back as 1932, Charles MacDowell, a former WIB colleague, had told me of the work German scientists were doing to harness atomic energy. He thought of it not in military terms, but as a development which offered tremendous industrial possibilities. I never learned what came of his efforts to explore the matter. I have often shuddered, though, at what would have been the fate of the world had the Germans succeeded in harnessing nuclear power before we did.

The second hint came during World War Two, when Mrs. Roosevelt asked me to see a young scientist who had come to her with a matter she felt was of the utmost urgency. The young man was in a highly nervous state. All I could get from him was that he was engaged in developing a secret process at the University of Chicago, and that he was convinced his work was being obstructed. I could learn no more, but I had heard enough to know that this matter was not in my bailiwick. I asked Dr. Conant to see the troubled physicist. Later, I realized that the young scientist had been involved in the breakthrough experiments on nuclear chain reactions, which were carried on at the University.

From the moment we stepped into the atomic age, it was clear that America could not long retain a monopoly on nuclear energy. It was equally clear that the problems presented by its discovery, as Secretary of State Byrnes said before the United Nations General Assembly in January, 1946, could not be solved by any one nation. "They are the common responsibility of all nations." The control of this cosmic force demanded international coöperation of a character never before achieved in world society. I did not then imagine, as I followed the early discussions on this subject, that I would be called upon to help solve this most crucial problem of our age.

The first step toward the formulation of a plan to control atomic energy was taken in January, 1946, when Byrnes appointed a committee to investigate the problems involved. This committee consisted of Undersecretary of State Acheson, Dr. Conant, Dr. Vannevar Bush, former Assistant Secretary of War John McCloy, and Major General Leslie Groves, who had headed the Manhattan District—the code name for the A-bomb project—to study the problem of atomic control. The committee was assisted by a board of consultants headed by David Lilienthal, then Chairman of T.V.A.

Then, early in March, Byrnes told me that President Truman wished me to serve as the American Representative on the United Nations Atomic Energy Commission, created by resolution of the United Nations to draft the American proposals for a system of international control. He stressed the importance of this task, and urged me to accept.

My first reaction was to decline. For more than five years I had been working, virtually on a full-time basis, in the war production program. I was looking forward to a rest. I also felt that the task Byrnes was offering me required a younger man; I was then in my seventy-sixth year. I went down to Hobcaw to think things over. But I soon realized that I could not decline. I sent word to Byrnes and returned North immediately to confer with him and other officials, and to begin studying the issues with which I would be dealing. But then, the situation was suddenly confused by the un-authorized publication of the report of the Acheson-Lilienthal group.

This report, which laid the basis for a system of international control of atomic energy, proved indispensable in formulating specific plans. But it was, in Acheson's words, a "rough sketch," "a sort of working paper." The report defined itself as "a place to begin, a foundation on which to build." It did not pretend to offer a definitive program; for example, it did not deal with the problem of enforcement—a problem which I considered crucial.

Nonetheless, the report was immediately interpreted as the official statement of American policy. And when, a day or two after its release, Sir Alexander Cadogan told me that he had been informed by Acheson that the United States would offer the Acheson-Lilienthal report to the United Nations Atomic Energy Commission as a basis for discussion, I immediately went to Acheson for clarification.

I could not understand why Cadogan, the British representative on the UNAEC, should have been informed of the United States's intention, about which I, the American Representative, was kept ignorant. Nor could I see the purpose of my appointment if the United States plans on atomic control had already been decided upon. When Acheson confirmed what Cadogan had told me, I told him plainly that he would then have to find another messenger boy, because Western Union didn't take anybody at my age. I had never served as a messenger or mouthpiece before, and did not intend to start now.

I asked for an appointment with President Truman. When I saw the President, I handed him the following letter:

March 26, 1946

My dear Mr. President:

I was, of course, very much gratified that you should have expressed such great confidence in me as to appoint me the United

States representative on the United Nations Atomic Energy Commission. I do not underestimate either the honor or the responsibility but, as I have become more familiar with the situation, there are certain elements of it which are causing me concern, and which I, therefore, want to discuss with you. As I understand my duties and authority, they consist presently solely of the obligation of representing the United States policy on atomic energy, as communicated to me by you directly or through the Secretary of State, before the United Nations Organization. I see nowhere any duty or responsibility on me to participate in the formation of that policy.

This situation has been brought very forcibly to my attention by the press announcements of the report rendered by Mr. Acheson's Committee. I do not underestimate the effect of this publication in the United States or in the world at large, and while I have not had an opportunity to examine the report with care and cannot state my own definite views with respect to it, the letter from Secretary Byrnes to me transmitting the report states that it was unanimously recommended by a Committee headed by the Under Secretary of State. This brings the report pretty close to the category of the United States Government policy.

I have no doubt that the public feels that I am going to have an important relation to the determination of our atomic energy policy. There is no legal basis for this view and now that the Under Secretary of State's Committee Report has been published, the determination of policy will be greatly affected by the contents of this report. Even the superficial and incomplete examination of the subject that I have been able to make in the last few days convinces me that this report is likely to be the subject of considerable and rather violent differences of opinion. Its publication, which I understand to have been unauthorized, does not render the situation any less difficult.

These are the things that have been bothering me, and I wanted to talk them over with you before coming to a final conclusion myself as to whether, in the circumstances, I can be useful to you. I will need a little more time to reflect. As it presently stands, I think that embarrassment all around would be avoided if you would ask Chairman Connally of the Foreign Relations Committee to postpone any action on confirmation of my appointment until I have had a little more time to think things over.

Respectfully yours,

Bernard M. Baruch

In discussing our interview in his memoirs, President Truman has suggested that I was trying to infringe on his Presidential prerogative to determine policy. He has written that he read me a lecture on the powers of the Presidency, and admonished me that he and he alone would make policy. His recollection in this matter is, regrettably, inaccurate. Far from giving me any such lecture, Truman was most affable, and plainly anxious for me not to withdraw from the task. When the question arose about who was to draft the atomic proposals, he made this exact and characteristic reply: "Hell, you are!"

I understood this remark as an expression of his confidence in me, and his reliance upon me to give him my best advice as to what our policy should be. I appreciated, of course, that the final policy decision had to come from him—and, to his everlasting credit, the one President Truman made was sound.

Byrnes echoed the President's attitude. At a meeting with him, attended also by John Hancock, Byrnes remarked, as Hancock noted in a memo summarizing this talk, that he "depended upon Baruch to take the initiative, develop the plans, and carry the initiative in the creation of a policy which . . . [Baruch] might have approved by the President as . . . [Baruch] might wish."

With my position clarified, and fortified further by this expression of the President's and Byrnes's confidence, I assembled my team of alternates and fellow workers. I turned once again to John Hancock and Herbert Swope. I also called on Ferd Eberstadt and Fred Searls, head of Newmont Mining Corporation and a former assistant to Byrnes in OWM. These men put aside their private interests to serve with me. Without them, I could not have carried on the work.

By and large, public reaction to the appointment of me and

my colleagues was gratifying. But, of course, approval was not unanimous. In scientific circles particularly, there was disappointment and dissatisfaction at my selection. I had hoped that the State Department board of scientific consultants would continue to serve in that capacity as advisers to me; and I asked Byrnes to request them to do so. They declined for a variety of reasons. There were also the usual aspersions on "Wall Streeters," and one or two men displayed some pique, apparently because they felt they should have been given the job.

Beyond these personal reactions, however, there appeared to be a sincere conviction among scientists that only a scientist could cope with the problem of controlling the atom. Vannevar Bush, a distinguished scientist, and also my friend, was a man who never let friendship keep him from speaking his mind. He told me pointblank that, in his opinion, I was the most unqualified man in the country for the task.

"Doc, you couldn't be more right," I said. "Put on your hat and let's go tell the President, and that will let me out."

"If you get out," Bush protested, "the damn thing will blow up."

"If I stay in, I'm unqualified, and if I get out, it will blow up," I said. "What do you want me to do?"

"Oh, hell," Bush exploded, "stay in."

I could understand the concern of the scientists, and I tried not to be offended by their initial patronizing attitude. I was well aware of my ignorance about nuclear science. But I could not agree with Niels Bohr, who said to me, "Why not leave the question of atomic control to the scientists? They wouldn't destroy the world."

Quite apart from the implication in Bohr's remark that scientists were wiser or more noble than others when it came to dealing with the world's fate, I rejected his assumption that the fundamental problem in the control of nuclear energy is scientific. Albert Einstein once declared that the control of nuclear energy is an ethical and political problem. This was exactly my view. The problem, as I have said, is "a problem of the heart of men." At its root lies the question of man's willingness to stop killing his fellow man, to forge a society in which force is not the arbiter of disputes. To control the atom, men must learn to control the brute which lives in man.

Once I got to work, however, I found scientists who were willing to help. R.F. Bacher, Arthur H. Compton, C.A. Thomas, and Harold Urey rendered invaluable aid to me by serving on the Scientific Panel. So did J. Robert Oppenheimer, who had played so vital a role in the development of the atomic bomb. His is one of the most brilliant minds I have ever encountered. I remember a two-hour lecture he gave at my request to acquaint other representatives of the Atomic Energy Commission with the ABC's of atomic energy. For sheer intellectual virtuosity, it was a performance that could hardly be surpassed.

General Groves and General Thomas F. Farrell also gave important assistance. But the scientist on whom I relied most was the late Dr. Richard C. Tolman, of the California Institute of Technology, whose services I enlisted with Conant's help. I never knew a wiser man.

Both Acheson and Lilienthal were also very helpful and coöperative. Lilienthal, although reluctant at first to continue working on the atomic energy problem, later offered to do anything he could to help. I struck up a warm friendship with this man, who ultimately became the first chairman of the United States Atomic Energy Commission.

Before he was confirmed for this post, Lilienthal was subjected to violent attack, with Senator Kenneth McKellar acting as his chief tormenter. Lilienthal came to me in a despondent mood, regretting that he had ever entered public service. I tried to encourage him, and told him that he was permitting his critics to take the initiative. They, rather than he, were defining his views. I suggested that he seize the first opportunity to state his own convictions, which was the same kind of advice I had tried to give Mr. Wilson on the ship coming home from Paris. It was advice I myself have always tried to follow—never to let my critics say what is in my own mind. Lilienthal took it. Next day, he appeared before the Senate committee holding hearings on his nomination, and delivered that memorable statement of his philosophic faith which stirred the nation and subdued his enemies.

3

With the aid of all these men, and with the Acheson-Lilienthal report as a guide, we set to work to elaborate a plan for the international control of atomic energy. Most of the next two months were spent in study and in conference with scientists, technical experts, State Department aides, military advisers, specialists of every kind. The most complex questions had to be answered, and a staggering variety of information obtained.

There was no question on the basic principle of international control. How to effect it was the problem—how, for the first time, to provide international jurisdiction which would be effective. Where, for example, should such jurisdiction begin? With the ownership of mines containing fissionable ore, or at the point where fissionable materials were refined from the ores? What means could be devised to detect violations? And how could we provide an effective system of inspection without encouraging espionage or infringing upon the legitimate privacy of nations? How could we propose a scheme which would provide ultimate effective control, without jeopardizing the American national interest until that control was achieved? Should the plan be limited to atomic weapons, or include biological and chemical weapons of mass destruction as well? And what form should the agreement take—a UN resolution or a conventional treaty?

These were some of the questions confronting us. But central to all of them was the question of enforcement, of preventing any

agreement on control of atomic energy from becoming another in
the long line of history's empty declarations and gestures. The
lesson of the League and the fight over Article X of the Covenant
—the record of meaningless disarmament agreements and renunciations of war—were very much in my mind. If I had learned anything out of my experiences in international affairs, it was that
world peace is impossible without the force to sustain it. Consequently, I insisted that any plan for the control of atomic energy
contain provision for sanctions against those who violated the rules.

Many people, among them Dean Acheson, had little faith in the
efficacy of sanctions. Violations would have to be dealt with
through juridical processes, Acheson said, which seemed to me to
beg the question. Acheson felt that we could do no better than to
rely upon an inspection system to detect violations and warn us
against any potential atomic attack. An effective system of inspection could, it was estimated, provide us with a twelve months'
warning period at best; more likely it would be only three months.
(Today we measure it in minutes.)

But I insisted that a warning system was not enough; if peace
were to be more than an interlude between wars, we would have
to invoke penalties against would-be aggressors.

The question of sanctions brought us up against the issue of
the veto in the Security Council. Any member, by exercising its
veto, could prevent the UN from acting against violation of the
atomic agreement. Consequently, we proposed that once the atomic
control agreement was ratified, the veto power could not be exercised against the application of penalties invoked under it.

Day after day we wrestled with these and other issues. Finally,
on June 7th, we completed a "Statement of United States Policy."
I took this document to Secretary Byrnes, who approved it, and
then the two of us went over to the White House to submit it to
President Truman. I asked him to read it in my presence, so that
I could answer any questions he might have. President Truman
read the statement of policy. As he read, he initialed each para-

graph, and at the end he wrote out his formal approval and signed his name. He did not change a word.

We discussed the crucial questions of sanctions and the veto. I pointed out that in the last analysis the only penalty we could invoke against a nation found guilty of transgression was war. Mr. Truman was absolutely firm on this. "I quite agree with you," he said. He went on to declare that if the world had followed Henry Stimson in his call for sanctions against Japan at the time she invaded Manchuria, the Second World War might never have occurred.

I was tremendously impressed with President Truman on this occasion. His grasp of the subject was sure. He displayed an understanding of the plan, and a determination to make it work.

I want to underscore that no man ever received more encouragement and support from his chief than I did from President Truman during my service on the Atomic Energy Commission. I say this as one who has had serious disagreement with him on other matters, and as one whose personal relationship with him has been ruptured.

When we left the meeting, the President returned the approved "Statement of United States Policy" to me with a memo saying that it was for my guidance as the Representative of the United States on the Atomic Energy Commission of the United Nations. The memo went on:

> . . . I want you to have authority to exercise your judgment as to the method by which the stated objectives can be accomplished.
>
> If as negotiations progress you conclude that there should be changes in this statement of policy, I will expect you to advise me and to frankly give me your views.
>
> I know that you will keep me advised as to the negotiations. However, I want you to know that I am relying upon you to exercise your own discretion in those negotiations, subject only to the general statement of policy attached, unless you should receive through the Secretary of State a further statement of policy.

A few days after delivering the policy statement to the President, Swope, Eberstadt, and I were sitting on a park bench discussing the address I was to give before the UNAEC in presenting the American plan for control of atomic energy. I said I wanted to convey, in my opening remarks, my conviction that the question the delegates were about to debate was a matter of life and death for the world.

A day or so later, Swope called me on the phone and said, "I've got your opening line. It comes from the best possible source—the Bible." Thus it was that on June 14th, I rose before the assembled members of the United Nations Atomic Energy Commission and said:

> We are here to make a choice between the quick and the dead. That is our business.
>
> Behind the black portent of the new atomic age lies a hope which, seized upon with faith, can work our salvation. If we fail, then we have damned every man to be the slave of Fear. Let us not deceive ourselves: We must elect World Peace or World Destruction.
>
> Science has torn from nature a secret so vast in its potentialities that our minds cower from the terror it creates. Yet terror is not enough to inhibit the use of the atomic bomb. The terror created by weapons has never stopped man from employing them. For each new weapon a defense has been produced, in time. But now we face a condition in which adequate defense does not exist.
>
> Science, which gave us this dread power, shows that it *can* be made a giant help to humanity, but science does *not* show us how to prevent its baleful use. So we have been appointed to obviate that peril by finding a meeting of the minds and the hearts of our peoples. Only in the will of mankind lies the answer. . . .
>
> In this crisis, we represent not only our governments but, in a larger way, we represent the peoples of the world. We must remember that the peoples do not belong to the governments but that the governments belong to the peoples. We must answer their demands; we must answer the world's longing for peace and security. . . .

In our success lies the promise of a new life, freed from the
heart-stopping fears that now beset the world. The beginning
of victory for the great ideals for which millions have bled and
died lies in building a workable plan. Now we approach fulfillment of the aspirations of mankind. At the end of the road lies
the fairer, better, surer life we crave and mean to have. . . .

The peoples of these democracies gathered here have a particular concern with our answer, for their peoples hate war. They
will have a heavy exaction to make of those who fail to provide
an escape. They are not afraid of an internationalism that pro-
tects; they are unwilling to be fobbed off by mouthings about
narrow sovereignty, which is today's phrase for yesterday's isolation.

The basis of a sound foreign policy, in this new age, for all
the nations here gathered, is that anything that happens, no
matter where or how, which menaces the peace of the world, or
the economic stability, concerns each and all of us.

I went on, then, to outline the American plan for the control
of atomic energy. It called for the creation of an International
Atomic Development Authority "to which should be entrusted all
phases of the development and use of atomic energy starting with
the raw materials and including—

1. Managerial control or ownership of all atomic-energy activities potentially dangerous to world security.

2. Power to control, inspect, and license all other atomic activities.

3. The duty of fostering the beneficial uses of atomic energy.

4. Research and development responsibilities of an affirmative
character intended to put the Authority in the forefront of
atomic knowledge and thus to enable it to comprehend, and therefore to detect, misuse of atomic energy."

The Authority was to have the right of free access at all times
for inspection; and, by a system of rapid and effective punishment,
it was to provide "a program not composed merely of pious

thoughts but of enforceable sanctions—an international law with teeth in it."

". . . The matter of punishment lies at the very heart of our present security system," I said. Any nation guilty of illegal possession or use of atomic bombs, or of illegal possession of materials suitable for use in bombs, or of seizure of Authority plant or property, or any other violation, would be liable to "immediate, swift and sure punishment. . . ." "Penalization is essential. . . ." "There must be no veto to protect those who violate their solemn agreements not to develop or use atomic energy for destructive purposes."

After a system of effective controls was brought into operation by successive stages, the United States would cease the production of bombs, and dispose of its existing stock pile of bombs according to the terms of the agreement.

I concluded my presentation of the American plan with this statement:

> In the elimination of war lies our solution, for only then will nations cease to compete with one another in the production and use of dread "secret" weapons which are evaluated solely by their capacity to kill. This devilish program takes us back not merely to the Dark Ages but from cosmos to chaos. If we succeed in finding a suitable way to control atomic weapons, it is reasonable to hope that we may also preclude the use of other weapons adaptable to mass destruction. When a man learns to say "A" he can, if he chooses, learn the rest of the alphabet too.
> Let this be anchored in our minds:
> Peace is never long preserved by weight of metal or by an armament race. Peace can be made tranquil and secure only by understanding and agreement fortified by sanctions. We must embrace international cooperation or international disintegration.
> Science has taught us how to put the atom to work. But to make it work for good instead of for evil lies in the domain dealing with the principles of human duty. We are now facing a problem more of ethics than of physics.
> The solution will require apparent sacrifice in pride and in

position, but better pain as the price of peace than death as the price of war.

This, then, was our proposal for the control of atomic energy, of which General Eisenhower was to say: "In truth, it demands nothing of others which the United States is not willing to give to others." It was a proposal unprecedented in its generosity. The United States offered to surrender a weapon it alone possessed, and to share its secrets, on only one condition—that every nation be guarded against its destructive use.

4

In the following weeks, the details of the American plan were spelled out to the UNAEC. The reaction to our proposals was overwhelmingly favorable among the United Nations, except, of course, for the Communist bloc. In the United States, public opinion upheld the plan by a large majority. But there was criticism in some quarters that the plan was too generous, that we were giving away too much. And a few, of whom Walter Lippmann was representative, criticized our proposal dealing with the veto. They failed to understand that in this lay the very heart of the American position.

A few days after the presentation of the American plan, Andrei Gromyko presented the Russian proposals, which were elaborated in a series of closed meetings during the last week of July and the first week of August. In brief, the Soviet plan called merely for an international convention outlawing the production and use of atomic weapons, and requiring the destruction of all atomic weapon stockpiles. The Russians were adamantly against any system of international inspection, control, and punishment; they refused even to consider surrender of the veto, protesting that this did violence to national sovereignty.

Of course it did! Every treaty involves some diminution of sovereignty. For myself, I believed it was time to start freeing ourselves from the fetish of national sovereignty. Just as the doctrine of unbridled laissez faire is no longer applicable to twentieth-century America and the world, so the extreme dogma of national sovereignty is no longer applicable in an age when the lives and destinies of nations are inextricably bound together. Naturally, the international control of atomic energy involves the surrender of some portion of sovereignty to a higher sovereignty—to an instrument of world order.

I summed up the differences between the American and Soviet positions in a letter to Mr. Truman on July 2nd:

> The Russian-Polish position boils down to this—that they would like to agree not to use atomic weapons, to cease their production, and to destroy our stockpile of bombs in advance of adequate measures of control and safeguards. If and when we have done this, they are ready to discuss arrangements for exchange of scientific information and the formation of international controls, inspection, licensing, surveys and general overall look-see.
>
> Our position, as you know, is that we want to start at the bottom of all atomic energy—the raw materials out of which fissionable materials can be made. These must be controlled or owned or a grip gotten upon them by every device of human ingenuity before atomic energy, the product of these raw materials, gets started on its way. We must be sure it will move into peace and not into war.
>
> If we accept the Russian position, the atomic race would really then be on, because there would be nothing but the so-called good faith of nations' pious wishes and no enforcement or knowledge of what anyone else was doing.
>
> I think we should stand firm on the position we have taken, in order that, through no compromise, will false hopes be raised among peaceful peoples, leaving any malevolent nation or nations in a position to destroy the peaceful nations. I am sure you concur in this.

President Truman was in complete accord with me. He replied on July 10th:

>   . . . It is my opinion that we should stand pat on our program.
> . . . We must have assurance that the raw materials from which
> atomic energy can be released are controlled at the source and I
> am of the opinion that we should not under any circumstances
> throw away our gun until we are sure the rest of the world can't
> arm against us.

After the American and Soviet plans had been presented, the detailed negotiations began. I and my associates were, at the outset, hopeful that an agreement would be reached, within a few months, if the Russians were acting in good faith. John Hancock, always cautious, estimated that it would take a year. John Foster Dulles, whose counsel we sought, thought the chances of agreement were good if only because the Russians would not want to isolate themselves from the rest of the world, and would therefore go along with world public opinion.

Our optimism proved unwarranted. From all the subsequent alarums and excursions, the diplomatic maneuvers, the envenomed tirades of Andrei Vishinsky, the stolid debating of Gromyko—from all these, one central fact emerged: The Russians would not countenance an effective system of international control of nuclear energy.

The Russians could not argue that the American proposals were unworkable, or that they did not provide the protection to which all nations were entitled. A Scientific and Technical Committee of the Atomic Energy Commission, on which the Russians were represented, had already agreed unanimously that effective control was scientifically feasible. Yet the Russians would not yield, nor would we surrender our basic principle.

By mid-September, after three months of intense debate and discussion, it was clear that deliberations were deadlocked. On September 17th, I prepared another lengthy report to President Truman on the American and Russian positions. "We see no possibility of reconciling these views," I wrote. "Agreement could be effected only through a drastic change in the Soviet position or through a sacrifice by us of the very principles which were unanimously endorsed by the United Nations last January and restated in your instructions to me. Abandonment of those principles would mean defrauding the peoples of the world."

I went to Washington to present my report to the President and to discuss the situation with him. It was at this point that a storm broke over the American proposals—not from the direction of the Russian Politburo, but from the President's own Cabinet.

In a move that was as ill-timed as it was ill-considered, Secretary of Commerce Wallace called for the United States to scrap its atomic proposals. A week earlier, Wallace had attacked American policy toward Russia in an address at Madison Square Garden. The resulting furor was compounded by uncertainty over whether or not Truman had endorsed the speech. Now, on September 17th, the same day that I prepared my report, Wallace released a letter, written some weeks earlier to President Truman, in which he elaborated his criticism of our Russian policy.

Much of this letter was taken up with an attack on our atomic energy plan. He characterized it as "one-sided," "not workable," "self-righteous," "take it or leave it"—one which the Russians could not accept. Attacking the step-by-step principle, Wallace called for a single package under which we would destroy all our bombs and surrender all our secret information without any guarantees of protection.

Wallace's letter was a bombshell. Byrnes was then attending a Foreign Ministers Conference in Paris, trying to negotiate peace settlements; I was trying to conduct equally difficult negotiations in the United Nations. Wallace's letter threatened to torpedo both these efforts. When an important Cabinet officer speaks out, as Wallace had done, in direct conflict with established policy, world opinion is bound to be confused.

On the morning of September 18th, I went to the White House in company with Hancock and Assistant Secretary of State Clayton. I had intended to report on the state of the negotiations at the UN,

but I told the President that this could wait; it was more important
to discuss the Wallace matter. The President was pleasant but grim,
and expressed himself pungently on the disclosure of the Wallace
letter. Hancock, as was his custom, dictated a memorandum of the
meeting immediately after it adjourned. I quote from Hancock's
memo:

> He [Baruch] told the President in a very firm but very friendly
> manner that so far as he could see there were three choices open
> to us. First, a full retraction on the part of Mr. Wallace; second,
> an utter repudiation of Mr. Wallace's statements; or third, that
> we resign, as our usefulness was ended. The President told us
> of his plan to see Wallace, asked us not to be in a hurry about
> resigning, and told us that he thought his action in the afternoon
> would be satisfactory to us. Mr. Baruch used some such words
> as these—that our position was in no wise an ultimatum but that
> we still saw only those three courses open.

President Truman saw Wallace that afternoon. The President
was, no doubt, in something of a dilemma. He was anxious to retain Wallace in the Cabinet because the Secretary had a political
following and elections were coming up. On the other hand, he
could not keep him at the high cost to national unity and international confidence which was threatened. What President Truman
said to Wallace that afternoon I do not know; but as a result of
it, Wallace pledged to remain silent until the Foreign Ministers
Conference was ended, in about a month.

But meanwhile, Byrnes communicated with the President from
Paris advising that Wallace would have to go or that he too would
resign. That did it. On the 20th, Truman asked for and received
Wallace's resignation.

I have always maintained that every man has a right to be wrong
in his opinions. But no man has a right to be wrong in his facts.
Wallace was wrong in his facts. He was wrong in asserting that
under our proposals the United States alone would determine the
timing of the transition and the sequence of steps to be taken in

developing atomic controls. He was wrong in his assertion that the Soviet plan went further than the American proposal in providing safeguards against violation. And he was wrong in asserting that the United States refused to modify its plan. We were ready to strengthen our proposals and to negotiate any details which did not violate the basic principle of our mandate.

Wallace's attack, launched from his privileged position in the Cabinet, created public uncertainty and divisiveness where unity was essential. In the hope that some of the harm could be undone, I telephoned Wallace and invited him to meet with me. Wallace stalled for several days, but after several phone calls and telegrams, he finally came to New York with his aide, Philip Hauser. With Swope, Hancock, and Eberstadt present, I went over Wallace's position point by point, showing him where he had been misinformed. I quote again from the notes Hancock made immediately following the meeting: "As Mr. Wallace was about to leave, he summed up his view of the discussion by stating: 'It is obvious that I was not fully posted.' "

Before leaving, Wallace expressed his regret that he had not consulted with me earlier. He agreed to make a public statement correcting his misunderstanding and expressing his endorsement of the policy approved by the President. Hauser and Swope prepared the statement; but after it was drawn, Wallace reneged. Thereafter, he carried on an increasingly militant attack against American foreign policy. His views were overwhelmingly rejected when he sought the Presidency in 1948.

5

Wallace was not the only one anxious to conciliate the Russians. I, myself, tried in every way during the negotiations in the AEC to ease Russian suspicions and convince them of America's good faith. I understood and sympathized with the Russian obsession with security, ravaged as their country had been in the war.

In the face of Soviet intransigeance, some of my colleagues had urged me to denounce the Russians, to force an early vote and make the break. But I refused. I kept insisting that we must make every conceivable effort to reach an agreement. I told Eberstadt and Swope one day, after a long session, "I don't care what they call me or what they think of me. They may think I'm a senile old fool, but I'm not going to give the Russians or anyone else the chance to say that we did not explore every possible avenue in the search for agreement." For a while, we even entertained the thought of going to Moscow to appeal to Stalin personally. George Kennan, the Russian specialist, another of the experts whose views we constantly sought, thought it might be a good idea.

During those months of debate, I came to appreciate how well Soviet diplomats serve their government. I could not help but admire Gromyko's ability. I came to know him rather well, spending many hours in private, informal talks with him, both then and since. In private I found him always pleasant, even when he was most obdurate.

Once I asked Gromyko why it was that the American plan was not published in full in the Soviet press. Didn't this mean, I inquired, that the Soviets were unwilling for their people to know exactly what we proposed? "Oh, no," Gromyko answered, "it's because of a shortage of newsprint." But when I offered to provide all that was needed if Gromyko would promise full publication, he was silent.

My years and my amateur status as a diplomat gave me the prerogative of speaking in a very undiplomatic style. I used to tell Gromyko, "Can't you see it's to your interest as well as ours to agree to this plan? Someday the Russian people are going to hold your government responsible if we fail to control the atom."

For all his dour looks, Gromyko is not without a sense of humor. I took him to the second Joe Louis-Billy Conn fight, and when the champion, making up for his poor showing in the first encounter, was pounding poor Conn from pillar to post, Gromyko leaned over and remarked, "Conn must wish he had the veto."

After six months of debate on the control of atomic energy, I was ready to concede that further debate was hopeless. My associates had been pressing me to call for a vote, and at last I agreed. The vote was scheduled for December 30th. Just before I entered the committee chamber, Sir Alexander Cadogan called me aside, and told me that His Majesty's Government could not support the American position.

To say the least, I was shocked. The British had stood firmly with the United States from the very beginning. I could not understand this reversal, unless they were trying to bluff us into putting off a vote. As I heard Sir Alexander's words, however, I could feel the color leave my face. I told him in the plainest language, and in the presence of others, that if Britain walked out on us, I would denounce her in terms that would make "perfidious Albion" sound like words of praise.

Cadogan, who was only following his instructions, took it all with perfect diplomatic aplomb. We then went in to take the vote. The bluff having failed, Britain voted with the United States and eight other nations in support of the American plan. Poland and Russia abstained.

With the issue now before the United Nations Security Council, I felt that my work was over, and on January 4, 1947, I submitted my resignation to the President. Mr. Truman replied:

Dear Mr. Baruch:

The Secretary of State has handed me your letter of resignation as the Representative of the United States on the Atomic Energy Commission.

At first I was reluctant to accept the resignation. However, upon reflection, I have to agree with the correctness of the conclusions stated in your letter. The recent action of the General Assembly of the United Nations placed the responsibility for the consideration of disarmament proposals primarily upon the Security Council, where Senator Austin will represent the United States. I am impressed by the fact that, with one exception, the governments represented on the Security Council have the same representatives on the Atomic Energy Commission.

I know how tremendously interested you have been in the accomplishment of the task assigned you, and when you tell me that you believe your task is completed and that the work should now be taken over by Senator Austin, I accept your decision.

I wish to congratulate you most heartily on having secured the acceptance by the Commission of the United States proposal. It is inevitable that members of the Commission representing many governments should have differences of opinion as to the best approach to a solution of this problem. That our proposal should finally be accepted by a vote of ten to nothing, with two states abstaining, is a tribute to the fairness of our proposal. At the same time, it is convincing evidence of your skill and patience in presenting the proposal.

I wish you would extend to those who have been associated with you in this most important service my sincere appreciation of their efforts. Your own efforts in this matter only furnish additional evidence of your unselfish devotion to your country.

Very sincerely yours,
Harry S. Truman

In the almost fifteen years which have elapsed since the United States offered its plan for the control of nuclear energy, the deadlock with the Soviet Union has persisted. And yet, the need for effective control has grown more urgent with each passing year. Today the United States and the Soviet Union each have nuclear arsenals capable of destroying the world. Nor is the nuclear club as exclusive as it once was; almost any nation can make atomic bombs today. We must face the fact that the scientific know-how of developing nuclear energy is no longer secret. Within the foreseeable future, many nations, especially those who aspire to first rank, will have armed themselves with nuclear weapons. France's insistence on developing such weapons is a case in point.

What, then, will be the danger of nuclear war when many countries are armed with the H-bomb? Not long ago, the world was thrown into a sudden panic by the erroneous story that Argentina was making atomic bombs. No one imagined that our southern neighbor was embarked on a course of world conquest. Still, no thoughtful statesman or citizen could avoid a chill of fear when he visualized what ultimate catastrophe might result if some mad, power-hungry dictator, even in a small nation, should become inflamed with dreams of glory, or if two small countries owning the bomb should become embroiled in a war.

I often tried to drive this point home with Gromyko, and I never miss a chance to impress it whenever I talk to the Russians now. The fact is that the atomic bomb makes all nations equal, just as the Smith & Wesson revolver made all men equal on the old frontier. When the Russians begin to understand this, they may show themselves more amenable to accepting a workable plan for atomic control.

Many people claim it is no longer possible to devise a system of international control. They argue that, in the past decade, stockpiles of bombs and fissionable materials have been created and techniques developed which are impossible to detect. I reject this contention. It is one of despair and defeat. I am certain that it is still scientifically and technologically feasible to devise an effective system of control. We must not settle for less. In this case, it is not better to accept half a loaf. To do so would be to lull the world into a false sense of security, jeopardizing our own survival.

The control of atomic energy remains one of the crucial elements in the making of a durable peace. As long as the threat of atomic destruction hangs over the world, there can be no peace; but if we can abolish nuclear weapons by a system of effective and enforceable controls, we will have taken a long step toward the abolition of war itself.

In the atom we have a power for tremendous good as well as evil. The uses of nuclear energy—in science, medicine, industry, agriculture, transportation—are limitless. If we could but devote the atom to peace, we would have a tremendous weapon to use in the only war worth fighting—the war against hunger, poverty, and disease.

XX

The Cold War

THE IMPASSE OVER the control of atomic energy foretold a continuing deadlock between Russia and the West on all the other questions of peace-making. It took four years to win the war, but in the fifteen years since, we have not yet been able to win the peace.

It is easy to blame the Kremlin for this. If the Soviet leaders had not been suspicious, intransigent, and hostile, the alliance which brought military victory was fully capable of erecting a durable peace. If the Kremlin had only recognized and reciprocated our own peaceful intentions and motives, the world would not now be divided into armed camps, expending its resources on creating frightening instruments of destruction.

All this is true, yet it ignores our own responsibility for the present state of affairs. When the war ended, we expected peace to follow as the day the night. We did not realize that as much courage and effort and discipline would be required to win the peace as had been needed to win the war. We relied on good intentions, forgetting that in this imperfect world the road to defeat, if not to hell, is easy, and that hell itself is paved with such intentions.

We Americans have always been naïve about war and peace. I

remember my teachers extolling that great Roman, Cincinnatus, who twice saved Rome from her enemies, and who, each time, returned to his plow after the foe was routed. This is the way we Americans have been brought up to regard wars—as a temporary interruption of our normal, peaceful pursuits, to which we hasten to return as quickly as possible. Our whole national make-up assumes a sharp division between war and peace. This assumption may have been valid in the early years of our national life, but it no longer conforms to reality.

In the twentieth century, the major fact of life has been war. There has scarcely been a year when we have not been threatened by it, or preparing for it, or fighting it, or recovering from its consequences. Today we live in a state which is neither peace nor war, and we will in all probability go on living in this state, if worse does not occur, for many years to come.

In 1945, we Americans did not understand that reality—the continuity of war and peace. We had suffered a million casualties, and had spent over three hundred billion in a terrible conflict. Now, we thought, it was time to get back to our plows, our lathes, our offices, and get on with the ways of peace. That meant getting rid of all the inconveniences, restraints, and disciplines associated with war, disciplines which we consider alien to our free way of life.

But what we failed to realize is that these disciplines are as essential to the waging of peace as they are to the waging of war. Speaking before the United Jewish Appeal in February, 1946, I urged, "Don't let us be the first to disarm! Don't scuttle and run militarily, economically, or spiritually. Don't let us dodge the duty which lies upon us of helping to keep the world's peace. We must be strong."

But we did scuttle and run. We shut our eyes to the needs of peace. We dismantled our military forces, thus opening the door to Soviet advances and paving the way for the cold war—and the hot one in Korea.

Along with dismantling our armed forces, we scrapped the structure of economic controls with far greater dispatch than the time it took to create it. Instead of devoting our productive power and economic resources to the peace-making, we went off on a spree. Following the war, Congress cut taxes by six billion dollars. The Little Steel Formula, which had kept wages and prices in uncertain check through the last half of the war, was abandoned in the face of an epidemic of major strikes. Labor got its wage increases. Industry got its price increases, which, as usual, more than offset increased labor costs. The consumer, who has no lobby, paid the bill.

All of this was done under the justification of returning to peace-time economic ways—though we did not yet have peace. It was meant to encourage business and stimulate production. But business needed no artificial stimulation through tax reduction in 1946, just as it did not need it in 1953, when we again needlessly and unwisely reduced taxes. The tax cut, the wage increases, the abandonment of price controls and priority powers were all part of a race for selfish advantage. The end result was to let inflationary forces loose in the economy, to the detriment of all.

To me, all this was sheerest economic folly. I played my familiar role of dissenter in opposing the tax cut and the abrogation of the Little Steel Formula. I also testified in vain before Congress in support of continuing price controls. My economic thinking was expressed in this excerpt from a memo written to President Truman on February 13, 1946:

> For purposes of economic thinking, we are still at war. We certainly are not at peace. In the transition period we will require the same effort . . . to meet the demands for food, clothing, housing and transportation for the world as we did in war. . . . This means that everyone will have for at least a year to work harder than ever and above all, there should be no strikes or lockouts [the steel strike was then on] for any cause until there is some near approach of supply to . . . demand. . . . When prices and wages are advanced to the new plateau, they must be held there by every device. Everything which has caused the present inflation must be undone—wages must be held in line; the $6,000,-000,000 tax reduction . . . should be restored; rationing and

controls must be continued in order that the longest purse or the biggest pull may not get the short production. There must be no leaks in the dike. . . .

The American people should be told exactly how we stand, what to do and why. There must be no sudden shifts until we are sure of the future. Wherever there is sure full production we can let these controls go. The wage earner will, in the end, get more if he produces more. Now he is being fooled into believing that he is getting more because he is getting more dollars which in turn buy less than they did before. If inflation is not controlled, the dollar will buy less not alone day by day, but hour by hour and minute by minute.

This prophecy has proved accurate enough. Since the end of the war, consistently inflationary policies have pyramided the national debt to astronomical proportions, slashed the value of the dollar, eroded savings, dislocated the economy, increased the burden of taxes, and injured most those people least able to afford it—the pensioners, savers, and white-collar workers. Inflation has unbalanced the budgets, not only of individuals and governments, but of hospitals, schools, colleges, and institutions of every kind.

Despite the pervasiveness of inflation, however, and its obviously damaging effect, we have never been able to find a leader able or willing to mobilize the people against it. Some believed they could keep inflation under control, or that they could escape its consequences. This is one of the supreme fallacies of our time. Once inflation gets under way, no one can escape its harmful effects.

I tried to impress this upon President Truman at the time we were throwing over anti-inflationary checks at the end of the war. Although he later courageously vetoed a tax reduction bill, at this point he did not fight the tax cut. Nor was he able to hold the line on wages. During the steel strike at the beginning of 1946, the President, through John Snyder, then head of the Office of War Mobilization and Reconversion, called on me for help in trying to reach a settlement. I met with Benjamin Fairless and other steel leaders, urging them not to turn down the President's proposals. But the steel people were not coöperative. At a White House meeting with the President, I warned that an inflationary settlement of the steel strike would spread through the entire economy and push wage and price levels up to new and higher plateaus.

President Truman disagreed. At most, he said, it would cause a "bulge" which could easily be held. I dissented. "There's no holding it," I declared. In his characteristic homely way, Mr. Truman asked, "Ain't I the boss?" He never doubted that he was. "No, Mr. President," I replied. "In this matter, no one is the boss; the laws of economics are."

After the meeting, I summed up my views in a note to President Truman: "There is only one way to avoid inflation and that is not to let it start. . . . No one has ever yet been able to control inflation. If it can be controlled upon the new plateau to which you are going, it will be the first time in history."

There was not much of an audience for such anti-inflation prescriptions. Nor was there much attention paid to a proposal I made before the House Banking and Currency Committee in March, 1946, for the creation of a High Court of Commerce, a sort of economic council, to decide questions at issue between economic groups whose quarrels jeopardized the well-being of the entire nation.

The idea of such a tribunal seems to me worth consideration today, in the light of labor-management wars which not only grow more bitter and prolonged, but whose effects on noncombatant consumers, on the nation as a whole, and on our world position grow more injurious. The steel strike of 1959, which not only immobilized the entire industry but caused many related industries to grind to a halt, throwing hundreds of thousands out of work, is a case in point.

The power of labor and management is such today that neither can win a clear-cut victory over the other. Inasmuch as a sense of responsibility is not particularly well-developed in either, the question is whether the nation can sit by while they fight it out—during which time the country suffers, and in the end pays the cost of these labor-industry wars. The legislation we now have is evidently inadequate to settle disputes and to protect the national interest. Consequently, some sort of tribunal along the lines I have suggested seems to me to deserve study as a possible solution.

2

In view of the power vacuum we helped to create when the war ended, it is not surprising that the Soviets moved in to fill it and to frustrate our hopes for peace.

As the Soviets thwarted an atomic agreement, lowered their Iron Curtain in Eastern Europe, and broke one promise after the other in those early postwar years, it became clear that they were waging war against us. It was a new kind of war, to be sure, in which the guns were silent; but our survival was at stake nonetheless. It was a situation that soon came to be known as the "cold war," a phrase I introduced in a speech before the South Carolina legislature in April, 1947.

I was indebted to Herbert Swope for this graphic expression, which caught the public imagination and became a part of the language. Swope had suggested the phrase a year before, but I was reluctant then—when I was serving on the United Nations Atomic Energy Commission—to characterize the United States-Soviet relationship in such a fashion; I was anxious not to excite Russia's almost pathological suspicion and fear of us. Indeed, I still hoped that we could establish amicable relations with the Russians.

For all that I reject Marxist ideology and condemn Communist authoritarianism, I have always felt sympathetic toward the Russian people who have suffered so much at the hands of domestic and foreign tyrants. I have always tried to understand the point of view of these people. At the war's end, with the help of Professor D.F. Fleming, I made a series of studies to try to find out how I would feel on various issues if I were a Russian. From these studies, and from my contacts with Soviet representatives, I came to understand something of Russian immaturity, with its accompanying suspicions and fears, and to take into account the legitimate grievances and demands of the USSR. Certainly the unequal sacrifices Russia was called upon to make in fighting the common foe—the incredible suffering of her people and the terrible punishment to her land —must be remembered in dealing with the Soviet.

I have always advocated playing square with the Russians. After I had completed the rubber report in 1942, Harry Hopkins, who was on his way to Moscow, asked me what I thought about fulfilling a promise we had made to deliver a tire-making factory to the Russians. He pointed out that the factory was badly needed at home, and that there was doubt that it could be dismantled, shipped, reassembled, and put into production in time. Did I think, he asked, that we should tell the Russians they couldn't have the factory after all?

"Did we promise it to them?" I asked.

"Yes, we did," Hopkins said.

"Then we must carry out our promise," I told him. "If we expect the Soviets to live up to their pledges, we must live up to ours meticulously."

Later, Hopkins told me that President Roosevelt had been very pleased with my attitude. To me, this still seems the only honorable way for a great nation like ours to approach relationships with other powers.

But as the ice jams of the cold war piled up, for the third time in my life America was faced with a threat to her peace and security. And once again, for the third time, I took up the banner of preparedness.

By 1947, I was publicly calling for mobilization of our economic, political, and spiritual resources. Before a Special Senate Committee Investigating the National Defense Program, I advocated such measures as universal military training; a work-or-fight law, in the event of war; stand-by legislation to ration, to control prices, wages, production, and priorities; stockpiling of critical materials; the unification of hemisphere defense; increased defense expenditures; and stepped-up scientific and technological research.

This call for preparedness was heeded no more in 1947 than it had been in 1937. And in 1947, as earlier, it was our weakness which invited aggression. Not until we were caught in the Korean War, in 1950, did we begin to rebuild our armed strength. In the eyes of many experts, our strength is still inadequate.

In the years before Korea, we were, paradoxically, willing to spend billions to help reconstruct Europe's war-ravaged economy; but we were unwilling to tax ourselves and accept the disciplines required to make ourselves and Europe secure from the threat of Soviet domination. I could see no sense in this. Testifying before a Senate Committee in support of the Marshall Plan in January, 1948, I pointed out that it would do no good to restore the European economy with our dollars only to see Europe hijacked by the Russians. Our foreign aid program, I said, should be integrated into a comprehensive program in which our own defenses were made secure while Europe welded itself into a political, economic, and defense union. I went even further. If our Allies created such a defense union, I proposed that the United States pledge unequivocally to help defend it against aggression. "By guarantee," I said, "I mean a firm promise to go to war in joint defense if any nation is attacked."

This was, I believe, one of the first times such a proposal had been publicly made. Some Senators told me later that they were fearful the American public would not stand for such a commitment. Others told me they were glad I had said what they had not felt free to say. General Marshall, then Secretary of State, told me he wished that he had said what I had. He told me that British Foreign Secretary Bevin, on hearing a radio report of my testimony, had telephoned him from London to inquire whether my call for a guarantee of West Europe's freedom reflected official American thinking. Marshall assured him that it did.

In this testimony, I vigorously endorsed the principle of foreign aid. "There is no place left to which . . . [Europe can] turn for regeneration except to America," I said. "We must answer that call or we shall fail civilization . . . and thus fail ourselves."

Still, while I favored American aid to the Allies, I did not believe we should try to restore Europe by loans, grants, subsidies, or bonuses, but rather by the "helpfulness which insists upon self-help." I felt that Europe had to be disabused of the notion that our resources were limitless, and that all that was required to set the world right was to borrow money from us.

What Europe needed, obviously, was to restore her production, to get her people back to work, her factories going, her fields growing, her cities rebuilt, her people fed, clothed, and housed. Loans and grants would help, but we need not have relied entirely upon them. It would have been just as effective in restoring Europe's economy, and much less costly for us, had we reduced these loans and grants and agreed instead to purchase all the non-perishable raw materials, produced anywhere, by anyone, which could not be sold in normal commercial markets. This proposal would have given us something for the money we advanced to Europe. Yet it was rejected on the grounds that it would swamp us in surpluses. But surpluses, as I have said before, should never frighten us. They are invaluable when properly managed.

In supporting the Marshall Plan, I insisted that responsibility lay on both sides, in receiving as well as in giving. Europe had the responsibility of integrating her economy, of rebuilding and unifying her defenses, of relieving us as quickly as possible of the burden we were carrying. But Europe has been laggard in fulfilling these obligations. Even the effort which she has put into military coöperation, as represented by NATO, has never been adequate. NATO still is not the defense force it was intended to be.

In view of Europe's economic well-being today, I think it is time for her to reduce her dependence on American aid. But countries are a lot like men. Sometimes there is no getting rid of them, once they have secured a beachhead on your generosity.

It is time, too, for the United States to stop looking upon foreign aid as a means of winning the friendship of other countries. The simple fact is that you cannot buy friends, and in trying to purchase popularity, one often earns only contempt. The Western alliance can be cemented not by American dollars, but by mutual interest and a common dedication to freedom.

Our foreign aid program, from the beginning—and, indeed, much of American policy since the end of the war—shows little evidence of having been thought through in terms of the over-all problems facing America. One crucial reason why peace has eluded us is because we failed to devise the global strategy which its winning required. Whatever one may say about F.D.R., one tribute all historians must pay him and his aides—General Marshall, Admiral King, General Arnold—they saw the war in its global dimensions and developed the necessary world-embracing strategy to win it. The global vision never fogged.

But the truth is that when it came to peace, we never thought through the problems, much less formulated an over-all policy. We have not made our basic decisions according to our own timetable or master plan, but rather on an emergency basis as the result of challenge. The big decisions have been emergency decisions. We have certainly responded bravely to such challenges as Berlin and Korea, but we cannot go on from crisis to crisis. Sooner or later, indecision—or the wrong decision taken in haste—will be fatal.

In this age, when events move so rapidly, when the issues confronting us are so complex, the need for a carefully defined strategy to wage the peace is imperative. For a long time, I have advocated that the problems of peace-making should be centralized in one government agency. As long ago as 1945, I proposed to President Roosevelt that he appoint an Advisory Peace Council, which would be responsible for studying the problems of peace in all their interrelationship and for recommending over-all policy to the President.

President Roosevelt liked the idea. He spoke of including, on this Council, several persons not burdened with official duties. He said that he wanted me to serve on it, and he had in mind naming James Byrnes as Chairman and Sam Rosenman as counsel. This discussion took place shortly before I flew to London.

In my report to Mr. Truman when I returned from London, I took up the proposal with him. Truman said he liked the idea of an advisory group on peace policy, and that he would act on it as soon as he got his "team" in. It took more time than that, but in 1947 the main idea behind my proposal—the creation of what I called a General Staff for Peace—was implemented with the establishment of the National Security Council.

The National Security Council, however, has not performed as expected. This is primarily due to the fact that its members, which include the President, the Vice-president, and the heads of major executive departments, are already overburdened with responsibilities which take all their time. They simply cannot devote the hours required to think through the numerous and complex problems of the world crisis. Washington probably has the greatest concentration of first-class minds in the country, but less thinking goes on there than in most other places, simply because there is no time for study and reflection.

There have been many proposals made to revamp the National Security Council. I myself would like to see it strengthened and reconstituted. I have long advocated that its membership be expanded to include all former Presidents, and men of such caliber as James Conant, Omar Bradley, John McCloy, and David Sarnoff—who would sit in constant deliberation over all the problems of the peace, with no other responsibility to distract their thoughts and energies. I think such a reorganization would permit the National Security Council to function as a genuine General Staff for Peace.

3

By the end of President Truman's first term, the hopes for en-during peace had faded. The country was disillusioned and frus-trated by the cold war, and a great deal of recrimination was focused on the President. His domestic policies had also antagonized a large part of the public.

As the 1948 elections approached, the President was at the nadir of his popularity. He had been deserted successively by the less ardent New Dealers, most of the Party bosses, Mr. Roosevelt's sons, and the conservative Southern Democrats. As Jonathan Daniels ob-serves in his biography of Mr. Truman, "It was the fashion then to walk out on Truman." He meant it literally, speaking particularly of desertions from the rear rows when the President spoke to the American Society of Newspaper Editors in April, 1948.

As the convention approached, Truman supporters were hard to find—and those in sight were not very sanguine about his pros-pects for reëlection. Indeed, a good part of the Democratic Party was ready to deny him renomination.

In the months preceding the convention, I was visited by a num-ber of Democrats, some of them supposedly friends of the President, and others identified with the liberal wing of the Party. All of them wanted to discuss the chances of ditching President Truman, and the prospects of doing so. They tried to enlist me in this effort, and one or two even had the notion that I ought to go to the Presi-dent and try to persuade him to withdraw.

The man whom many of these visitors had fixed on to succeed Truman as the leader of the Democratic Party was General Eisen-hower. Despite my affectionate regard for Eisenhower, I could not countenance this proposal to dump the President—quite apart from the fact that none of those seeking to boom Eisenhower for the Democratic nomination had the slightest idea whether he would accept, or where he stood on the issues confronting us.

To all my callers I gave the same reply. I told them that the effort to unseat President Truman would fail, that he would most certainly be renominated, that control of the party machinery, which always lies in the President's hands, would guarantee this. Whether they liked it or not, I said, Mr. Truman would be the nominee, and it seemed to me that a party man could best serve his party by supporting him.

I intended to. There was much in Mr. Truman's policy with which I disagreed. But if I could not support everything in his record as President, still I saw nothing in that record which deserved rebuff and insult from his own party. He had shown qualities of greatness during his first term; he had risen notably to the challenge of his high office. The Truman Doctrine, the Berlin Airlift, the Marshall Plan were achievements to be admired.

I was as ready to support President Truman in 1948 as I had been in 1940, when he had been hard pressed to win renomination to the Senate against the bid of Governor Lloyd Stark. At that time, F.D.R. had tried to get Truman to withdraw from the primary race, and Truman's prospects looked very bleak. According to Jonathan Daniels' account of that primary fight, Truman did not even have funds to pay the postage on campaign literature. At the request of James Byrnes and Bennett Clark, the senior Senator from Missouri, I contributed to Truman's campaign. Truman won by fewer than eight thousand votes. After the election, he came up to my apartment in the Carlton Hotel with Bennett Clark to thank me for my help. He told me that it had been the toughest fight he had ever waged, and that he would never forget my support. Later—when he was asked about this incident—President Truman said that he knew nothing of it.

Toward the end of June, 1948, I went to see Mr. Truman at the White House. We discussed the opposition he faced within the Democratic Party. I repeated what I had told my callers about the certainty of his renomination. I then said that I had some suggestions which might improve his chances for reëlection, and failing that, might serve to hold the Party together.

I suggested, first, that he go to Philadelphia in person to accept the nomination, rather than accept it at the White House or at his home in Independence. The effect on the Party of his personal acceptance would be good, I felt, showing both his modesty and courage. I suggested also that he seize the initiative at the outset by announcing to the convention his intention of calling a special session of Congress, and by challenging the Republicans to use that session to fulfill their platform promises.

President Truman listened attentively as I spoke. When I had concluded, he rose from his chair and walked up and down in front of his desk, swinging his arms vigorously. "You've got something there," he said. "You've got something there."

After I left Mr. Truman's office, I called on Clark Clifford, the President's special counsel, and Secretary of the Treasury John Snyder. I repeated to both of them the suggestions I had made to the President. Snyder, a close friend of the President, was immensely pleased with my interest and support. He went on to tell me of the difficulties he was having in raising money to bring the Missouri delegation to Philadelphia. To his delight, I promised to contribute the sum he needed.

A few days later Clark Clifford came up to New York. While there, he paid me a call, and asked me to elaborate on the suggestions I had made to President Truman. This I did.

Within a few days, I left for Europe. I was hoping to visit Russia; Gromyko had invited me several times, promising me complete freedom to see whatever and whomever I wanted. At that time, however, the United States was not encouraging its citizens to visit Russia; and so I had consulted Secretary Marshall on whether or not I ought to go. He gave me tentative approval, and said that in the event he had to change his mind, he would advise me in London. I visited Paris, and then the Hague, where my brother Herman was American Ambassador. He was a staunch Truman supporter and one of the few who thought the President would be reëlected.

Then I went over to London, where I received a message from General Clay in blockaded Berlin to "come see your beleaguered friend." But I fell ill with a severe attack of gout, and had to take a plane for home. My Russian trip was off. I am sure, however, that Gromyko always thought my illness was feigned, and that Washington had killed my visit.

During my absence, the Republicans had nominated Thomas E. Dewey and were confident of victory. The Democrats, however, came to their convention in Philadelphia a divided party, anticipating defeat. The proposed candidacy of Henry Wallace threatened to siphon off important segments of New Deal support. The South was on the verge of bolting over the civil rights issue.

The President, acting along the lines I had suggested, came to Philadelphia and waited for what he knew was inevitable—his nomination. It came after midnight of the third day, and was accomplished over determined Southern protest. But accomplished it was, and on the first ballot at that.

The President appeared before the convention at two o'clock in the morning. It may be that no candidate has ever accepted the nomination from such an unenthusiastic gathering of delegates. Before he was through, however, Truman had brought them all to a roaring pitch of excitement.

It was a rough, angry, fighting speech. "Senator Barkley and I will win this election, and make these Republicans like it, don't you forget that," he said. He went on to make a bitter, cutting attack on the Eightieth Congress and the Republican platform. Then he produced the dramatic challenge:

On the twenty-sixth day of July, which out in Missouri we call "Turnip Day," I am going to call Congress back and ask them to pass laws to halt rising prices, to meet the housing crisis—which they are saying they are for in their platform.

At the same time, I shall ask them to act upon other vitally needed measures, such as aid to education, which they say they are for; a national health program; civil rights legislation, which they say they are for; an increase in the minimum wage, which I doubt very much they are for; extension of the Social Security coverage and increased benefits, which they say they are for; funds for projects needed in our program to provide public power and cheap electricity. . . .

"Now, my friends," he concluded, when the tremendous applause from this last statement died down, "if there is any reality behind that Republican platform, we ought to get some action from a short session of the Eightieth Congress. They can do this job in fifteen days, if they want to do it. . . . What the worst Eightieth Congress does in its special session will be the test. The American people will decide on the record."

With this rousing finale, President Truman's campaign was launched. From Europe I cabled Clifford my congratulations on Truman's convention speech and his handling of the renomination. "The President's stock is going up," I said.

I returned to the United States shortly after the convention. I was in bed for some time recovering from the attack of gout. When I was up again, I went one day to the opening of New York International Airport. President Truman and Governor Dewey were both present. As I took my seat, Dewey came over and inquired, "Baruch, what have you got to say about our campaign?"

"*Our* campaign," I said. "I'm for the Democratic ticket, Tom."

After the ceremonies, I went over to shake hands with President Truman. "That was a wonderful job you did at Philadelphia, Mr. President," I said. "I haven't had a chance to congratulate you, other than by the cable I sent. But you handled it beautifully."

To my utter astonishment, Truman looked at me as though he had never seen me before. I went back to my seat dumbfounded. I was at a loss to explain his conduct.

I was even more surprised to receive the following letter, a few weeks later, from the President:

August 19, 1948

Dear Mr. Baruch:

I was talking with Senator McGrath yesterday and he suggested that it would be very greatly to the advantage of the Democratic organization if you would agree to serve on the Finance Committee. I hope you will be willing to do that.

Sincerely yours,
Harry Truman

P.S. Congratulations on your birthday today.

I replied on August 27th:

The delay in answering your letter of August 19th has been due to the fact that when I returned to town you had gone on what I am sure is a much needed vacation.

In regard to my going on the Finance Committee, I have never yet served on any committee of the Party, nor have I ever made a political statement. As you well know, that is not because of lack of interest, but over the years my friends have agreed with me that my methods were perhaps the best. Roosevelt, among others, thoroughly agreed with me. . . .

What I had told the President was true. I had made it a rule never to serve on committees, particularly fund-raising committees for political purposes. I did not expect the President to take my declining very hard, but it miffed him—or perhaps, as Jonathan Daniels has put it, he "mistook . . . an old preference for a new desertion." In any case, he replied as follows on August 31st:

My dear Mr. Baruch:

I read your letter of the twenty-seventh with much disappointment. A great many honors have been passed your way, both to you and your family, and it seems when the going is rough it is a one-way street. I am sorry that this is so.

Sincerely yours,
Harry Truman

The fact is that in more than forty years of public life I have always declined the honors which often accrue for party loyalty.

I have declined ambassadorships and an assortment of other appointments. I never accepted a party post; and any public position I undertook was not on the basis of reward, but rather the opportunity for service in difficult and trying times.

What I found particularly hard to understand, in Mr. Truman's letter, was his evident belief that I was hostile to him. We had enjoyed excellent relations while I was serving on the UN Atomic Energy Commission. I had, moreover, championed his renomination, and offered suggestions as to the tactics he might follow.

After my initial anger and resentment at the President's letter had cooled, I decided not to reply. Mutual friends who knew of the President's letter were unhappy about it. Louis Johnson told me heatedly that he would get Truman to retract it, and John Snyder was also apologetic. But I was content to let the matter rest, and to attribute it to the pressures which beset the President during the campaign. I certainly did not want to get involved in any controversy which would add to the President's problems.

I have only myself to blame for the fact that this matter led to an open break between the President and myself. Just a few days before the election, Westbrook Pegler came into possession of a garbled version of the correspondence between Mr. Truman and me. Pegler asked me, over the telephone, if I would let him see the originals. I refused. But in discussing the matter with Pegler, whom I knew well and to whom I thought I was speaking in confidence, my resentment at Mr. Truman's unjust charge—a resentment which had never quite stopped smouldering—flared again, and I characterized his letter in harsh terms.

Next day, the papers carrying Pegler's column appeared with blazoned headlines in which my angry words were quoted. Coming as it did on the eve of the election, the story created a sensation and precipitated the breach which I never intended to create between President Truman and myself.

When I was a boy, my mother used to admonish me to keep my

tongue between my teeth when I was angry. I had followed that rule most of my life. This was one time I didn't, and I have regretted it.

There has been only one occasion, since this incident, when I saw President Truman. In May, 1951, I had made an address at Virginia Military Institute in honor of George Marshall, dealing in it with the question of foreign affairs. The President wrote to express his appreciation of my tribute to Marshall, whom he admired as greatly as I did, and to say that I had added something to an understanding of the Administration's foreign policy. Shortly afterward, I was visiting the Marshalls at their Virginia home. I was ready to return to New York when Mrs. Marshall said: "The President has called. He is going to come down and he told me to keep you here."

When the President arrived, he was accompanied by Justice and Mrs. Vinson. He was cordial, and we sat around in a circle talking for awhile. Then, as the President was ready to leave, I said to him: "Mr. President, I regret very much that any wedge should have been driven between us."

Mr. Truman replied: "I'll see that it doesn't happen again." Then, as he walked off, he turned and shook a finger at me. "That's a promise," he said, and grinned.

But it was the last time we spoke.

President Truman's second term was filled with crises and tainted with bitterness. He had done the right thing by intervening in Korea; yet, in at least one sense, his Administration had invited that aggression by failing to maintain our military strength. Despite the clear-cut designs of the Communists, President Truman did not support adequate military or economic preparedness programs. Indeed, even after the Korean War started and Congress, for the first time in my experience, enacted legislation which would have permitted effective control of the economy, President Truman did not employ the powers Congress had given him. Except for those whose sons, brothers, and husbands were fighting in Korea, the home front hardly knew there was a war.

The President had other second-term troubles: the revelations of Communist espionage at home; the whole sensational business of the Alger Hiss trials, and the controversies that followed in their wake; the corruption within the Administration, which led to widespread publicity about five per centers, mink coats, and deep freezes; the outcry over the dismissal of General MacArthur; and, finally, the spectacular rise of Senator Joe McCarthy.

But even his critics must concede that Mr. Truman represents, and represents strikingly, the capacity of a man to rise to great challenges and opportunities. No one can deny that he made the hard decisions, and made them well: the Truman Doctrine, the Marshall Plan, the Berlin Airlift, the response to aggression in Korea.

All in all I have no doubt that history will rank Mr. Truman far up among those Presidents who have served their country with distinction.

XXI

The World We Face

As I THINK of the Presidents I have known, from Woodrow Wilson to Dwight Eisenhower, what impresses me is the increasing complexity and burden of the office they held. This, of course, reflects not only the increased complexity of the world in which we live, but the changing role of America in it. In my lifetime, the United States has become the world's first power. In consequence, all the world's problems impinge upon us. Fifty years ago, a President could make an inaugural address, as Woodrow Wilson did, without one reference to foreign affairs. Today, the President must be concerned and informed—because our fate is involved—with revolution in Asia, political developments in Africa, economic crises in Latin America.

Never before has the world faced such peril as it faces today. In earlier days, war and conflict, no matter how brutal, did not threaten to extinguish life. Today war does threaten such extinction. I doubt that any President has ever been confronted with so many and so delicate and so complex problems as Eisenhower, or presided at a time of greater peril. His successor's task, in all likelihood, will be even more onerous.

I first heard Dwight Eisenhower's name in the early thirties, when a report on guayule rubber he had written for the Secretary of War came to my attention. Eisenhower was then a major, a career officer, sweating out the Army's usual slow promotions, and suffering the added frustration of serving in an armed force that was skeletonized and all but ignored in the transcendent crisis of the depression.

What a startling, fantastic turn his life took in one brief decade! Within ten years he was Supreme Commander, leading the Allied Armies in history's greatest war. In another ten years, he was President of the United States and the acknowledged leader of the Free World.

Eisenhower's spectacular rise was no accident. General Marshall chose him, over many of his seniors, to lead the Allied forces because he recognized his talents and abilities. These abilities were applied to the huge job of coördinating the mighty effort of men and machines necessary to defeat Germany, and to the thorny task of creating unity among the Allied forces; both of these General Eisenhower did supremely well. Even Field Marshal Lord Alanbrooke, Chief of the Imperial General Staff and one of the General's severest critics, had to admit that he was ". . . a past master in the handling of allies, entirely impartial and consequently trusted by all." To which Arthur Bryant, the British historian who edited the Alanbrooke war diaries, added: "For all his good nature, the Supreme Commander was a tough 'West Pointer'. . . . Nor, in the hour of crisis, was the Supreme Commander unworthy of the men he led. Calamity acted on Eisenhower like a restorative and brought out all the greatness in his character."

One of the things that struck me on my trip to Europe during the war was the affection which GI's, not notably fond of brass hats, had for General Eisenhower. Certainly no man in public life elicits affection and trust as he does. And this is because people respond to his essential decency and humanity.

These qualities were never better defined than by his reaction to the horrors of the German concentration camps. Appalled and sickened by these factories of death, and knowing how short our memories are, he insisted that the American public be told, in full detail, the terrible story of what had transpired. He called in the representatives of the press and enjoined them to report the full truth of Auschwitz, Buchenwald, and the other death camps. When I asked Walker Stone, the Scripps-Howard editor, to describe what he had seen, he said, "You can't describe it. You have to see it and smell it."

It is a tribute to America and her military tradition that we can produce men such as Eisenhower, Marshall, MacArthur—great commanders who are nevertheless humane men dedicated to democratic ideals. We have had great soldiers; but we have had no militarism, no glorification of war, no men on horseback. It is quite possible, indeed, that no group of men has better served America and her democratic traditions than our military leaders.

That is why I have always resented the consignment of military men to the status of second-class citizens in time of peace; and I reject the notion that there is such a thing as the "military mind." Most of the "military minds" I have met have been top-notch minds, the kind that would permit a man to succeed in any field.

A man who exercises top command in the modern military machine must be expert in more than tactics, strategy, logistics, and other elements of military science. If he is to rise in his profession, he must be a student of economics, international affairs, history, social psychology, the sciences, and a number of other subjects. Since modern war and defense involve a coalition of allies, with all that this means in terms of conflicting national views, ambitions, and needs, a top commander must be skilled in politics and diplomacy. By the time a man rises to the top in the military, he must have displayed great ability and acquired the broadest experience. By then, he is anything but debarred from a career in civil affairs.

Eisenhower is a striking example of this process. During the war, and later with NATO, he was not only a military commander in the traditional sense, but a political leader, helping to build and preserve the Western alliance. He did the job superbly. Quite apart from his military attainments, it was his ability to inspire unity and create a sense of common purpose that marked him as the only one considered to head NATO when it was organized.

General Eisenhower and I became close friends after the war. I saw him frequently at Columbia University, as I had when he was Chief of Staff, and developed a warm affection and regard for him. One question which interested us both, and which we often discussed, was the relationship between the individual and his government—how to strike a balance between laissez faire and paternalism. The discussions between us on this subject, while Eisenhower was president of Columbia, led him to initiate a study of the problem at the Univeristy. Out of such conversations I gained an appreciation of his ability, and of his quick and open mind.

In view of his achievements and the public's enthusiasm for him, it was all but inevitable that Eisenhower should be injected into the political scene in 1948. Ever since he returned from the war, he had been under heavy pressure from political leaders of both parties to carry their flag. "How do you make these people understand I'm not interested?" he once asked me.

"I give you General Sherman," I said.

He did issue a Sherman-like statement in 1948, but in 1952 he had little alternative except to run for the party which represented his views. No man can withstand unremitting pressure of the kind he was subjected to, especially when those who were determined that he run were appealing to his sense of duty, which was always paramount.

The country was fortunate in the choice it was offered in 1952. Adlai Stevenson certainly is one of the outstanding men in public life today. During the campaign, both he and General Eisenhower were kind enough to ask my views. I told them both that in my opinion the control of inflation, the strengthening of our defenses, and the securing of peace were the major goals.

I myself concluded that, apart from the advantages which might accrue from a change after so long a Democratic tenure, General Eisenhower could best provide the leadership which the attainment of these goals required. I also felt that he could bring unity to the country. It is still too early to evaluate Eisenhower as President. But no one can deny his great achievement in ending the rancor, the bitterness, and the divisiveness which existed in the nation before he became President. Above all, he must surely be lauded and remembered for his tireless efforts to obtain a just settlement with Russia and bring peace to the world.

2

We can be grateful that, during the Eisenhower years, none of the perils that ring us like so many time bombs have exploded. It cannot be said, however, that we have used these years gained to defuse those bombs. They still go on ticking. We have still to resolve the problems upon whose solution our future depends. We have not yet chained up the destructive power of the atom. Nor have we yet solved the crucial question of Germany's future.

In 1945, on my return from Europe, I identified the German issue as "the key to the whole peace." I wrote in my report to President Truman that unless the victors could reach agreement on the future of our erstwhile enemy, there could be no peace in Europe. And this is still true today. As long as the Soviet Union threatens Berlin and rejects unification of Germany except on Russian terms, Europe must remain a potential tinderbox.

After fifteen years, the issue of Germany is still central to the issue of peace. But events of these years have compelled most of us to revise our views on her treatment. When I was a boy, they used to say that "only a mule and a milepost never changed its mind." I have never wanted to be included in that category, and I have changed my mind on German policy.

In 1945, I favored the strictest control over our recent enemy. This was in sharp contrast with my attitude after the First World War, when I had advocated leniency and fought against the punitive terms that France and Great Britain sought to impose. I remember how my father had disagreed with me then, insisting that Germany merited the harshest kind of justice and that she would never reform. I made allowances for my father's bitterness, since he was a refugee from Prussian militarism and had always insisted that Germany suffered from a malady which could be cured only by radical surgery.

But during World War Two, I often thought of my father's estimate of his homeland and found myself agreeing with him. I was appalled, like every civilized man, by German atrocities. On my trip to Eisenhower's and Patton's headquarters, I had seen some of the ravages of war and had recalled my tour of the battlefields with President Wilson after the First War. Here it was again, spread before my eyes for the second time—the ruin and desolation visited upon the earth by German aggression.

I came back from Europe advocating the strictest controls until Germany had proved her right to rejoin the world community. For a time I even sympathized with Henry Morgenthau's radical plan to reduce Germany to a pastoral economy, but I soon saw that this was not practicable. Nevertheless, I strongly urged that the military class, and the Junker landholders who formed the backbone of it, must be broken up. I even advocated that if German labor were to be used for reparations, the first to be chosen should be the Junkers, the General Staff, and the rest of the ruling clique.

One of the bitterest ironies of our time is that our former enemies, Germany and Japan, should become our allies, while our former allies, Russia and China, should become our presumptive enemy. The irony, again, is that Russia, which did so much to defeat Hitler's Germany, should be responsible for the policy which has led to rebuilding Germany; and that Germany herself, which once united the West and Russia against her, is now the focus of their disunity.

Like most Americans, I was distressed at this turn of events. But in the face of Soviet policy, we have had no other choice than to help rebuild West Germany. The security of America and of the Free World cannot permit Soviet domination of Germany; the security of Western Europe would be hopeless with Russia along the Rhine.

To say that I am happy about the resurgence of West Germany would be untrue. To be sure, Chancellor Adenauer's leadership and whole-hearted commitment to democracy has given us reason for confidence; and the courage and will for freedom of the Berliners have won our admiration. But the bitter memories and the mistrust have not yet been entirely eradicated.

If Germany's economic and political integration into Free Europe can be fully accomplished, there will be less cause to fear her and much reason to hope that she will become a responsible and trustworthy member of the world community. But the central issue remains—until the West and Russia come to an agreement on Germany, there can be at best an uneasy truce in the heartland of the Continent.

The East-West conflicts over Germany and over the issue of nuclear controls are not the only threats to peace. On the mainland of Asia, a new monolith has risen. Communist China, confident and ruthless, is potentially more of a menace to the Free World than Russia, who must by now be entertaining serious apprehensions over this protégé's power and purpose. How shall we deal with Red China? And how shall we deal, too, with the explosive forces of the new nationalism which have erupted in the former colonial areas of the world, and which the Communists are exploiting? How can we prevent the instability of these new nations from jeopardizing peace, and how can we help them attain stability and win them to our side?

The contest between East and West may well be decided by the so-called uncommitted nations of the world, most of which have only recently thrown off their colonial status. Field Marshal Smuts, commenting on the aspirations of colonial peoples, once remarked, "The masses are on the trek." They are indeed; and, as I reminded the Field Marshal, when we met at Chequers in 1945, they want not only political independence but the economic and social opportunities which freedom promises. The peoples of Africa and Asia have taken seriously the slogans under which the great wars were fought. They have been exposed to the world. Their sons and daughters have gone away to be educated in Western colleges, where they have absorbed the ideas and ambitions inherent in the peoples of the Free World. Western education has already helped to mold the characters and arm the will to freedom of a long list of colonial leaders who have brought, or are bringing, their people to independence.

While we must applaud and encourage the effort of former colonials to be free, we must remember that it takes time for peoples to learn to govern themselves. I always remember Woodrow Wilson's words: "Liberty is not itself government. In the wrong hands, in hands unpracticed, undisciplined, it is incompatible with government." Self-discipline will be needed to make liberty meaningful for newly liberated peoples.

It also takes time and much experience for economically underdeveloped nations to give their peoples the standard of living they have been taught to expect will come with independence. But if they are promised too much and given too little, the resulting situation will certainly open the way to Communist control. They will find themselves then subject to an imperialism which makes the Western colonialism of the nineteenth century appear benevolent and disinterested, by comparison.

3

On so many of the great unsettled questions which have plagued us since the end of the war, we appear to have operated on the assumption that time is working for us, that all our problems will be resolved by time. But will they? We cannot forever escape the hard decisions which must be made. To believe that time necessarily favors us may be a dangerous form of wishful thinking.

The belief that time is our ally presumably rises out of our basic American optimism, our conviction that progress is inevitable. Such a belief may have been justified in the past when, no matter how violently mankind spun through various cycles—war and peace, enslavement and liberty, depression and prosperity—everything emerged as net progress, at least in a material sense. It may have been two steps forward and one back, and there were many detours, but men were able to keep to the main road of progress. No matter what follies were committed, they had time to clean up the debris and begin building all over again.

Today, however, there is grave doubt whether civilization, as we know it, could survive the kind of cyclical breakdowns we have experienced in the past. Could our economic and political system withstand another depression on the scale of 1929? Could the planet itself, let alone a single nation, survive another general war—this one fought with nuclear weapons?

This is why we must, while there is still time, arrive at decisions on the problems confronting us. This is why we must devise some system to replace the cycles of spasm and counter-spasm which have characterized human history until now. I believe it can be done. Not the immediate creation of Utopia, to be sure, but a system of progress and stability without relapse.

If we are to do this, as I have often said, we must pass three tests. The first is a test of values. What do we believe in? What are our goals? Unless we stop to determine what it is that we as a nation wish to achieve, we shall not find our way.

The second is a test of reason. Can we think through the problems besetting us, and analyze the ways in which they may be solved? That is how progress is attained. We must learn to understand the natural laws which govern human affairs, adapting these laws to our own use, and when that is not possible, adapting ourselves to these laws.

Until now, it must be admitted, we have been more successful in using reason to seek out truth in chemistry, physics, and medicine than in mastering the laws governing human institutions. We have learned to control the atom, but the problems of government still bedevil us. Some deny there are natural laws governing human affairs. I do not. Certainly in reading history, one cannot help being struck by the recurrence of certain patterns, such as the abuse of power, the failure that results from tinkering with money, the curious mass madnesses that sweep over people.

But even when we discover basic truths about human affairs, it is another thing to overcome human failings—the greed, hatred, sloth, or whatever it is that keeps us from acting on those truths. In a laboratory, men follow truth wherever it may lead. In human relations, men have a supreme talent for ignoring truth, and denying facts they do not like. That is why the ancient messenger who brought bad tidings was put to death.

We would all do well to echo Thomas Huxley's prayer: "God give me strength to face a fact even though it slay me."

And here we come to the third test—in many ways the most difficult of all. This is the test of self-discipline. Even when we know what is right, too often we fail to act. More often we grab greedily for the day, letting tomorrow bring what it will, putting off the unpleasant and unpopular. We blame the nation's troubles on others—Russia, the government, labor, business—whatever our favorite whipping boy may be. But it is far more likely that we will find the source of our national trials in our own failure as individuals to discipline ourselves to do what the nation's well-being demands.

I suppose most people would excuse this failure on the grounds that what they do has no bearing on America's fortunes—that it is only what "important" people do that matters. How wrong they are! For one thing, each of us—farmer, clerk, teacher, banker, nurse, mechanic, engineer—is important. Each of us, to the extent that we do our chosen work well, has a valuable contribution to make to the community. For another, each of us, no matter what our calling or status, shares equally in the responsibilities of citizenship. And a democratic system cannot endure unless its citizens fulfill these responsibilities, chief among which is the responsibility to exercise self-restraint.

It is all very well to blame inflation on the government, but isn't it caused fundamentally by our selfishness and self-indulgence? Isn't it true that our defenses are insecure because we as individuals are unwilling to bear the burdens involved? We understand the danger of Russian aggression. We know her capabilities and the tremendous advances she has made in the technology of war, and we know that the prospects of peace will grow less if she outdistances us in military and economic strength. Yet we have failed to enact those measures which would make our defenses secure.

There are many people who claim the American economy simply cannot afford to do all that is required to meet the Soviet challenge. But the American economy met the demands of two World Wars, without seriously impairing the highest standard of living the world has ever known. I believe we *are* capable of maintaining a deterrent nuclear power second to none. I believe our conventional forces *can* be built up to handle any foreseeable contingency. I believe it is *not* too late to close whatever missle gap the Russians may have opened.

But there is no point in deceiving ourselves. An effective defense may mean higher taxes. An effective defense may mean that we will have to defer many of the goals we would like to reach. It may mean inconvenience and even sacrifice—but this is a small price to pay.

We are faced here with a question of determining priorities. I have no doubt that we can meet our defense requirements and still provide our people with what they need, if not all they want. Peace is not going to come overnight; at best it will be a long haul, and we must begin to learn how to pace ourselves now. The Russians' objectives have not altered, despite the hot winds and the cold which blow from the Kremlin. We must be prepared to carry the burden of defense for a long time.

It may sound old-fashioned to talk of values, reasoning, and self-discipline, but these fundamental attributes lie at the heart of the democratic dilemma. No democracy can long endure unless its people pass these tests. Nor can we exempt ourselves from them on the ground that government will do what has to be done. The government cannot do what we as individuals leave undone, any more than it can undo our mistakes.

In my long life, I have seen the relationship between the individual and his government radically altered in America. In my youth, it was heretical to question the doctrine of laissez-faire and its premise that government must be kept out of the nation's social and economic life. Today, the old kind of "do-nothing government" is dead. Government intervention has been made necessary by the growing complexity of society.

I point to an analogy I have frequently made—the little town of my boyhood which needed no traffic light to direct its few horses and buggies on Main Street, in contrast to the chaos which would ensue if there were no traffic signals in New York or Chicago today. Government acts as the traffic cop in modern America, regulating the flow and cross-flow of economic and social forces. But traffic jams can develop from too many signals, or signals that are not properly coördinated, just as they can from no signals at all. Government can over-regulate. Government intervention, once considered a panacea for all our ills, has proved not to be so.

Government is not a substitute for people, but simply the instrument through which they act. And if the individual fails to do his duty as a citizen, government becomes a very deadly instrument indeed.

The greatest blessing of our democracy is freedom. But in the last analysis, our only freedom is the freedom to discipline ourselves.

4

As I look back over my long life, nearly a century of time, I marvel at the changes which I have seen. America was an adolescent, unfinished country when I was born. The first transcontinental railroad had been completed less than two years before my birth, and the passing of the American frontier did not occur until almost ten years after. As a child, I listened to my great-grandmother tell stories of the American Revolution—stories which she had heard from her mother who lived through it—and of the War of 1812, which was part of her own girlhood memories. Through the eyes of these relatives and my own life, I have enjoyed a virtual eyewitness account of our country's development since Independence.

Comparing the world in which I live now with the one into which I was born, I might just as well have been born one hundred and ninety, instead of ninety, years ago. Scarcely anything we now consider indispensable to normal living existed in the world of my birth. It was a world without automobiles or airplanes; without radio, television, or movies; without miracle drugs, electric home appliances, fountain pens, or frozen foods.

The rate of our progress—of material progress—staggers the imagination. It took men thousands of years to find a substitute for the oxcart, but in fifty years they have learned how to fly above the earth and to explore the very precincts of the moon. Every day we learn of some fantastic new development in medicine, transportation, communication.

Still, I have noticed that some people—young people in particular —take the wonders of this age pretty much for granted. I suppose that this is so because it is hard to sustain a sense of fantasy in the face of new marvels which science and technology pour out week after week. But when one can look back as far as I can, and remember that the working of a kitchen water tap once filled him with wonder, he can truly appreciate the fantastic changes which have taken place and gain the true perspective of age.

I have had a long, long life—a full one and a good one. Sometimes I stop whatever I am doing to wonder at the good fortune I have had in this lengthy pilgrimage. I have had a loving family, many devoted and loyal friends, good health (and what a blessing to have it still), all the material comforts a man could want (and these are by no means unimportant). But above all, I have had the opportunity to serve my country. That has meant most to me.

America has always been considered the Land of Opportunity. It has given its citizens advantages and liberties which no other people can claim. I cannot say that I have discharged the debt I owe this country for what it has given me, but in good conscience I can say I have tried.

Index

417